THE NEUROPSYCHOLOGY OF THIRST:

NEW FINDINGS AND ADVANCES IN CONCEPTS

THE NEUROPSYCHOLOGY
OF THIRST:

NEW FINDINGS AND
ADVANCES IN CONCEPTS

EDITED BY   ALAN N. EPSTEIN, HARRY R. KISSILEFF

and ELIOT STELLAR

UNIVERSITY OF PENNSYLVANIA, PHILADELPHIA, PENNSYLVANIA

 V. H. WINSTON & SONS

1973   Washington, D.C.

DISTRIBUTED BY THE HALSTED PRESS DIVISION OF

JOHN WILEY & SONS

New York   Toronto   London   Sydney

V. H. Winston & Sons, Inc., Publishers
1511 K St. N.W., Washington, D. C. 20005

Distributed solely by Halsted Press Division, John Wiley & Sons, Inc.,
New York.

Library of Congress Cataloging in Publication Data:

The Neuropsychology of thirst.

    Based on a symposium prepared for the meeting of the AAAS, held
in Philadelphia, Dec. 28–29, 1971.
    Includes bibliographies.
    1. Thirst–Congresses. 2. Psychology, Physiological–Congresses.
I. Epstein, Alan N., ed. II. Kissileff, Harry R., ed. III. Stellar,
Eliot, 1919–   ed. IV. American Association for the Advance-
ment of Science. [DNLM: 1. Neurophysiology–Congresses.
2. Thirst–Congresses. WI102 N503 1971]
QP139.N48   612'.391   73-10257
ISBN 0-470-24350-3

Printed in the United States of America

CONTENTS

LIST OF CONTRIBUTORS

Numbers in parentheses indicate the pages on which the authors' contributions begin.

Bengt Andersson, Karolinska Institutet, Stockholm, Sweden. (113)

Elliott M. Blass, Johns Hopkins University, Baltimore, Maryland. (37)

Alan N. Epstein, University of Pennsylvania, Philadelphia, Pennsylvania. (315)

John L. Falk, Rutgers University, New Brunswick, New Jersey. (225)

Alan E. Fisher, University of Pittsburgh, Pittsburgh, Pennsylvania. (243)

James T. Fitzsimons, University of Cambridge, Cambridge, England, and University of Pennsylvania, Philadelphia, Pennsylvania. (3)

John A. Harvey, University of Iowa, Iowa City, Iowa. (293)

Harry R. Kissileff, University of Pennsylvania, Philadelphia, Pennsylvania. (163)

David Lehr, M.D., New York Medical College, New York, New York. (307)

Gordon J. Mogenson, University of Western Ontario, London, Ontario, Canada. (119)

Keith Oatley, University of Sussex, Brighton, England. (199)

Jeffrey W. Peck, University of Utah, Salt Lake City, Utah. (99)

Paulette E. Setler,* University of Cambridge, Cambridge, England. (279)

Gerard P. Smith, Cornell University Medical College, Westchester Division, White Plains, New York. (231)

Eliot Stellar, University of Pennsylvania, Philadelphia, Pennsylvania. (xiii)

Edward M. Stricker, University of Pittsburgh, Pittsburgh, Pennsylvania. (73)

Philip Teitelbaum, University of Pennsylvania, Philadelphia, Pennsylvania. (143)

Elliot S. Valenstein, University of Michigan, Ann Arbor, Michigan. (155)

*New mailing address: Department of Pharmacology, Smith Kline & French Laboratories, 1500 Spring Garden St., Philadelphia, Pa. 19101.

ACKNOWLEDGMENT

This book is published under the sponsorship of the International Commission on the Physiology of Food and Fluid Intake, an agency of the International Union of the Physiological Sciences.

Jacques LeMagnen, *Chairman of the Commission*
Alan N. Epstein, *Secretary*
Miguel R. Covian
James T. Fitzsimons
Elzbieta Fonberg
Gordon Mogenson
Yutaka Oomura
Mauricio Russek
Kamal Sharma

PREFACE

Early in 1971, William Bevan, Executive Director of the American Association for the Advancement of Science, invited Eliot Stellar and his colleagues at the Institute of Neurological Sciences at the University of Pennsylvania to prepare a symposium for the meeting of the AAAS that was held in Philadelphia at the end of that year. We accepted the invitation because we had some genuine news about thirst that we wanted to give to our friends in brain-behavior research. Work on the physiological psychology and neurology of drinking behavior had moved fast since the problem was last reviewed at the Florida Symposium (Wayner, 1964) and at the New York Academy of Sciences (Morgane, 1969). We were working with refreshed concepts and a broad range of new techniques. Bevan's invitation was therefore very welcome. It also provided the occasion and the travel funds to bring James Fitzsimons back to Philadelphia, where he was Visiting Professor of the Institute from the end of December 1971 through January 1972. This book is the result of our symposium, entitled "Thirst: New Findings and Advances in Concept" and held at the Warwick Hotel on December 28 and 29, 1971.

Although it has been thoroughly rewritten and edited, the book follows the symposium in format and authorship. We distinguished three areas of major advance in work on the neuropsychology of thirst and divided the material into three parts. First we consider the double depletion hypothesis of thirst (Part I) that has emerged from our recognition that a qualitatively different kind of thirst arises from depletions of the two major body water compartments of the mammalian body. Cellular dehydration and extracellular volume loss both stimulate thirst. Each depletion appears to do so by an independent physiological mechanism that employs separate receptive systems in the forebrain. We then consider broader issues (Part II) of motivation including the problem of the hypothalamic mechanisms of motivation as posed by studies of electrically elicited behavior, and the related issue of thirst phenomena that are not linked to body water needs. Thirdly, the possible neuropharmacological mechanisms of thirst are discussed (Part III). Both the cholinergic and the adrenergic possibilities are considered, with emphasis on their relationships to the brain mechanisms of cellular and extracellular thirst and to angiotensin as a possible natural hormone of thirst. J. T. Fitzsimons has provided a historical introduction especially for this book, and one of us (A.N.E.) has expanded his summary remarks into a review of the double depletion hypothesis and an attempt to foresee some of the research opportunities that lie ahead.

The book is not an exhaustive treatment of the problem of thirst. Thirst for fluids other than water is not reviewed; the relations of thirst to feeding are not adequately treated, nor is the problem of thirst as a habit or symptom. We have attempted to repair some of the gaps in our treatment by inviting comments from several of our colleagues (Andersson, Valenstein, Falk, and Lehr) whose work was very much a part of the symposium but who were not with us. They gave us what will surely be among the most interesting parts of the book by focusing on the important controversies that are alive in our field.

Despite its deficiencies, we are proud of this book. First, we are proud of it as a product of our colleagueship. The editorship of this book is the result of two generations of companionship in science. Epstein was Stellar's student at Johns Hopkins 20 years ago, and Kissileff was Epstein's student at Pennsylvania a decade ago when all three were associated in the Institute of Neurological Sciences. And secondly, we are proud of how well the book represents the state of our art. It captures the essential qualities of current research on the neuropsychology of thirst. These chapters reveal our field to be a multidisciplinary assault on an important problem that requires concepts and skills from psychology, physiology, neurology, pharmacology, and biology. Furthermore, it shows the study of thirst to be an area of basic research that combines the joy of discovery, the satisfaction of understanding, and the hope of final success. It invites the younger investigator to join the search.

Alan N. Epstein
Harry R. Kissileff
Eliot Stellar

July, 1973

REFERENCES

Morgane, P. J. (Ed.) Neural regulation of food and water intake. *Annals of the New York Academy of Sciences,* 1969, **157**, 531–1216.
Wayner, M. J. (Ed.) *Thirst: Proceedings of the First International Symposium on Thirst in the Regulation of Body Water.* Oxford: Pergamon Press, 1964.

INTRODUCTION

Eliot Stellar
University of Pennsylvania

The striking advances in the study of thirst in the last decade represent the convergence of four great traditions in the sciences of physiology and behavior. As the history of science has shown, when the pieces of one part of a puzzle begin to fall in place, they begin to fit together with other parts that were at first thought to be unrelated. As the picture grows, the scope of the problem addressed grows, so that while knowledge is accumulating rapidly, progress seems slow. Then there is the last step when all avenues of knowledge converge, and not only is the problem solved, but at last it can be stated in simple terms. We are at the threshold of this last step in the study of thirst, and it is a good time to look back at our converging traditions.

The first tradition is Claude Bernard's idea of the constancy of the internal environment, expanded by Cannon (1932) to the concept of homeostasis, and refined by Adolph (1943) into the more precise concept of physiological regulation. It has been a great advance to think of thirst and the ingestion of water as a behavior that serves in the regulation of the internal environment, and this identifies the adaptive and evolutionary significance of thirst and classifies it with other regulatory mechanisms serving in maintaining temperature, blood sugar, pH, etc. In this way, the study of thirst profits from the adaptation of control theory to our understanding of regulatory mechanisms. Thirst, of course, is not the only mechanism at work in meeting challenges to body fluid balance. By the same token, some cases of thirst are nonhomeostatic or nonregulatory and indeed pose new problems of regulation for the organism.

The second great tradition behind the modern study of thirst is the concept of biological drive, of instinct or motivation. To C. J. Warden (1931) we owe the behavioristic definition of biological drive as measured, for example, with the obstruction box. It was Lashley (1938), however, in his paper "An Experimental Analysis of Instinctive Behavior," who used the term instinct as a synonym for motivated behavior and postulated excitatory mechanisms in the brain as the underlying biological mechanism. In a similar behavioristic vein, Richter (1942–43) thought of motivated behavior as self-regulatory behavior and thus helped tie these first two traditions together. The great advance in thinking of thirst as a biological drive, as self-regulatory behavior, or as motivated behavior, is that it can be classified with hunger, specific hunger, sexual behavior, maternal behavior, migration, homing, and a host of other biological drives. Not only are the same kinds of multifactor, biological mechanisms at work in each case, but also the same behavioral measurements, and thus the same behavioral concepts, apply in all cases.

A third tradition is the history of thought about the nature of hedonic experience, the sensations of pleasure and pain, of hunger and thirst, etc. Modern experimental approaches owe their beginnings to William James (1894), who tried to understand the basis of emotional experience as man's awareness of his own autonomic responses. Despite his many controversies with James, Cannon (1932) also wanted to address himself directly to the basis of experience, not only emotion, but hunger and thirst as well. For Cannon, identification of local factors such as dryness of the mouth gave the answer to his primary question about the basis of thirst sensation. His important contribution, however, was not in his theory, but rather his successful use of methods of experimental physiology to investigate the sensations of thirst and hunger. Even more direct focus on the experimental study of hedonic processes was the goal of P. T. Young's (1949) investigative work. He took choice and preference as direct measures of hedonic processes in animals. Certainly in man we know of thirst as a state of great discomfort and the slaking of thirst as a great source of pleasure. We may now be far enough advanced as a science in psychology to be willing to infer similar, although not identical, experiences of discomfort and pleasure in our physiological and behavioristic studies of water-deprived animals.

Finally, there is the tradition of the study of the nervous system as the great integrative organ of physiology and behavior. Most important for our thinking is the work of Sir Charles Sherrington (1906) and his concept of excitatory and inhibitory states in the activity of the spinal cord. Philip Bard (Bard, 1928; Bard & Mountcastle, 1947) took Sherringtonian concepts into the diencephalon and cerebral cortex in his investigations of the role of the hypothalamus and the limbic system in sexual behavior and emotional behavior. In the same vein, Ranson and his colleagues (Hetherington & Ranson, 1942), adapting the stereotaxic method developed for man by Horsely and Clarke to use with animals in the 1930's, investigated the role of deep structures of the brain by lesions, stimulation, and local heating and cooling of the hypothalamus. As a result, we now think of thirst and other motivated behaviors in terms of excitatory and inhibitory mechanisms in the brain that we can reach with electrodes for lesion or stimulation or intracranial cannulae for chemical injection, particularly in sites in the hypothalamus and preoptic areas. Thus a concept of the neurological mechanisms is emerging, revealing anatomical loci, neuroendocrine relations, and possibly specific neurotransmitters that may serve as the basis for specific neural codes, distinguishing thirst and drinking from other behaviors.

We still have some way to go before the convergence of these physiological, behavioral, psychological, and neurological traditions solve the problem of thirst. Facts are accumulating rapidly on all fronts, but at the same time, the problem is broadening in scope. Where we used to think of just one thirst, now we must think of four or five thirsts: (*a*) the thirst of cellular dehydration, (*b*) the thirst of hypovolemia, (*c*) prandial or dry-mouth thirst, (*d*) psychogenic polydipsia, and (*e*) the drinking of palatable solutions. All are not necessarily regulatory: different sensory and internal environment states are involved. There are probably somewhat different neurological mechanisms in each case, and the sensation and hedonic experiences may be rather different in each case. All lead to drinking, however; and while in that sense, at least, they all may be classified under the general rubric of thirst, our current research holds the promise of leading to a simplified and unified theory of thirst.

REFERENCES

Adolph, E. F. *Physiological regulations.* Lancaster, Pa.: Jacques Cattell Press, 1943.

Bard, P. A diencephalic mechanism for the expression of rage with special reference to the sympathetic nervous system. *American Journal of Physiology,* 1928, **84,** 490–515.

Bard, P., & Mountcastle, V. B. Some forebrain mechanisms involved in the expression of rage with special reference to suppression of angry behavior. *Research Publication Association Nervous and Mental Disease,* 1947, **27,** 362–404.

Cannon, W. B. *The wisdom of the body.* New York: Norton, 1932.

Hetherington, A. W., & Ranson, S. W. The spontaneous activity and food intake of rats with hypothalamic lesions. *American Journal of Physiology,* 1942, **136,** 609–617.

James, W. The physical basis of the emotions. *Psychological Review,* 1894, **1,** 516–529.

Lashley, K. S. An experimental analysis of instinctive behavior. *Psychological Review,* 1938, **45,** 445–471.

Richter, C. P. Total self-regulatory functions in animals and human beings. *Harvey Lectures,* 1942–43, **38,** 63–103.

Sherrington, C. S. *The integrative action of the nervous system.* London: Constable, 1906.

Warden, C. J. (Ed.) *Animal motivation studies.* New York: Columbia University Press, 1931.

Young, P. T. Food seeking drive, affective process, and learning. *Psychological Review,* 1949, **56,** 98–121.

THE NEUROPSYCHOLOGY OF THIRST:

NEW FINDINGS AND ADVANCES IN CONCEPTS

PROLOGUE

SOME HISTORICAL PERSPECTIVES IN THE PHYSIOLOGY OF THIRST

James T. Fitzsimons
University of Cambridge
and
University of Pennsylvania

INTRODUCTION

Scientific interest in the physiology of thirst goes back at least to Albrecht von Haller (1708-1777), who wrote on "Fames et Sitis" (1764) in his great treatise on physiology published in Berne between 1757 and 1765. He assembled all that was then known about the subject and made extensive reference to earlier authors, including his teacher Herman Boerhaave (1668-1738) whose book *Institutiones Medicae,* published in 1708, had much influenced Haller.

It was not until the nineteenth century, however, that any significant experimental work was done on the physiology of thirst. During this century the three principal classical theories concerning the origin of the sensation were laid down, though right up to and including the work of W. B. Cannon, there was considerable confusion as to whether it was the sensation or the changes in the body fluids giving rise to the sensation that was under investigation. Nevertheless, by the First World War the three theories had been clearly stated. They were:

1. Thirst is a generalized sensation arising from the loss of body water.
2. Thirst is a sensation of local origin referred to the mouth and throat.
3. Thirst arises from stimulation of a thirst center in the brain.

Not one of these theories is incompatible with the other two, and it is clear that elements of all three were often present in the ideas of early workers. It is convenient, however, to trace the development of each theory separately when considering this early period.

FIG. 1. *Albrecht von Haller* (1708–1777). Haller was born in Berne. A precocious and talented youth, he decided on medicine as a career and went to Tübingen in 1723 and from there to Leyden in 1725, where he studied under Boerhaave and the anatomist B. Albinus. Having taken his M.D. in 1727, he visited England, then Paris where he was acquainted with J. B. Winslow the anatomist, and finally Basel where he studied under Bernoulli. Invited by George II as Elector of Hanover to the Chair of Anatomy, Surgery, and Botany in the newly founded University of Göttingen in 1736, he remained there until 1753, when he retired to Berne to occupy himself with writing, poetry, and other learned pursuits. The *Elementa Physiologiae Corporis Humani* was compiled after his retirement between 1757 and 1765. In it he gave an excellent account of the dry-mouth theory of thirst and made an extensive compilation of all previous writings on hunger and thirst. A devout and religious man, he died in 1777.

THE THEORY THAT THIRST IS A SENSATION
OF GENERAL ORIGIN

In the course of the nineteenth century it became established that the principal stimulus to drinking is dehydration of the tissues. Dupuytren's famous experiment (cited by Rullier, 1821) in which the thirst of a dehydrated dog was relieved by intravenous water, a similar observation by François Magendie (1823) in a patient suffering from rabies, and the relief afforded by placing

FIG. 2. *François Magendie* (1783-1855). Magendie was born in Bordeaux. He studied medicine in Paris, where he came under the influence of Boyer, Bichat, Dupuytren, and Cuvier, and he graduated in 1808. He was appointed physician at the Hôtel-Dieu in 1830 and Professor at the Collège de France in 1831. He was a pioneer experimental physiologist and founded the first French journal devoted to physiology, *Journal de Physiologie Expérimentale et Pathologique,* of which 10 volumes in all appeared between 1821 and 1831. Magendie's most famous discovery was the functions of the dorsal and ventral roots of the spinal cord. He believed that thirst is a general sensation, but the belief was not apparently based on experiment. However, he did show that intravenous water could relieve thirst in man when he treated a case of rabies by this means in 1823. His most famous protégé was Claude Bernard, who succeeded him at the Collège de France when he died in 1855.

FIG. 3. *Claude Bernard* (1813–1878). Bernard was born in St Julien (Rhône). After attending school he worked for a time in Lyons as a pharmacist's assistant, where he wrote a vaudeville, *La Rose du Rhône*. He later wrote a play *Arthur de Bretagne* which was published in 1886 after his death. He went to Paris in order to pursue a literary career, but he was dissuaded from this by an unusually percipient critic who advised Bernard to study medicine. He became Magendie's "interne" at the Hôtel-Dieu, and in 1841 Magendie appointed him to be his "préparateur" at the Collège de France, so impressed was he by Bernard's talents. After Magendie's death in 1855, Bernard succeeded him to the Chair of Experimental Medicine at the Collège de France. He also held Professorships of General Physiology at the Sorbonne and at the Muséum d'Histoire Naturelle. His achievements and influence are well known. He was not only a talented experimenter. He was also a great theoretician, as witness that most seminal of physiological doctrines, the constancy of the internal environment being a necessary condition for an existence independent of the external physical environment. On the basis of experiments on animals with gastric or esophageal fistulas, he concluded that thirst is a general sensation aroused by a general need for water, and that oropharyngeal dryness is just one of the causes of drinking and that it is by no means an essential one. Bernard died of a renal disorder in 1878. (Photograph courtesy of Jacques Le Magnen.)

water directly into the stomach (Bernard, 1856) or the intestine (Schiff, 1867), thereby bypassing the mouth and throat, showed that restoring the water content of the dehydrated tissues is crucial for relief of thirst and that the passage of water through the oropharynx is not essential. Indeed, Claude Bernard (1856) demonstrated that if ingested water escapes through an opening in either the esophagus or the stomach, the dog and horse continue to drink until exhausted, rest a little while, and then start to drink again. Wetting the oropharynx without subsequent absorption of water into the body is not alone sufficient to assuage thirst.

A clinical report by Thomas Latta of Leith which appeared in the *Lancet* of 1832, and which contains his experiences during the great cholera epidemic of 1832, is interesting for a number of reasons. It contains excellent descriptions of the circulatory collapse and thirst produced by the severe diarrhea and of the dramatic relief afforded by intravenous fluids: "The poor patient, who but a few minutes before was oppressed with sickness, vomiting, and burning thirst is suddenly relieved from every distressing symptom [Latta, 1832, p. 275]." The date of the report and the fact that severe diarrhea mainly depletes the extracellular fluid make Latta's observations on thirst in cholera and its relief by intravenous "muriate and subcarbonate of soda" (i.e., a mixture of saline and sodium bicarbonate) perhaps the earliest, albeit unwitting, to be devoted to the subject of extracellular thirst.

Claude Bernard, who was Magendie's pupil and then his successor at the Collège de France, and Moritz Schiff, also a pupil of Magendie, followed the latter's view (Magendie, 1817) that thirst is an internal sensation, though they recognized that dryness of the mouth and throat may also cause drinking. Both emphasized the importance of tissue dehydration, and both made a careful distinction between the need for water and the sensation aroused by this need (Bernard, 1856; Schiff, 1867). Schiff had also studied under François Achille Longet in Paris, and he refers to the latter's statement (Longet, 1842) that bilateral section of the glossopharyngeal and lingual nerves, or section of the vagi, does not affect the manifestations of thirst. Schiff, who was then in Florence, added some observations of his own on the lack of effect of denervation of the pharynx on thirst (Schiff, 1867). Schiff's conclusions summarized a view widely held at the time: "Thirst being therefore above all a general sensation arising from the lack of water in the blood and not to be identified with the feeling of dryness at the back of the throat . . . everything shows that the local pharyngeal sensation can be missing and nevertheless thirst be very lively [p. 42]."

What the nature of the need is, i.e., what the immediate stimulus to thirst is, was the subject of investigation by André Mayer in Paris and by Hugo Wettendorff in Brussels at the turn of the century. Mayer (1900), later to hold chairs in Strasbourg and at the Collège de France, found that the dog's serum osmolality measured by cryoscopy was higher after a 5- to 9-day period of water deprivation than it was before, and he suggested that this increase might be the

FIG. 4. *Moritz Schiff* (1823–1896). Schiff was born in Frankfurt-am-Main, in which city he attended the Senkenberger Institute. He obtained the M.D. degree at Göttingen in 1844 and afterwards studied comparative anatomy under Magendie and Longet, at the Museum in Paris. He was Professor of Microscopic Anatomy and Pathology in Berne from 1855 to 1862, Professor of Physiology in Florence from 1863 to 1876, and Professor of Physiology in Geneva from 1876. He was an influential teacher and a productive researcher. He is best known for having shown that the effects of thyroidectomy in the dog can be alleviated by a graft of thyroid tissue (1884). He believed, on the basis of oropharyngeal denervation and bypass experiments on animals with intestinal fistulae, that thirst is a general sensation arising from lack of water in the tissues.

stimulus to drink. Mayer was at pains to point out that the increase in osmolality was mainly accounted for by the "albuminoïdes" and not by the salts. In fact the proportion of total osmotic pressure attributed to the organic matter in the serum was astonishingly high, but even allowing for error it seems that water deprivation leads to a proportionately greater increase in the plasma protein concentration than in the crystalloid concentration.

FIG. 5. *Hugo Wettendorff* (1857-1935). After graduating
in medicine at the Université Libre de Bruxelles in 1893,
Wettendorff worked for a while at the Institut Solvay de
Physiologie. He presented his thèse d'agrégation, "Modifications du Sang sous l'Influence de la Privation d'Eau:
Contribution à l'Étude de la Soif," in 1901 and was awarded
the degree Docteur Spéciale en Sciences Physiologiques. His
thesis was published in 1901 in the Travaux du Laboratoire
de Physiologie, Instituts Solvay, but an earlier note was
communicated to the Société des Sciences Médicales et
Naturelles de Bruxelles on March 2, 1900, and was published,
with additions, in April of the same year in the Journal
médicale de Bruxelles. This, of course, was after André
Mayer's communication to the Société de Biologie de Paris,
made in February 1900 and to which Wettendorff quite
properly refers. Unfortunately for the subject, after his
brilliantly prescient statement of the cellular dehydration
theory of thirst, Wettendorff turned to more clinical matters,
specializing in orthopedics and developing an interest in
physical education and the treatment of disease of the bones
by marine cures and other nature methods. (Photograph,
courtesy of Jean Wettendorff).

Wettendorff (1901) also measured freezing point depressions in the serum taken from dogs deprived of water and obtained similar results. He was, however, more impressed by the smallness of the changes in the first day or so of water deprivation, and he suggested that the reason for this was that water is withdrawn from the tissues as dehydration progresses. He suggested that it is this loss of water from the tissues that is actually the cause of thirst in water deprivation—the first explicit statement that cellular dehydration is an important stimulus to thirst. Wettendorff also claimed that the thirst of hemorrhage could be accounted for by withdrawal of water from the tissues. He was certainly aware, therefore, that there are, in the words of a classical paper by Adolph, Barker, and Hoy (1954), multiple factors in thirst.

THE NEUROLOGY OF THIRST UP TO 1918

The nineteenth century also saw the emergence of the idea of a thirst center in the central nervous system. It is of course implicit in all theories of thirst that the nervous system is in some way involved in the sensation. In 1806, Charles-Louis Dumas of Montpellier wrote of the irritant effect of the blood on the nervous system. By 1861, Longet was suggesting that only the hindbrain and midbrain are concerned in hunger and thirst because, he claimed, anencephalic babies appear to experience hunger during the short time they live. In the earlier decades of the century, Franz Joseph Gall and Johann Caspar Spurzheim had suggested that the brain is composed of as many separate anatomical systems as there are distinct cerebral functions—the doctrine of phrenology or craniology (Dumesnil, 1935; McHenry, 1969). Phrenology, however, became as discredited as speculations on the seat of the soul because of the extreme views and charlatanism of many of its practitioners. Gall in fact had to leave Vienna, and he migrated to Paris, where he had a successful practice. Nevertheless, despite opposition to the whole concept of localization of function in the cortex from physiologists of the caliber of Marie Jean Pierre Flourens, professor of comparative anatomy at the University of Paris, and of Longet, considerable progress had already been made in identifying the function of subcortical structures. The idea of localization of function in the brain was therefore becoming more respectable by the second half of the century.

Julien Jean César Legallois had described the respiratory function of the medulla in 1812. Flourens gave this concept anatomical precision by defining the limits of the *"noeud vital"* or the respiratory center, in 1822. In 1849 Bernard described the phenomenon of *"piqûre diabète,"* the glycosuria shown by C. Eckhard in 1903 to result from sympathetic activation induced by puncture of the floor of the fourth ventricle. In 1871, Philip Vasiljevich Ovsjannikov identified the medullary vasomotor center.

Evidence of localization of cortical function was also accruing. Jean Baptiste Bouillaud in 1825, and then in 1861 Pierre Paul Broca, the surgeon and anthropologist, localized speech to the third left frontal convolution. The clinical observations of the English neurologist John Hughlings Jackson on the nature of epileptiform convulsions made from 1861 onwards, then the experiments of Theodor Fritsch and Eduard Hitzig in 1870 in Berlin, followed by the much more meticulous observations of Sir David Ferrier, started at the West Riding Lunatic Asylum in 1873, on electrical stimulation of the cortex, consolidated the notion of localization of function in the brain.

In 1881 when we come to Nothnagel's suggestion of a thirst center in the brain, it was generally agreed that specific brain functions have precise anatomical localization, and that the vital functions of respiration, cardiac control, and vasomotor control are represented in the medulla. Carl Wilhelm Hermann Nothnagel (1881), then in Jena, but later to go to Vienna, described primary polydipsia in a 35-year-old man immediately following head injury. There had been no loss of consciousness, and the excessive thirst and drinking preceded any increase in urine flow. Nothnagel explicitly excluded the possibility that oropharyngeal factors were responsible for thirst—the mouth and throat remained moist, and ice afforded no relief whatsoever. The immediate cause of thirst was considered to be central stimulation of a "*durstcentrum*" in the pons or medulla. The hindbrain was considered to be the most likely site, because other vital centers are located here and this is the region where nerves from the pharynx enter the central nervous system. Also considered suggestive were the site of pain at the back of the head and neck, and the occurrence of miosis; but Nothnagel himself admitted that this was all rather inconclusive.

In 1897, Stephen Páget read a paper before the Clinical Society of London entitled, "On cases of voracious hunger and thirst from injury or disease of the brain." He considered the cases of 14 patients, 9 taken from the literature, including Nothnagel's case, and 5 new ones. Paget thought that it was reasonable to postulate the existence of special centers for hunger and thirst which he localized to the temperosphenoidal lobe close to Broca's speech area in the inferior frontal gyrus from the fact that 3 patients were aphasic. All the patients recovered, which, Paget argued, indicated "that these centres of hunger and thirst, if they do exist, are not situated in the immediate neighbourhood of the vital centres [Paget, 1897, p. 119]." Though he did not refer to Brown and Schäfer's paper of 1888 on hyperphagia after temporal lobectomy in the monkey, Paget's clinical notes obviously complemented the experimental findings in the monkey.

Mayer and Wettendorff wrote more extensively on thirst than any of their predecessors. Wettendorff (1901) considered that thirst originates in the tissues themselves and that though the nervous system is the "seat of the conscious perception of the sensation [p. 474]," it is acting merely as the receiving and coordinating center for nervous impulses coming from the dehydrated tissues. Thirst is general in the sense that all the tissues contribute to the sensation, but Wettendorff conceded that the sensation may be referred to the oropharynx, since the mucosa is here exposed to the desiccant action of air during breathing and speaking and it is the route by which water enters the body.

FIG. 6. *Carl Wilhelm Hermann Nothnagel* (1841–1905). Nothnagel was born at Alt-Lietzegöricke in the Mark Brandenburg in Germany. He studied medicine under Traube and Virchow in Berlin and graduated in 1865. He was then assistant to Ernst von Leyden in Königsberg in East Prussia before becoming Professor in Freiburg from 1872, Professor in Jena from 1874, and finally Professor of Special Pathology, Therapeutics, and Clinical Medicine in Vienna from 1882 until his death from a heart attack in 1905. He is best known for his *Handbook of Special Pathology and Therapeutics,* published in 24 volumes between 1894 and 1905. In 1881, while he was in Jena he described his famous case of primary polydipsia and, to account for the symptom, suggested that there is a "durst-centrum." He was a gifted lecturer and orator and was a member of the Austrian parliament. He also had a large private practice which included kings and emperors.

Mayer's (1901) hypotheses were more elaborate. He considered that drinking was just one of a series of regulatory mechanisms that protect the animal from the effects of an abnormally high osmotic pressure. He described a number of circulatory changes that follow injection of solutions of different tonicity into blood vessels or into the stomach and which, according to him, would tend to restore the osmotic pressure to normal by affecting intestinal absorption and renal excretion in the appropriate way. The circulatory changes are mediated by bulbar centers, and only when they prove insufficient to restore the osmotic pressure of the blood does regulation by thirst intervene. Since both the circulatory changes and drinking serve to restore the osmotic pressure of the blood to normal, it seemed reasonable to regard all these changes as being subserved by a *"centre régulateur de la pression osmotique du sang"* located in the medulla. As for the question of a cerebral center for thirst, Mayer reserved judgement, merely pointing out that a conscious phenomenon demands cerebral participation.

When Erich Leschke, clinical assistant at the Charité in Berlin, wrote on thirst in 1918, little more was known about the neural structures involved, though by now interest had shifted from the hindbrain to the gray matter at the base of the brain as the principal focus for the nervous control of water metabolism. In a long article published in 1886, Otto Kahler reported that puncture of the floor of the fourth ventricle followed by the application of silver nitrate to the damaged site would sometimes produce lasting polyuria in the dog. Kahler was still very much influenced by Bernard's *"piqûre diabète,"* but in the same paper Kahler also concluded from an analysis of the clinical and pathological material then available that lasting polyuria never resulted from involvement of structures in the floor of the fourth ventricle or cerebellum, but that it not infrequently followed damage to the gray matter in the region of the pituitary. By 1912 when Alfred Erich Frank, then in Minkowski's laboratory in Breslau, wrote on the relationship of the pituitary to diabetes insipidus, the role of the pituitary was reasonably firmly established, though the manner of its action was misunderstood. George Oliver, a physician from Harrogate, and Edward Albert Schäfer (later Sharpey-Schafer), then at University College, London, had reported in 1895 that pituitary extracts were pressor. The first report implicating the neurohypophysis in water metabolism was a communication to the Physiological Society in 1901, in which Rudolph Magnus, later Professor of Pharmacology at Utrecht but at the time working in Edinburgh, and Schäfer stated that pituitary extracts were diuretic in the anesthetized dog. In the Croonian lecture of 1909, Schäfer elaborated on this diuretic action and suggested that polyuria after damage to the base of the brain was attributable to hypersecretion of hormone from irritation to the pituitary. Frank followed Schäfer in attributing the polyuria of diabetes insipidus to pathological hyperfunction of the pituitary, and though the irritative hypersecretion hypothesis was invalidated by the independent reports of F. Farini and R. von den Velden in 1913 (see Fisher, Ingram, & Ranson, 1938) of the antidiuretic action of pituitary extracts in unanesthetized patients, these reports merely reinforced the belief that the pituitary was involved in water metabolism.

FIG. 7. *André Mayer* (1875–1956). Mayer was born in Paris. He entered medical school at the age of 16 and later studied science at the Sorbonne under Albert Dastre, Claude Bernard's favorite student. His early work was concerned with the constancy of the internal . environment, and this culminated with his famous monograph on thirst which appeared in 1900. For the first time a basic physiological drive was related to a measurable physicochemical variation in the body. He did fundamental work on the chemical structure of protoplasm and developed the first synthetic medium for the culture of bacteria. When the war broke out in 1914, Mayer immediately volunteered and saw service as battalion surgeon during the first battle of the Marne and then later at Verdun. He was recalled from the front to help organize the Allied Chemical Warfare Service after the first poison gas attack by the Germans. When the war ended, he became Professor of Physiology at Strasbourg in 1919, Professor at the Collège de France in 1922, and codirector with Jean Perrin of the Institute for Biophysics and Biochemistry in 1929. Between the wars he did important work on cellular respiration, including work on the hyperthermia produced by 2, 4–dinitrophenol, and he also continued the study of regulatory mechanisms, especially those involved in food intake. His interest in nutrition found expression not only in the laboratory but also in the activities of various international bodies, such as the Red Cross, in the relief of poverty and malnutrition. He and Frank McDougall were largely instrumental in the setting up of the Food and Agriculture Organization Conference in 1945, and to the end of his life he retained a passionate and active concern for the suffering of the poor and undernourished. He died after a short illness in 1956.

However, even as significant evidence in favor of an endocrine role for the pituitary in water metabolism was becoming available (e.g., Cushing, 1912), Jean Camus and Gustave Roussy, of Paris, reported to the Société de Biologie in 1913 that damage to the tuber cinereum without injury to the pituitary would cause polyuria in the dog. The considerable controversy that arose between those who believed that destruction of the neurohypophysis was essential in the induction of experimental diabetes and those who believed that damage to the base of the brain was critical was only finally resolved by the classical studies of C. Fisher, W. R. Ingram, and S. W. Ranson, of Northwestern University, on experimental diabetes insipidus, published in 1938, which established that damage to any part of the supraoptico-hypophysial system would give rise to polyuria.

The reason for the controversy between the "hypothalamists" and the "pituitarists" need not concern us. Leschke (1918) himself rejected the idea that pituitary failure was a significant factor in polyuria, but perhaps because of the controversy, his attention was firmly fixed on this region of the brain. He said that all the evidence was in favor of an important role for the basal part of the hypothalamus in the pathology of water output and, therefore, in thirst. He distinguished between primary polydipsia, which he called nervous or psychogenic, and secondary or diabetic polydipsia. He said that we have to imagine reflexes at several levels for the regulation of water and solute metabolism, with the lowest level in the medulla, the next in the floor of diencephalon, and the highest, which alone is associated with consciousness, in the cerebral cortex. Leshke was therefore firmly committed to the idea of a nervous center or of nervous centers for thirst. He pointed out that anesthesia of the mouth did not alter thirst induced by intravenous hypertonic saline and that, conversely, neither atropine nor gargling with hypertonic saline would induce thirst. He explicitly excluded stimulation of nerve endings in the mouth by changes in the composition of the blood as being the origin of the sensation of thirst.

Leshke's 1918 affirmations on the mechanisms of thirst were very much in the tradition of Magendie, Bernard, Schiff, Wettendorff, and Mayer. It is ironic that they were published in the same year that Walter Bradford Cannon, in his Croonian lecture to the Royal Society, took up the diametrically opposite point of view, coming down heavily in favor of a local or oropharyngeal theory of thirst. It is perhaps even more ironic and deeply saddening that Leshke at the time was attached to the IIIrd Corps of the German Army, and that Cannon was serving on the other side as a Major in the United States Army.

THE INFLUENCE OF W. B. CANNON AND THE THEORY THAT THIRST IS A SENSATION OF LOCAL ORIGIN

Dry-mouth theories of thirst have been extant for as long as scientific interest in the subject itself, and very clear statements are to be found much earlier than 1918. In his textbook on the comparative physiology of domestic animals, published in 1854, G. Colin gave a particularly good account. "The sensation that causes animals to take liquids derives from the general state of the economy, or rather the state of the blood, from excessive sweating . . . . This state of the blood stimulates the nervous system and diminishes or delays the secretions, including those of the pharyngeal mucosa . . . . The fact that thirst is relieved . . . by injection of water into the veins or by introduction of liquid directly into the stomach, does not disprove localization of the sensation to the mucosa of the throat . . . for penetration of water into the blood in sufficient quantity makes it less stimulating and gives it suitable qualities to reestablish the secretions to their normal state and in particular those of the pharyngeal mucosa [p. 434]."

Walter Bradford Cannon was George Higginson Professor of Physiology at Harvard and had already published his classical book, *Bodily Changes in Pain, Hunger, Fear and Rage,* when he was invited to give the Croonian lecture for 1918. In his opening remarks Cannon said that his studies had been interrupted by military service and that he was breaking with custom by presenting some ideas and observations on the physiological basis of thirst, which, though incomplete, might prove interesting and suggestive. Such was the authority and richly deserved reputation of Cannon that his remarks then and subsequently exerted a quite disproportionate influence on the subject. It was doubly unfortunate that the timing of the lecture coincided with the start of American hegemony in science, the United States having been relatively untouched by the World War, then in its final months. It meant that one theory of thirst came to be regarded as "the physiological basis of thirst" and that earlier work on the systemic factors and on the neurology were largely ignored.

Cannon's view, set down at the end of his lecture, was that the " . . . water supply is maintained because we avoid, or abolish, by taking water or aqueous fluid, the disagreeable sensations which arise and torment us with increasing torment if the salivary glands, because of a lowering of the water-content of the body lack the water they need to function, and fail therefore to pour out their watery secretion in sufficient amount and in proper quality to keep moist the mouth and pharynx [Cannon, 1919, p. 307]." Cannon had earlier (Cannon & Washburn, 1911–12) proposed that hunger is not a "general sensation," but that it is the consequence of contractions in the stomach, to which region the sensation is referred. He claimed that thirst is also a local sensation, since it is universally described as "an experience of dryness and stickiness in the mouth and throat [Cannon, 1919, p. 292]." He strongly criticized the views of those who, he claimed, had concluded that thirst is a general sensation, citing many of the experiments we have already considered, including those of Dupuytren, Magendie, Bernard, Longet, and Schiff. However, as put by A. V. Wolf in his monograph of 1958, "A perusal of Cannon's own paper reviewing evidence before and since Bernard can have the unsettling effect of leading a disinterested reader to draw conclusions quite opposed to Cannon's [p. 66]." It must also be said that Cannon advanced little new evidence in support of his theory that

FIG. 8. *Walter Bradford Cannon* (1871-1945). Cannon was born in Prairie du Chien, Wisconsin. He graduated in medicine at Harvard in 1900 and succeeded Bowditch as Professor of Physiology at Harvard in 1906. His studies on the gastrointestinal tract and then on the sympathetic nervous system led to the notion of homeostasis and also generated an interest in emotional behavior and experience. His view that hunger and thirst are local sensations dominated thinking in this field until very recently.

oropharyngeal dryness is the essential factor in thirst, other than showing that thirst may be associated with a diminution in salivary flow.

Between the wars a number of papers by various authors appeared in which the relationship between salivary flow and thirst was considered under a variety of conditions and after the various drugs which affect the rate of salivation. For the most part these papers were devoted to the rather sterile object of confirming or refuting the dry-mouth theory of drinking. In advocating the dry-mouth theory in such strong terms, Cannon had performed a disservice because he had deflected interest from the more important questions of the nature of the changes in the body fluids that underlie thirst and the neurological mechanisms activated by these changes. He had focused attention on one aspect only of the sensation and had put out of court consideration of other possible mechanisms.

Wettendorff (1901) had been nearer the truth when he distinguished between true thirst arising from lack of water in the tissues, and false thirst or dryness of the mouth and throat that we associate with true thirst through experience. The mouth and throat are usually dry in states of general dehydration, but moistening this region without restoring tissue water does not afford more than transient relief. On the other hand, dryness from local factors such as speaking, smoking, eating certain foods, etc., causes false thirst in which there is no tissue dehydration and which is relieved by local application of water.

The controversy has lost all force because it is now generally agreed, largely on the basis of analysis of the lateral hypothalamic syndrome, that a dry mouth is neither necessary nor sufficient to account for drinking in all circumstances.

THE MODERN PERIOD

In recent times inquiry into the mechanisms that make animals drink has followed several paths, some of which lead back to classical theories, while others explore completely new ground. Thirst continues to occupy the attention of physiologists and others as a subject that is intrinsically interesting and also as a means of understanding motivated behavior in general. The themes that have been evident during this time are:

1. The elucidation of the anatomy and interrelationships of the neural structures involved in drinking.

2. The elaboration of a complicated but ill-understood neuropharmacology of thirst.

3. The investigation of the quantitative relationships between thirst stimuli and drinking responses, and the demonstration that the urge to drink is multifactorial.

4. The increasing awareness that part of thirst may be hormonally mediated through the renin-angiotensin system.

THE NEUROLOGY OF THIRST SINCE 1921

Between the two World Wars, two important innovations in technique were introduced which revolutionized the investigation of the neurological mechanisms of feeding behavior. These were: (a) the stereotaxic placement of lesions, and (b) electrical stimulation in the conscious animal.

Following the earlier speculations on a thirst center in the nervous system, attention was diverted, as we have seen, to a consideration of the possible endocrine role of the hypothalamo-pituitary region in water metabolism, culminating with the monograph of Fisher, Ingram, and Ranson in 1938. In an important paper on experimental diabetes in the dog, published in 1921, Percival Bailey and Frédéric Bremer, working in Harvey Cushing's laboratory at Harvard, claimed that minute lesions in "the parainfundibular region of the hypothalamus provokes with certitude . . . a polyuria which appears in the first two days," and that, "there is no evidence at present that the lesion acts by the intermediation of the pituitary [p. 803]." As E. Anderson (1969) said, its publication "was akin to a manifesto protesting the prevailing views on the pituitary as Cushing had presented them in his monograph on *The Pituitary Body* and replacing the role of the pituitary with that of the hypothalamus [p. 5]," and this of course from Cushing's own laboratory. Much more significant in the present context were Bailey and Bremer's (1921) remarks "that polyuria can be preceded by thirst. It is not necessarily preceded by it. The polyuria may appear and persist without any intake of water. But at any rate the polydipsia is not consecutive to the polyuria. The only possible way to reconcile these facts is to suppose that the nervous lesion produces at once thirst and polyuria [p. 797]." However, the question of whether polydipsia is primary or secondary to the polyuria remained rather a side issue in the elucidation of the role of the supraoptico-hypophysial system in diabetes insipidus, and appeared to be resolved in favor of the latter.

A major impetus to research into feeding behavior was the reintroduction during the 1930's by Ranson and his school of the stereotaxic method of making lesions in restricted parts of the brain, first described by Sir Victor Horsley and R. H. Clarke in 1908. The freehand method of lesioning was far too imprecise even in the larger animal to allow thorough exploration of subcortical structures. The stereotaxic method made reproducible lesions in large numbers of animals possible, and in particular, it allowed small animals, notably the rat, to be used for this type of work. The harvest was not long forthcoming. A. W. Hetherington and Ranson reported hypothalamic obesity in the rat in 1939 (see Hetherington & Ranson, 1942); in 1943, J. R. Brobeck, J. Tepperman, and C. N. H. Long argued that obesity after ventromedial hypothalamic lesions was caused by overeating; and in 1951, B. K. Anand and J. R. Brobeck described aphagia following lesions in the lateral hypothalamus, and introduced the idea of a lateral feeding center and a medial satiety center operating together to control intake of energy. During the 1950s, descriptions of altered water intake after hypothalamic damage also appeared. J. A. F. Stevenson and his colleagues (Stevenson, Welt, & Orloff, 1950), A. D. Keller and his colleagues (Witt, Keller, Batsel, & Lynch, 1952), P. Teitelbaum and E. Stellar (1954), and B. Andersson and S. M. McCann (1956) all reported diminished or absent thirst after lesions or ablations in different parts of the hypothalamus.

The syndrome of aphagia and adipsia caused by lateral hypothalamic damage was studied in detail by Teitelbaum and Stellar (1954) and by Teitelbaum and Epstein (1962). These studies and the experiments derived from them are now classical (see Kissileff, this volume). They have laid to rest the old disputes between the upholders of the dry-mouth theory and those who supported the various general and central theories, by showing that regulatory drinking is abolished by bilateral lesions in the lateral hypothalamus but that dry-mouth drinking is largely unaffected.

FIG. 9. *Walter Rudolph Hess.* Hess was born in Frauenfeld, Switzerland. After completing his medical studies at the University of Zurich in 1906, he practiced for a while as an ophthalmologist. His interest in physiology was such that he joined the staff at the Institute of Physiology in Zurich in 1913, becoming Professor in 1917. His main work has been on the nervous integration of autonomic functions. On the basis of electrical stimulation experiments in conscious animals, he was able to demonstrate that the diencephalon is capable of integrating and directing complicated autonomic reactions, including feeding. For this work he was awarded the Nobel prize in physiology and medicine in 1949. Hess became Professor Emeritus in 1951.

The second important innovation in technique was the development of methods of electrical stimulation of brain structures in the unanesthetized animal, notably by W. R. Hess in Zurich, also during the 1930's. In the course of his studies Hess showed that the diencephalon integrates complicated autonomic reactions and that it plays a part in sensory and associative functions formerly ascribed to the cerebral cortex alone. Hess' book, *Das Zwischenhirn,* published in 1949, contains descriptions of electrically induced behavior of various sorts, including feeding, in the cat. An earlier report in 1943 by Hess' associate M. Brügger was devoted to electrically induced feeding, and in it Brügger commented on the increased drinking that was sometimes seen with electrode placements near the mamillothalamic tract.

The most significant experiments on electrically induced drinking were carried out by Bengt Andersson and his colleagues (Andersson, 1952; Andersson & McCann, 1955, 1956) in Stockholm during the 1950's. Andersson applied Hess' technique of electrical stimulation of brain structures in the conscious animal through previously implanted electrodes to a study of diencephalic function in the goat, sheep, and dog. His earlier experiments were concerned with the neurohormonal regulation of milk ejection following the work of G. W. Harris (1955), but in 1955 Andersson and McCann reported that stimulation near the anterior columns of the fornix would cause polydipsia in the goat. These observations have been widely confirmed in a variety of species and are now classical.

Also of very great interest and significance, not only in the physiology of thirst but also for motivated behavior in general, was the observation by J. Olds and P. M. Milner (1954) that if rats were given the opportunity to stimulate themselves electrically through electrodes implanted along the course of the medial forebrain bundle, they would do so for hours on end—apparently the sensation is pleasant. Stimulation through the same electrode by the experimenter may also cause drinking, so that with suitable electrode placements, concurrent self-stimulation and drinking can be obtained (Mogenson & Stevenson, 1966). The intermingling of systems subserving drive and reward could account for the urgency of thirst and ensure that the most vigorous efforts would be made to assuage it, obviously of tremendous benefit to the animal.

Recently the stability of neural systems for drinking and other behavior has been questioned. It has been suggested that electrical stimulation simply raises the level of motivation in a nonspecific way, the actual behavior depending on what courses of action are available to the animal (Valenstein, Cox, & Kakolewski, 1970). On the whole, the evidence favors the view that there are distinctive anatomical representations of drinking and feeding in the hypothalamus (see Mogenson, this volume). Another aspect of the same problem is the possible optimization of behavior when several drives are present simultaneously. As Brobeck (1960) said, E. F. Adolph (1947b) seems to have introduced the "idea that animals show priorities, competition and compromises in their regulation of the several variables contributing to homeostasis [Brobeck,

1960, p. 1200]." The modulation of electrically induced drinking by stimulation or lesioning elsewhere in the nervous system, and the quantitative study of behavior in richer environments than the usual metabolism cage with a water spout, are approaches currently employed that will surely throw light on the hierarchical organization of behavior in the nervous system.

The history of the investigation of the physiology of thirst up to the early 1950's is summarized in Figure 12, which emphasizes the intellectual relations (or lack of them) among the major workers in the field.

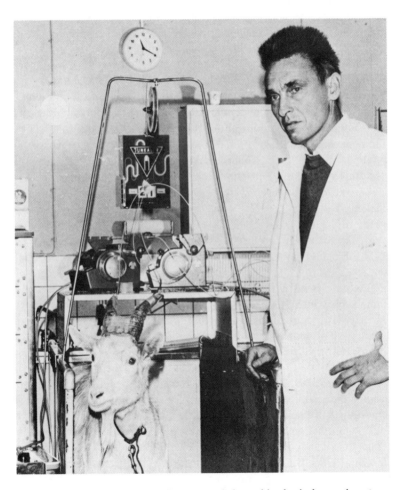

FIG. 10. *Bengt Andersson.* Andersson carried out his classical experiments on electrically induced drinking in the goat at the Veterinärhögskolan in Stockholm in the early 1950's. This was a dramatically successful application of the techniques developed by W. R. Hess to stimulate the brain structures in conscious and cooperative animals. Andersson succeeded U. S. von Euler to the Chair of Physiology at the Karolinska Institute in 1971.

FIG. 11. *Edward F. Adolph.* Adolph's classical work on ingestive behavior and problems of fluid balance have emphasized the importance and fruitfulness of measurement in this field. In two influential volumes, *Physiological Regulations* (1943) and *Physiology of Man in the Desert* (1947a), as well as in his many papers, he has laid the foundations of modern work on the multifactorial nature of thirst stimuli. He continues to be active in the Department of Physiology at the University of Rochester, New York.

NEUROPHARMACOLOGY OF THIRST

A major advance in the analysis of ingestive behavior was the introduction of the chronic brain cannula. In 1952 Andersson reported that hypertonic NaCl injected directly into the hypothalamus through a permanently implanted cannula would cause the water-replete goat to drink. The solutions were exceedingly hypertonic, and the effect was probably due to a nonspecific stimulation of neurons. However, this method of applying active substances to

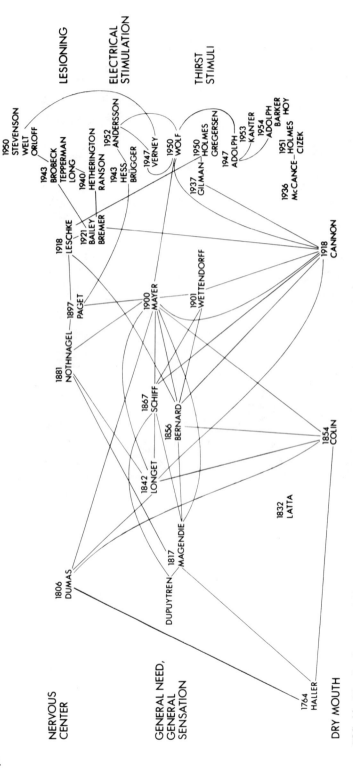

FIG. 12. The development of ideas on the physiology of thirst between about 1750 and 1950. The dates above the names are those of the principal writings by these authors. The line between names indicates that an author has referred to the work of the previous man. The three principal classical theories are listed on the left, and the broad areas of inquiry in the 1950s are given on the right. The diagram is to chronological scale. The horizontal stratification of names gives an indication of which aspect of the problem the particular writer was concerned with.

neural tissue in conscious animals has proved to be of the utmost value. In 1960 S. P. Grossman, then at Yale, described remarkably specific effects produced by crystalline chemicals applied to the lateral hypothalamus through a permanent cannula. He found that adrenergic agents caused eating and cholinergic agents drinking. In another pioneering study published the same year Epstein (1960) reported that local anesthetics injected directly into the ventromedial nuclei would elicit feeding in satiated animals, and injected into the lateral hypothalamic regions would suppress eating in hungry animals. Other early studies were carried out by N. E. Miller and his colleagues and by A. E. Fisher and J. N. Coury.

The advantages of this method of investigating neural function are: flexibility, selectivity, and reversibility. Neural excitants or depressants can be administered in graded amounts, and usually the effects produced wear off after a time, allowing for retesting with the same substance or testing with another substance. Antagonistic effects may be elicited from the same anatomical locus by using different pharmacological agents or by combining agonists with selected antagonists. Where specific behavior can be elicited with a pharmacologically active substance, the behavior is likely to be accompanied by fewer side effects than follow electrical stimulation, which inevitably affects all neural structures present. The possible involvement of various neurotransmitters in specific behavior can be investigated using the appropriate antagonists. The advantage of selectivity is well illustrated by the recent use of 6-hydroxydopamine to lesion catecholaminergic systems in the brain. U. Ungerstedt (1970) has reported complete adipsia and aphagia after 6-hydroxydopamine induced degeneration of the nigrostriatal dopamine system, and he believes that destruction of this system may underlie the lateral hypothalamic syndrome.

It is not the purpose of this chapter to review the present knowledge concerning the neuropharmacology of behavior which has emerged in the past 10 years. This is dealt with in the chapters by Fisher, Setler, and Harvey (this volume). It is worth pointing out, however, that there was no neuropharmacology of ingestive behavior worth talking about prior to the first use of the intracranial cannula in the late 1950s.

THE STIMULI TO THIRST

The study of stimulus-response relationships follows in the tradition of Mayer and Wettendorff, but it was not until one-third of a century later with the publication of Alfred Gilman's paper, "The Relation between Blood Osmotic Pressure, Fluid Distribution and Voluntary Water Intake," in the *American Journal of Physiology* of 1937 that further significant work was done. Short notes by rather few workers including F. Arden in 1934 and S. Janssen in 1936 had preceded this paper, but as Gilman (1937) said: "The influence of general body hydration and the distribution of body fluids upon thirst has received scant attention [p. 323].″ It seems surprising to us that 37 years separates Gilman's paper from those of Mayer and Wettendorff, but the reason is evident in the second sentence of Gilman's paper: "Recent investigations have centered around the old controversy as to whether thirst is a general or localized sensation [p. 323]." The malevolent influence of Cannon's lapse 19 years previously was still working. It seems significant that Gilman refers to Cannon's paper of 1918 and to Mary F. Montgomery's paper of 1931 for the early evidence but mentions neither Mayer nor Wettendorff.

Gilman, as is well known, studied the relationship between water intake and serum osmolality and specific gravity after equiosmolar amounts of hypertonic saline or hypertonic urea, and found that it is cellular dehydration rather than an increase in cellular osmotic pressure per se that is the true stimulus to thirst. He therefore placed Wettendorff's inspired guess on an experimental footing.

The bulk of the work on cellular dehydration as a stimulus to drinking has been carried out since the war and is reviewed elsewhere in this volume (see chapter by E. M. Blass). Suffice it to say here that Gilman's conclusion that cellular dehydration is a true thirst stimulus stands and that thanks to the work of Peck and Novin (1971) and of Blass and Epstein (1971) we now know that the sensitive receptors lie in the lateral preoptic region.

In the course of work on the quantitative aspects of thirst stimuli, it became apparent that cellular dehydration alone could not always explain why an animal drinks. Despite the ancient belief that hemorrhage causes thirst, J. H. Holmes and A. V. Montgomery, in a paper published as recently as 1953, reported the failure of loss of blood to cause thirst in the dog or in man. On the other hand reports of thirst and excessive drinking in states of Na deficiency started appearing in the literature from 1935 onwards, though Gilman wrote in 1937 concerning Na depletion that "seemingly, despite the anhydremia and the striking dry appearance of the oral mucous membranes and the probable lack of salivary secretions, these dogs did not experience the sensation of thirst [p. 327]." A deficit of Na of course leads to a loss of ECF (extracellular fluid) and an increase of ICF (intracellular fluid). In a classical study of Na deficiency performed on himself and two other subjects, R. A. McCance wrote in 1936 that "their sense of flavour and taste was affected. E. interpreted this aberration or lack of sensation as thirst. She complained of it constantly and drank freely without obtaining any relief. R.A.M. recognized the feeling as distinct from thirst ... R.B.N. was not so much troubled by this sympton but felt it from time to time. He noted once that he was 'Thirsty all morning—drank a lot but water seems to make little difference' and on another day reported that he had a 'funny feeling in the mouth' [pp. 249–250]."

In McCance's experiment, the only study carried out on human beings, it is evident that the subjects had some difficulty deciding whether they were thirsty or whether it was some other sensation they were experiencing. In all the animal experiments referred to, the subjects only had water available. Since it was well

FIG. 13. *Curt Richter.* Richter's entire scientific career, 50 years of research, has been spent at Johns Hopkins. He began his work there as a graduate in psychology (PhD. 1921) and was Professor of Psychobiology in the Department of Psychiatry until his formal retirement in 1959. Fortunately, his emeritus status has not interrupted his work as Director of the Laboratory of Psychobiology. His contributions to the physiology of behavior are best summed up by an old pupil and colleague of his at Johns Hopkins, Eliot Stellar, who wrote: "A behaviorist with an organismic point of view, he saw that motivated behavior could be of adaptive value in the survival of the organism because of its essential contribution to the maintenance of the internal environment. Starting with the conceptualizations of Claude Bernard and with Cannon's homeostasis, Richter conceived of motivated behavior as self-regulatory behavior in the sense that it may correct deviations of the internal environment in cooperation with more automatic physiological mechanisms. ... In his extensive investigations, Richter was able to show that the organism actually is sensitive to many of its own physiological needs and will develop motivated behavior appropriate to the correction of those needs and the maintenance of the internal environment [Stellar, 1960]."

Richter's name is associated particularly with Na appetite and his extensive investigations have thrown much light on the phenomenon. He did early, definitive work on other problems that still occupy students of thirst (specific hungers, preference-aversion functions, the poisoning phenomena, endocrine-behavior relations) and he was a pioneer in the study of periodic phenomena. These continue to be his major interest.

known at this time, owing above all to the studies of C. P. Richter (1956), that animals, at least, show a well-marked Na appetite when they are Na-deficient, none of the Na depletion experiments could be interpreted as compelling evidence in favor of a second stimulus to thirst, additional to the by then well-established cellular stimulus.

Nevertheless, a unitarian (i.e., cellular dehydration) theory of thirst was becoming more and more unsatisfactory owing to the work of G. S. Kanter (1953), and of J. H. Holmes and M. I. Gregersen (1950a, 1950b) in the early 1950's and above all to the penetrating analyses of E. F. Adolph and his colleagues. The coup de grâce came in the classical paper "Multiple Factors in Thirst," by Adolph, J. P. Barker, and P. A. Hoy, published in 1954, in which it was stated that "the adequate stimulus to drinking was not osmotic pressure alone, not chloride concentration alone, not sodium concentration alone, not extracellular volume alone, not intracellular volume alone. But evidence can be found that each of these factors was effective at times. The receptor or battery of receptors, correspondingly, was not just an osmoreceptor, just a volume receptor, just a chlororeceptor etc. . . . the hope that all drinking may represent response to one trigger has evaporated [p. 561]."

It was in order to investigate the possibility that extracellular dehydration might be an additional thirst trigger that I introduced the technique of sequestering ECF by a Starling mechanism using hyperoncotic polyethylene glycol and other colloids. An advantage the procedure has over Na depletion is that it causes an early functional extracellular hypovolia (i.e., affecting water immediately as well as the electrolytes) instead of causing first an early extracellular hypotonicity followed by a secondary and delayed hypovolia such as occurs in developing Na deficiency. Observations could therefore be made on water intake early in the experiment before a Na appetite developed, which usually takes several hours. As is now well established, hyperoncotic sequestration of extracellular fluid is a potent stimulus to thirst as well as to Na appetite. (See chapter by E. M. Stricker, this volume).

We are now entitled to refer to the double depletion hypothesis of regulatory thirst, since loss of cellular water or of extracellular water is a sufficient stimulus to drink. When the loss affects both the cellular and the extracellular water, the signals from the two compartments are additive in their effects on drinking. As far as extracellular control is concerned, we believe that the receptors are located in the vasculature, probably in the low-pressure capacitance vessels including the atria of the heart. This is obviously a field for future endeavor, and a start has already been made by Stanislaw Kozłowski in Warsaw to find the elusive extracellular volume receptor.

The most recent development in the quantitative study of drinking behavior has been application of control theory to describe the various physiological mechanisms which ensure the stability of the milieu intérieur. This is considered in the chapter by Keith Oatley (this volume), who was one of the first to apply this type of analysis to thirst.

THE ENDOCRINOLOGY OF THIRST

The development of our understanding of the neurological mechanisms of thirst was closely tied in with research into the causes and mechanisms of diabetes insipidus, as has already been discussed. Thirst in diabetes insipidus is in the vast majority of cases secondary to loss of body water, and this is also true of thirst in a number of other endocrine disorders, whether these be produced by hypersecretion or hyposecretion of hormone. Thirst in these instances may be regarded as symptomatic in the sense that a normally functioning mechanism is responding to a deficit of body fluid.

Recent evidence suggests a more direct involvement of an endocrine system in thirst (Fitzsimons, 1971). Some years ago I found that ligation of the inferior vena cava just below the liver is a less effective stimulus to drinking in the nephrectomized rat than it is in either the normal rat or the rat made anuric by ureteric ligation (Fitzsimons, 1964). I suggested that "the kidneys play a part in the response, possibly by release of renin or some other renal factor (p. 480)." Further evidence in support of this hypothesis was the finding that constriction of the abdominal aorta above the renal arteries (or the renal arteries themselves) caused drinking, but not when the constriction was placed below the level of the renal arteries or when the aorta was constricted after previous removal of the kidney. Drinking therefore depends to a considerable extent on alterations in the blood supply to the kidneys, but urine formation is not essential. A thirst-inducing factor localized to the cortex of the kidney was found to be identical with renin, which was known to cause increased fluid intake in the rat (e.g., Masson, Corcoran, Page, & del Greco, 1953). It became of considerable interest to study the action of angiotensin itself on thirst mechanisms. In the first series of experiments in Cambridge, Barbara Simons and myself found that intravenous infusion of angiotensin II caused drinking in the water-replete rat, and then Alan Epstein and ourselves found that direct injection of angiotensin into the brain in p-mole quantities would also cause the rat to drink. It soon became clear that angiotensin is much the most potent dipsogenic substance so far discovered and, unlike its closest rival carbachol, which is dipsogenic only in the rat, angiotensin causes drinking in a variety of animals including the rat, the monkey, the dog, the cat, the goat, the rabbit, and the pigeon. It also lowers the threshold of drinking to cellular or to extracellular stimuli to thirst, and it therefore seems possible that its physiological role is to provide additional activation of thirst mechanisms in the presence of these stimuli. The puzzle of why intracranial renin, renin substrate, and angiotensin I should also be highly dipsogenic when it is believed that all physiological actions of the renin-angiotensin system are mediated through angiotensin II, was partly elucidated by the discovery of a cerebral renin-angiotensin system (Fischer-Ferraro, Nahmod, Goldstein, & Finkielman, 1971; Ganten, Minnich, Granger, Hayduk, Brecht, Barbeau, Boucher, & Genest, 1971). The components of this intrinsic system ensure the local generation of angiotensin II when any one of the other dipsogens is injected, though whether this in fact explains their dipsogenic action is not known. We are presently investigating the possibility by using antibodies and competitive blockers to the agonists. However, the physiological role of the cerebral renin-angiotensin system, its relationship to the renal renin-angiotensin system, and the function of either or both systems in the normal control of water intake remain wide-open questions at present. It may be that the cerebral renin-angiotensin system is a neurotransmitter mechanism particularly involved in the neural systems responsible for drinking. In this connection it is extremely interesting that there is a high degree of correlation between angiotensin and noradrenaline concentrations in different parts of the brain, particularly in view of the fact we have recently found in Cambridge that intracranial angiotensin-induced drinking is attenuated by pretreatment with 6-hydroxydopamine (a drug which destroys catecholaminergic neurones) or by treatment with certain catecholaminergic antagonists, notably the dopamine blockers haloperidol and spiroperidol (see chapter by Paulette Setler). This dependence of the dipsogenic action of angiotensin on the integrity of a known neurotransmitter system must surely be significant.

Whether either or both of these renin-angiotensin systems is involved in the control of water intake then remains uncertain, but involvement of the better known renal renin-angiotensin system would be particularly fitting since it would provide a link between the control of body water through thirst and the control of body Na through renin-angiotensin-aldosterone, aldosterone itself causing renal retention of Na and possibly increased Na appetite as well. The kidney would therefore be the key organ in the coordination of body fluid homeostasis as well as being the principal excretory organ. We have some indication that blood-borne angiotensin gets into the CSF, and ventricular administration of angiotensin is highly effective at causing drinking (see chapter by A. N. Epstein). Blood-borne angiotensin may also penetrate the blood-brain barrier in certain restricted regions of the brain, for example, the subfornical body, and stimulate thirst neurones directly, as is the case for some of the pressor actions of angiotensin on other regions of the brain where the barrier is lacking, and of course a peripheral angiotensin-sensitive drinking receptor has yet to be ruled out. It is evident that if the cerebral renin-angiotensin system is found to play the principal role in water intake, my original simple hypothesis of a renal control of extracellular thirst will have to be extensively modified if not abandoned. Clearly an enormous amount of research is needed here as in so many other aspects of that supremely important activity, the taking of water into the animal. The fascination of the search is evident to us all, and the disciples of many sciences meet together to pursue this end.

REFERENCES

Adolph, E. F. *Physiological regulations.* Lancaster, Pa.: Jaques Cattell Press, 1943.
Adolph, E. F. *Physiology of man in the desert.* New York: Interscience, 1947. (a)
Adolph, E. F. Urges to eat and drink in rats. *American Journal of Physiology,* 1947, **151**, 110–125. (b)

Adolph, E. F., Barker, J. P., & Hoy, P. A. Multiple factors in thirst. *American Journal of Physiology*, 1954, 178, 538−562.

Anand, B. K., & Brobeck, J. R. Hypothalamic control of food intake in rats and cats. *Yale Journal of Biology and Medicine*, 1951, 24, 123−140.

Anderson, E. Earlier ideas of hypothalamic function, including irrelevant concepts. In W. Haymaker, E. Anderson, & W. J. H. Nauta (Eds.), *The hypothalamus*. Springfield, Ill.: Charles C Thomas, 1969. Pp. 1−12.

Andersson, B. Polydipsia caused by intrahypothalamic injections of hypertonic, NaCl-solutions. *Experientia*, 1952, 8, 157−159.

Andersson, B., & McCann, S. M. A further study of polydipsia evoked by hypothalamic stimulation in the goat. *Acta Physiologica Scandinavica*, 1955, 33, 333−346.

Andersson, B., & McCann, S. M. The effect of hypothalamic lesions on the water intake of the dog. *Acta Physiologica Scandinavica*, 1956, 35, 312−320.

Arden, F. Experimental observations upon thirst and on potassium overdosage. *Australian Journal of Experimental Biology and Medical Science*, 1934, 121−122.

Bailey, P., & Bremer, F. Experimental diabetes insipidus. *Archives of Internal Medicine*, 1921, 28, 773−803.

Bernard, C. *Leçons de physiologie expérimentale appliquée à la médicine faites au Collège de France.* Vol. 2. Paris: Baillière, 1856. Pp. 50−51.

Blass, E. M., & Epstein, A. N. A lateral preoptic osmosensitive zone for thirst in the rat. *Journal of Comparative and Physiological Psychology*, 1971, 76, 378−394.

Brobeck, J. R. Regulation of feeding and drinking. In *Handbook of Physiology*. Section 1. *Neurophysiology*. Vol. 2. Washington, D. C.: American Physiological Society, 1960. Chap. 47, pp. 1197−1206.

Brobeck, J. R., Tepperman, J., & Long, C. N. H. Experimental hypothalamic hyperphagia in the albino rat. *Yale Journal of Biology & Medicine*, 1943, 15, 831−853.

Brown, S., & Schäfer, E. A. An investigation into the functions of the occipital and temporal lobes of the monkey's brain. *Philosophical Transactions of the Royal Society (London), Series B*, 1888, 179, 303−329.

Brügger, M. Fresstrieb als hypothamisches Symptom. *Helvetica Physiologica et Pharmacologica Acta*, 1943, 1, 183−198.

Camus, J., & Roussy, G. Polyurie expérimentale par lésions de la base du cerveau. La polyurie dite hypophysaire. *Comptes Rendus des Séances de la Société de Biologie*, 1913, 75, 628−633.

Cannon, W. B. The physiological basis of thirst. *Proceedings of the Royal Society (London), Series B*, 1919, 90, 283−301.

Cannon, W. B., & Washburn, A. L. An explanation of hunger. *American Journal of Physiology*, 1911−12, 29, 441−454.

Colin, G. *Traité de physiologic comparée des animaux domestiques*. Vol. 1. Paris: Baillière, 1854. P. 434.

Cushing, H. *The pituitary body and its disorders.* Philadelphia: Lippincott, 1912.

Dumas, C. L. *Principes de physiologie ou introduction à la science expérimentale, philosophique et médicale de l'homme vivant.* (2nd ed.) Vol. 1. Paris: Mequignon-Marvis, 1806. P. 181.

Dumesnil, R. *Histoire illustrée de la médicine.* Paris: Plon, 1935.

Epstein, A. N. Reciprocal changes in feeding behavior produced by intrahypothalamic chemical injections. *American Journal of Physiology*, 1960, 199, 969−974.

Fischer-Ferraro, C., Nahmod, V. E., Goldstein, D. J., & Finkielman, S. Angiotensin and renin in rat and dog brain. *Journal of Experimental Medicine*, 1971, 133, 353−361.

Fisher, C., Ingram, W. R., & Ranson, S. W. *Diabetes insipidus & the neurohormonal control of water balance: A contribution to the structure and function of the hypothalamic-hypophyseal system.* Ann Arbor, Mich.: Edwards, 1938.

Fitzsimons, J. T. Drinking caused by constriction of the inferior vena cava in the rat. *Nature*, 1964, 204, 479−480.

Fitzsimons, J. T. The hormonal control of water and sodium intake. In L. Martini & W. F. Ganong (Eds.), *Frontiers in neuroendocrinology,* 1971. New York: Oxford University Press, 1971. Pp. 103–128.

Frank, E. Ueber Beziehungen der Hypophyse zum Diabetes insipidus. *Klinische Wochenschift,* 1912, **49**, 393–397.

Ganten, D., Minnich, J. L., Granger, P., Hayduk, K., Brecht, H. M., Barbeau, A., Boucher, R., & Genest, J. Angiotensin-forming enzyme in brain tissue. *Science,* 1971, **173**, 64–65.

Gilman, A. The relation between blood osmotic pressure, fluid distribution and voluntary water intake. *American Journal of Physiology,* 1937, **120**, 323–328.

Grossman, S. P. Eating and drinking elicited by direct adrenergic or cholinergic stimulation of hypothalamus. *Science,* 1960, **132**, 301–302.

Haller, A. von. Fames et Sitis. In *Elementa physiologiae corporis humani.* Vol. 6. Berne: Sumptibus Societatis Typographicae, 1764. Pp. 164–187.

Harris, G. W. *Neural control of the pituitary gland.* London: Edward Arnold, 1955.

Hess, W. R. *Das Zwischenhirn.* Basel: Benne Schwabe, 1949.

Hetherington, A. W., & Ranson, S. W. The spontaneous activity and food intake of rats with hypothalamic lesions. *American Journal of Physiology,* 1942, **136**, 609–617.

Holmes, J. H., & Gregersen, M. I. Observations on drinking induced by hypertonic solutions. *American Journal of Physiology,* 1950, **162**, 326–337. (a)

Holmes, J. H., & Gregersen, M. I. Role of sodium and chloride in thirst. *American Journal of Physiology,* 1950, **162**, 338–347. (b)

Holmes, J. H., & Montgomery, A. V. Thirst as a symptom. *American Journal of the Medical Sciences,* 1953, **225**, 281–286.

Horsley, V., & Clarke, R. H. The structure and the functions of the cerebellum examined by a new method. *Brain,* 1908, **31**, 45–124.

Janssen, S. Pharmakologische Beeinflussung des Durstes. *Archiv für experimentelle Pathologie und Pharmakologie,* 1936, **181**, 126–127.

Kahler, O. Die dauernde Polyurie als cerebrales Herdsymptom. *Zeitschrift für Heilkunde,* 1886, 7, 105–219.

Kanter, G. S. Excretion and drinking after salt loading in dogs. *American Journal of Physiology,* 1953, **174**, 87–94.

Latta, T. Letter from Dr. Latta to the Secretary of the Central Board of Health, London, affording a view of the rationale and results of his practice in the treatment of cholera by aqueous and saline injections. *Lancet,* 1832, **2**, 274–277.

Leschke, E. Ueber die Durstempfindung. *Archiv für Psychiatrie und Nervenkrankheiten,* 1918, **59**, 775–781.

Longet, F. A. *Anatomie et physiologie du système nerveux de l'homme et des animaux vertébrés.* Vol. 2. Paris: Fortin, Masson, 1842. Pp. 326–327.

Longet, F. A. *Traité de physiologie.* Vol. 1. Paris: Masson, 1861. P. 32.

Magendie, F. *Précis elémentaire de physiologie.* Vol. 2. Paris: Mequignon-Marvis, 1817. P. 33.

Magendie, F. Histoire d'un hydrophobe, traité a l'Hôtel-Dieu de Paris, au moyen de l'injection de l'eau dans les veins. *Journal de Physiologie expérimentale et pathologique, par F. Magendie,* 1823, 3, 382–392.

Magnus, R., & Schäfer, E. A. The action of pituitary extracts upon the kidney. *Journal of Physiology (London),* 1901, **27**, IX-X.

Masson, G. M. C., Corcoran, A. C., Page, I. H., & del Greco, F. Angiotensin induction of vascular lesions in desoxycorticosterone-treated rats. *Proceedings of the Society for Experimental Biology and Medicine,* 1953, **84**, 284–287.

Mayer, A. Variations de la tension osmotique du sang chez les animaux privés de liquides. *Comptes Rendus des Séances de la Société de Biologie,* 1900, **52**, 153–155.

Mayer, A. *Essai sur la soif: Ses causes et son mechanisme.* Paris: Felix Alcan, 1901.

McCance, R. A. Experimental sodium chloride deficiency in man. *Proceedings of the Royal Society (London), Series B,* 1936, **119,** 245–268.

McHenry, L. C. *Garrison's history of neurology.* Springfield, Ill: Charles C Thomas, 1969.

Mogenson, G. J., & Stevenson, J. A. F. Drinking and self-stimulation of the lateral hypothalamus. *Physiology and Behavior,* 1966, **1,** 251–254.

Montgomery, M. F. The role of the salivary glands in the thirst mechanism. *American Journal of Physiology,* 1931, **96,** 221–227.

Nothnagel, H. Durst und Polydipsie. *Archiv für pathologische Anatomie und Physiologie,* 1881, **86,** 435–447.

Olds, J., & Milner, P. M. Positive reinforcement produced by electrical stimulation of septal area and other regions of rat brain. *Journal of Comparative and Physiological Psychology,* 1954, **47,** 419–427.

Oliver, G., & Schäfer, E. A. On the physiological action of extracts of pituitary body and certain other glandular organs. *Journal of Physiology (London),* 1895, **18,** 277–279.

Paget, S. On cases of voracious hunger and thirst from injury or disease of the brain. *Transactions of the Clinical Society of London,* 1897, **30,** 113–119.

Peck, J. W., & Novin, D. Evidence that osmoreceptors mediating drinking in rabbits are in the lateral preoptic area. *Journal of Comparative and Physiological Psychology,* 1971, **74,** 134–147.

Richter, C. P. Salt appetite of mammals: Its dependence on instinct and metabolism. In *l'Instinct dans le comportement des animaux et de l'homme.* Paris: Masson, 1956. Pp. 577–629.

Rullier, P. Soif. In *Diction(n)aire des sciences médicales par une société de médecins et de chirurgiens.* Vol. 51. Paris: Panckoucke, 1821. Pp. 448–490.

Schäfer, E. A. The functions of the pituitary body. *Proceedings of the Royal Society (London), Series B,* 1909, **81,** 442–468.

Schiff, M. *Leçons sur la physiologie de la digestion faites au Muséum d'Histoire Naturelle de Florence.* Vol. 1. Florence: Loescher, 1867. Pp. 41–42.

Stellar, E. Drive and motivation. In *Handbook of Physiology.* Section 1. *Neurophysiology.* Vol. 3. Washington, D. C.: American Physiological Society, 1960. Chap. 62, p. 1503.

Stevenson, J. A. F., Welt, L. G., & Orloff, J., Abnormalities of water and electrolyte metabolism in rats with hypothalamic lesions. *American Journal of Physiology,* 1950, **161,** 35–39.

Teitelbaum, P., & Epstein, A. N. The lateral hypothalamic syndrome: Recovery of feeding and drinking after lateral hypothalamic lesions. *Psychological Reviews,* 1962, **69,** 74–90.

Teitelbaum, P., & Stellar, E. Recovery from the failure to eat produced by hypothalamic lesions. *Science,* 1954, **120,** 894–895.

Ungerstedt, U. Is interruption of the nigrostriatal dopamine system producing the lateral hypothalamic syndrome. *Acta Physiologica Scandinavica,* 1970, **80,** 35–36A.

Valenstein, E. S., Cox, V. C., & Kakolewski, J. W. Re-examination of the role of the hypothalamus in motivation. *Psychological Review,* 1970, **77,** 16–31.

Wettendorff, H. Influence de la soif sur certaines propriétés du sang chez les animaux. *Journal médicale de Bruxelles,* 1900, April 5, No. 14, 1–9.

Wettendorff, H. Modifications du sang sous l'influence de la privation d'eau: Contribution à l'étude de la soif. *Travaux du Laboratoire de Physiologie, Instituts Solvay,* 1901, **4,** 353–484.

Witt, D. M., Keller, A. D., Batsel, H. L., & Lynch, J. R. Absence of thirst and resultant syndrome associated with anterior hypothalamectomy in the dog. *American Journal of Physiology,* 1952, **171,** 780. (Abstract)

Wolf, A. V. *Thirst: Physiology of the urge to drink and problems of water lack.* Springfield, Ill.: Charles C Thomas, 1958.

PART I:
THE DOUBLE DEPLETION
HYPOTHESIS OF THIRST

1

CELLULAR-DEHYDRATION THIRST: PHYSIOLOGICAL, NEUROLOGICAL, AND BEHAVIORAL CORRELATES[1]

Elliott M. Blass[2]
Johns Hopkins University

INTRODUCTION

Cellular dehydration is caused by the net loss of cellular fluid. Its most common natural occurrence is during water deprivation when extremely hypotonic fluid is lost insensibly from lungs and skin (Newburgh & Johnson, 1942). Cellular water is also lost during diarrhea (Gamble, 1947; Danowski & Elkinton, 1951) and following the ingestion of foods (especially those rich in salt) which increase extracellular fluid concentration (Winkler, Danowski, Elkinton, & Peters, 1944). This last condition has been successfully exploited in the experimental control of cellular dehydration. Hypertonic solutions which do not effectively permeate cell membranes are introduced into the extracellular space. This exaggerates the gradients between extracellular and cellular phases, and an osmotic withdrawal of cellular fluid is produced (Gilman, 1937; Holmes & Gregersen, 1950a, 1950b; Fitzsimons, 1961a, 1963). In response, a complex of physiological and behavioral effectors is activated which minimizes further cellular fluid depletion and restores the contracted cellular phase to its normal volume. Hypertonic urine is excreted by the kidney, eliminating excess solute; water is drunk; and incompatible behaviors such as eating, which would tend to dehydrate the cellular phase further, are attenuated.

Traditionally, body fluid maintenance has been considered to be mainly the job of the kidney. Consequently renal morphology and physiology have received considerable scrutiny, and it is now rather well established that this system is

[1] This work was supported by USPHS grant in aid of research NS 09305.

[2] I am grateful to Lorraine Blass, James Fitzsimons, and Bert Green for their helpful comments on an earlier draft of this manuscript.

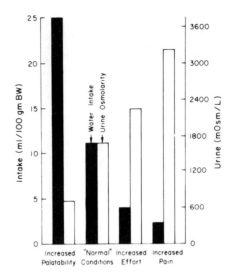

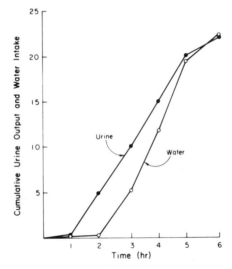

FIG. 1. *Upper panel,* compensation by the kidney for behavioral excess or deficiencies; *lower panel,* development of polydipsia in response to the primary polyuria of diabetes insipidus. (Upper panel, after Miller, 1967. Lower panel, after Richter, 1935.)

fully capable, for short time spans, of maintaining fluid balance with remarkable precision. However, as explicitly stated by Adolph (1950), the kidney by itself cannot maintain fluid balance, for it is primarily concerned with eliminating excess body fluid constituents while conserving those that may be in scarce supply. And the kidney cannot add new water to the body fluid reserves.

Behavior, particularly drinking, is therefore required to correct fluid deficits. Normally, both renal and behavioral effectors operate synergistically and unobtrusively to yield positive fluid balance and thereby provide the animal freedom to indulge a normal range of pursuits. However, the burden carried by each effector may, through natural or experimental hardships, be dispropor- tionately exaggerated. Two such instances are presented in Figure 1 which demonstrate the compensatory capacites of each system and suggest that the balance struck in health is the product of two actively controlled systems and is not fortuitous. The contribution of one mechanism may be emphasized simply by reducing the effectiveness of the other. As seen in the upper portion of Figure 1, renal output is matched to behavioral excesses or deficits. Rats drinking saccharin in excess of body fluid needs compensate by excreting copious amounts of dilute urine. On the other hand, rats that voluntarily reduce intake when forced to climb a steeply inclined plane to reach water or when obliged to drink from a spout which also delivers 0.4 milliamperes of direct current, conserve water by eliminating concentrated urine (Miller, 1967). Similarly, distortion of renal function is rather quickly corrected behaviorally. As an example, animals (as shown in the lower portion of Figure 1) or patients with diabetes insipidus who can no longer conserve water efficiently, compen- sate by enhanced intake and thereby survive in good health (Richter, 1935; Holmes & Gregersen, 1948). Behavioral adjustments, therefore are rapid and precise in response to demands that exceed renal functional capacity.

Specifically, behavior is required to maintain normal cellular volume, and its contributions to this end serve as the major theme of this chapter. The most salient behavioral characteristic, drinking, is best understood and will be closely examined with particular reference to its physiological and neurological foundations. It will be shown that the behavioral mechanism is as sensitive and responsive to cellular dehydration as is the renal system. Behaviors other than drinking which defend the cellular phase from extensive dehydration or overhydration and the direct influence of behavior on excretion will also be examined.

In addition, a subtheme is developed which shows cellular dehydration to be but one of a number of controls of drinking. Each control appears mediated by neural systems which are anatomically separable, and the different physiological controls, mediated by their own afferent neurologies, give rise to behavioral states which differ qualitatively.

PHYSIOLOGICAL CONSIDERATIONS

Elevated osmotic pressure as a correlate of drinking was first reported by Mayer in 1900. Wettendorff (1901), working independently, also noted such an increase during water privation, but was struck by its modesty. To Wettendorff, the small effect reflected a withdrawal of water from tissues into the vasculature, and he suggested therefore that loss of tissue fluid so altered the characteristics of cells that they collectively produced the general sensation of thirst. These early reports of thirst as a sensation of general origin with a specific physiological basis were not accorded their full due. Research labored under the vast influence of Walter Cannon (1918, 1932) who argued strongly that thirst and therefore drinking could be best understood by analyzing the characteristics of signals arising from the dried mouth (see Fitzsimons' introductory chapter in this volume for a comprehensive treatment of the issue of "local sign"). And so it remained until 1937, when Gilman discovered that dogs drank twice as much water following infusions of hypertonic saline, which dehydrates cells, as they did following equiosmotic infusions of urea, which does not. The power of Gilman's analysis is conveyed in Figure 2, which emphasizes the essential similarity and the essential difference in fluid balance between urea and saline treatments. Since the infusions were equiosmotic, identical increases in cellular concentration were produced (see ordinate). However, this endpoint was reached by two entirely different routes. Sodium chloride, by virtue of its rigorous exclusion from the cellular phase, gave rise to an increase in effective osmotic pressure causing the osmotic shift of cellular fluid into the extracellular phase. As shown in the left-hand panel, hypertonic equilibrium was achieved at the expense of cellular fluids. Urea, per contra, as shown in the right-hand panel, diffuses freely into most cells, simultaneously increasing cellular and extra-cellular concentration, and expanding cellular and extracellular phases. That copious drinking was elicited only by NaCl led Gilman (1937) to observe, "After

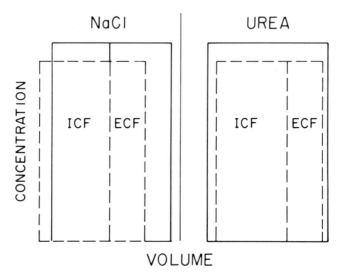

FIG. 2. Consequences of infusions of hypertonic NaCl (*left-hand panel*) and equiosmotic urea (*right-hand panel*) on body fluid balance as shown in Gamble diagrams. Broken lines in each panel represent the system at isotonicity. Solid lines represent equilibria at termination of infusions. *ICF*, intracellular fluid; *ECF*, extracellular fluid.

administration of hypertonic NaCl and urea the increases in blood osmotic pressure were the same. The essential difference between the two groups of experiments was in the water content of the cell. The logical conclusion to draw from the above results is that cellular dehydration rather than an increase in cellular osmotic pressure *per se* is the stimulus of true thirst [p. 327]." This conclusion is of considerable generality, as it has held for every mammal tested including man (Wolf, 1950).

Gilman's classical finding was confirmed and clarified by Holmes and Gregersen (1950b), who pointed out that one could not discern whether drinking elicited by hypertonic saline reflected the activation of a cellular control or whether it was specifically in response to hypernatremia or hyperchloremia. They showed that copious drinking was confined to solutions, nonelectrolyte as well as electrolyte, excluded from cells. Moreover, drinking was not determined either by serum sodium or serum chloride levels, as both were quite low following infusions of hypertonic sucrose or sorbitol, both potent dipsogens. Taken together, these findings reinforced Gilman's notion of cellular dehydration as an adequate drinking stimulus.

Although drinking caused by a variety of solutions proved highly reproducible, those investigators who sought to quantify the relationship between cellular dehydration and drinking were plagued by the extreme variability in drinking, regarding both timing and amount. Some dogs, according to Holmes and Gregersen (1950a), drank the amount required to render the body fluids isotonic, others not nearly enough, still others far too much. Variability bore no relationship to size of animal, as dogs of identical body weight differed by as much as threefold in their drinking to a given stimulus. Yet drinking of individual animals to cellular dehydration was not haphazard. The copious drinker who was immediately overresponsive to the initial dehydration consistently overdrank across many replications covering up to 2 years. The small drinker also remained consistent; behavior did not appear modified over time. Furthermore, intake of a given animal was not fixed, for it was always commensurate with dosage, although differences between large and small drinkers held. Kanter (1953) was also impressed by variability among animals, noting that dogs which drank little to the initial dehydration would quite consistently drink little to subsequent dehydrations. Because most of their osmoregulation was renal, such animals were classified as maximal internal regulators. Others, the minimal internal regulators, generally drank to isotonicity and excreted a copious and relatively dilute urine. Kanter then went on to show that when water was withheld, excretion did not differ between the two groups as to timing, volume, or concentration. He logically reasoned that variability in behavior must be primary and not secondary to a differential osmotic diuresis.

The extreme variability in the drinking response to cellular dehydration was an embarrassment to those who viewed cellular dehydration as the exclusive control of drinking. It is problematic when one considers that mammals are 69%

water by body weight, that approximately 67% of the water is cellular, and that body weight is maintained with considerable constancy throughout most of life (Elkinton & Danowski, 1955). Yet according to the above work, precise behavioral control was wanting. Support for the theory was further eroded by Adolph and colleagues (Adolph, Barker, & Hoy, 1954), who found water deprivation to be a more powerful stimulus for drinking than cellular dehydration and asserted that drinking was under the control of multiple factors, and by Novin (1962), who observed significant drinking in water-deprived rats despite a minimal increase in brain conductivity (an indirect measure of cell dehydration). On the other hand, who could deny the potency of cellular dehydration as a dipsogen causing intense thirst in man and eliciting motivated behavior in subhumans (O'Kelly & Heyer, 1948)?

In short, as of the early 1960s the quantitative relationship between cellular dehydration and drinking remained obscure, and the more general problem as to how cellular fluid balance was achieved through drinking stayed unresolved. This dilemma reflected, in part, the fascination of renal physiologists with the complexities of the kidney, generally to the exclusion of the behavioral contributors to water balance. Equally, it reflected the psychologists' insistence on examining drinking and its adjunctive behaviors, often without recourse to their physiological bases. Each camp therefore conveyed but half a story which, when related alone, could not specify how water balance was finally achieved. The bridge between the two groups was provided, the quantitative dilemma resolved, and an extracellular control identified when Fitzsimons elegantly demonstrated that deficits in cellular fluid could be precisely restored through drinking (Fitzsimons, 1961a, 1963), and that depletion of the vasculature could reliably cause drinking without changes in osmotic pressure (Fitzsimons, 1961b) (see Stricker's chapter, this volume, on the extracellular controls of drinking).

Fitzsimons reasoned that the quantification of drinking and the restoration of balance remained elusive because previous investigators of drinking had neglected to take into full consideration the renal defense against cellular dehydration. Normally, a given osmotic challenge is immediately acted upon by the kidney and is continually modified. Therefore, in animals with intact kidneys, the dipsogenic stimulus is not amenable to quantitative specification over time; only an approximation can be realized. Consequently quantitative expressions of drinking must incorporate a series of independent parameters reflecting renal modifications of the stimulus. This makes the tacit assumption that ingestion does not modify excretion (an erroneous assumption, as will be shown below) and that excretion per se does not influence ingestion. Accordingly, Fitzsimons performed the converse of Kanter's analysis, namely, he studied drinking in the absence of the renal influence. By nephrectomizing rats to eliminate the renal contribution to osmoregulation, and by administering intravenous infusions of hypertonic solutions to produce a specifiable degree of cellular dehydration which now could be assuaged only through drinking, Fitzsimons (1961a, 1963) carried out two exhaustive series of experiments which have served greatly to clarify the conditions which lead to cellular thirst as well as those which relieve such thirst.

Figure 3 presents some of the essential findings of the Fitzsimons experiments, and its details merit our attention. In the first place it replicates, in nephrectomized rats, the main result of Holmes and Gregersen: not all substances are effective in eliciting drinking. Indeed the sine qua non for drinking under these circumstances was cellular dehydration. Drinking was elicited by NaCl, Na_2SO_4 and the nonelectrolyte sucrose, all of which are rigorously excluded from cells. Fructose, glucose, and methyl glucose, all of which enter cells freely, did not cause excessive drinking despite as much as a 15% increase over initial osmolality. Urea was intermediate. This is revealing, as we now know that urea, although it freely enters most cells, does not freely cross the blood-brain barrier (Reed & Woodbury, 1962). Such a condition would tend to dehydrate the brain including, presumably, central thirst osmoreceptors.

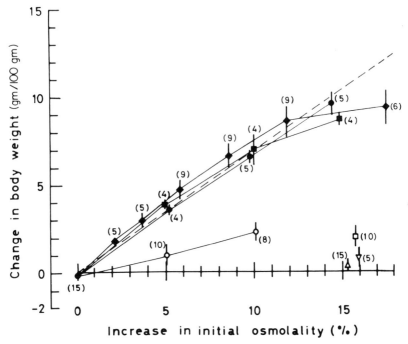

FIG. 3. The relationship between percentage increase in osmolality produced by injection of various substances and the net fluid intake of nephrectomized rats allowed to drink to satiety. The broken line delineates the theoretical relationship predicted by Equation (3) for an osmotically effective substance and represents dilution of the injected solution to isotonicity and restoration of cell size. Vertical bars are twice the standard errors of the means; the numbers of results are given in parentheses, $\bullet$ = NaCl; $\blacklozenge$ = Na_2SO_4; $\blacksquare$ = sucrose; $\circ$ = urea; $\triangle$ = glucose; $\triangledown$ = methyl glucose; $\square$ = fructose. (Data from Fitzsimons, 1971. Used by permission of the Physiological Society.)

In addition to confirming cellular dehydration as a potent drinking stimulus, Fitzsimons discovered that intake was remarkably consistent from rat to rat and that it increased uniformly among nephrectomized rats in response to increased systemic osmotic pressure. A unifying theme emerged to account for these sudden consistencies, namely, that in the absence of renal modulation of the osmotic challenge, drinking is sustained until normal cellular volume returns (as inferred from the restoration of the body fluids to isotonicity). A recent exposition by Fitzsimons (1971), which formally characterizes drinking to cellular dehydration, can hardly be improved upon, and its logic and notations will be followed below. Simply stated, if an anuric mammal of a given body weight, whose water content (w) is known, receives an injection of hypertonic solution (s), then the water necessary to restore normal cellular volume may be determined as follows:

Let w = body water, and b = the water load introduced into the body with the solute, both expressed in ml/100 g BW.

Let s = the introduced solute load in μ osmole/100 g BW.

Let c and c' = initial and final body concentrations in μ osmole/ml HOH.

Then

$$c' = \frac{cw + s}{w + b} \tag{1}$$

and

$$\text{percent increase in osmolality} = 100\left[\frac{cw + s}{c(w + b)} - 1\right] \tag{2}$$

As it is highly unlikely that osmotically active material is released idiogenically with the physiological doses utilized by Fitzsimons, it is reasonable to assume that changes in cellular volume accurately reflect changes in osmolality. Therefore, setting the percent increase in Equation (2) equal to zero, then

$$b_{iso} = s/c \tag{3}$$

That is, the amount of fluid necessary to restore isotonicity is equal to the solute injected (μ osmole/100 g BW) divided by the original body fluid concentration (290 μ osmole/ml HOH).

For example, if $s = 870$ μ osmole/100 g BW, then 3 ml water/100 g BW are required to accommodate the solute load as isotonic fluid (i.e., to reduce percent increase to zero). The behavioral contribution to the increase in body weight may range from nil, in the case where the solute is injected in isotonic form, to 100% in the event of crystaloid ingestion. Note that the dependent variable is expressed as increase in body weight rather than amount drunk. The latter does not take into account the fact that water lost from lungs, gastrointestinal tract, and skin is no longer available for dilution; the former does and may therefore be used to evaluate the cellular dehydration hypothesis of drinking. That

$b_{iso} = s/c$ is an accurate predictor of behavior in anuric rats is seen from Figure 3. It is clear that when the effective solute load cannot be excreted, drinking continues until the body fluids are restored to isotonicity and, presumably, normal cellular volume is reinstated. The dashed line in the figure represents the theoretical increase in body weight due to water retention required to achieve isotonicity. When increases in osmolality are no greater than 10%, the actual gains in weight conform very closely to the predicted values.

To Fitzsimons, this suggested that drinking was initiated by cellular dehydration, and was arrested by cellular rehydration—no long-term inhibitory mechanisms need be invoked to account for the cessation of drinking. However, the fluid withdrawn from the cells was accommodated in an expanded extracellular phase. It was possible, therefore, that extracellular expansion per se, rather than cellular rehydration, arrested drinking. In a direct test of this alternative, Fitzsimons infused substantial volumes of isotonic saline into nephrectomized rats, causing gross extracellular hypervolia.[3] Yet, as shown in Table 1, drinking to cellular dehydration remained normal. Extracellular overhydration, therefore, does not appear normally to contribute to the offset of drinking; no long-term inhibitory mechanisms appear to be active to stop this form of drinking. This is not to denigrate the contributions of the well-known oropharyngeal and gastric factors which produce intermittent and often quite lengthy pauses in drinking. It is to emphasize rather that drinking to cellular dehydration finally ceases only when cellular balance is restored.

Fitzsimons then called attention to the fact that the standard techniques of inducing cellular dehydration by the abrupt increase in body fluid concentration follow a rather artificial time course for developing thirst, one which is highly unlikely to occur naturally. Dehydration is a more gradual process, and Fitzsimons thought it worthwhile to evaluate whether rate of depletion was an

---

[3] The suffix "volia" as used in this chapter refers to alterations in both interstitial and vascular fluids.

TABLE 1

The Effect of Expanding Body Fluids on Drinking Induced by
Hypertonic NaCl in Nephrectomized Rats

Isotonic NaCl (ml/100 g initial body H_2O)	2 M NaCl injected (ml/100 g postinfusion body wt.)	Increase in initial osmotic pressure (%)	Water drunk (ml/100 g postinfusion body H_2O)	Fluid balance (g/100 g postinfusion body H_2O)
0	0.805	13.8	10.98	8.95 ± 0.64 (10)
3.09	0.819	13.8	10.3	8.98 ± 0.92 (6)
10.03	0.824	13.6	10.24	8.16 ± 1.33 (9)

Note.—From Fitzsimons (1961).

important factor. He found that it was not. As shown in Figure 4, drinking was determined by percentage increase in osmotic pressure and bore no relationship whatever to rate of infusion or concentration. Furthermore, the thresholds for eliciting drinking to cellular dehydration were found to be quite low in the rat—on the order of 1.6 to 2.4% increase over initial osmotic pressure and, like

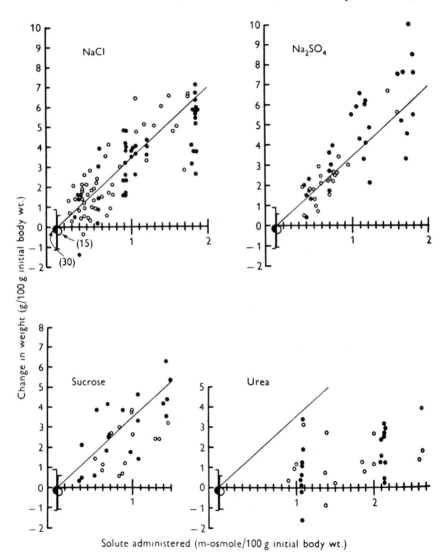

FIG. 4. The relations between the amounts of different solutes administered by rapid injection (•) or by slow infusion (○) and the changes in weight of nephrectomized rats in 6 hours. Each point is one observation except the controls, which are mean values ± SD with the number of observations in parentheses. The controls were given 0.154 M NaCl. (Data from Fitzsimons, 1963. Used by permission of the Cambridge University Press.)

amount drunk, independent of rate. These findings accord well with the earlier reports of Wolf (1950), who found that drinking in dog and man occurred after a 1 to 2% rise in osmotic pressure. They are significant, for they suggest that rats, which do not always enjoy unlimited access to water, do not adapt to the slowly developing dehydrational stimulus in terms of threshold or amount drunk.

The issue of adaptation was also tested directly by Fitzsimons, who found that the amount of water drunk by nephrectomized rats in 30 hours to a given degree of cellular dehydration was invarient whether water was made available immediately or following a 24-hour delay. By contrast, withholding water for 24 hours from rats with intact kidneys caused a 75% reduction in drinking. This is of great significance for it emphasizes the synergistic action of the renal and behavioral osmoregulatory systems. Nephrectomized rats are deprived of the renal defense, and their sole avenue towards regulation is behavioral. Normal rats, on the other hand, by excreting excess solute in hypertonic urine, realize a fair degree of renal osmoregulation, and the amount required to restore isotonicity by drinking is reduced accordingly. Yet animals are penalized when relying exclusively on renal osmoregulation, for there is an accompanying loss of other electrolytes, particularly potassium, and negative fluid and electrolyte balances are realized. Ironically, this state is also reached in the 24-hour food-deprived rat, even with water continuously available, and it is actually independent of the initial degree of cellular dehydration. Why is drinking so severely attenuated, especially in view of the lack of adaptation in the anuric rat? This strikes me as a cardinal issue, for although the physiological determinants of thirst and drinking have been identified and a number of their interactions investigated (Corbit, 1968; Fitzsimons & Oatley, 1968; Stricker, 1969; Blass & Fitzsimons, 1970), very little is known of the conditions that terminate drinking under more normal circumstances. (This issue will be developed in more detail in a later section of this chapter).

In summary, Fitzsimons' analyses have revealed an extremely sensitive behavioral system, activated selectively by hypertonic substances to mobilize drinking. The system does not adapt and, in the anuric rat, drinking persists until excess solute is diluted to isotonicity, i.e., until normal cellular volume is reinstated. Drinking, therefore, reflects degree of cellular depletion, not rate; cessation infers restoration and not inhibition from an expanded extracellular compartment.

NEUROLOGICAL CORRELATES

The burden of analyzing the neurology of thirst is lightened considerably by the excellence of recent reviews by Stevenson (1967, 1969) and Fitzsimons (1966). Their comprehensiveness allows me to focus on changes in conceptualizations of central thirst mechanisms, especially in the approaches to the neurological bases of drinking to cellular dehydration.

Two issues may be raised at the outset to direct this analysis: How is the signal of cellular dehydration detected and integrated to produce motivated drinking behavior? Does drinking in response to cellular dehydration reflect the activation of central osmoreceptors, sensitive to their own hydrational state, or are there central units which, as Wettendorff suggested in 1901, receive information from all dehydrated tissues? Stated differently, is the thirst arising from cellular dehydration of a central or a peripheral origin?

The earliest suggestions of central thirst centers appeared in 1881. Voit (1881) suggested a neural mediator of drinking, and Nothnagel (1881) reported a patient who, after being kicked in the stomach by a horse and hitting the back of his head on the road when he fell, became exceedingly thirsty. That little urine loss had ensued prior to drinking presented to Nothnagel the possibility of a primary thirst center. The neurological mediation of thirst has since received considerable attention. Preliminary information was essentially of a clinical origin and consisted largely of reports describing aberrant drinking following central traumas, especially to the brainstem. But it was not until the thirties when the Horsley-Clarke stereotaxic instrument became generally available that the experimental analysis focused on specific brain loci. The issue of a primary central thirst mechanism was in dispute, and much of the original research focused on a specific aspect of this problem: Was the excessive drinking in diabetes insipidus, produced by destruction of the median eminence, primary or secondary to a primary polyuria? Indeed the question has only very recently been resolved by the work of Barbara Simons (1968), now Barbara Rolls, which clearly favors the primacy of polyuria in diabetes insipidus.

After World War II, however, attention quickly centered on the hypothalamic and limbic systems as critical neurological mediators of drinking. Confidence in central mediation of drinking was buoyed by reports of an active role for the hypothalamus in the modulation of antidiuretic hormone secretion. Fisher, Ingram, and Ranson (1935) discovered that stereotaxically placed lesions of the supraoptico-hypophyseal tracts caused the copious urination characteristic of diabetes insipidus. Verney's (1947) wonderful analysis implicated central osmoreceptors in the vicinity of the supraoptic nuclei, sensitive to their own hydrational level, in the control of antidiuretic hormone release. Evidence for central thirst mediators accumulated rapidly in the postwar era. Brügger (1943) elicited copious feeding and drinking in cats by electrical stimulation of various hypothalamic loci; Andersson and his colleagues (Andersson & McCann, 1955a, 1955b; Andersson & Wyrwicka, 1957; Andersson, Larsson, & Persson, 1960), in an important series of experiments, elicited drinking under similar circumstances in goats (indeed goats performed a learned response to obtain water during electrical stimulation); and Greer (1955) reported the case of a rat which drank 400 ml in 24 hours during intermittent stimulation in the vicinity of the paraventricular nuclei. In short, drinking as well as other homeostatic behaviors was soon conceptualized as being mediated centrally rather than peripherally (Stellar, 1954), and today there is a wealth of data demonstrating that electrical and chemical stimulation can elicit motivated drinking from a variety of hypothalamic and limbic loci (Fitzsimons, 1966; Grossman, 1967; Stevenson, 1967, 1969). These data are important in their own right, as they have demonstrated the involvement of various rhinencephalic and diencephalic systems in thirst. In addition they have provided direction for those investigators interested in determining the functional neurology of the various components of thirst—a case in point being the elegant analysis of angiotensin-sensitive loci in the rat forebrain by Epstein, Fitzsimons, and Rolls (1970). But the students of stimulus-bound drinking have not, until very recently, addressed themselves to the question of how electrical and chemical stimuli realize their efficacy as thirst stimuli. Is it by activating select neurological mediators of cellular thirst, of extracellular thirst, or of angiotensin, or is it perhaps by activating a common path? These are important issues, and as can be seen in later chapters in this text by Mogenson, Fisher, and Setler, a start has been made on studying the specificity of drinking caused by electrical and chemical stimulation.

Data obtained by the lesion technique were, in general, consistent with the stimulation studies in that they tended to verify the relevance of an anatomical area to drinking. But they too were difficult to interpret. Again, the problem of specificity: Were alterations in drinking, produced by a lesion, due to the interruption of fibers mediating one or the other forms of thirst? Was motivation generally impaired? Did the lesions interfere with motor functions? Such questions generally remained unanswered when only ad libitum drinking was studied, for under this circumstance the functional stimulus (cellular, extra-cellular, or nonhomeostatic) could not be specified. Until a brain-damaged animal is tested with a variety of drinking stimuli, the contributions of an area to homeostatic drinking must remain unknown. As of the early sixties such analyses had not been undertaken, and because Fitzsimons (1961b) and Stricker (1966) had yet to discover the extracellular controls of drinking, a neurology of drinking emerged without reference to its underlying physiology. Although drinking was routinely enhanced, attenuated, or eliminated by various central manipulations, the contributions of diverse loci remained unspecified. Indeed, the issue of central versus peripheral detection mechanisms remained completely unresolved. Fortunately an example of the exacting form of analysis required to identify the contribution of a neural system to thirst was soon provided by Epstein and Teitelbaum (1964), and we may now speak with considerable certainty of the involvement of the lateral hypothalamic area in the hydrational controls of drinking.

Rats with well-placed lateral hypothalamic lesions neither eat nor drink, for 4 to 5 days postoperatively. But if the rat is kept alive by intubation, recovery ensues, feeding and then drinking are reinstated, and daily intake of water returns to normal (Teitelbaum & Epstein, 1962; Epstein, 1971). Yet, more specific tests after the recovery of ingestive behavior reveal that such rats suffer permanent deficits in drinking to dehydration. Epstein and Teitelbaum (1964) demonstrated that rats with lateral hypothalamic lesions are permanently impaired in drinking caused by water deprivation or cellular dehydration. Later Fitzsimons (1966) and Stricker and Wolf (1967) reported that such animals also drink less in response to extracellular dehydration. Actually the only time such animals drink is when they eat dry food and then only to facilitate the passage of dry food through the dry mouth (Kissileff & Epstein, 1969).

We have seen the beginning of the experimental separation of the neurological controls of drinking. Lateral hypothalamic integrity is not required for drinking in response to certain nonhomeostatic cues, but is required for drinking to deficits in either the cellular or extracellular phases. Could the separation be extended? That is, are there different neurological mediators subserving the various physiological controls of drinking, or is all homeostatic drinking mediated by a single neural substrate which includes the lateral hypothalamic area? The work of Blass and his colleagues favors the former alternative. They found that the neurological mechanisms underlying drinking to cellular dehydration could be uncoupled rostral to the lateral hypothalamic area. Rats made hyperdipsic by septal lesions did not drink more than normal rats to cellular dehydration, were overresponsive to hypovolia caused by intraperitoneal injections of hyperoncotic colloid (Blass & Hanson, 1970), and have since been found to be selectively overresponsive to angiotensin (E. M. Blass, A. Nussbaum, & D. G. Hanson, 1973, unpublished observations). On the other hand, rats with lesions of the frontal pole area did not drink or drank substantially less than normal to cellular dehydration, yet were not at all deficient in drinking to intravascular depletions (Blass, 1968).

Did the alterations in drinking which followed various lesions reflect an interruption of pathways mediating one or more aspects of drinking? In the case of cellular dehydration, were specialized receptors, sensitive to their own hydrational state, destroyed? It is quite unlikely that central thirst osmo- receptors reside in the lateral hypothalamic area, for Epstein (1960) had but little success in eliciting drinking by local lateral hypothalamic stimulation with very concentrated solutions of sodium chloride. However, encouraging evidence for central thirst osmoreceptors was provided by Andersson's laboratory. Andersson (1953) and his colleagues (Andersson & McCann, 1955b) demon- strated that copious drinking could be elicited from goats by injecting 0.2 ml of hypertonic saline into the perifornical region of the hypothalamus. However, saline, the only test stimulus used, was extremely hypertonic and, at .45 M, well outside the physiological range; and because other responses like milk ejection and antidiuresis also appeared, Andersson himself cautioned: "As, however, other effects were sometimes seen in association with polydipsia from the injections, conclusive proof had not been obtained for the view that the osmotic stimulus was the adequate stimulus to the tissue producing the response [Andersson & McCann, 1955b, p. 343]."

Recently, however, compelling evidence for the existence of central thirst osmoreceptors has been presented, almost simultaneously, by Peck and Novin (1971) and by Blass and Epstein (1971). Herein lies a lovely example of the internal validation process of the scientific community. The two groups worked independently, Peck and Novin at UCLA, Blass and Epstein at Pennsylvania, and, until the final stages of analysis, without knowledge of each other's experiments. Moreover, different experimental subjects were used: rabbits by the California investigators, rats in Philadelphia. Also two entirely different experimental paths were followed which led to the same conclusion, namely, that the lateral preoptic area (LPO) meets the requirements of a central osmoreceptive zone for thirst. Both of these studies will now be presented in some detail.

The point of departure for the Blass and Epstein analysis was Blass' 1968 finding that extensive ablation of the frontal pole area, which incorporated the LPO, produced a specific deficit in drinking to cellular dehydration in rats. Attention was then focused on the LPO as the critical area, for Andersson and Larsson (1956) had earlier reported that transverse sections caudal to the preoptic area in the dog abolished drinking to cellular dehydration, yet had little effect on drinking to water deprivation which dehydrates both compartments.

Accordingly, Blass and Epstein destroyed tissue in and about the LPO. The results of their experiments are shown in Figure 5, where the drinking of

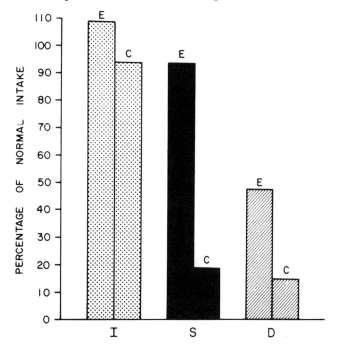

FIG. 5. The consequences of various forebrain lesions on drinking to cellular dehydration (*C*) and extracellular dehydration (*E*). Drinking is expressed as a percentage of normal rats' intake. *I*, ineffective; *S*, separation; *D*, double deficit. (From Blass & Epstein, 1971. Used by permission of the American Psychological Association.)

brain-damaged rats to extracellular and cellular dehydration is presented as a percentage of the amount drunk by normal rats. Three groups of rats which differed in their drinking to hydrational challenges were created by the lesions. Rats in Group D sustained a double deficit. They were markedly deficient in drinking to both cellular and extracellular depletions. The lesions of these rats were found to invade the medial forebrain bundle rostral to the lateral hypothalamic area at the level of the globus pallidus and, presumably, interfered with all thirst afferents as they funneled into the lateral hypothalamus. This will be discussed in more detail below. Group I designates rats with ineffective lesions. Such rats drank normally to both challenges. Finally rats in Group S (separation lesions) sustained a severe and permanent impairment in drinking to cellular dehydration but were essentially normal in their drinking to hypovolia, which suggests that the effects seen earlier by Blass (1968) in rats with massive frontal pole area lesions were attributable to the ablation of the LPO.

Figure 6 is a montage of the reconstructions of the anterior, center, and posterior aspects of the effective lesions (Group S). Nine of ten rats in Group S shared a bilateral common locus of destruction of the anterior-medial portion of the LPO at the level of the anterior commissure. Note that although the lesions varied considerably in shape and extent, the communality of damage was seen only at this level. There was no common overlap at the more rostral or caudal extents of the lesions. It is clear therefore that these rats possess at least two characteristics which distinguish them from normal: bilateral destruction of the anterior medial portion of the LPO, and a severe attenuation of the drinking response to cellular dehydration.

Figure 7 shows the reconstructions of the centers of all ineffective lesions (Group I) with the critical area from Group S superimposed. In not a single instance was there bilateral destruction of this area in rats with ineffective lesions, even though a few of the more extensive lesions destroyed considerable tissue either medial or lateral to the anterior-medial portion of the LPO, and in a number of instances overlapped the critical area unilaterally.

The agreement is all the more remarkable when the lesion data provided by Peck and Novin (1971) are taken into consideration. In Figure 8, the smallest effective lesion of the 3 rabbits which drank considerably less than normal to cellular dehydration, but which drank normally to water privation, are compared to the largest bilaterally symmetrical lesions in the bed nucleus of the stria terminalis or the far lateral portion of the LPO of the 25 rabbits who continued to drink normally. Here as in the Blass-Epstein (1971) study, the common locus of destruction in animals that did not drink to cellular dehydration was the anterior-medial portion of the LPO. Not one of the 25 rabbits that drank normally to cellular dehydration sustained damage to this critical area. Both studies agree that very little tissue of the critical area need remain functional in order for normal drinking to cellular dehydration to occur. It should be noted, however, that the challenges utilized by Blass and Epstein and by Peck and Novin were rather severe, and it is conjecture whether rats or rabbits with little

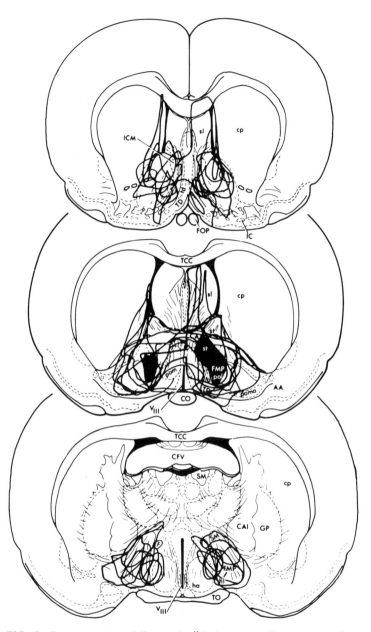

FIG. 6. Reconstruction of "separation" lesions (area of common overlap, seen only at level of anterior commissure, is darkened). Note lack of common overlap at most rostral and caudal aspects of lesions. Abbreviations: *TCC*, truncus corporis callosi; *CFV*, commissura fornicis ventralis; *SM*, stria medularis thalami; *sl*, nucleus septi lateralis; *cp*, nucleus caudatus putamen; *CA*, commissura anterior; *CAI*, capsula interna; *GP*, globus pallidus; *st*, nucleus interstitialis striae terminalis; *FMP*, fasciculus medialis prosencephali; *pom*, nucleus preopticus medialis; *pol*, nucleus preopticus lateralis; *td*, nucleus tractus diagonalis [Broca]; *TD*, tractus diagonalis [Broca]; *poma*, nucleus preopticus magnocellularis; *CO*, chiasma opticum; *AA*, area amygdala anterior. (From Blass & Epstein, 1971. Used by permission of the American Psychological Association.)

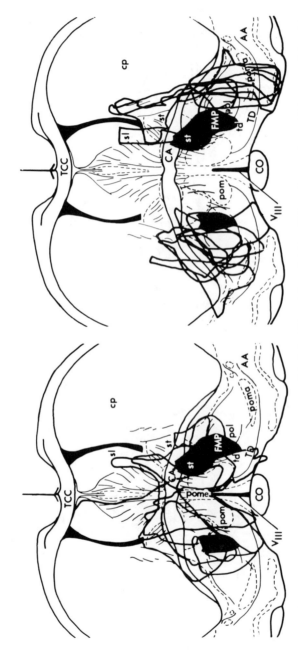

FIG. 7. Reconstruction of all ineffective lesions medial (*left side*) and lateral (*right side*) to the anterior-medial aspect of the LPO. Area of common overlap from Group S is superimposed. Anatomical abbreviations as in Figure 6; *pome*, nucleus preopticus medianus. (From Blass & Epstein, 1971. Used by permission of the American Psychological Association.)

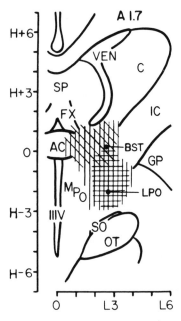

FIG. 8. Schematic frontal section through the posterior border of the anterior commissure to show the extent of lesions abolishing and sparing drinking after i.v. hypertonic saline. (*Vertical striping*, the tissue bilaterally destroyed by the smallest lesion producing the deficit; *horizontal striping*, the tissue bilaterally destroyed by the largest lesion centered in LPO and which produced no deficit; *diagonal striping*, tissue bilaterally destroyed by the largest lesion centered in *BST*, which produced no deficit. Abbreviations as in Figure 9. (From Peck & Novin, 1971. Used by permission of the American Psychological Association.)

critical tissue remaining would drink normally to threshold increases in osmotic pressure.

Is the LPO just another relay converging upon the LHA, or does it possess characteristics unique to osmoreceptors? A number of lines of evidence will now be developed which strongly support the conclusion that osmoreceptors mediating drinking are in the LPO.

Fundamental to any demonstration of osmosensitivity for thirst is the finding that drinking to the exclusion of all other behaviors must be activated by solutions which are excluded from cells. This criterion was rigorously followed by Peck and Novin, and by Blass and Epstein. Indeed it served as the basis of the

Peck and Novin experiment. In an exhaustive analysis Peck and Novin surveyed over 600 brain loci through chronically indwelling stainless steel cannulae with hypertonic saline and with sucrose, both of which are excluded from cells, and with hyperosmotic urea, which is not.

Consistent behaviors were induced from only 49 of the 600 brain loci tested. And of the 49 sensitive loci, only 6 were osmosensitive, i.e., drinking and drinking only was elicited by saline *and* sucrose but not by urea, and equal amounts were drunk to equiosmotic injections of sucrose or saline. The six, the filled circles in Figure 9, were closely clustered in the LPO ventral and caudal to the anterior commissure. Injections of 1.15 osmolal saline or sucrose at these loci elicited a mean response of 29 grams of water; equiosmotic urea caused an intake of only 3 grams. Filled squares represent sensitive loci from which other oral behaviors such as feeding and gnawing could be elicited with saline only. They were, in general, caudal to the LPO and probably represent the nonspecific activation of high-order dorsal and lateral hypothalamic neurons mediating these behaviors. Finally, the open circles represent areas which were insensitive, and it is important to note that included in the ineffective drinking loci was the supraoptic area where the osmoreceptors for the secretion of antidiuretic hormone are located. The important criterion of selectivity was, therefore, fulfilled only when the cannulae terminated in the LPO. The contrast between the specific elicitation of drinking from the 6 LPO loci with the arousal of diverse behaviors from a variety of other loci is impressive. It supports the assertion that the drinking elicited by injections of hypertonic solutions into the LPO was by virtue of the specific activation of thirst osmoreceptors by osmotically effective stimuli. It does not support the possibility that this drinking reflected the nonspecific activation of neural systems generally involved in ingestive behavior.

In addition to being activated selectively, the area appears to be quite sensitive. Blass and Epstein (1971) were able to elicit drinking consistently with bilateral injections of 0.18 M NaCl even when only 1 μl was injected. This concentration approaches the physiological range. If we assume that before drinking occurred the injected solute was diluted in a volume of extracellular fluid that was at least several times the volume of the injected solution, then the increase in effective osmotic pressure that was stimulating drinking was in, or very close to, the upper limits of the physiological range.[4]

Drinking elicited by local LPO dehydration therefore bears some of the physiological characteristics of that caused by systemic cellular dehydration, namely, selectivity of activation and sensitivity. Local LPO dehydration also produced alterations in behavior, which were remarkably similar to those caused by systemic dehydration. Drinking under each condition was motivated. When the drinking tube was removed from its customary location and moved to a new place, the animal searched for it after the injection. Moreover, when a hand was

---

[4] We have recently elicited drinking by stimulating the LPO, bilaterally, with .165 M NaCl (E. M. Blass unpublished observations).

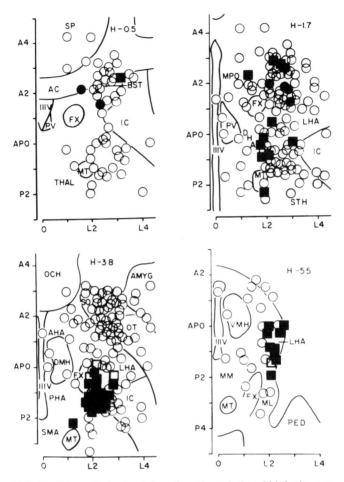

FIG. 9. Schematic horizontal sections through the rabbit brain onto which are projected injection loci within .3 mm of the section. Symbols: ● = osmosensitive; ■ = sensitive to saline only; □ = sensitive to any injection; ○ = insensitive to 1.15 osmolal saline. Abbreviations: *AC*, anterior commissure; *AHA*, anterior hypothalamic area; *AMYG*, amygdala; *BST*, n. interstitialis striae terminalis; *C*, caudate nucleus; *DHA*, dorsal hypothalamic area; *DMH*, n. dorsomedialis hypothalami; *FF*, fimbria of fornix; *FX*, fornix; *GP*, globus pallidus; *HPC*, hippocampus; *IC*, internal capsule; *LHA*, lateral hypothalamic area; *LPO*, lateral preoptic area; *ML*, n. mammillaris lateralis; *MM*, n. mammillaris medialis; *MPO*, medial preoptic area; *MT*, mammillothalamic tract; *OCH*, optic chiasm; *OT*, optic tract; *PED*, basis pedunculi; *PHA*, posterior hypothalamic area; *PV*, n. paraventricularis; *SMA*, supramammillary area; *SO*, n. supraopticus; *SP*, septum; *STH*, subthalamus; *THAL*, thalamus; *VMH*, n. ventromedialis hypothalami; *VEN*, lateral ventricle; *III V*, third ventricle. (From Peck & Novin, 1971. Used by permission of the American Psychological Association.)

cupped over the spout, the rat stepped over the obstacle and drank. In addition, Peck and Novin (1971) found that in two rabbits with osmosensitive placements, intracranial cellular dehydration caused the animals to choose distilled water over the normally preferred isotonic saline solution, a choice routinely made to systemic cellular dehydration. This specific appetite for water is further evidence for the activation of thirst osmoreceptors and against the notion of a general activation.

Certain behavioral and physiological characteristics are therefore common to drinking caused by LPO or systemic cellular dehydration. Blass and Epstein (1971) then asked if the conditions producing satiety are similar. Recall the important point made by Fitzsimons (1961) that drinking ceases only with the restoration of isotonicity. It was reasoned therefore that if the lateral preoptic area is the central osmosensitive zone for thirst, then rehydrating the LPO should arrest drinking in the systemically dehydrated rat. This prediction was borne out, as seen in Figure 10. The left-hand panel represents drinking induced by 2 ml intraperitoneal injections of 2 M saline. The unbroken line is drinking when no intracranial injection was made. The inhibitory effect of distilled water delivered to the LPO at the onset of drinking and at 1, 6, and 8 minutes

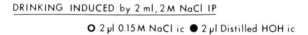

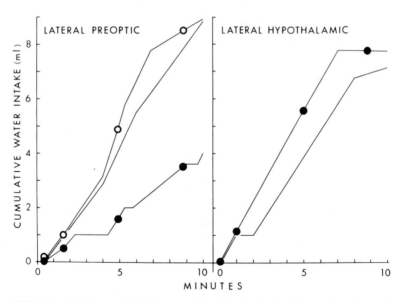

FIG. 10. Inhibition of drinking to cellular dehydration by bilateral injections of distilled water (●) into the LPO. Inhibition was specific to distilled water in LPO as neither isotonic saline (○) in LPO nor distilled water in LHA (right-hand panel) were effective. (From Blass & Epstein, 1971. Used by permission of the American Psychological Association.)

thereafter, is represented by the closed circles. This is a highly reproducible phenomenon as the mean intake of six rats was reduced from 6.3 ml in 10 minutes when no intracranial injections were made, to 3.4 ml when distilled water was injected bilaterally into the LPO. It was not the injection per se which caused inhibition, for isotonic saline delivered to the LPO exerted no inhibitory effect. The effect was anatomically specific. Distilled water injected into the lateral hypothalamic area was ineffective in reducing drinking (right-hand panel). Moreover, the inhibition was physiologically specific as well. Distilled water was effective in the LPO as an inhibitor of drinking only when drinking was in response to cellular dehydration, but not when it followed intraperitoneal injections of renin. In addition to showing physiological specificity, this demonstrated that injections of distilled water into the LPO did not cause a global debilitation which could have hampered ingestive behavior. The finding that the eating of a liquid diet was also resistant to intracranial injections of distilled water argues further for the specificity of the effect.

Together the Peck-Novin and Blass-Epstein studies strongly suggest that the LPO contains osmosensitive cells which serve as the sensors for the neurological system that mobilizes drinking in response to cellular dehydration. This form of drinking was specifically eliminated in rats and rabbits by destruction of the anterior medial portion of the LPO. Drinking in the hydrated animal was elicited selectively by microliter injections of osmotically active substances into the LPO. This area is sensitive as solutions approaching the physiological range were effective. Drinking appeared normal and motivated. No signs of stress were ever observed, and rabbits were shown to choose water over the normally preferred isotonic saline. Lastly, rehydration of the LPO specifically attenuated drinking in response to systemic cellular dehydration. It is likely that these are the exclusive osmoreceptors for thirst. However, it is premature to exclude the possibility that osmoreceptors in the pancreas (Inchina & Finkinshtein, 1964) or in the hepatic portal vein, described by Haberich (1968) in the modulation of antidiuretic hormone secretion, also contribute to thirst.

In addition to discovering thirst osmoreceptors per se, these studies have made inroads in identifying a functional neurology underlying behavioral contributions to the maintenance of normal cellular balance. From Peck and Novin (1971) we learn that the preference of water over saline by the dehydrated rabbit may be initiated by the preoptic osmosensitive system. Therefore, there is now no need to postulate additional sets of detectors in order to account for this specific choice behavior. Similarly the observations of drinking following local cellular dehydration of the LPO in rabbits and rats, otherwise in positive fluid balance, coupled with the fact that bilateral rehydration of the LPO arrests drinking in grossly dehydrated rats, provides a neurological basis for Fitzsimons' analysis. If cells in the lateral preoptic area respond like all other cells to changes in their osmotic ambience, then systemic infusion of hypertonic solutions dehydrates all cells including osmoreceptors. This is the necessary and sufficient stimulus for cell dehydration thirst. Drinking ensues, and water reenters the cells along an osmotic gradient, which is maintained until enough has been drunk to restore the cellular phase, including the osmoreceptors, to normal. This appears to be the necessary and sufficient condition to terminate drinking. It does not preclude the contribution of peripheral oropharyngeal and gastric inhibitory mechanisms which may account for the often lengthy pauses in drinking. Rather it strongly suggests that the ultimate cessation described by Fitzsimons reflects the return of the proposed osmosensitive cells in the lateral preoptic area to normal.

Our understanding of the neural integration of signals arising from LPO is very inadequate. As mentioned earlier, the only area which has received the experimental analysis necessary to identify its involvement in cellular dehydration thirst has been the lateral hypothalamus, where all thirst afferents appear to coalesce.

The merger of thirst afferents appears to be complete rostral to the LHA. This is seen in Figure 11, which presents the lesions of four rats with double deficits which drank neither to cellular nor to extracellular depletions (Blass & Epstein, 1971). While the lesions varied considerably in shape and extent, they

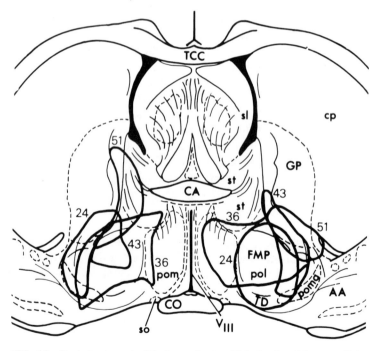

FIG. 11. Posterior aspect of lesions of rats which drank neither to cellular dehydration nor to extracellular dehydration (Group D). (The lesions of two rats [43 and 51] fully spared the head of the LPO bilaterally, and did not extend into the lateral hypothalamic area. *F,* columna fornices.) (From Blass & Epstein, 1971. Used by permission of the American Psychological Association.)

all shared a common locus of destruction bordered by the globus pallidus, internal capsule, and the dorsolateral portion of the posterior LPO. It is particularly important to note that in the case of rats 43 and 51, this marked the posterior terminus of the lesion. The lateral hypothalamic area was undamaged in so far as we could discern using light microscopy. These rats are of considerable interest as they were similar to the classic "recovered-lateral" in that drinking to hydrational challenges appeared permanently impaired. They differed, however, to the extent that their duration of recovery into stage IV was only 3 to 4 days, and they were able to survive by rapidly developing the prandial style of drinking (Kissileff, 1969).

Much remains to be learned from this preparation by contrasting its behavior with the global deficits of the "recovered laterals," and with the specific deficit of the animal with LPO damage.

BEHAVIORAL CORRELATES

This anatomical consideration discussed above relates directly to a perplexing behavioral problem. If cellular and extracellular afferents converge upon the LHA, do they give rise to a single unified sensation of thirst or do the various physiological stimuli, each exerting control through separate neurological afferents, produce qualitatively different forms of thirst?

Evidence has recently been produced which favors the latter alternative (Burke, Mook, & Blass, 1972). As shown in the left-hand portion of Figure 12, rats, following water privation, drank as much of mildly bitter quinine solutions (.01% and .001%) as they did of water. However, when cellular dehydration was superimposed upon water privation, quinine intake was actually reduced while water intake increased considerably. The decrease was state-dependent, for as seen in the right-hand panel, intravascular depletion, in combination with water deprivation, enhanced both quinine and water intake.

It was not as if the rats were not motivated to drink or were particularly debilitated. Cellular dehydration was produced via intravenous infusion and without any untoward discomfort; the animals were quite alert and returned to the drinking tube repeatedly. Considerable displacement behavior was in evidence following ingestion of QHCL. Some rats recoiled from the spout and, in a few exaggerated cases, drank while in the supine position, a behavior reminiscent of the poisoned rat's response to poisoned fluids. These observations mark the first evidence for separate sensations of thirst, and suggest that the afferents do not coalesce to form a unified sensation of thirst.

To this point drinking to cellular dehydration and the maintenance of normal fluid balance have been described under ideal conditions, i.e., with fluid freely available. Such circumstances are generally not the rule, and there are many occasions when cellular integrity is forfeited in deference to other balances. Accordingly, we shall consider regulation of cellular fluid in a more general biological context, placing particular emphasis on the behavioral contributions.

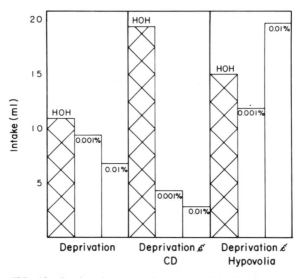

FIG. 12. Intake of water and quinine hydrochloride (0.01 and 0.001%) following: *left-hand panel,* water deprivation alone; *center panel,* water deprivation in combination with cellular dehydration; *right-hand panel,* water deprivation in combination with hypovolia. (From Burke, Mook, & Blass, 1972. Used by permission of the American Psychological Association.)

Normally the environment places many different demands on the animal, which must arrange its priorities accordingly. For example, water is lost by the dehydrated animal during feeding. The animal is not inflexible in its defense of the cellular space to the exclusion of this other demand. It has long been established that cellular dehydration attenuates feeding—attenuates but does not eliminate, despite the fact that to eat causes a further embarrassment to the cellular space. When, however, water is made available and the animal has drunk, it will eat. This has been very nicely shown by Deaux and Kakolewski (1971) in an extensive analysis, part of which is presented as Figure 13. Latencies to eat, and serum osmolalities of 23-hour water- but not food-deprived rats, given 3, 6, or 9 ml of water to drink, are presented. The latencies for the 6- and 9-milliliter groups are short indeed. But to my way of thinking the most impressive aspect of this figure is the fact that eating occurred here despite the persistence of frank dehydration, normal serum osmolality being approximately 290 m Osm/KG. In other words, rats, albeit sensitive to very small increases in osmotic pressure, voluntarily undergo further dehydration in order to meet their energy demands. A balance is struck. When no constraints are applied, energy exchanges and fluid balances are maintained with great precision. However, this precision is in a sense a luxury, for in more normal circumstances strict cellular balance must be forfeited. Under the conditions described above, rats voluntarily tolerated a 6% increase in osmolality in order to eat. It is also the case, however, that the sacrifice is not open-ended. A compromise is reached, for eating did not occur when osmolalities were at 317.2 m Osm/KG, and amount eaten was proportional to amount drunk.

A similar compromise is realized in defending the vascular volume. According to Stricker (1969) hypovolic rats stop drinking water well in advance of intravascular restoration. An extensive array of data has been presented by Stricker to support the idea that cellular overhydration inhibits drinking, and that the inhibition is graded in proportion to vascular depletion; i.e., a greater degree of cellular overhydration is required to terminate drinking to severe intravascular depletions. Again, a trade-off. Degree of overhydration is not absolute, but is reasonably flexible to accommodate the more severe hypovolia. On the other hand, cellular overhydration is not fully open-ended. Rats do not

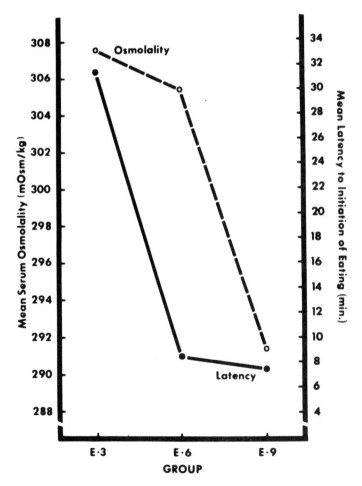

FIG. 13. Mean serum osmolality (*left-hand scale*) and mean latency to initiate eating for rats given 3, 6, of 9 ml of water to drink. (From Deaux & Kakolewski, 1971. Used by permission of the American Psychological Association.)

voluntarily overhydrate themselves beyond 130.5 mEq Na/liter even in the face of intravascular depletion combined with caval ligation—a stimulus which caused up to 160 ml intake of isotonic saline (Stricker, 1971). The fact that a lower limit is defended is of considerable significance, for if it were violated, and the rats continued to drink water, they would succumb to water intoxication.

I believe that Stricker has detailed a fundamental characteristic of the hydrational controls of drinking, and we now have evidence that it may actually be called into effect whenever deprivation occurs. Adolph et al. (1954) reported that water-deprived rats do not nearly make up their fluid deficit when drinking water in the absence of food and, as indicated earlier, Fitzsimons (1971) reported that rats that are in cellular dehydration also undergo voluntary dehydration. We have analyzed the Adolph phenomenon, to discover that this failure may be attributed to cellular overhydration (E. M. Blass & W. G. Hall, 1973, unpublished data). Figure 14 shows the intake of water and of isotonic saline of water-deprived rats made anuric by ureteric ligation just prior to fluid restoration. Table 2 presents the blood measures of these rats, of similarly deprived rats prevented from drinking, and of rats with food and water available

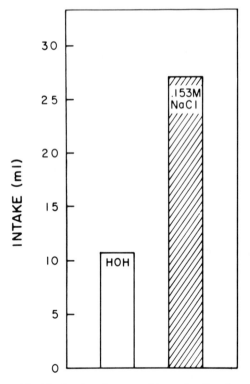

FIG. 14.   Intake of water and isotonic saline, by 24-hour food- and water-deprived anuric rats. (E. M. Blass, W. G. Hall, unpublished observations.)

TABLE 2

Mean Plasma Sodiums and Hematocrits of Rats Following
Various Deprivation and Rehydration Schedules

Condition	Drink	Na	Hct.
Ad libitum	HOH	142	45.4
24-hour food and water privation	nothing	142.5	49
24-hour food and water privation[a]	HOH	134	49
24-hour food and water privation[a]	.153 M NaCl	143	45

[a]Made anuric at start of drinking test.

ad libitum. Rats drinking water stopped within the first half hour of testing, generally not to resume again. Their intake was less than half that of the saline group, and they made up 20% of the fluid deficit. Table 2 presents a strong case for the inhibition of drinking by cellular overhydration. Plasma sodiums were quite low in comparison to normal; yet hematocrits were elevated. That is, drinking stopped in the face of persistant hypovolia. Yet the system is precisely sensitive to the hypovolic challenge. This is inferred from the saline tests where drinking continued until the extracellular deficit was restored, for here drinking was not opposed by cellular overhydration. The paradox of plenty in the face of an impoverished extracellular phase is appreciated by intact rats drinking water. They excrete about 25% of their intake as extremely dilute urine within 1 hour after completion of drinking, despite the fact that they do not make good their fluid deficit.

And now we come full circle. Recall the difficulties which renal regulation presented to earlier students of thirst. Now, however, owing to the analyses of Fitzsimons, drinking in the absence of renal regulation is better understood. Some have felt it opportune therefore to investigate the impact of drinking per se on renal function. The important work of Nicolaïdis (1969) bears on this issue. Nicolaïdis overhydrated anaesthetized rats by intubation of water, causing a brisk diuresis. He then irrigated the mouth with either 1 to 3 ml water or 5% saline and discovered, as seen in Figure 15, that the passage of fluids through the mouth exerted a profound effect on diuresis, water enhancing urine output and saline diminishing it. It was as if the water conservation mechanism anticipated the consequences of ingestion and responded accordingly. This was extended by Kakolewski, Cox, and Valenstein (1968), who observed a profound antidiuresis in overhydrated rats within 2 minutes after the initiation of feeding. The short latencies, according to Kakolewski et al., rule out postingestional absorption mechanisms or the dehydrating effects of food in the stomach. The electro-physiological data obtained by Nicolaïdis are complementary, for increases in

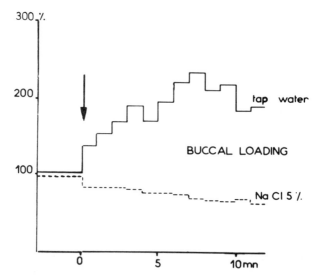

FIG. 15. The effects of oral loading of 1 to 3 ml tap water (*solid line*) or 5% NaCl (*dashed line*) on urine flow in overhydrated rats. (Data from Nicolaïdis, 1969. Used by permission of the New York Academy of Sciences.)

the firing of supraoptic units caused by 0.2 ml intracarotid infusion of 1 M saline were very similar indeed to those produced by irrigating the mouth with 4 ml of 1 M saline. Renal output, therefore, is affected appropriately by the passage of substances through the oropharynx as marked changes in urine flow precede fluid absorption. Whether the mechanisms are innate or reflect a conditioned response demands empirical resolution.

These reports of behavioral and physiological accommodation and interactions are impressive. They are cardinal examples of Stellar's (1954) excellent insight into the multiple controls of motivated behavior. They indicate the complexity of the behavioral effectors, and call attention to behavioral-physiological synergisms. They also make the important point that at issue is the maintenance of normal cellular volume and that drinking is but one of a number of effectors which act in concert to realize this end.

SUMMARY, CONCLUSIONS, AND FUTURE DIRECTION

We have seen that in the absence of the kidneys, rats made thirsty by infusions of hypertonic solutions drink until isotonicity is restored. However, restoration to isotonicity is incidental. Methyl glucose, glucose, and fructose, all of which freely enter cells, failed to elicit drinking. The critical stimulus is, therefore, cellular dehydration, and it is believed that drinking finally stops when the cellular phase, particularly the cells of the lateral preoptic area, is restored to normal volume. The system is quite sensitive. In normal animals as little as a 1 to 2% increase in osmotic pressure causes drinking and also leads to the release of antidiuretic hormone (ADH). Balance in the normal animal is therefore realized through the contributions of renal and behavioral effectors, and recent evidence suggests that the passage of fluid or food through the mouth may directly modulate ADH release.

Because there is a certain degree of closure on the drinking of animals faced with a pure cellular stimulus, some have started to inquire how cellular balance fits into the larger homeostatic scheme. Rats are quite flexible in their maintenance of cellular balance. They voluntarily undergo excessive cellular overhydration in the face of a persistent extracellular deficit, and excessive dehydration is endured when the thirsty rat eats. Also, a start on the neurology has been made. The lateral preoptic area appears to be the central osmosensitive zone for thirst and its efferents pass through the lateral hypothalamic area. The details of a functional neurology have not been worked out, and nothing is known about the neural or peripheral mechanisms which allow the animal to voluntarily overhydrate or dehydrate the cellular space.

The outline of the dynamics of a possible mechanism responsive to cellular dehydration is presented as Figure 16. It should be noted at the outset that this

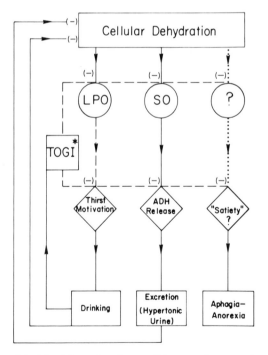

FIG. 16. Schematic of a possible control system in the behavioral and renal defenses against cellular dehydration. *TOGI*, Temporary Oropharyngeal-Gastric Inhibition.

circuit is considerably simplified to serve as a guide toward conceptualizing and directing future research.

A 1 to 2% decrease in cellular volume is detected, presumably, by osmosensitive units in the supraoptic and lateral preoptic areas. Supraoptic arousal controls the release of antidiuretic hormone from the posterior pituitary. ADH, in turn, acts directly on the distal tubules of the kidney to conserve water, thereby causing the excretion of concentrated urine.

It is presumed that activation of the LPO osmoreceptors is directly involved in the sensation of thirst in man and in motivated behavior in subhumans. Evidence for man is, of course, lacking but is suggestive for rats and rabbits. Accordingly, the assertion that activation of the LPO is the only source of the thirst of cellular dehydration is, although highly likely, premature (see section on neurological correlates) and the connection is presented in the model as a dashed line. Another reason for the dashed line is that the functional neurology mediating signals arising from LPO is unknown, save for the fact that the lateral hypothalamic area is somehow involved.

The intervening variable of thirst is necessary, at this point of our understanding, for we simply do not know the relationship between the subjective feeling caused by cellular dehydration, the willingness to work for water, and the amount drunk. While rate of drinking, in rats at least, is constant, suggesting that LPO osmoreceptors could respond in an "on-off" manner (Stellar & Hill, 1952; Corbit & Luschei, 1969), our subjective experiences of thirst are of increasing discomfort with increasing deprivation and, in rats, operant rate on a VI 60' schedule is commensurate with degree of dehydration (Wayner, Brown, Kitayama, & Gray, 1970). Moreover, drinking temporarily stops well before the cellular deficit is repaired.

In any event, drinking occurs and the synergism of behavioral and physiological effectors ultimately restores normal cellular volume. However, because ingestion is far more rapid than excretion, there is phase-advance in the behavioral system, involving feedback from oral metering (Bellows, 1939), taste of ingested fluid (Mook, 1963), and stomach distention (Adolph, 1950; Towbin, 1949) which summate to temporarily inhibit drinking. We may currently assume that these inputs are realized at an integrative level rather than at the receptors, for drinking initially stops even though the cellular space remains rather severely contracted. However, it certainly is possible that the receptors themselves are affected. This speculation gains support from Nicolaïdis' (1969) report of alterations in rate of firing of neurons in the supraoptic-paraventricular area when the mouth was irrigated by various fluids.

The third vertical column in Figure 16 represents the voluntary decrease in feeding caused by cellular dehydration. Here the connections are dotted rather than dashed, for there is not a shred of evidence for the existence of a central inhibitory mechanism for the inhibition of feeding by dehydration. That alterations in feeding are commensurate with changes in fluid intake could be reasonably explained by the action of peripheral mechanisms (e.g., altered salivary flow). Moreover, the little information available regarding the neurology of this system is discouraging, for Kissileff's (1969) data suggest that some rats, "recovered" from lateral hypothalamic lesions, increased feeding when "over-hydrated" experimentally. Consequently the influence of the temporary signals, arising from drinking, on feeding is also presented as a dotted line.

While the diagram has been useful in summarizing the behavioral dynamics of rehydration and in pointing out some of the more prominent lacunae in our understanding, a number of other factors, omitted from the figure, must be noted before this summary of the "simpler" hydrational control is brought to a close. No horizontal connections have been made between the columns. It is not at all known whether LPO activity "drives" that of SO. Nor is it established whether the integration of the various thirst signals influences ADH release independent of supraoptic activity. Further, it is not known whether drinking per se influences feeding. Similarly the consequences of supraoptic activity on drinking have yet to be established, although a recent report by Barbara Rolls (1971) has clearly demonstrated that exogenous ADH does not affect the drinking response.

The future calls for resolution of the problems presented above. Our neurological understanding is rudimentary, for only receptors and one possible synaptic link have been identified. Attention must now also focus on interactions between depletions of the different phases and alterations in behavior (Burke et al., 1972) as well as on the interactions that Nicolaïdis (1969) has demonstrated between oral afferents and renal effectors.

REFERENCES

Adolph, E. F. Thirst and its inhibition in the stomach. *American Journal of Physiology,* 1950, **161**, 374–386.

Adolph, E. F., Barker, J. P., & Hoy, P. A. Multiple factors in thirst. *American Journal of Physiology,* 1954, **178**, 538–562.

Andersson, B. The effect of injections of hypertonic NaCl-solutions into different parts of the hypothalamus of goats. *Acta Physiologica Scandinavica,* 1953, **28**, 188–201.

Andersson, B., & Larsson, S. Water and food intake and the inhibitory effect of amphetamine on drinking and eating before and after prefrontal lobotomy in dogs. *Acta Physiologica Scandinavica,* 1956, **38**, 22–30.

Andersson, B., Larsson, S., & Persson, N. Some characteristics of the hypothalamic "drinking centre" in the goat as shown by the use of permanent electrodes. *Acta Physiologica Scandinavica,* 1960, **50**, 140–159.

Andersson, B., & McCann, S. M. Drinking, antidiuresis and milk ejection elicited by electrical stimulation in the goat. *Acta Physiologica Scandinavica,* 1955, **35**, 191–201. (a)

Andersson, B., & McCann, S. M. A further study of polydipsia evoked by hypothalamic stimulation in the goat. *Acta Physiologica Scandinavica,* 1955, **33**, 333–346. (b)

Andersson, B., & Wyrwicka, W. The elicitation of a drinking motor conditioned reaction by electrical stimulation of the hypothalamus of the goat. *Acta Physiologica Scandinavica,* 1957, **41**, 194–198.

Bellows, R. T. Time factors in water drinking in dogs. *American Journal of Physiology,* 1939, **125**, 87–97.

Blass, E. M. Separation of cellular from extracellular controls of drinking in rats by frontal brain damage. *Science,* 1968, **162**, 1501–1503.

Blass, E. M., & Epstein, A. N. A lateral preoptic osmosensitive zone for thirst in the rat. *Journal of Comparative and Physiological Psychology,* 1971,**76**, 378–394.

Blass, E. M., & Fitzsimons, J. T. Additivity of effect and interaction of a cellular and extracellular stimulus of drinking. *Journal of Comparative and Physiological Psychology,* 1970, **70**, 200–205.

Blass, E. M., & Hanson, D. G. Primary hyperdipsia in the rat following septal lesions. *Journal of Comparative and Physiological Psychology,* 1970, **70**, 87–93.

Brügger, M. Fresstrieb als hypothalamisches. *Helvetica Physiologica et Pharmacologica Acta,* 1943, **1**, 183–198.

Burke, G. H., Mook, D. G., & Blass, E. M. Hyperreactivity to quinine associated with osmotic thirst in the rat. *Journal of Comparative and Physiological Psychology,* 1972, **78**, 32–39.

Cannon, W. B. The physiological basis of thirst. *Proceedings of the Royal Society (London),* Series B, 1918, **90**, 283–301.

Cannon, W. B. *The wisdom of the body.* New York: Norton, 1932.

Corbit, J. D. Cellular dehydration and hypovolaemia are additive in producing thirst. *Nature,* 1968, **218**, 886–887.

Corbit, J. D., & Luschei, E. S. Invariance of the rat's rate of drinking. *Journal of Comparative and Physiological Psychology,* 1969, **69**, 119–125.

Danowski, T. S. and Elkinton, J. R. Exchanges of potassium related to organs and systems. *Pharmacological Review,* 1951, **3**, 42–58.

Deaux, E., & Kakolewski, J. W. Character of osmotic changes resulting in the initiation of eating. *Journal of Comparative and Physiological Psychology,* 1971, **74**, 248–253.

Elkinton, J. R., & Danowski, T. S. *The body fluids: Basic physiology and practical therapeutics.* Baltimore: Williams & Wilkins, 1955.

Epstein, A. N. Reciprocal changes in feeding behavior by intrahypothalamic chemical injections. *American Journal of Physiology,* 1960, **199**, 969–974.

Epstein, A. N. The lateral hypothalamic syndrome: Its implications for the physiological psychology of hunger and thirst. In E. Stellar & J. M. Sprague (Eds.), *Progress in physiological psychology,* Vol. 4. New York: Academic Press, 1971. Pp. 263–317.

Epstein, A. N., Fitzsimons, J. T., & Rolls, B. J. Drinking induced by injection of angiotensin into the brain of the rat. *Journal of Physiology (London),* 1970, **210**, 457–474.

Epstein, A. N., & Teitelbaum, P. Severe and persistent deficits in thirst produced by lateral hypothalamic damage. In M. J. Wayner (Ed.), *Thirst.* London: Pergamon Press, 1964. Pp. 395–406.

Fisher, C., Ingram, W. R., & Ranson, S. W. The relation of the hypothalamico-hypophyseal system to diabetes insipidus. *Archives Neurology and Psychiatry,* 1935, **34**, 124–163.

Fitzsimons, J. T. Drinking by nephrectomized rats injected with various substances. *Journal of Physiology (London),* 1961, **155**, 563–579. (a)

Fitzsimons, J. T. Drinking by rats depleted of body fluid without increase in osmotic pressure. *Journal of Physiology (London),* 1961, **159**, 297–309. (b)

Fitzsimons, J. T. The effect of slow infusions of hypertonic solutions on drinking and drinking thresholds in rats. *Journal of Physiology (London),* 1963, **167**, 344–354.

Fitzsimons, J. T. The hypothalamus and drinking. *British Medical Bulletin,* 1966, **22**, 232–237.

Fitzsimons, J. T. The physiology of thirst: A review of the extraneural aspects of the mechanisms of drinking. In E. Stellar & J. M. Sprague (Eds.), *Progress in physiological psychology.* Vol. 4. New York: Academic Press, 1971. Pp. 119–201.

Fitzsimons, J. T., & Oatley, K. Additivity of stimuli for drinking in rats. *Journal of Comparative and Physiological Psychology,* 1968, **66**, 450–455.

Gamble, J. L. Deficits in diarrhea. *Journal of Pediatrics,* 1947, **30**, 488–494.

Gilman, A. The relation between blood osmotic pressure, fluid distribution and voluntary water intake. *American Journal of Physiology*, 1937, **120**, 323–328.

Greer, M. A. Suggestive evidence of a primary "drinking center" in hypothalamus of the rat. *Proceedings of the Society of the Experimental Biology and Medicine*, 1955, **89**, 59–62.

Grossman, S. P. Neuropharmacology of central mechanisms contributing to the control of food and water intake. In C. F. Code (Ed.), *Handbook of physiology. Sec. 6. Alimentary canal. Vol. 1. Food and water intake.* Washington, D. C.: American Physiological Society, 1967. Pp. 287–302.

Haberich, F. J. Osmoreception in the portal circulation. *Federation Proceedings*, 1968, **27**, 1137–1141.

Holmes, J. H., & Gregersen, M. I. Origin of thirst in diabetes insipidus. *American Journal of Medicine*, 1948, **4**, 503–510.

Holmes, J. H., & Gregersen, M. I. Observations on drinking induced by hypertonic solutions. *American Journal of Physiology*, 1950, **162**, 326–337. (a)

Holmes, J. H., & Gregersen, M. I. Role of sodium and chloride in thirst. *American Journal of Physiology*, 1950, **162**, 338–347. (b)

Inchina, V. I., & Finkinshtein, Y. D. Osmoreceptors and baroreceptors of the pancreas. *Fiziologicheskii Zhurnal SSSR*, 1964, **50**, 301–303.

Kakolewski, J. W., Cox, V. C., & Valenstein, E. S. Short-latency antidiuresis following the initiation of food ingestion. *Science*, 1968, **162**, 458–460.

Kanter, G. S. Excretion and drinking after salt loading in dogs. *American Journal of Physiology*, 1953, **174**, 87–94.

Kissileff, H. R. Oropharyngeal control of prandial drinking. *Journal of Comparative and Physiological Psychology*, 1969, **67**, 309–319.

Kissileff, H. R., & Epstein, A. N. Exaggerated prandial drinking in the "recovered lateral" rat without saliva. *Journal of Comparative and Physiological Psychology*, 1969, **67**, 301–308.

Mayer, A. Variations de la tension osmotique du sang chez les animaux prives de liquides. *Comptes Rendus des Séances de la Société de Biologie*, 1900, **52**, 153–155.

Miller, N. E. Behavioral and physiological techniques: Rationale and experimental designs for combining their use: In C. F. Code (Ed.), *Handbook of physiology. Sec. 6. Alimentary canal. Vol. 1. Food and water intake.* Washington, D. C.: American Physiological Society, 1967. Pp. 51–61.

Mook, D. G. Oral and postingenstional determinants of the intake of various solutions in rats with esophogeal fistulas. *Journal of Comparative and Physiological Psychology*, 1963, **56**, 645–659.

Newburg, L. H., & Johnson, M. W. Insensible loss of water. *Physiological Review*, 1942, **22**, 1–18.

Nicolaïdis, S. Early systemic responses to orogastric stimulation in the regulation of food and water balance: Functional and electrophysiological data. *Annals of the New York Academy of Sciences*, 1969, **157**, 1176–1203.

Nothnagel, H. Durst and Polydipsie. *Virchow's Archiv für Pathologische Anatomie und Physiologie und Klinische Medizin*, 1881, **86**, 435–447.

Novin, D. The relation between electrical conductivity of brain tissue and thirst in the rat. *Journal of Comparative and Physiological Psychology*, 1962, **55**, 145–154.

O'Kelly, L. I., & Heyer, A. W., Jr. Studies in motivation and retention. I. Retention of a simple habit. *Journal of Comparative and Physiological Psychology*, 1948, **41**, 466–478.

Peck, J. W., & Novin, D. Evidence that osmoreceptors mediating drinking in rabbits are in the lateral preoptic area. *Journal of Comparative and Physiological Psychology*, 1971, **74**, 134–147.

Reed, D. J., & Woodbury, D. M. Effect of hypertonic urea on cerebrospinal fluid pressure and brain volume. *Journal of Physiology* (*London*), 1962, **164**, 252–264.

Richter, C. P. The primacy of polyuria in diabetes insipidus. *American Journal of Physiology*, 1935, **112**, 481–487.

Rolls, B. J. The effect of intravenous infusion of antidiuretic hormone on water intake in the rat. *Journal of Physiology (London)*, 1971, **219**, 331–339.

Simons, B. J. Cause of excessive drinking in diabetes insipidus. *Nature,* 1968, **219**, 1061–1062.

Stellar, E. The physiology of motivation. *Psychological Review,* 1954, **61**, 5–22.

Stellar, E., & Hill, J. H. The rat's rate of drinking as a function of water deprivation. *Journal of Comparative and Physiological Psychology,* 1952, **45**, 96–102.

Stevenson, J. A. F. Central mechanisms controlling water intake. In C. F. Code (Ed.), *Handbook of physiology.* Sec. 6. *Alimentary canal.* Vol. 1. *Food and water intake.* Washington, D. C.: American Physiological Society, 1967. Pp. 173–190.

Stevenson, J. A. F. Neural control of food and water intake. In W. Haymaker, E. Anderson, & W. J. H. Nauta (Eds.), *The hypothalamus.* Springfield, Ill.: Charles C Thomas, 1969. Pp. 524–621.

Stricker, E. M. Extracellular fluid volume and thirst. *American Journal of Physiology,* 1966, **211**, 232–238.

Stricker, E. M. Osmoregulation and volume regulation in rats: Inhibition of hypovolemic thirst by water. *American Journal of Physiology,* 1969, **217**, 98–105.

Stricker, E. M. Inhibition of thirst in rats following hypovolemia and/or caval ligation. *Physiology and Behavior,* 1971, **6**, 293–298.

Stricker, E. M., & Wolf, G. The effects of hypovolemia on drinking in rats with lateral hypothalamic damage. *Proceedings Society of Experimental Biology and Medicine,* 1967, **124**, 816–820.

Teitelbaum, P., & Epstein, A. N. The lateral hypothalamic syndrome: Recovery of feeding and drinking after lateral hypothalamic lesions. *Psychological Review,* 1962, **69**, 74–90.

Towbin, E. J. Gastric distention as a factor in the satiation of thirst in esophagustomized dogs. *American Journal of Physiology,* 1949, **159**, 533–541.

Verney, E. B. The antidiuretic hormone and the factors which determine its release. *Proceedings of the Royal Society (London), Series B,* 1947, **135**, 25–106.

Voit, C. von. Physiologie des allegemeinen stoffwechsels und der ernährung. *Hermanns Handbuch der Physiologie,* 1881, **6**, 566.

Wayner, M. J., Brown, F. M., Kitayama, M., & Gray, M. Effects of salt arousal of drinking and water deprivation on performance of CRF and VI-1 schedules of reinforcement. *Physiology and Behavior,* 1970, **5**, 99–109.

Wettendorff, H. Modifications du sang sous l'influence de la privation d'eau: Contribution à l'étude de la soif. *Travaux du Laboratoire de Physiologie, Instituts Solvay,* 1901, **4**, 353–484.

Winkler, A. W., Danowski, T. S., Elkinton, J. R., & Peters, J. P. Electrolyte and fluid studies during water deprivation and starvation in human subjects, and effect of ingestion of fish, of carbohydrate, and of salt solutions. *Journal of Clinical Investigation,* 1944, **23**, 808–815.

Wolf, A. V. Osmometric analysis of thirst in man and dog. *American Journal of Physiology,* 1950, **161**, 75–86.

2

THIRST, SODIUM APPETITE, AND COMPLEMENTARY PHYSIOLOGICAL CONTRIBUTIONS TO THE REGULATION OF INTRAVASCULAR FLUID VOLUME[1]

Edward M. Stricker
University of Pittsburgh

The long-term regulation of body fluid volume is a complex phenomenon involving prominent behavioral responses as well as more subtle physiological mechanisms. Given this fact, it is perplexing to consider that the various behaviors subserving body fluid regulation generally have been investigated in laboratories separate from those pursuing related physiological issues. Perhaps this unfortunate parochialism is an inevitable consequence of the arbitrary division of scientific inquiry into separate academic disciplines of psychology, physiology, and biology. Whatever the explanation, because of this odd tradition it is worth stating explicitly that behavioral and physiological mechanisms make complementary contributions to the regulation of body fluid volume, and that it is often difficult to evaluate and appreciate fully the one aspect of regulation without at the same time considering the other. Consequently, although this book is oriented towards drinking behavior and thirst, some physiological mechanisms of volume regulation will be considered briefly at the onset of this chapter. These considerations are intended to provide a perspective for the behavioral work described afterwards and also, because certain aspects of this work are more advanced than related studies of ingestive behavior, to provide a model for studying drinking behavior.

[1] The research reported in this paper was supported in part by research grants APA—248 from the National Research Council of Canada and GB—28830 from the National Science Foundation of the United States.

PHYSIOLOGICAL MECHANISMS OF VOLUME REGULATION

Considering how essential intravascular circulation is to life, it is not surprising that there are elaborate mechanisms for insuring the constancy of the pressure and volume of this fluid (for recent reviews emphasizing individual features of this regulation, see Gauer, Henry, & Behn, 1970; Guyton, Coleman, Fourcade, & Navar, 1969; Guyton, Granger, & Taylor, 1971; Houdas, 1969; Mason & Bartter, 1968). These mechanisms support the circulation at several different levels. For example, there are the dynamics of fluid exchange at the capillary, involving the Starling equilibrium of forces due to capillary pressure, colloid osmotic pressure, and lymphatic drainage. In addition, there are controls intrinsic to the circulation, such as the adjustment of cardiac output to venous return, the autoregulation of blood flow in peripheral tissues, and the direct effects of arterial pressure on glomerular filtration and urinary output. There are also cardiovascular reflexes involving the autonomic nervous system, adrenal medullary secretions, and other vasomotor controls. Finally, there are various endocrine influences on renal function, especially in response to internal needs for water and sodium. These latter contributions to volume regulation are relatively slow in comparison with the above reflex mechanisms, but they are similar in many respects to the gross adjustments in fluid intake which complement them. Both aspects of nutrient balance will be emphasized in the present discussion.

Antidiuretic Hormone

Only in the last generation of scientific work has it been recognized that specific endocrinologic events resulting from changes in the circulation actively contribute to the maintenance of body fluid volume and composition. With regard to the endocrine influence on renal water loss, it was first observed that increased antidiuretic material was present during dehydration (e.g., Gilman & Goodman, 1937), and later, in the classic work by Verney (1947), it was demonstrated that this material was a hormone controlled by a central osmoregulatory system. However, additional stimuli for antidiuretic hormone (ADH) secretion were sought because water conservation also was observed to accompany sodium depletion and adrenal insufficiency, despite the loss of osmotic material (e.g., Leaf & Mamby, 1952). Ultimately, specific volume regulatory mechanisms were implicated by reports that circulating levels of ADH increased following controlled blood loss (see review by Share, 1969), and that the renin-angiotensin system also provided an effective stimulus for ADH secretion (see review by Malvin, 1971). These and other results clearly demonstrated that ADH contributes to the reduced urinary water loss following a reduction of circulatory volume, as by hemorrhage or other iso-osmotic loss of body fluids, by obstruction of the venous return to the heart, or by sodium deficiency (see reviews by Gauer & Henry, 1963; Smith, 1957). As might be expected, overhydration of intravascular or intracellular fluids reduces ADH secretion.

Osmoregulation Versus Volume Regulation

The persistence of hyponatremia during salt deficiency and of hypernatremia during water deficiency indicates that body fluid composition may be sacrificed in the interests of fluid volume preservation. Similarly, it is well known that a high plasma osmolality (and volume) due to the infusion of hypertonic solutions results in greater urine flow than occurs when equally elevated plasma osmolality (but low volume) results from loss of body water. More specific investigations have revealed that relatively small losses of blood volume can increase ADH secretion and abolish the diuresis expected following water infusions (e.g., Arndt, 1965; Rydin & Verney, 1938). These findings indicate that, with regard to ADH secretion and renal function, volume regulation may have a higher priority than osmoregulation (see reviews by Gauer, 1968; Grossman, 1957).

Aldosterone

With regard to the endocrine influence on renal sodium loss, it was first observed that adrenal cortical extracts prevented the severe symptoms of sodium depletion in adrenalectomized animals (e.g., Harrison & Darrow, 1938), and subsequent work has revealed the important role of the renin-angiotensin-aldosterone system in the control of sodium excretion and the regulation of intravascular fluid volume (see reviews by Davis, 1962; Gross, Brunner, & Ziegler, 1965). This complex system is excited by multiple stimuli arising during sodium depletion, such as hyponatremia, hypovolemia, renal arterial hypotension, and renal sympathetic neural activity. Briefly, these stimuli promote the release of renin from granular juxtaglomerular cells located within the walls of afferent renal arterioles. Renin is a proteolytic enzyme that reacts with angiotensinogen (renin substrate) in the plasma to form the decapeptide angiotensin I, which is rapidly hydrolized into the active octapeptide angiotensin II. This latter substance is a potent vasoconstrictor and also provides an excellent stimulus for the secretion of aldosterone from the zona glomerulosa of the adrenal cortex (see reviews by Peart, 1965; Vander, 1967). Secretion of aldosterone, the principle sodium-conserving hormone, is also stimulated by ACTH and altered plasma electrolyte levels during sodium deficiency (see reviews by Blair-West, Coghlan, Denton, Goding, Wintour, & Wright, 1963; Mulrow, 1966).

Volume Receptors

Receptor mechanisms in the control of these endocrine systems have been identified (e.g., Hodge, Lowe, & Vane, 1966; Share, 1968; also reviews by Gauer & Henry, 1963; Tobian, 1967; Welt, 1960). One baroreceptor mechanism appears to be located on the low pressure side of the circulation, in the right atrium and in the adjacent walls of the great veins. Small to moderate changes in blood volume primarily affect the venous system and these highly distensible vascular structures. More pronounced volume deficits extend the effects to the high-pressure side of the circulation, and important arterial receptors have been located in the aortic arch and the carotid sinus and have been inferred in the juxtaglomerular apparatus of the kidneys. Impulses generated in the atrial, aortic, and carotid receptor areas are transmitted via the vagus and glosso-pharyngeal nerves to the medullary vasomotor centers; then, they appear to stimulate central ascending pathways involved in blood pressure regulation and ADH secretion, and descending pathways involved in catecholamine release from the adrenal medulla, activation of renal sympathetic nerves, and secretion of renin. Of course, local reduction of intra-arteriolar pressure also increases renin secretion from the juxtaglomerular cells. It is interesting to note that the secretions of both ADH and renin increase rapidly following small losses of blood volume, whereas larger or more prolonged changes appear to be required for stimulating aldosterone secretion (e.g., Share, 1968; Stricker & Leenen, unpublished observations, 1972). Thus, marked antidiuresis may precede renal sodium retention following acute or progressive loss of circulatory volume (e.g., Fitzhugh, McWhorter, Estes, Warren, & Merrill, 1953; Stricker & Jalowiec, 1970).

In summarizing these brief sketches of the physiological contributions to volume regulation, there are several general points that can be made. First, there is an increased retention of both water and sodium following the loss of body fluids. Second, hormones obviously are of great importance to the renal mechanisms controlling water and sodium loss following body fluid depletion. Third, multiple (and, in some instances, common) factors stimulate the secretions of the antidiuretic and antinatriuretic hormones. Fourth, volume regulation can take precedence over osmoregulation when these control systems are in conflict. And fifth, baroreceptor mechanisms stimulate the secretions of ADH and renin in response to small deficits in blood volume, whereas larger and more prolonged deficits additionally activate the biosynthesis and secretion of aldosterone. These findings have important parallels in the behavioral responses to reduced circulatory volume.

BEHAVIORAL MECHANISMS OF VOLUME REGULATION

The above considerations have been concerned primarily with the conservation of water and sodium following the reduction of extracellular fluid volume. Of course, in times of need not only must the animal minimize further fluid loss, but it must replenish its deficits as well. This is the goal of ingestive behaviors motivated by thirst and sodium appetite: to increase water and sodium intakes, respectively, in order to maintain their balances and thereby achieve regulation of body fluids.

Thirst

Early research on the behavioral contribution to the regulation of body fluid volume generally may be characterized as attempts to demonstrate in the laboratory that hypovolemia was a stimulus for thirst, a fact that many workers had accepted without such demonstration on the basis of intuition and clinical experience. Controlled hemorrhage typically was used in these studies as a simple and direct means of reducing circulatory volume, but it had only inconsistent success in producing thirst. In retrospect, these results are not surprising; following a small blood loss, plasma volume might be restored within minutes by fluid transfers from the interstitial space, whereas with larger hemorrhages animals might be sent into hypotensive shock which, with the added complication of anemia, was not the most desirable preparation for studies of behavior. Nevertheless, the inconsistencies in the data left some nagging doubts, and it remained for concerned experimenters to devise a procedure for permanently depleting the intravascular fluid volume without so debilitating the animal that it could not behave.

Two procedures have accomplished this reliably. The first produced permanent deficits of intravascular fluid volume by sodium depletion. Sodium loss decreases the effective osmolality of extracellular fluid, thereby upsetting the flux of water across the cellular membrane; the accumulation of water within cells reestablishes osmotic equilibrium at the expense of extracellular fluid volume. In one important experiment (Holmes & Cizek, 1951), dogs depleted of body sodium by a diuretic were observed to remain hypovolemic and polydipsic for weeks while maintained on a sodium-deficient diet, but plasma volumes and daily water intakes returned to normal with restoration of sodium to the animals. These findings have been replicated and extended using other techniques for inducing sodium depletion (e.g., Cizek, Semple, Huang, & Gregersen, 1951; Falk, 1966; Stricker, 1966).

Using a different approach, Fitzsimons (1961) produced an extravascular sequestration of extracellular fluid within rats by injecting hyperoncotic colloidal solutions intraperitoneally and observed that drinking occurred despite the absence of changes in the osmolality of their body fluids. In an extension of this work, we found that the colloidal solutions leached plasma out of the circulation, with controlled levels of hemoconcentration produced in direct proportion to the concentration of the colloidal solution that was administered (Stricker, 1966, 1968). As indicated in Figure 1, water intakes of rats receiving subcutaneous injections of various hyperoncotic polyethylene glycol (PG) solutions correlated highly with associated plasma deficits. There were no changes in plasma osmolality or intracellular hydration produced by this isotonic transfer of protein-free plasma fluid into the interstitium, and all animals displayed increased thirst over a broad range (5 to 35%) of plasma deficits. These and other results strongly suggest that thirst-motivated drinking provides a behavioral component of the volume-regulatory response of rats to plasma deficits.

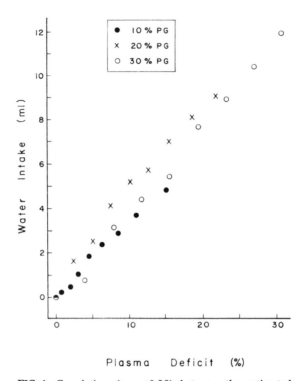

FIG. 1. Correlation (r = +0.98) between the estimated plasma deficits and the observed water intakes of rats injected subcutaneously with 5 ml of 10%, 20%, or 30% PG solutions. Each point represents the mean value from 11 animals. (From Stricker, 1968. Reproduced with permission of Pergamon Press.)

A second stimulus for thirst that arises from changes within the vascular compartment has been identified in recent work by Fitzsimons and his colleagues. They have found that infusion of angiotensin into hydrated rats initiates drinking, with water intake increasing in proportion to the amount of angiotensin that is infused (Fitzsimons & Simons, 1969). In addition, activation of the renin-angiotensin system in rats, as by partial constriction of the abdominal aorta or a renal artery, or total ligation of the inferior vena cava, also produces thirst (Fitzsimons, 1969). Angiotensin appears to mediate thirst following these and other experimental disruptions of normal circulatory function since the excessive drinking usually observed is abolished by bilateral nephrectomy (Fitzsimons, 1969; Gutman, Benzakein, & Livneh, 1971; Houpt & Epstein, 1971).

Plasma renin activity rises proportionally with increasing volume deficits following PG treatment (see Table 1), to levels that are comparable to those associated with thirst following total ligation of the inferior vena cava (Stricker

& Leenen, unpublished observations, 1972). In contrast to the latter preparation, however, it is important to note that hypovolemic rats drink increased amounts of water whether they are nephrectomized or have intact kidneys (see Table 2; also, Fitzsimons, 1961; Fitzsimons & Stricker, 1971; Peck, 1971). Thus, the deficits in circulatory volume following PG treatment must provide a

TABLE 1

Estimated Deficits in Plasma Volume (ΔV), Plasma Renin Activities (PRA), and Water Intakes Following 30% PG Treatment in Rats

Time following treatment (hours)	ΔV	PRA (mμg/ml)		Intake (ml)	
		Control	30% PG	Control	30% PG
1	4%	3.07 ± 0.23[a]	12.97 ± 2.17*	0.0 ± 0.0	1.5 ± 0.7*
2	8%	7.43 ± 0.93	39.76 ± 5.71*	0.1 ± 0.1	3.2 ± 0.6*
4	16%	4.70 ± 0.81	75.30 ± 4.51*	0.8 ± 0.3	5.6 ± 0.4*
8	32%	16.11 ± 1.76	143.07 ± 24.32*	0.8 ± 0.7	8.9 ± 1.2*

Note. – The treatment consisted of a subcutaneous injection of 5 ml 30% PG or 0.15 M NaCl (control) solution. Plasma renin activity was measured with a radioimmunoassay for angiotensin I and is expressed as millimicrograms of angiotensin I that was generated per milliliter of plasma per 3-hour incubation. Data from Stricker (1968), and from Stricker & Leenen (unpublished observations, 1972).
[a]Mean ± S.E.; N = 3 to 6 per group.
*$p < .005$ in comparison with control values.

TABLE 2

Effect of Nephrectomy on Thirst Elicited by Ligation of the Inferior Vena Cava (IVC) or by 30% PG Treatment in Rats

Treatment	N	Water intake (ml)
Intact control	14	1.0 ± 0.4[a]
Nephrex control	11	4.6 ± 0.9*
IVC ligation[b]	22	11.5 ± 0.9
Nephrex + IVC ligation	18	3.9 ± 0.5*
30% PG[c]	19	9.4 ± 0.6
Nephrex + 30% PG	19	8.7 ± 0.9

Note.– Intakes were recorded 6 hours after the treatments.
[a]Mean ± S.E.
[b]The ligature was placed below the liver and above the kidneys.
[c]Subcutaneous injection of 5 ml 30% PG solution.
*$p < .001$ in comparison to respective intact controls.

stimulus for thirst in addition to angiotensin, one which survives nephrectomy and is capable of mediating thirst in the absence of the renin-angiotensin system. The afferent signal of this dipsogenic stimulus is presumed to originate in the altered baroreceptor activities that result from regional changes in blood pressure following the loss of intravascular fluid volume.

As the above results indicate, renal and nonrenal components of the complex stimulus for hypovolemic thirst can be separated experimentally and shown to be effective independently of each other and of the third stimulus for thirst, intracellular dehydration (as discussed in the preceding chapter by Blass). However, under normal circumstances these stimuli do not occur in isolation, and multiple stimuli are present for thirst. How do they interact? As indicated in Figure 2, the water intakes of rats suffering concurrent cellular dehydration and hypovolemia clearly are proportional to both intravascular and intracellular dehydrations and approximate the arithmetic sums of the intakes obtained when the PG and hypertonic NaCl treatments are administered separately (Stricker, 1969; also, Corbit, 1968; Oatley, 1964). Additional work has demonstrated the

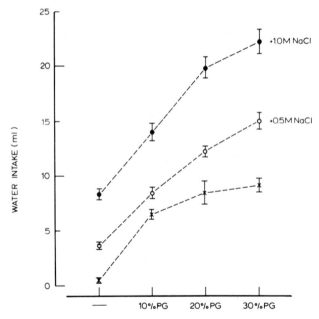

FIG. 2. Effect of pretreatment with 0.5 M or 1.0 M NaCl solution on mean water intakes of rats after sham, 10%, 20%, or 30% PG injections (N = 8 to 12 in each group). Hypertonic NaCl solutions were injected (2% body weight, ip) 2 hours before injections of the PG solutions (5 ml, subcutaneous). Drinking water was made available 8 hours later, and intakes were recorded for 1 hour. (From Stricker, 1969. Reproduced with permission of the *American Journal of Physiology.*)

additive effect on thirst of the other combinations of stimuli (e.g., Fitzsimons & Simons, 1969; Stricker, 1971c).

Satiety and Inhibitory Mechanisms

In addition to considering the physiological bases of thirst, consideration also should be given to the physiological consequences of water intake: the fate of ingested water and its effects on thirst.

Ingested water is distributed in proportion to the existing volumes of the body fluid compartments. Thus, approximately two-thirds of ingested water becomes part of the intracellular fluid volume (omitting renal effects), whereas less than one-tenth of it becomes plasma fluid. This distribution of water is desirable when thirst arises from cellular dehydration, since the cellular deficits are readily repaired and satiety is thereby conferred (e.g., Fitzsimons, 1963); but it is less appropriate for thirst arising from intravascular dehydration, since only a small fraction of the ingested water remains in the circulation. In the latter situation, the rate of repletion is so low that drinking by animals with large plasma deficits might be disrupted by water intoxication before hypovolemia could be repaired. However, recent experiments have revealed that hypovolemic rats stop drinking water, despite the continued presence of substantial plasma volume deficits, with no more than an 8 to 10% dilution of body fluids (Stricker, 1969). This inhibition of hypovolemic thirst does not appear at a fixed level of dilution but at one which increases as a function of plasma deficit; that is, rats with larger plasma deficits drink and retain more water, as if more dilution were required to inhibit further drinking (Stricker, 1968, 1971c).[2] In contrast, it is interesting to note that hypovolemic rats given 0.15 M NaCl solution to drink instead of water consume this isotonic fluid continuously and at much higher rates than they do water (see Figure 3, left) and, since it remains extracellular, restore their plasma volumes most effectively (Stricker & Jalowiec, 1970).

A similar inhibition of thirst induced by angiotensin also has been demonstrated (Stricker, 1971c). For example, in recent experiments that are summarized in Figure 3 (center), rats ingest much more of an isotonic NaCl solution than water following total ligation of the inferior vena cava (IVC)[3]. In further tests, rats given combined PG injection and IVC ligation treatments showed even greater thirst, and consequently drank to a greater degree of

---

[2] Note that drinking by hypovolemic animals may be sustained if ingested water is excreted. This probably accounts for the polydipsia of sodium-depleted dogs that was observed by Holmes and Cizek (1951). Evidently, chronic plasma deficits in these animals were sufficient to stimulate thirst despite some level of osmotic dilution, but were not so large as to eliminate or severely retard renal excretion of the water load.

[3] This treatment does not elicit sodium appetite in rats (Stricker, 1971b), and thus the observed differences between the intakes of water and 0.15 M NaCl solution reflect some inhibitory influences of the ingested water rather than augmentation of saline intake by sodium appetite.

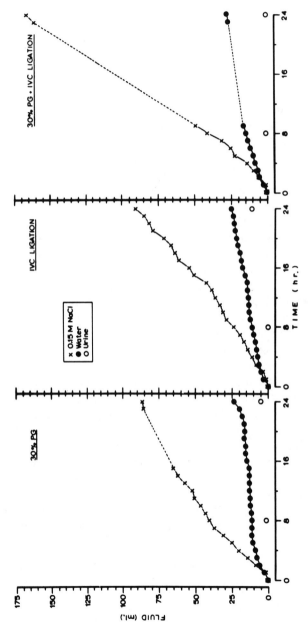

FIG. 3. Cumulative mean volumes of fluid ingested by rats given only water or 0.15 M NaCl solution to drink following (*left*) subcutaneous injection of 30% PG solution, (*center*) total ligation of the inferior vena cava (IVC) below the liver and above the kidneys, and (*right*) combined IVC ligation and 30% PG injection treatments (*N* = 9 to 18 in each group). Dotted lines represent intervals, during which data were not collected. Mean urine outputs 8 and 24 hours after treatment, when water was the drinking fluid, also are presented (note the oliguria in rats given either PG injection or IVC ligation treatment, and the anuria in rats given both treatments). (From Stricker, 1971c.)

dilution, than animals given either treatment alone. Curiously, this dilution was achieved by increased retention of ingested water rather than by increased water intakes (see Figure 3, right). The increased thirst of these rats was demonstrated most clearly when 0.15 M NaCl was offered as the drinking fluid and body fluid dilution was thereby avoided; this complex treatment elicited more drinking with fluid retention than any other experimental procedure known.[3] For example, the rat pictured in Figure 4 (left) drank over 300 ml saline in 24 hours following combined PG injection and IVC ligation treatment, yet excreted only 97 ml urine and thus displayed a massive peripheral edema. These findings emphasize the extreme potency of this preparation as a stimulus for thirst, while the contrast between this animal and the similarly treated rat given water to drink (see Figure 4, right) reflects the comparable strength of the inhibitory mechanism associated with body fluid dilution.

It should be noted that the inhibition of water intake in rats given PG injection and/or IVC ligation treatments is associated with a reduction of the effective osmotic pressure of body fluids, or the concomitant intracellular overhydration, rather than with a reduction of total osmotic pressure (Stricker, 1971c). Although the exact mechanism of inhibition still is unknown, it clearly cannot be attributed to a general debilitation, because rats showing little interest in water will ingest large amounts of saline; indeed, the inhibitory influence on water intake in thirsty oliguric animals prevents their overhydration from progressing to the extreme dilutional state associated with water intoxication.

Sodium Appetite

Sodium appetite is a strong motivation to seek and ingest sodium that apparently is innate, at least in rats (see reviews by Denton, 1965; Wolf, 1969). It does not seem to be associated readily with some peripheral cue, as "dry mouth" is with thirst or gastric filling is with hunger and satiety, nor does it commonly occur in Western societies due to the abundance of salt in our foods. Thus, sodium appetite usually is not recognized and reported by most human subjects during sodium deficiency (Henkin, Gill, & Bartter, 1963). Perhaps it is for these reasons that sodium appetite has received relatively little experimental attention since the pioneering work of Richter, in contrast with the long history of research and interest in thirst.

Richter (1936) first demonstrated the sodium appetite of rats in response to uncontrolled losses of sodium following adrenalectomy. This finding has been replicated and extended in many laboratories, perhaps most elegantly in a series of experiments by Denton and his colleagues, who have integrated their studies of sodium appetite with their important research on the control of aldosterone secretion in intact sodium-deficient sheep (see reviews by Blair-West et al., 1963; Denton, 1965). In these and other experiments it has been observed repeatedly that animals suffering negative external sodium balances will develop a sodium appetite. But sodium appetite also will appear if need occurs without external loss. For example, in traumatized tissues damage to capillary and cellular

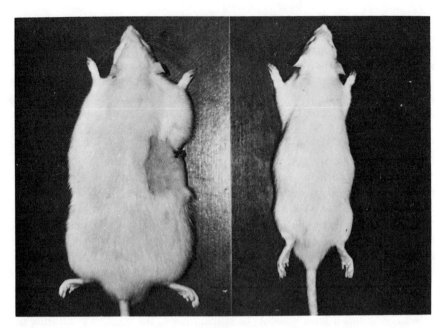

FIG. 4. A representative rat given only (*left*) 0.15 M NaCl solution or (*right*) water to drink following combined total ligation of the inferior vena cava and subcutaneous injection of 30% PG solution. Photographs were taken 24 hours after the experimental treatments. (From Stricker, 1971c.)

membranes can result in an extensive loss of protein-rich plasma fluid into a local edema, altered plasma sodium and potassium concentrations, activation of the renin-angiotensin-aldosterone system, and other changes generally reminiscent of sodium depletion (e.g., Fox & Baer, 1947; Jalowiec & Stricker, 1970a); such experimental trauma also evokes increased thirst and sodium appetite in rats (see Table 3; also, Braun-Menendez & Brandt, 1952). Finally, there is a third paradigm in which sodium appetite paradoxically becomes associated with excess body sodium rather than with sodium deficiency. This unusual circumstance can be produced experimentally by elevating circulating mineralocorticoid levels; then, despite the absence of need, rats will ingest and retain large amounts of sodium and, in consequence, may become polydipsic, edematous, and hypertensive (e.g., Hall & Hall, 1965; Rice & Richter, 1943).

Because of the distinctive taste of sodium-containing foods, and perhaps because of the then-current experimental emphasis on peripheral controls of feeding, it was initially presumed that the appetite for sodium was mediated by taste factors. For example, Richter (1939) noted that sodium deficient adrenalectomized rats had a lower preference threshold for dilute saline solutions than intact rats and attributed this to an increased sensitivity to the taste of salt. This hypothesis was strongly challenged, however, when Pfaffmann and Bare (1950) showed that the sensory thresholds for saline solutions, as determined from recordings of gustatory afferent discharges, were virtually identical in intact and adrenalectomized rats. This important study, together with later work on the same problem (e.g. Koh & Teitelbaum, 1961; Nachman & Pfaffmann,1963), demonstrated that sodium deficiency does not alter the sensitivity of the taste receptors and thus suggested that the increased sodium appetite was mediated by other factors. Perhaps as a result of these findings, the past 20 years of research on sodium appetite has been oriented towards its contribution to regulation, although recent studies have finally clarified the contribution of gustatory factors to sodium appetite (e.g. Mook, 1969; Smith, Holman, & Fortune, 1968).

The role of sodium appetite in the maintenance of internal body sodium levels was clearly demonstrated by Epstein and Stellar (1955), who showed that adrenalectomized rats consumed more NaCl solution after an ion-exchange resin (which reduced the amount of ingested salt reaching the body) was placed in their gastrointestinal tracts, and by Denton and Sabine (1961), who showed that sodium deficient sheep rapidly consumed almost exactly the amount of sodium required to repair their deficits. Since then, detailed studies of the behavioral and physiological responses of intact animals to controlled sodium need have been accomplished under a variety of acute testing conditions, each involving external sodium loss or internal redistribution of body fluids while avoiding traumatic insult to tissues. In one example that is most relevant to the present discussion, it was found that, subsequent to a more rapidly developing thirst, PG-treated rats would begin to display sodium appetite by ingesting even unpalatable concentrated NaCl solutions (Figure 5; also, Stricker & Jalowiec, 1970; Stricker & Wolf, 1966). It is interesting to note that whereas hypovolemic rats consume little additional water after the first 6 to 10 hours when it is the only drinking fluid available (Figure 3, left), rats offered 0.51 M NaCl solution

TABLE 3

Effect of Tissue Trauma on Thirst and
Sodium Appetite in Rats

Treatment	N	Water (ml)	3% NaCl (ml)
1.5% Formalin, 2.5 ml[a]	15	41.0 ± 2.6*	18.4 ± 1.6*
Control	15	19.4 ± 3.2	2.6 ± 0.9
Traumatic injury[b]	10	56.8 ± 3.4*	13.8 ± 1.1*
Control	10	21.8 ± 2.3	3.5 ± 1.0

Note. – Intakes were recorded 24 hours after the treatments. Food was absent during the testing periods. Data from Fitzsimons & Stricker (1971), and from Stricker (unpublished observations, 1969).

[a]Administered by subcutaneous injection.

[b]A high unilateral tourniquet was applied to one hind leg for 5 hours and then was released.

*p < .001 in comparison with respective controls.

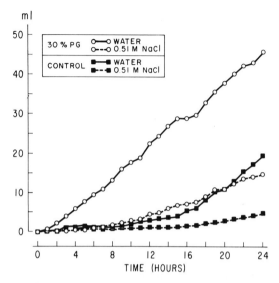

FIG. 5. Cumulative mean volumes of water and 0.51 M NaCl ingested by rats during food deprivation (control) and after subcutaneous injection of 30% PG solution (N = 8 in each group). (From Stricker, 1971b.)

and water to drink show no apparent inhibition of thirst. It would appear that by alternating their intakes of the fluids, rats alternatively decrease (following water ingestion) and increase (following saline ingestion) the osmolality of their body fluids, thereby avoiding prolonged osmotic dilution and actually obtaining a fluid mixture that approximates the isotonic NaCl solution that is optimal for restoring plasma volume. The complementary physiological mechanisms of water and sodium homeostasis are indicated in Figure 6; hypovolemic rats are oliguric and retain virtually all ingested sodium until plasma volumes are restored, at which time sodium concentrations rise abruptly to normal levels and sodium balance stabilizes despite continued sodium intake.

The delayed appearance of sodium appetite in hypovolemic rats, and their continued ingestion of saline following plasma volume repletion, evidences a lag in the relationship between sodium need and intake. Separate theories have attributed these and related observations to the slow transport of sodium from and to brain cells (Denton, 1966) or, more generally, some reservoir (Stricker & Wolf, 1969) specifically involved in sodium appetite. At present, the physiological changes which might affect such sodium transport mechanisms or otherwise stimulate sodium appetite are not known. Mentioned most frequently in this regard are hypovolemia, hyponatremia, and elevated circulating levels of aldosterone. Each of these potential stimuli normally is present during sodium deficiency, and each has been strongly implicated in the control of sodium appetite, although consideration of these issues is not without controversy. Thus, hypovolemia appears to elicit sodium appetite reliably in rats, as

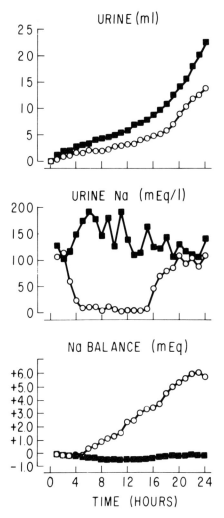

FIG. 6. Cumulative mean volumes of urine excreted, mean urine sodium concentrations, and cumulative mean sodium balances (i.e., sodium intake minus urine sodium) of rats during food deprivation (control) and after subcutaneous injection of 30% PG solution ($N = 8$ in each group). All rats were given continuous access both to water and to 0.51 M NaCl solution (mean fluid intakes are presented in Figure 5). Note that plasma restoration was complete 16 to 20 hours after PG injection treatment. (From Stricker, 1971b.)

indicated above; however, this effect does not occur without a considerable delay (Stricker & Jalowiec, 1970; Stricker & Wolf, 1966), and furthermore, prevention of plasma volume deficits by dextran infusion during sodium depletion does not affect the development of sodium appetite in sheep (Denton, Orchard, & Weller, 1971). Hyponatremia appears to potentiate the sodium appetite of sodium-deficient rats (Jalowiec & Stricker, 1970b; Stricker & Wolf, 1966); however, hyponatremia produced in the absence of sodium depletion by intragastric water loads does not elicit sodium appetite in rats (Stricker & Wolf, 1966), and furthermore, hypernatremia does not seem to affect sodium appetite in sodium-deficient sheep (Beilharz, Bott, Denton, & Sabine, 1965; Beilharz, Denton, & Sabine, 1962; Beilharz & Kay, 1963; although preliminary evidence suggests that it does reduce sodium appetite in hypovolemic rats—Stricker, unpublished observations, 1971). Elevated mineralocorticoid levels appear to stimulate sodium appetite in rats (Fregly & Waters, 1966; Rice & Richter, 1943; Wolf & Handal, 1966); however, it is well known that sodium appetite develops in adrenalectomized rats (Richter, 1936), and furthermore, aldosterone does not seem to elicit sodium appetite in sheep or rabbits, the only other experimental animals that have been tested (Denton, Nelson, Orchard, & Weller, 1969).

In short, multiple stimuli may exist for sodium appetite, as for thirst, but they may be difficult to identify because none of them are necessary for, or immediately associated with, increased sodium ingestion. Alternatively, other factors than those considered above, also present during sodium depletion, may be important. However, such additional possibilities as increased levels of angiotensin or ACTH have been examined, and they appear to be neither necessary nor sufficient for eliciting sodium appetite (Bott, Denton, & Weller, 1967; Braun-Menendez & Brandt, 1952; Fitzsimons & Stricker, 1971; Jalowiec, Stricker, & Wolf, 1970; Stricker, 1971b). It is evident that much work remains to be done on this problem, using approaches other than those described above. For example, the mysterious disappearance of sodium appetite which occurs during anuria (see Table 4; also, Fitzsimons & Stricker, 1971), when understood, may reveal important mechanisms in the stimulation and control of sodium appetite.

In summarizing these considerations of thirst and sodium appetite, there are several general statements that can be made about the behavioral contributions to volume regulation. First, there is an increased intake of both water and sodium following the loss of body fluids. Second, the same endocrine systems that are involved in the renal conservation of water and sodium also are of great importance to the control of water and sodium intake, both indirectly (i.e., by minimizing further nutrient losses and conserving ingested fluid) and directly (e.g., the effects of angiotensin and aldosterone on thirst and sodium appetite, respectively). Third, multiple (and, in some instances, common) factors may be involved in the controls of thirst and sodium appetite. Fourth, drinking behaviors subserving volume regulation can take precedence over those involved in osmoregulation when these control systems are in conflict, although not to an unlimited extent. And fifth, thirst is an immediate behavioral response to

TABLE 4

Effects of Anuria on Thirst and Sodium Appetite Elicited
by 30% PG Treatment in Rats

Treatment	N	Water (ml)	3% NaCl (ml)	Urine (ml)
30% PG	10	46.4 ± 3.6^{a}	11.3 ± 1.4	17.0 ± 2.7
"	13	$28.7 \pm 1.7*$	ABSENT	$7.5 \pm 1.4*$
" + nephrectomy	7	$21.6 \pm 1.6*$	$0.0 \pm 0.0*$	$0.0 \pm 0.0*$
" + ureter ligation	5	$23.9 \pm 2.0*$	$0.2 \pm 0.2*$	$0.0 \pm 0.0*$
" + bladder puncture	5	$27.0 \pm 3.6*$	$0.4 \pm 0.1*$	$0.0 \pm 0.0*$
" + IVC ligation	5	$31.8 \pm 3.1*$	$0.0 \pm 0.0*$	$0.0 \pm 0.0*$
" + 30% PG	5	$36.3 \pm 1.6*$	$0.6 \pm 0.2*$	$0.0 \pm 0.0*$

Note.— Intakes and urine volumes were recorded 24 hours after the treatments. Data from Stricker (1971b), and from Stricker (unpublished observations, 1970).

[a]Mean ± S.E.

$*p < .001$ in comparison with intact rats given a single subcutaneous injection of 5 ml 30% PG solution and ad libitum access to water and 3% NaCl solution.

hypovolemia, but later, after a considerable delay, sodium appetite also appears. These two appetitive behaviors, together with complementary physiological mechanisms, ultimately restore circulatory volume to normal.

Neurological Substrates

Many of the physiological parameters that have been considered to be involved in the control of thirst and sodium appetite are represented schematically in Figure 7. Proceeding from left to right, intracellular dehydration activates a neural system controlling thirst that leads to increased water intake, which rehydrates cells and thereby removes the stimulus for thirst. This is a single-loop negative-feedback system in which a stimulus initiates a behavioral response that results in the removal of the initiating stimulus. Overdrinking does not occur, and thus no inhibitory system involving osmotic dilution is necessary in the control of osmoregulatory thirst. In contrast, when hypovolemia activates the neural system controlling thirst, the increased water intake has little effect on the initiating stimulus. Cells become overhydrated as body fluid osmolality is lowered, and if water is the only drinking fluid that is present, some aspect of body fluid dilution eventually activates a system inhibiting thirst and further water intake. Similarly, if ingestion only of hypertonic NaCl solution is permitted, cells become dehydrated and some aspect of body fluid concentration eventually activates a system inhibiting sodium appetite. In either situation, hypovolemia continues because both water and sodium are necessary to repair plasma volume deficits. Finally, if ingestion of both water and hypertonic NaCl solution is permitted, osmotic dilution and inhibition of thirst are avoided, as are osmotic concentration and inhibition of

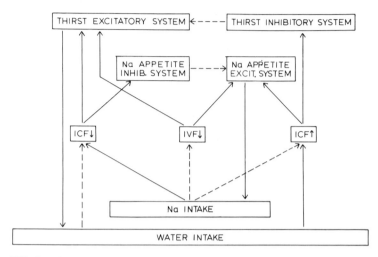

FIG. 7. Schematic representation of some physiological mechanisms that appear to control thirst, sodium appetite, and satiety. Solid arrows indicate stimulation, dashed arrows indicate inhibition. *IVF,* intravascular fluid; *ICF,* intracellular fluid.

sodium appetite, and water and saline intakes proceed until plasma volume is restored.

It should be noted that in the interests of simplicity this complex schema omits entirely the respective influences of angiotensin and aldosterone on thirst and sodium appetite, and also does not indicate that sodium appetite is not immediately associated with the proposed stimuli. Nevertheless, the schema is useful in summarizing the body fluid factors which appear to elicit thirst and sodium appetite, and in drawing attention to four major hypotheses: (*a*) that thirst and sodium appetite are interdependent in restoring plasma deficits; (*b*) that some factor associated with osmotic dilution (cellular overhydration?) could inhibit hypovolemic thirst but potentiate sodium appetite; (*c*) that some factor associated with osmotic concentration (cellular dehydration?) could inhibit sodium appetite but stimulate osmoregulatory thirst; and (*d*) that appetitive neural structures are involved in mediating these appetitive drives. Various experimental evidences in support of the first three hypotheses have been mentioned or discussed in the preceding paragraphs; the fourth hypothesis will now be considered.

With regard to thirst, there is ample evidence for the existence of hypothalamic osmoreceptors (see review by Blass in the preceding chapter). Receptors for hypovolemic thirst have not been located as yet, although they may be identical to the peripheral baroreceptor mechanisms demonstrated in the control of ADH and renin secretions. Studies of central mechanisms have focused on the hypothalamus (e.g., Nicolaïdis, 1970), not only because of this structure's involvement in vasomotor control (see review by Hilton, 1966), but also, and more specifically, because early reports demonstrated that adipsia resulted from destruction of the ventrolateral hypothalamic area (Andersson & McCann, 1956; Montemurro & Stevenson, 1957). More recently, permanent deficits in the thirst responses to specific regulatory demands have been observed in rats with lateral hypothalamic lesions (Epstein & Teitelbaum, 1964; Stricker & Wolf, 1967) as well as in rats suffering damage to more rostral structures (Black, 1971; Blass & Epstein, 1971; Peck, 1971). However, each of these experiments studied the drinking responses of brain-damaged rats during relatively brief (1 to 6 hour) testing conditions, which may have been restrictive. For example, more prolonged tests reveal appropriate drinking to plasma volume deficits and/or elevated angiotensin levels in rats recovered from lateral hypothalamic damage which had not responded at all during the first 6 hours of these tests (see Figure 8; comparable results also have been demonstrated for

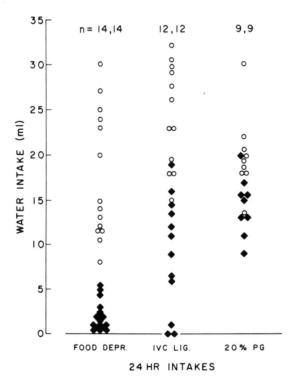

FIG. 8. Individual water intakes of control rats (o), or rats recovered from lateral hypothalamic damage (♦), during 24 hours following sham treatment (food deprivation), total ligation of the inferior vena cava (IVC), or subcutaneous injection of 20% PG solution. Note that most of the water was consumed by intact rats during the first 6 hours following the experimental treatments, whereas lesioned rats consumed 0 to 2 ml during this period. (From Stricker, 1971a.)

osmoregulatory thirst following treatment with hypertonic NaCl solution). Thus, it appears possible that hypothalamic tissue might be essential to the more general motivational aspects of the early behavioral response to homeostatic imbalance but not to the ultimate appearance of regulatory drinking behaviors, and that effector pathways involving other neural areas can mediate thirst during dehydration (Stricker, 1971a).

Angiotensin may elicit thirst by sensitizing or directly stimulating the above osmoreceptor or baroreceptor reflexes, or by activating specific angiotensin-sensitive substrates in the brain. In this regard, the finding that thirst is elicited by angiotensin injected directly into the brain had implicated various limbic structures in the control of thirst (Epstein, Fitzsimons, & Rolls, 1970), although it now appears that drinking was produced by the migration of angiotensin into the ventricles (Johnson, 1972). These latter results are consistent with Andersson's (1971) recent work suggesting that the ependymal layer of the ventricles is sensitive to angiotensin. Thus, angiotensin may not normally have to penetrate brain tissue and reach sensitive inner structures in order to stimulate thirst. Alternatively, the discovery of a renin-angiotensin "system" within the brain (Ganten, Minnich, Granger, Hayduk, Brecht, Barbeau, Boucher, & Genest, 1971) allows for the possible stimulation by local angiotensin of structures remote from the ventricles.

Careful exploration within the hypothalamus has not revealed a specific site whose damage leads to increased drinking and osmotic dilution in PG-treated rats (Black, 1971). In addition, whereas preliminary evidence had suggested impaired inhibition of thirst in hypovolemic rats with lesions of the septal area (Blass & Hanson, 1970), later work has indicated that septal damage does not, in fact, lead to an exaggerated drinking response to all treatments producing plasma deficits (Hanson, 1970). Thus, although separate neural mechanisms have been postulated for a system mediating the inhibition of thirst elicited by hypovolemia or angiotensin, no structure has been identified as yet. However, it should be noted that, as with the control of ADH secretion (Johnson, Zehr, & Moore, 1970), overhydration and osmotic dilution may simply minimize the osmoregulatory contributions to thirst and thereby demand a greater volume regulatory stimulus to provoke drinking (i.e., osmotic dilution may reduce the stimulation of thirst rather than inhibit it), and thus separate neural mechanisms for inhibition may not exist.

With regard to sodium appetite, Wolf (1964, 1967, 1968a, 1968b, 1971; also, Novakova & Cort, 1966) has demonstrated the crucial importance of ventral hypothalamic structures in an impressive series of experiments. Other limbic structures also have been implicated (e.g., Chiaraviglio, 1971; Covian & Antunes-Rodrigues, 1963; Gentil, Mogenson, & Stevenson, 1971), although an integrated neural system controlling sodium appetite remains to be specified.

To summarize, investigation of the neural substrates mediating thirst and sodium appetite are still preliminary, although there is considerable interest in this problem and already there have been exciting research discoveries. Not only is basic neuroanatomical work progressing, but neurophysiological recording and stimulation studies continue to reveal new information about possible neural control systems. It can be anticipated that neurochemical analyses will become more common and prove to be as revealing of the neural systems controlling thirst and sodium appetite as they already have of those systems controlling hunger (e.g., Ungerstedt, 1971).

SUMMARY

Elaborate mechanisms have evolved for insuring the integrity of the circulation by maintaining the volume and composition of the intravascular fluid. These involve controls intrinsic to the circulation as well as neural reflex and endocrine mechanisms affecting both physiological and behavioral responses to body fluid need. With regard to the latter, the maintenance of homeostasis is particularly influenced by the excretion and intake of water and sodium, the major constituents of the extracellular fluid. Accordingly, the present discussion of volume regulatory mechanisms has focused on the secretion of antidiuretic hormone, the activity of the renin-angiotensin-aldosterone system, and the complementary behaviors motivated by thirst and sodium hunger.

Multiple overlapping factors are involved in the control of water and sodium balances. For example, cellular dehydration (via osmoreceptor activity), hypovolemia (via baroreceptor activity), and angiotensin all stimulate ADH secretion during dehydration, and each of these factors appears to stimulate thirst as well. Hypovolemia and angiotensin also are important in the control of aldosterone secretion during sodium deficiency, along with ACTH and altered electrolyte levels, and some of these same factors appear to be involved in eliciting sodium appetite as well. Thus, interdependent systems stimulate the ingestion and retention of water and sodium when circulatory volume is depressed.

Water and sodium balances may be adjusted in order to subserve volume regulation or osmoregulation of body fluids. Volume regulatory demands usually predominate when these systems are in conflict, but not to an unlimited extent. For example, the hypovolemic animal, thirsty and oliguric, progressively dilutes its body fluids when it is given only water to drink, but ultimately its thirst is inhibited despite continued plasma deficits. This animal needs both water and sodium to restore its plasma volume. Appropriate to these needs, sodium also is ingested and conserved by the kidney. Ingestion of NaCl solution together with water avoids excessive dilution or concentration of body fluids and thereby permits the intakes to continue without inhibition. Eventually, sufficient fluid is ingested and retained for plasma deficits to be repaired. The stimuli for the acquisition and retention of water and sodium then subside, and both appetitive behaviors and renal function return to normal.

REFERENCES

Andersson, B. Thirst – and brain control of water balance. *American Scientist,* 1971, **59**, 408–415.

Andersson, B., & McCann, S. M. The effect of hypothalamic lesions on the water intake of the dog. *Acta Physiologica Scandinavica,* 1956, **35**, 312–320.

Arndt, J. O. Diuresis induced by water infusion into the carotid loop and its inhibition by small hemorrhage: The competition of volume–and osmocontrol. *Pflüger's Archiv für die gesamte Physiologie des Menschen und der Tiere,* 1965, **282**, 313–322.

Beilharz, S., Bott, E., Denton, D. A., & Sabine, J. R. The effect of intracarotid infusions of 4 M NaCl on the sodium drinking of sheep with a parotid fistula. *Journal of Physiology (London),* 1965, **178**, 80–91.

Beilharz, S., Denton, D. A., & Sabine, J. R. The effect of concurrent deficiency of water and sodium on the sodium appetite of sheep. *Journal of Physiology (London),* 1962, **163**, 378–390.

Beilharz, S. & Kay, R. N. B. The effects of ruminal and plasma sodium concentrations on the sodium appetite of sheep. *Journal of Physiology (London),* 1963, **165**, 468–483.

Black, S. L. Hypothalamic lesions, hypovolemia, and the regulation of water balance in the rat. Unpublished doctoral dissertation, McMaster University, 1971.

Blair-West, J. R., Coghlan, J. P., Denton, D. A., Goding, J. R., Wintour, M., & Wright, R. D. The control of aldosterone secretion. *Recent Progress in Hormone Research,* 1963, **19**, 311–363.

Blass, E. M., & Epstein, A. N. A lateral preoptic osmosensitive zone for thirst in the rat. *Journal of Comparative and Physiological Psychology,* 1971, **76**, 378–394.

Blass, E. M., & Hanson, D. G. Primary hyperdipsia in the rat following septal lesions. *Journal of Comparative and Physiological Psychology,* 1970, **70**, 87–93.

Bott, E., Denton, D. A., & Weller, S. The effect of angiotensin II infusion, renal hypertension and nephrectomy on salt appetite of sodium-deficient sheep. *Australian Journal of Experimental Biology and Medical Science,* 1967, **45**, 595–612.

Braun-Menendez, E., & Brandt, P. Aumento del apetito especifico para la sal provocado por la desoxicorticosterona. I. Caracteristicas. *Revista de la Sociedad Argentina de Biologia,* 1952, **28**, 15–23.

Chiaraviglio, E. Amygdaloid modulation of sodium chloride and water intake in the rat. *Journal of Comparative and Physiological Psychology,* 1971, **76**, 401–407.

Cizek, L. J., Semple, R. E., Huang, K. C., & Gregersen, M. I. Effect of extracellular electrolyte depletion on water intake in dogs. *American Journal of Physiology,* 1951, **164**, 415–422.

Corbit, J. D. Cellular dehydration and hypovolaemia are additive in producing thirst. *Nature,* 1968, **218**, 886–887.

Covian, M. R., & Antunes-Rodrigues, J. Specific alterations in sodium chloride intake after hypothalamic lesions in the rat. *American Journal of Physiology,* 1963, **205**, 922–926.

Davis, J. O. The control of aldosterone secretion. *Physiologist,* 1962, **5**, 65–86.

Denton, D. A. Evolutionary aspects of the emergence of aldosterone secretion and salt appetite. *Physiological Reviews,* 1965, **45**, 245–295.

Denton, D. A. Some theoretical considerations in relation to innate appetite for salt. *Conditional Reflex,* 1966, **1**, 144–170.

Denton, D. A., Nelson, J. F., Orchard, E., & Weller, S. The role of adrenocortical hormone secretion in salt appetite. In C. Pfaffmann (Ed.), *Olfaction and taste, III.* New York: Rockefeller University Press, 1969. Pp. 535–547.

Denton, D. A., Orchard, E., & Weller, S. The effect of rapid change of sodium balance and expansion of plasma volume on sodium appetite of sodium-deficient sheep. *Communications in Behavioral Biology,* 1971, **6**, 245–258.

Denton, D. A., & Sabine, J. R. The selective appetite for Na+ shown by Na+-deficient sheep. *Journal of Physiology (London)*, 1961, **157**, 97–116.

Epstein, A. N., Fitzsimons, J. T., & Rolls, B. J. Drinking induced by injection of angiotensin into the brain of the rat. *Journal of Physiology (London)*, 1970, **210**, 457–474.

Epstein, A. N., & Stellar, E. The control of salt preference in the adrenalectomized rat. *Journal of Comparative and Physiological Psychology*, 1955, **48**, 167–172.

Epstein, A. N., & Teitelbaum, P. Severe and persistent deficits in thirst produced by lateral hypothalamic damage. In M. J. Wayner (Ed.), *Thirst in the regulation of body water.* Oxford: Pergamon Press, 1964. Pp. 395–406.

Falk, J. L. Serial sodium depletion and NaCl solution intake. *Physiology and Behavior*, 1966, **1**, 75–77.

Fitzhugh, F. W., Jr., McWhorter, R. L., Jr., Estes, H. E., Jr., Warren, J. V., & Merrill, A. J. The effect of application of tourniquets to the legs on cardiac output and renal function in normal human subjects. *Journal of Clinical Investigation*, 1953, **32**, 1163–1170.

Fitzsimons, J. T. Drinking by rats depleted of body fluid without increase in osmotic pressure. *Journal of Physiology (London)*, 1961, **159**, 297–309.

Fitzsimons, J. T. The effects of slow infusions of hypertonic solutions on drinking and drinking thresholds in rats. *Journal of Physiology (London)*, 1963, **167**, 344–354.

Fitzsimons, J. T. The role of a renal thirst factor in drinking induced by extracellular stimuli. *Journal of Physiology (London)*, 1969, **201**, 349–368.

Fitzsimons, J. T., & Simons, B. J. The effect on drinking in the rat of intravenous infusion of angiotensin, given alone or in combination with other stimuli of thirst. *Journal of Physiology (London)*, 1969, **203**, 45–57.

Fitzsimons, J. T., & Stricker, E. M. Sodium appetite and the renin-angiotensin system. *Nature, New Biology*, 1971, **231**, 58–60.

Fox, C. L., Jr., & Baer, H. Redistribution of potassium, sodium and water in burns and trauma, and its relation to the phenomena of shock. *American Journal of Physiology*, 1947, **151**, 155–167.

Fregly, M. J., & Waters, I. W. Effect of mineralocorticoids on spontaneous sodium chloride appetite of adrenalectomized rats. *Physiology and Behavior*, 1966, **1**, 65–74.

Ganten, D., Minnich, J. L., Granger, P., Hayduk, K., Brecht, H. M., Barbeau, A., Boucher, R., & Genest, J. Angiotensin-forming enzyme in brain tissue. *Science*, 1971, **173**, 64–65.

Gauer, O. H. Osmocontrol versus volume control. *Federation Proceedings*, 1968, **27**, 1132–1136.

Gauer, O. H., & Henry, J. P. Circulatory basis of fluid volume control. *Physiological Reviews*, 1963, **43**, 423–481.

Gauer, O. H., Henry, J. P., & Behn, C. The regulation of extracellular fluid volume. *Annual Review of Physiology*, 1970, **32**, 547–595.

Gentil, C. G., Mogenson, G. J., & Stevenson, J. A. F. Electrical stimulation of septum, hypothalamus, and amygdala and saline preference. *American Journal of Physiology*, 1971, **220**, 1172–1177.

Gilman, A., & Goodman, L. The secretory response of the posterior pituitary to the need for water conservation. *Journal of Physiology (London)*, 1937, **90**, 113–124.

Gross, F., Brunner, H., & Ziegler, M. Renin-angiotensin system, aldosterone and sodium balance. *Recent Progress in Hormone Research*, 1965, **21**, 119–167.

Grossman, J. Volume factors in body fluid regulation. *Archives of Internal Medicine*, 1957, **99**, 93–128.

Gutman, Y., Benzakein, F., & Livneh, P. Polydipsia induced by isoprenaline and by lithium: Relation to kidneys and renin. *European Journal of Pharmacology*, 1971, **16**, 380–384.

Guyton, A. C., Coleman, T. G., Fourcade, J. G., & Navar, L. G. Physiologic control of arterial pressure. *Bulletin of the New York Academy of Medicine*, 1969, **45**, 811–830.

Guyton, A. C., Granger, H. J., & Taylor, A. E. Interstitial fluid pressure. *Physiological Reviews*, 1971, **51**, 527–563.

Hall, C. E., & Hall, O. Hypertension and hypersalimentation. I. Aldosterone hypertension. *Laboratory Investigation,* 1965, **14**, 285−294.

Hanson, D. G. Drinking by rats with septal-area lesions during acute hypovolemia. Unpublished doctoral dissertation, University of Pennsylvania, 1970.

Harrison, H. E., & Darrow, D. C. The distribution of body water and electrolytes in adrenal insufficiency. *Journal of Clinical Investigation,* 1938, **17**, 77−86.

Henkin, R. I., Gill, J. R., Jr., & Bartter, F. C. Studies of taste thresholds in normal man and in patients with adrenal cortical insufficiency: The role of adrenal cortical steroids and of serum sodium concentration. *Journal of Clinical Investigation,* 1963, **42**, 727−735.

Hilton, S. M. Hypothalamic regulation of the cardiovascular system. *British Medical Bulletin,* 1966, **22**, 243−248.

Hodge, R. L., Lowe, R. D., & Vane, J. R. Increased angiotensin formation in response to carotid occlusion in the dog. *Nature,* 1966, **211**, 491−493.

Holmes, J. H., & Cizek, L. J. Observations on sodium chloride depletion in the dog. *American Journal of Physiology,* 1951, **164**, 407−414.

Houdas, Y. L'autoregulation du volume plasmatique. *Journal of Physiology (Paris),* 1969, **61**, 43−74.

Houpt, K. A., & Epstein, A. N. The complete dependence of beta-adrenergic drinking on the renal dipsogen. *Physiology and Behavior,* 1971, **7**, 897−902.

Jalowiec, J. E., & Stricker, E. M. Restoration of body fluid balance following acute sodium deficiency in rats. *Journal of Comparative and Physiological Psychology,* 1970, **70**, 94−102. (a)

Jalowiec, J. E., & Stricker, E. M. Sodium appetite in rats after apparent recovery from acute sodium deficiency. *Journal of Comparative and Physiological Psychology,* 1970, **73**, 238−244. (b)

Jalowiec, J. E., Stricker, E. M., & Wolf, G. Restoration of sodium balance in hypophysectomized rats after acute sodium deficiency. *Physiology and Behavior,* 1970, **5**, 1145−1149.

Johnson, A. K. Localization of angiotensin in sensitive areas for thirst within the rat brain. Paper presented at the meeting of the Eastern Psychological Association, Boston, April 1972.

Johnson, J. A., Zehr, J. E., & Moore, W. W. Effects of separate and concurrent osmotic and volume stimuli on plasma ADH in sheep. *American Journal of Physiology,* 1970, **218**, 1273−1280.

Koh, S. D., & Teitelbaum, P. Absolute behavioral taste thresholds in the rat. *Journal of Comparative and Physiological Psychology,* 1961, **54**, 223−229.

Leaf, A., & Mamby, A. R. An antidiuretic mechanism not regulated by extracellular fluid tonicity. *Journal of Clinical Investigation,* 1952, **31**, 60−71.

Malvin, R. L. Possible role of the renin-angiotensin system in the regulation of antidiuretic hormone secretion. *Federation Proceedings,* 1971, **30**, 1383−1386.

Mason, D. T., & Bartter, F. C. Autonomic regulation of blood volume. *Anesthesiology,* 1968, **29**, 681−692.

Montemurro, D. G., & Stevenson, J. A. F. Adipsia produced by hypothalamic lesions in the rat. *Canadian Journal of Biochemistry and Physiology,* 1957, **35**, 31−37.

Mook, D. G. Some determinants of preference and aversion in the rat. *Annals of the New York Academy of Sciences,* 1969, **157**, 1158−1175.

Mulrow, P. J. Neural and other mechanisms regulating aldosterone secretion. In L. Martini and W. F. Ganong (Eds.), *Neuroendocrinology.* Vol. 1. New York: Academic Press, 1966. Pp. 407−444.

Nachman, M., & Pfaffmann, C. Gustatory nerve discharge in normal and sodium-deficient rats. *Journal of Comparative and Physiological Psychology,* 1963, **56**, 1007−1011.

Nicolaïdis, S. Résponses unitaires dans les aires antérieures et médianes de l'hypothalamus associées à des variations de pression artérielle et de volémie. *Comptes Rendu de l'Académie des Sciences (Paris)*, 1970, **270**, 839–842.

Novakova, A., & Cort, J. H. Hypothalamic regulation of spontaneous salt intake in the rat. *American Journal of Physiology*, 1966, **211**, 919–925.

Oatley, K. Changes of blood volume and osmotic pressure in the production of thirst. *Nature*, 1964, **202**, 1341–1342.

Peart, W. S. The renin-angiotensin system. *Pharmacological Reviews*, 1965, 17, 143–182.

Peck, J. W. Separation of kidney-dependent from kidney-independent extracellular thirsts by brain lesions in rats. Paper presented at the meeting of the Eastern Psychological Association, New York, April 1971.

Pfaffmann, C., & Bare, J. K. Gustatory nerve discharges in normal and adrenalectomized rats. *Journal of Comparative and Physiological Psychology*, 1950, **43**, 320–324.

Rice, K. K., & Richter, C. P. Increased sodium chloride and water intake of normal rats treated with desoxycorticosterone acetate. *Endocrinology*, 1943, **33**, 106–115.

Richter, C. P. Increased salt appetite in adrenalectomized rats. *American Journal of Physiology*, 1936, **115**, 155–161.

Richter, C. P. Salt taste thresholds of normal and adrenalectomized rats. *Endocrinology*, 1939, **24**, 367–371.

Rydin, H., & Verney, E. B. The inhibition of water-diuresis by emotional stress and by muscular exercise. *Quarterly Journal of Experimental Physiology*, 1938, **27**, 343–374.

Share, L. Control of plasma ADH titer in hemorrhage: Role of atrial and arterial receptors. *Amercan Journal of Physiology*, 1968, **215**, 1384–1389.

Share, L. Extracellular fluid volume and vasopressin secretion. In W. F. Ganong & L. Martini (Eds.), *Frontiers in neuroendocrinology*. New York: Oxford University Press, 1969. Pp. 183–210.

Smith, H. W. Salt and water volume receptors. *American Journal of Medicine*, 1957, **23**, 623–652.

Smith, M. H., Jr., Holman, G. L., & Fortune, K. H. Sodium need and sodium consumption. *Journal of Comparative and Physiological Psychology*, 1968, **65**, 33–37.

Stricker, E. M. Extracellular fluid volume and thirst. *American Journal of Physiology*, 1966, **211**, 232–238.

Stricker, E. M. Some physiological and motivational properties of the hypovolemic stimulus for thirst. *Physiology and Behavior*, 1968, **3**, 379–385.

Stricker, E. M. Osmoregulation and volume regulation in rats: Inhibition of hypovolemic thirst by water. *American Journal of Physiology*, 1969, **217**, 98–105.

Stricker, E. M. Drinking by rats following lateral hypothalamic damage. Paper presented at the meeting of the Society of Neuroscience, Washington, D. C., October 1971. (a)

Stricker, E. M. Effects of hypovolemia and/or caval ligation on water and NaCl solution drinking by rats. *Physiology and Behavior*, 1971, **6**, 299–305. (b)

Stricker, E. M. Inhibition of thirst in rats following hypovolemia and/or caval ligation. *Physiology and Behavior*, 1971, **6**, 293–298. (c)

Stricker, E. M., & Jalowiec, J. E. Restoration of intravascular fluid volume following acute hypovolemia in rats. *American Journal of Physiology*, 1970, **218**, 191–196.

Stricker, E. M., & Wolf, G. Blood volume and tonicity in relation to sodium appetite. *Journal of Comparative and Physiological Psychology*, 1966, **62**, 275–279.

Stricker, E. M., & Wolf, G. The effects of hypovolemia on drinking in rats with lateral hypothalamic damage. *Proceedings of the Society of Experimental Biology and Medicine*, 1967, **124**, 816–820.

Stricker, E. M., & Wolf, G. Behavioral control of intravascular fluid volume: Thirst and sodium appetite. *Annals of the New York Academy of Sciences*, 1969, **157**, 553–567.

Tobian, L. Renin release and its role in renal function and the control of salt balance and arterial pressure. *Federation Proceedings,* 1967, **26**, 48–54.

Ungerstedt, U. Adipsia and aphagia after 6-hydroxydopamine induced degeneration of the nigro-striatal dopamine system. *Acta Physiologica Scandinavica,* 1971, Supplement 367, 95–122.

Vander, A. J. Control of renin release. *Physiological Reviews,* 1967, **47**, 359–382.

Verney, E. B. The antidiuretic hormone and the factors which determine its release. *Proceedings of the Royal Society (London),* Series B, 1947, **135**, 25–106.

Welt, L. G. Volume receptors. *Circulation,* 1960, **21**, 1002–1008.

Wolf, G. Effect of dorsolateral hypothalamic lesions on sodium appetite elicited by desoxycorticosterone and by acute hyponatremia. *Journal of Comparative and Physiological Psychology,* 1964, **58**, 396–402.

Wolf, G. Hypothalamic regulation of sodium intake: Relations to preoptic and tegmental function. *American Journal of Physiology,* 1967, **213**, 1433–1438.

Wolf, G. Regulation of sodium intake after medial hypothalamic lesions. *Proceedings of the 76th Annual Convention of the American Psychological Association,* 1968, 281–282. (a)

Wolf, G. Thalamic and tegmental mechanisms for sodium intake: Anatomical and functional relations to lateral hypothalamus. *Physiology and Behavior,* 1968, **3**, 997–1002. (b)

Wolf, G. Innate mechanisms for regulation of sodium intake. In C. Pfaffmann (Ed.), *Olfaction and taste, III.* New York: Rockefeller University Press, 1969. Pp. 548–553.

Wolf, G. Neural mechanisms for sodium appetite: Hypothalamus positive – hypothalamofugal pathways negative. *Physiology and Behavior,* 1971, **6**, 381–389.

Wolf, G., & Handal, P. J. Aldosterone-induced sodium appetite: Dose-response and specificity. *Endocrinology,* 1966, **78**, 1120–1124.

DISCUSSION:
THIRST(S) RESULTING FROM
BODILY WATER IMBALANCES[1]

Jeffrey W. Peck
University of Utah

Three types of maldistribution of body water have been identified which generate signals inducing rats to drink: cellular dehydration, intravascular fluid volume depletion, and decreased vascular perfusion of the kidneys (apparently releasing renin and hence angiotensin). I refer to maldistributions of body water, for that describes how the drinking is elicited in the laboratory. The animal has suffered no absolute dehydration. Thus, hypovolemia is most commonly produced by introducing into the intraperitoneal or interstitial space a colloid to which basement membranes of capillaries are impermeable. The colloid causes an isotonic edema to accumulate, depleting other extracellular fluid spaces (especially plasma). Cellular dehydration is produced by adding to the extracellular fluid a solute to which cellular membranes are impermeable. The solute increases the effective osmotic pressure of the extracellular fluid, withdrawing water from cells. The renin-angiotensin system is activated by diverting blood flow from the kidneys.

Throughout the course of this work and as reviewed in the previous chapters, strong analogies have been made between the control of thirst and the control of the secretion of the antidiuretic hormone (ADH), reinforcing the interpretation that thirst is a response triggered just like internal responses for the homeostatic maintenance of bodily water balance. This analysis has now reached the point where several fundamental problems can be recognized and discussed with some reference to experimental evidence. In this brief contribution I would like to

[1] The original research reported in this article was performed while the author was a USPHS postdoctoral fellow (MH 24,556) with Alan N. Epstein at the University of Pennsylvania. The research was supported by USPHS grant NDS 03469 to A.N.E.

touch on the following: (a) Do the three signals described above account for all the data? (b) Are there three distinct sets of receptors for the signals generated by the three types of water imbalances? (c) Is the information derived from these receptors "line-labeled" throughout the thirst system? That is, on the basis of different behaviors elicited by the independent production of each of these deficits, must we (or can we) in fact talk about thirsts (plural), not just thirst? (d) Does it appear that thirst is organized, neurally, as one of several outputs (controls) of a center for regulating body water balance, the secretion of ADH being the most prominent other output? (e) Finally, how much has thirst as conceived on the model of homeostasis allowed us to explain why unstressed, unchallenged laboratory animals drink when they do?

SIGNALS: ANDERSSON'S OBJECTION TO OSMORECEPTION

Andersson (1971) has recently argued that the adequate stimulus for thirst and ADH release elicited by increases in the concentration of extracellular fluids (ECF) is not the cellular dehydration induced by those increases. He does not dispute the findings of Holmes and Gregersen (1950a, 1950b), in dogs, and of Fitzsimons (1961, 1963), in rats, who showed that the amount of drinking caused by intravenous solute loads corresponded to changes in the effective osmotic pressure of extracellular fluid, not to the changes in the concentrations of specific ions. This is the same adequate stimulus found by Verney (1947) for the secretion of ADH by dogs. Andersson points out, however, that extracellular fluid in brain is not typical of the interstitial fluid of the rest of the body: (a) a blood-brain barrier restricts transfer of solute to and from brain; and (b) the cerebrospinal fluid (CSF) is elaborated by active metabolic processes, and is not a passive ultrafiltrate of plasma such as interstitial fluid is.

Hypertonic sucrose is excluded from all bodily cells and causes thirst (Holmes & Gregersen, 1950a) and the release of ADH (Verney, 1947) when injected intravenously. Andersson and colleagues (Andersson, Olsson, & Warner, 1967; Olsson, 1969b) find that hypertonic sucrose introduced behind the blood-brain barrier, into the rostral portions of the third ventricle of goats, elicits neither thirst nor ADH release, although equally hypertonic solutions of various sodium salts, particularly sodium chloride, elicit both thirst and ADH release. They argue that at the level of brain receptors, it is the sodium concentration of brain extracellular fluid that matters, not the effective osmotic pressure. Andersson further argues that angiotensin releases ADH and causes thirst by increasing sodium transport through the cellular membrane of these same sodium receptors, for he finds that hypertonic sodium chloride and angiotensin show a multiplicative relationship when simultaneously introduced through the third ventricle (Andersson & Eriksson, 1971).

The case of urea is treated as the clinching argument. Urea penetrates most cells readily, but the blood-brain barrier only slowly. Hence, systemic urea dehydrates brain (Kleeman, Davson, & Levin, 1962). However, if urea dehydrates brain and yet causes negligible ADH release and little thirst (which misstates the case, as discussed below), then the receptors in brain mediating thirst and ADH release must not be osmoreceptors (i.e., cells sensitive to their own volume or concentrations of intracellular solutes).

There are flaws both in Andersson's arguments and in his evidence. Since urea dehydrates brain, the sodium concentration of the interstitial fluid of brain must increase. Hence, the postulate of sodium receptors rather than osmoreceptors is no advantage for explaining why urea causes so much less drinking than sodium chloride. After urea penetrates the blood-brain barrier it diffuses into neurons freely. Hence urea dehydrates brain cells, to be sure, but much less than does equiosmolar sucrose or sodium chloride, both of which are confined to ECF. And, in fact, urea has caused significant drinking equal to about one-third that of equiosmolar sodium chloride in all the major studies, and significant ADH release in one of the two major studies (Zuidema, Clarke, & Minton, 1956; Verney, 1947, is the exception). The drinking in the studies on rats could not have been secondary to an osmotic diuresis, for the rats were nephrectomized (Fitzsimons, 1961, 1963). These results should be taken as an argument that the receptors involved are indeed behind the blood-brain barrier, not as problems with the osmoreceptor theory.

However, there remains the question of whether to speak of osmoreceptors or of sodium receptors. As was summarized by Blass in this volume, hypertonic sucrose injected directly into the lateral preoptic areas of rabbits and rats does cause thirst. Furthermore, rehydrating this area or destroying it bilaterally has selective effects on thirst elicited by systemic cellular dehydration. The reduced drinking to cellular dehydration but not to other challenges when the lateral preoptic areas of rats were hydrated (Blass & Epstein, 1971) is particularly significant. It implies that dehydrating all cells in the body except those in the lateral preoptic area will result in no thirst. The lateral preoptic areas may not have been sufficiently stimulated by infusions through the third ventricle in Andersson's goats.

Questions can be raised about the specificity of effects and the locus of action of solutions containing highly abnormal concentrations of specific ions, such as Andersson and his colleagues have injected through the third ventricle. For instance, third-ventricular infusions of isotonic ammonium chloride caused antidiuresis (Olsson, 1969b), and isotonic potassium chloride caused drinking, antidiuresis, and natriuresis (Olsson, 1969a). These effects are unexplained if it is assumed that these solutions must act on either sodium receptors or osmo-receptors. Furthermore, polypnea accompanied the potassium chloride infusions (eating, when hyperosmotic solutions were used), and several sodium salts tried in earlier ventricular infusions were reported to cause interfering or debilitating side effects (Andersson, Jobin, & Olsson, 1967). It seems likely that all these intraventricular infusions nonspecifically stimulated neural tissue lying near the midline, and that this neural tissue happened to be involved (but not at the receptor level) in mediating ADH release and/or thirst.

The multiplicative effects of combining angiotensin and sodium chloride on thirst and ADH release are compatible with belief in such nonspecificity. Sodium chloride could be facilitating transmission in pathways otherwise activated by angiotensin. It would be interesting to know if angiotensin and potassium chloride (or ammonium chloride) were also multiplicative in Andersson's preparation. Non-specific effects (including eating and gnawing, as well as drinking) have been observed following injections of moderately hypertonic sodium chloride solutions directly into the hypothalamus of rabbits (Peck & Novin, 1971).

RECEPTORS

If we may tentatively conclude that the three types of signals summarized at the beginning of this article describe the control over drinking by changes in bodily fluids, are there three distinct receptors for the three types of signals? Inferences made from the analysis-of-variance independence of cellular dehydrational and hypovolemic thirst (Blass & Fitzsimons, 1970; Corbit, 1968; Fitzsimons & Oatley, 1968) do not prove that the hydrational signals act independently. Proof from such experiments would depend on the demonstration that asymptotic signal input into one system (e.g., cellular dehydration) would not preclude increased drinking to depletions of another system (e.g., hypovolemia).

Fitzsimons (1970) has argued that angiotensin might act to facilitate synaptic transmission in the neural pathway mediating responses to blood volume

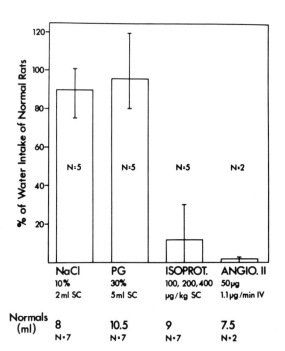

(*Continued*)

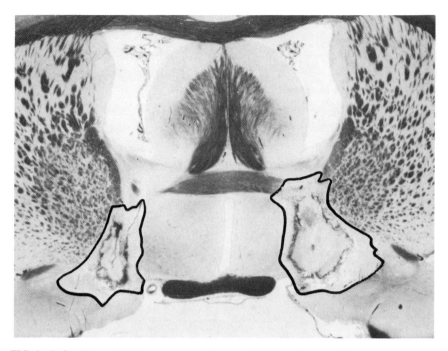

FIG. 1. *Left:* Mean drinking responses of rats with bilateral preoptic lesions to various dipsogens. Vertical lines indicate the range of the mean response for the five lesioned rats. Each injection was repeated twice (a total of six injections of isoproterenol). All injections were made 3 to 6 weeks postoperatively, and were separated by 2 to 4 days (longer after polyethylene glycol). The normal rats received injections in the same sequence. All injections were subcutaneous, except for angiotensin, which was infused intravenously through a jugular catheter for a total of 45 minutes. The mean 3-hour (isoproterenol, NaCl) and 8-hour (polyetheylene glycol, or "PG") water intakes of normal rats are indicated at the bottom. Isoproterenol depends entirely on the kidney (renin-angiotensin) for its dipsogenic activity. (Houpt & Epstein, 1971.) *Above:* A frontal section through the center of the lesions (outlined in black) in one of the rats giving the above responses. The extent of the lesions in this rat was less than any of the others giving this pattern of deficits. (From J. W. Peck, unpublished.)

depletion, and Andersson (1971) has argued that angiotensin and CSF sodium concentration effect the same receptors to cause thirst, ADH release, and natriuresis. Fitzsimons' argument is given some weight by the presence within brain of enzymes for converting substrate to angiotensin II (Ganten, Boucher, & Genest, 1971). Intracranial injections of precursors of angiotensin cause drinking (Fitzsimons, 1971). The natural argument is that endogenous brain angiotensin could be a neurotransmitter, with which circulating angiotensin might summate. I have recently found that large lesions centered in the lateral preoptic areas of rats abolish the thirst aroused by angiotensin (either injected intravenously or released by isoproterenol), while not markedly attenuating thirst induced by either vascular volume depletions (subcutaneous polyethylene glycol) or cellular

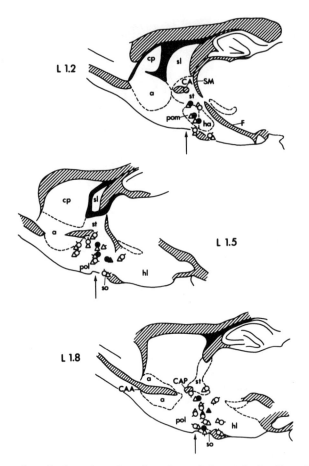

FIG. 2. Schematic sagittal sections through regions of the rat brain where low-threshold drinking (*circles*) or antidiuresis (*triangles*) was induced by unilateral injections of angiotensin. Placements where thresholds for both drinking and antidiuresis were obtained (on different occasions) are indicated by overlapping symbols. Antidiuresis was studied in unrestrained rats receiving a continuous intragastric infusion of 12 ml/hr through an indwelling catheter (see Figure 3). For the drinking tests, the injection cannula of the double-barreled intracranial cannula assembly (Epstein, Fitzsimons, & Rolls, 1970) was inserted and the rat allowed to assume a position indicating sleep before the injection. Arrows beneath the sections indicate the same anterior plane for each section. For clarity, a few nearly identical cannula placements have been omitted, most importantly for the lowest threshold ADH loci. *Filled symbols,* thresholds of 0.1 to 0.5 ng; *open symbols with added line,* thresholds of 1 to 5 ng; *plain open symbols,* thresholds greater than 10 ng. All injections were 2 μl. Note that the overlap between the lowest threshold placements for eliciting thirst and ADH release is small. *CA,* anterior commissure; *CAA,* anterior limb of anterior commissure; *CAP,* posterior limb of anterior commissure; *F,* fornix; *SM,* stria medullaris thalami; *a,* nucleus accumbens; *cp,* caudate nucleus; *ha,* anterior hypothalamic nucleus; *hl,* lateral hypothalamic nucleus; *pol,* lateral preoptic area; *pom,* medial preoptic area; *sl,* lateral septal nucleus; *so,* supraoptic nucleus; *st,* bed nucleus of stria terminalis. (From J. W. Peck & A. N. Epstein, unpublished.)

dehydration (subcutaneous sodium chloride) (see Figure 1). The result would argue against Andersson's hypothesis also. Thirst caused by cellular dehydration can also be abolished without markedly attenuating hypovolemic thirst (Blass & Epstein, 1971). Thus, it would appear that the three types of hydrational signals are separated at some point in the brain.

The presence within brain of enzyme systems for converting substrate to angiotensin II deserves further consideration. It is not unknown that the central nervous system uses as possible neurotransmitters compounds also produced in the periphery (i.e., adrenergic compounds), and it is possible that angiotensin introduced directly into brain by means of an intracranial injection stimulates neurons normally activated only by endogenous brain angiotensin acting as a neurotransmitter. Circulating angiotensin, if it is a dipsogen, may act elsewhere. The penetration from blood of labeled angtiotensin into brain parenchyma is not impressive (Volicer & Loew, 1971). Furthermore, angiotensin microelectro-phoretically introduced directly into the supraoptic nucleus strongly modifies the rate of the firing of neurosecretory neurons whereas intracarotid injections do not (Nicoll & Barker, 1971). These results suggest caution. On the other hand, the lowest threshold placement for the release of ADH by intracranial angiotensin in rats is not the supraoptic nucleus, but the lateral preoptic area about 0.7 mm above it (Figure 2). The lowest threshold area for eliciting thirst is somewhat rostral and medial to that; and if, as mentioned above (Figure 1), large bilateral lesions are placed in the latter region, thirst depending on angiotensin is markedly attenuated, while thirst in response to cellular dehydration or hypovolemia remains. Thus, the inference that blood-borne angiotensin normally acts on receptors in the preoptic area to cause thirst is supported.

THIRST(S)

The evidence currently suggests that there are three types of receptors sensitive to various aspects of the maldistribution of body water. Two of them appear to be located in the lateral preoptic area. The location of the third type (for hypovolemia) is unknown, but by analogy with receptors mediating ADH release to hypovolemia, they may be in the left atrium of the heart (Johnson, Zehr, & Moore, 1970). It would seem that the information supplied by each of these three kinds of receptors would be kept separate only if it made some difference in the behavior of the animal; that is, in its preferences. Different kinds of receptors could exist simply because redundancy is valuable.

Stricker, in this volume, has already demonstrated that thirst involves more than the ingestion of water; salt ingestion is important for restoring extracellular fluid volume. Hypovolemic rats, but not rats whose thirst is aroused by angiotensin, show salt appetites. However, the evidence is inadequate to suggest that this appetite is a direct consequence of hypovolemia. In the studies of Stricker and Wilson (1970) and of Krieckhaus and Wolf (1968), which apparently demonstrate such unlearned salt appetites, hypovolemia was induced by Formalin, which also causes hyponatremia. Salt appetite does not follow so promptly the hypovolemia induced without hyponatremia by hyperoncotic polyethylene glycol (Stricker & Jalowiec, 1970).

The problem of whether observed preferences for salt (following hypovolemia) or for water (following cellular dehydration) are unlearned and directly elicited by the specific deficits is reminiscent of the problem of specific subhungers, brought to the fore by Richter's (1943) classic experiments on the self-selection of diets. The intake of salt with water assures expansion of the ECF, and relief from hypovolemia, as Stricker has shown. The intake of water alone does not accomplish this, and in fact rehydrates cells to the extent that immediate further water intake is inhibited before blood volume is restored, as Stricker also showed. There seems to be no reason why activation of the renin-angiotensin system should not induce a salt appetite if hypovolemia does, for ingestion of water alone would be only marginally beneficial in either case. It may be that no salt appetite accompanies thirst induced by caval ligation, the most common method of activating the renin-angiotensin system in the laboratory, because ingestion of neither water nor salt can restore circulation through the kidneys in these rats. And it may be that salt ingestion follows hypovolemia because salt ingestion has beneficial consequences of the same learned sort now thought to explain the apparent specific subhungers (except that for salt in response to sodium *deficiency*) of rats (Rozin & Kalat, 1971). Studies such as Stricker and Wilson's (1970) with Formalin should be repeated with polyethylene glycol.

A way to eliminate the contamination of learning is to take advantage of the technique of intracranial injection. Assuming that preoptic injections of hypertonic solutions and angiotensin cause drinking by acting on their respective receptors, then at least with these two hydrational controls, tests of preference independent of possible beneficial or detrimental feedback can be performed. The procedure is, obviously, to confine the deficit to these brain regions by intracranial injections, and to record any preference shifts from solutions preferred ad libitum following the injections. An initial affirmative result—that cellular dehydration does elicit a preference for water over isotonic saline—was found in two rabbits following injections of hypertonic solutions in the lateral preoptic area (Peck & Novin, 1971). This study deserves replication. Clearly, the results of these studies should have great significance for attempts to trace how thirst is— or thirsts are—organized within the brain.

THIRST AND ADH

In the work summarized by Fitzsimons, by Blass, and by Stricker in this volume, the parallel between the control of ADH and the control of thirst in the regulation of bodily fluid balance has been strong; and in fact it has seemed valuable to view these controlled variables as dual activities of a single neural mechanism defending bodily fluid balance (Miller, 1965). This notion has been attacked recently by Mendelson, Feinberg, and Berman (1971), who separated antidiuretic and dipsogenic loci in the rat hypothalamus. However, their work with electrical stimulation left unclear whether they were stimulating different systems, as they thought, or just separate outputs of a single center.

Although it still has not been directly demonstrated, the inference from work with cats with small islands of hypothalamic tissue (Woods, Bard, & Bleier, 1966) and dogs with restricted arterial supply (Jewell & Verney, 1957) was that osmoreceptors controlling ADH secretion must be in or near the supraoptic nuclei. The pioneering studies of Andersson (1953; Andersson & McCann, 1955) and all subsequent work have confirmed that this area does not importantly contribute to thirst. The inference is that osmoreceptors controlling ADH release and osmoreceptors controlling thirst are probably different populations. We now have evidence that this may also be true for angiotensin-sensitive neurons. Lateral preoptic injections of angiotensin elicit both drinking (Epstein, Fitz-simons, & Rolls, 1970) and antidiuresis (Figure 3); however, as mentioned above (Figure 2), the lowest threshold placements are different for the two responses. Antidiuresis is elicited with lowest threshold (0.1 ng in 2 μl, unilaterally) from placements caudally in the lateral preoptic area, dorsal to the supraoptic nucleus. Drinking is elicited with lowest threshold (0.1 ng in 2μl) from placements more rostrally and medially located in the preoptic areas where 10 to 100 times more angiotensin is required to elicit antidiuresis. One must conclude that if separate populations of receptors can be inferred depending on whether antidiuresis or drinking is the response of interest, then it is less likely that there is a center for bodily water balance than that these receptors initiate separate and non-communicating neurological systems.

THIRST AND HOMEOSTASIS

The parallel between the homeostatic control of ADH secretion and the control of drinking by bodily fluid imbalances has fostered great advances in the study of thirst. The indication that these responses are not, in fact, both products of a single brain mechanism for maintaining bodily water balance causes one to pause, and then to look for possible differences in the control of these responses. There are two that are obvious. The first is that, before drinking, the animal faces the problem of selection of appropriate goal objects, which is never a factor in internal homeostatic responses. The second is that some temporary signal of satiety must be imposed between ingestion of water and the actual correction of the fluid imbalance by the ingested water; for internal homeostatic responses, the (negative) feedback is the reduction of the same signal that initiates the response. In other words, at least two more sets of receptors seem to intervene in the case of thirst, one to give positive feedback (appropriate goal) and the other negative (stopping the behavior, and anticipating the reduction of the stimulus to the receptors originally sensing the deviation in internal body state).

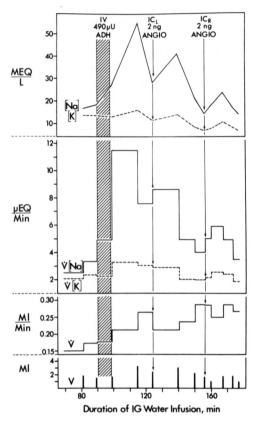

FIG. 3. Antidiuresis induced by unilateral injections of angiotensin into the lateral preoptic area. In this rat natriuresis and kaluresis accompanied the antidiuresis. In other rats natriuresis, but not kaluresis, accompanied the antidiuresis. In still other rats, neither natriuresis nor kaluresis was observed. In each case, however, intravenous infusions of ADH sufficient to produce an equivalent antidiuresis also produced the same pattern of changes in ionic excretion. Furthermore, median eminence lesions abolished both the antidiuresis and the change in ionic excretion. In this rat an 8-minute infusion, 15 μU/100 g/min (*shaded interval*) of Pitressin gave a somewhat larger decrease in urine flow and increase in ionic excretion than did 2 ng of angiotensin through either of two intracranial cannulas. *V*, volume of individual spontaneous urinations; $\dot{V}[Na]$, rate of sodium excretion, $\dot{V}[K]$, rate of potassium excretion. (The particular experiment was begun before urine flow in response to the continuous intragastric infusion of water had fully developed.) (From J. W. Peck & A. N. Epstein, unpublished.)

Although the model under which most of us have worked encompassed these considerations (Stellar, 1954), we have tended to divide the deviation from homeostatic set-point sensed by internal receptors ("drive"), from the positive feedback generated by external receptors ("appetite"), in a way that denies the latter the status of "true thirst" or "true hunger." This distinction when taken seriously implies separate brain mechanisms, yet the concept of "central motive state" (Stellar, 1954) suggests a single brain mechanism. While it is true that we can get rats to "drink" (Epstein, 1960) and "eat" (Epstein & Teitelbaum, 1962; Snowdon, 1969) without oropharyngeal sensations, we can also get rats to eat without "hunger" (Young, 1948).

We are not yet sure what role thirst considered strictly in terms of responses to bodily water imbalances plays in the drinking of unstressed laboratory rats. The hydrational controls of drinking surely have survival value, but the laboratory rat is not "nature's animal," and we do not treat it as such in generating phenomena we seek to understand (for instance, psychogenic polydipsia). When a laboratory rat wanders over to a water bottle before or after a spontaneous meal, is it responding to hydrational signals, or to dry mouth, or is its response a result of some other habit or need? We now have some confidence in our ability to define and measure what the signals of bodily water imbalance are, and we need to put this analysis to use to describe the spontaneous (unmanipulated) behavior of rats.

Rats recovered from lateral hypothalamic lesions respond very poorly, if at all, to hydrational challenges, but most hydrate themselves adequately by drinking while eating a dry diet (Epstein, 1971). These rats seem to be functionally desalivated, and drinking solely in response to a "dry mouth" (Kissileff & Epstein, 1969). This evidence can be looked at in two ways. The first is the way most of us have, which is to emphasize the failure of these rats to respond to bodily water imbalances (need), and so to emphasize the separateness of dry-mouth drinking from "true thirst" as controlled by the lateral hypothalamus. "Drive reduction" still lives in this argument, and we implicitly assume that dry mouth sets up a different sort of "drive" from the "true thirst" in response to bodily water imbalances.

The second way is to emphasize that these rats do drink in response to some signals. Provocative recent data suggest that it may be worthwhile to proceed on the assumption that this behavior is thirst. These data are, first, that structures rostral to the lateral hypothalamus (the lateral preoptic areas) appear to contain receptors for thirst, and that large lesions in the most caudal portions of the lateral preoptic areas abolish all three hydrational controls of drinking, without inducing the "recovery syndrome" that results from lesions centered in the lateral hypothalamus (Blass & Epstein, 1971; E. M. Blass, unpublished data; J. W. Peck, unpublished data). How these rats remain in water balance has not been analyzed, but reflection shows that the results can be interpreted as an extension of the explanation for the more restricted deficits that follow other lateral preoptic lesions, i.e., that pathways from receptors or the receptors themselves have been destroyed. Might not the permanent deficits from lateral hypothalamic lesions result in the main for the same reason, from lesioning the same pathways farther along? This suggestion carries the implication that the "thirst center"—if it is profitable to think of such a center (recall the question of thirst versus thirsts)—need not reside in the tissue destroyed by lateral hypothalamic lesions. Or if it does, control may be reorganized elsewhere following recovery, as is thought to happen with the control of food intake (Teitelbaum, 1971). In other words, permanent deficits in hydrational controls of drinking can be explained by arguing that sensory tracts are destroyed by lateral hypothalamic lesions, so that when thirst does recover (or is reorganized) following those lesions, these signals are still unavailable, while those from the oropharynx again become available. The evidence for recovery or reorganization of hunger (not just appetite) after lateral hypothalamic lesions is that these rats regulate body weight in response to dilutions of liquid diets with water, or to being placed in the cold (Epstein, 1971). But also recall that these rats lack the glucostatic control over food intake (Epstein & Teitelbaum, 1967), which is presumably a sensory loss, perhaps from receptors also in the preoptic areas (Blass, unpublished).

The compelling reason for considering this analogy with the neural organization of the control of food intake is provided by the results of Marshall, Turner, and Teitelbaum (1971), who showed that lateral hypothalamic lesions produce severe deficits in orientation to olfactory, visual, and somatosensory stimuli, partial recovery from which coincided with the start of recovery from complete aphagia and adipsia. Lateral hypothalamic lesioned rats, in short, show an inability to integrate sensory information with motor patterns in performing adaptive responses of almost any sort, but this general inability recovers. It seems that all motivated behaviors in these rats were similarly disrupted, and similarly recovered. The failure of *hydrational* controls over thirst to recover would be from irreparable damage to specific sensory pathways.

In summary, since the control of thirst is different from the control of secretion of ADH, it may be too restrictive to build a neurology around thirst as a strictly homeostatic-type response, to the extent that other causes of water intake are considered aberrations and not reflections of the *normal* mode of functioning of the thirst system. There is no real data at present to support such an argument. On the other hand, reinterpretation of the deficit and recovery from lateral hypothalamic lesions, in light of the provocative study of Marshall et al. (1971), seems to deny existence of a specific lateral hypothalamic "thirst center," in favor of a more general role of the lateral hypothalamus in the directive aspects of motivation. There seems to be no reason to deny that "dry mouth" in rats recovered from lateral hypothalamic lesions is thirst.

REFERENCES

Andersson, B. The effect of injections of hypertonic NaCl-solutions into different parts of the hypothalamus of goats. *Acta Physiologica Scandinavica*, 1953, **28**, 188–201.

Andersson, B. Thirst—and brain control of water balance. *American Scientist*, 1971, **59**, 408–415.

Andersson, B., & Eriksson, L. Conjoint action of sodium and angiotensin on brain mechanisms controlling water and salt balances. *Acta Physiologica Scandinavica*, 1971, **81**, 18–29.

Andersson, B., Jobin, M., & Olsson, K. A study of thirst and other effects of an increased sodium concentration in the 3rd brain ventricle. *Acta Physiologica Scandinavica*, 1967, **69**, 29–36.

Andersson, B., & McCann, S. M. A further study of polydipsia evoked by hypothalamic stimulation in the goat. *Acta Physiologica Scandinavica*, 1955, **33**, 333–346.

Andersson, B., Olsson, K., & Warner, R. G. Dissimilarities between the central control of thirst and the release of antidiuretic hormone (ADH). *Acta Physiologica Scandinavica*, 1967, **71**, 57–64.

Blass, E. M., & Epstein, A. N. A lateral preoptic osmosensitive zone for thirst. *Journal of Comparative and Physiological Psychology*, 1971, **76**, 378–394.

Blass, E. M., & Fitzsimons, J. T. Additivity of effect and interaction of a cellular and an extracellular stimulus of drinking. *Journal of Comparative and Physiological Psychology*, 1970, **70**, 200–205.

Corbit, J. D. Cellular dehydration and hypovolaemia are additive in producing thirst. *Nature*, 1968, **218**, 886–887.

Epstein, A. N. Water intake without the act of drinking. *Science*, 1960, **131**, 497–498.

Epstein, A. N. The lateral hypothalamic syndrome: Its implications for the physiological psychology of hunger and thirst. *Progress in Physiological Psychology*, 1971, **4**, 263–317.

Epstein, A. N., Fitzsimons, J. T., & Rolls (née Simons), B. J. Drinking induced by injection of angiotensin into the brain of the rat. *Journal of Physiology*, 1970, **210**, 457–474.

Epstein, A. N., & Teitelbaum, P. Regulation of food intake in the absence of taste, smell, and other oropharyngeal sensations. *Journal of Comparative and Physiological Psychology*, 1962, **55**, 753–759.

Epstein, A. N., & Teitelbaum, P. Specific loss of the hypoglycemic control of feeding in recovered lateral rats. *American Journal of Physiology*, 1967, **213**, 1159–1167.

Fitzsimons, J. T. Drinking by nephrectomized rats injected with various substances. *Journal of Physiology*, 1961, **155**, 563–579.

Fitzsimons, J. T. The effects of slow infusions of hypertonic solutions on drinking and drinking thresholds in rats. *Journal of Physiology*, 1963, **167**, 344–354.

Fitzsimons, J. T. The renin-angiotensin system in the control of drinking. In L. Martini, M. Motta, & F. Fraschini (Eds.), *The hypothalamus.* New York: Academic Press, 1970.

Fitzsimons, J. T. The effect on drinking of peptide precursors and of shorter chain peptide fragments of angiotensin II injected into the rat's diencephalon. *Journal of Physiology*, 1971, **214**, 295–303.

Fitzsimons, J. T., & Oatley, K. Additivity of stimuli for drinking in rats. *Journal of Comparative and Physiological Psychology*, 1968, **66**, 450–455.

Ganten, D., Boucher, R., & Genest, J. Renin activity in brain tissue of puppies and adult dogs. *Brain Research*, 1971, **33**, 557–559.

Holmes, J. H., & Gregersen, M. I. Observations on drinking induced by hypertonic solutions. *American Journal of Physiology*, 1950, **162**, 326–337. (a)

Holmes, J. H., & Gregersen, M. I. Role of sodium and chloride in thirst. *American Journal of Physiology*, 1950, **162**, 338–347. (b)

Houpt, K. A., & Epstein, A. N. The complete dependence of beta-adrenergic drinking on the renal dipsogen. *Physiology and Behavior*, 1971, **7**, 897–902.

Jewell, P. A., & Verney, E. B. An experimental attempt to determine the site of the neurohypophysial osmoreceptors in the dog. *Philosophical Transactions of the Royal Society of London*, 1957, **240B**, 197–324.

Johnson, J. A., Zehr, J. E., & Moore, W. W. Effects of separate and concurrent osmotic and volume stimuli on plasma ADH in sheep. *American Journal of Physiology*, 1970, **218**, 1273–1280.

Kissileff, H. R., & Epstein, A. N. Exaggerated prandial drinking in the "recovered lateral" rat without saliva. *Journal of Comparative and Physiological Psychology*, 1969, **67**, 301–308.

Kleeman, C. R., Davson, H., & Levin, E. Urea transport in the central nervous system. *American Journal of Physiology*, 1962, **203**, 739–747.

Krieckhaus, E. E., & Wolf, G. Acquisition of sodium by rats: Interaction of innate mechanisms and latent learning. *Journal of Comparative and Physiological Psychology*, 1968, **65**, 197–201.

Marshall, J. F., Turner, B. H., & Teitelbaum, P. Sensory neglect produced by lateral hypothalamic damage. *Science*, 1971, **174**, 523–525.

Mendelson, J., Feinberg, L. E., & Berman, J. Dissociation of diencephalic mechanisms controlling water intake and water retention in the rat. *American Journal of Physiology*, 1971, **220**, 1768–1774.

Miller, N. E. Chemical coding of behavior in the brain. *Science*, 1965, **148**, 328–338.

Nicoll, R. A., & Barker, J. L. Excitation of supraoptic neurosecretory cells by angiotensin II. *Nature New Biology*, 1971, **233**, 172–174.

Olsson, K. Effects of slow infusions of KCl into the 3rd brain ventricle. *Acta Physiologica Scandinavica*, 1969, **77**, 358–364. (a)

Olsson, K. Studies on central regulation of secretion of antidiuretic hormone (ADH) in the goat. *Acta Physiologica Scandinavica*, 1969, **77**, 465–474. (b)

Peck, J. W., & Novin, D. Evidence that osmoreceptors mediating drinking in rabbits are in the lateral preoptic area. *Journal of Comparative and Physiological Psychology*, 1971, **47**, 134–147.

Richter, C. P. Total self-regulatory functions in animals and human beings. *Harvey Lectures Series*, 1943, **38**, 63–103.

Rozin, P., & Kalat, J. W. Specific hungers and poison avoidance as adaptive specializations of learning. *Psychological Review*, 1971, **78**, 459–486.

Snowdon, C. T. Motivation, regulation, and the control of meal parameters with oral and intragastric feeding. *Journal of Comparative and Physiological Psychology*, 1969, **69**, 91–100.

Stellar, E. The physiology of motivation. *Psychological Review*, 1954, **61**, 5–22.

Stricker, E. M., & Jalowiec, J. E. Restoration of intravascular fluid volume following acute hypovolemia in rats. *American Journal of Physiology*, 1970, **218**, 191–196.

Stricker, E. M., & Wilson, N. E. Salt-seeking behavior in rats following acute sodium deficiency. *Journal of Comparative and Physiological Psychology*, 1970, **72**, 416–420.

Teitelbaum, P. The encephalization of hunger. *Progress in Physiological Psychology*, 1971, **4**, 319–350.

Verney, E. B. The antidiuretic hormone and the factors which determine its release. *Proceedings of the Royal Society (London), Series B*, 1947, **135**, 25–106.

Volicer, L., & Loew, C. G. Penetration of angiotensin II into the brain. *Neuropharmacology*, 1971, **10**, 631–636.

Woods, J. W., Bard, P., & Bleier, R. Functional capacity of the deafferented hypothalamus: Water balance and responses to osmotic stimuli in the decerebrate cat and rat. *Journal of Neurophysiology*, 1966, **29**, 751–767.

Young, P. T. Appetite, palatability and feeding habit: A critical review. *Psychological Bulletin*, 1948, **45**, 289–320.

Zuidema, G. D., Clarke, N. P., & Minton, M. F. Osmotic regulation of body fluids. *American Journal of Physiology*, 1956, **187**, 85–88.

INVITED COMMENT: OSMORECEPTORS VERSUS SODIUM RECEPTORS

Bengt Andersson
Karolinska Institutet, Stockholm

By courtesy of the editors, I have received the honor of an invitation to comment upon Section I of this book on thirst. Two conditions adhere to the flattering offer. The comments have to be brief, and they ought to be limited mainly to the aspects of my own work discussed by the authors. For these reasons my contribution is restricted to: (*a*) some comments upon the new evidence for osmoreceptors in the lateral preoptic area (LPO) which is extensively reviewed in the chapter written by Dr. Blass; and (*b*) an attempt to relate this work to recent studies in the goat which have given birth to the provocative suggestion that an alternative to osmoreceptors in Verney's (1947) sense may be a receptor system which responds to changes in the Na^+ concentration of the cerebrospinal fluid (CSF).

A more detailed presentation of the work in the goat is omitted since much of it is excellently reviewed in the chapter written by Dr. Peck. I am convinced that Dr. Peck understands that my enthusiasm for his subsequent criticism is less exuberant. However, also this negative criticism is agreeable on the whole, since there is nothing more unpleasant than to be hanged in silence.

Dr. Blass finds that compelling evidence for the existence of thirst osmoreceptors in the LPO has been presented simultaneously by Peck and Novin (1971) and by Blass and Epstein (1971). He concludes that herein lies a lovely example of the internal validation process of the scientific community. Peck and Novin have made an extensive stimulation/ablation study in the rabbit. Their main proof of specific osmosensitivity is based on the results of alternating injections of strongly hypertonic NaCl, sucrose, and urea solutions at many hundred sites in the hypothalamus and the preoptic region. They found that their criterion for specific osmosensitivity (thirst in response to NaCl and sucrose, but not to urea) was fulfilled at only six sites in the LPO, scattered among several times as many negative sites. The lack of response to so many injections into the "osmosensitive" area appears somewhat puzzling, as does the fact that drinking in response to *both* NaCl and sucrose in reality was obtained also at four sites more posterior in the hypothalamus.

In three out of 22 rabbits Peck and Novin found that bilateral lesions involving the LPO caused loss of the immediate thirst response to an extracellular load of hypertonic saline. However, drinking occurred at about an hour after the intravenous injection of hypertonic NaCl, and the lesions left the thirst response to 24-hour water deprivation completely unaltered. There is no reason to dispute this very interesting finding, especially since the same observation was made independently by Blass and Epstein (1971) in the rat. It may also be very unwise to argue against the apparently logical interpretation that these lesions destroyed the sensors which mobilize drinking to cellular dehydration but left the volumetric regulation of thirst intact. However, if this interpretation is correct, it follows that thirst elicited by 24-hour water deprivation in the rabbit lacks the stimulatory component of cellular dehydration. Unwise or not, having put forward the idea that the blood-liquor barrier may be of greater importance for the central control of fluid balance than the blood-brain barrier (Andersson, 1971), I cannot resist the temptation of questioning: Is it possible that the effective preoptic lesions impaired the vascular supply to the choroid plexa of the lateral and third ventricles? This may delay considerably the transfer of Na^+ from the systemic extracellular fluid to the CSF.

In his chapter Dr. Peck states that there are flaws both in my arguments and in my evidence for a central sodium-sensitive receptor system involved in the control of water balance (Andersson, 1971). Nothing could be more true. Much further work is needed either to prove or to disprove the existence of such receptors in the close vicinity of the third cerebral ventricle. But there seems to be some disagreement between Dr. Peck and me regarding the nature of these flaws. Dr. Peck finds it likely that *all* intraventricular infusions eliciting thirst and release of antidiuretic hormone (ADH) in the goat nonspecifically stimulate neural tissue near the midline, and that this neural tissue happens to be involved (but not at the receptor level) in mediating ADH release and/or thirst. He takes the infusions into the third ventricle of KCl (Olsson, 1969a) and of NH_4Cl (Olsson, 1969b) as examples. Dr. Olsson has not disputed the nonspecificity of these infusions. However, as for the corresponding infusions of hypertonic NaCl, the situation may well be different. The rate of infusion into the CSF of the third ventricle generally has been maintained at about 5% of the normal bulk flow of CSF in this species (Pappenheimer, Heisey, Jordan, & Downer, 1962). This means that 0.3 M NaCl (used in many of the experiments) on an average would cause about 5% increase in the Na^+ concentration of the CSF. Such infusions rapidly (within 1 to 3 minutes) induce cumulative drinking in goats in normal water balance, and an inhibition of the water diuresis in the hydrated animal. The only other obvious effects are natriuresis, which is most pronounced in the salt-supplemented, hydrated animal, and a moderate rise in the arterial blood pressure (Andersson, Eriksson, Fernández, Kolmodin, & Oltner, 1972). The rise in the CSF Na^+ concentration no doubt is much more than 5% close to the cannula outlet. However, the water balance of the animal is affected in the same manner when the NaCl is infused into the lateral cerebral ventricle. The only difference is that the latency time for the responses is prolonged and that the intensity of the effects becomes somewhat weaker.

Dr. Peck provides an explanation of the fact that intraventricular infusions of hypertonic sucrose elicits neither thirst nor ADH-release in the goat (Olsson, 1969b). He finds it unlikely that hypertonic sucrose infused into the third ventricle can act as an osmotic stimulus as far distantly as in the "osmosensitive" LPO. This assumption is probably correct. However, it then appears hard to explain in terms of the osmoreceptor theory the fact that intraventricular infusions of isotonic (Olsson, 1972a), or even hypertonic (Olsson, 1972b), monosaccharide and sucrose solutions can block completely the dipsogenic (Figure 1) and the antidiuretic effects of intracarotid infusions of hypertonic NaCl.

In Dr. Peck's opinion, also, the potentiation of the dipsogenic and the ADH-releasing effects seen during combined intraventricular infusions of NaCl and angiotensin II (Andersson, Eriksson, & Oltner, 1970), most likely reflects a

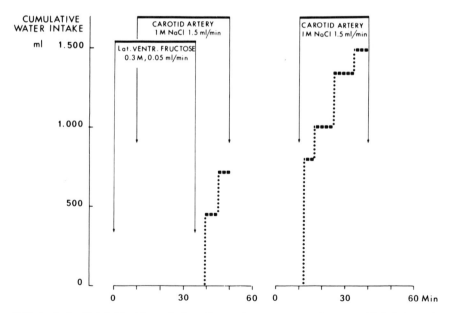

FIG. 1. *Left:* Total blocking of the dipsogenic response to intracarotid infusion of hypertonic NaCl by the infusion of isotonic fructose into the CSF of the lateral ventricle of a goat. Note that the animal starts to drink 4 min. after the discontinuation of the intraventricular infusion. *Right:* The dipsogenic response of the same animal to merely the intracarotid infusion of hypertonic saline. Interval between the experiments was two days.
(From Olsson, 1972b. Used by permission of Pergamon Press.)

nonspecific action of sodium. He suggests that NaCl might be facilitating transmission in pathways otherwise activated by angiotensin. That the facilitation might occur at receptor level appears equally possible at present. Whether then to speak about sodium receptors activated by angiotensin, or the reverse, will remain an academic question until we know much more about the phenomenon.

REFERENCES

Andersson, B. Thirst—and brain control of water balance. *American Scientist,* 1971, **59**, 408–415.

Andersson, B., Eriksson, L., Fernández, O., Kolmodin, C.-G., & Oltner, R. Centrally mediated effects of sodium and angiotensin II on arterial blood pressure and fluid balance. *Acta Physiologica Scandinavica,* 1972, **85**, 398–407.

Andersson, B., Eriksson, L., & Oltner, R. Further evidence for angiotensin-sodium interaction in central control of fluid balance. *Life Sciences,* Part I, 1970, 9, 1901–96.

Blass, E. M., & Epstein, A. N. A lateral preoptic osmosensitive zone for thirst. *Journal of Comparative and Physiological Psychology,* 1971, **76**, 378–394.

Olsson, K. Effects of slow infusions of KCl into the 3rd brain ventricle. *Acta Physiologica Scandinavica,* 1969, **77**, 358–364. (a)

Olsson, K. Studies of central regulation of secretion of antidiuretic hormone (ADH) in the goat. *Acta Physiologica Scandinavica,* 1969, **77**, 465–474. (b)

Olsson, K. On the importance of CSF Na^+ concentration in central control of fluid balance. *Life Sciences,* Part I, 1972, **11**, 397–402. (b)

Olsson, K. Further evidence for the importance of CSF Na^+ concentration in central control of fluid balance. *Acta Physiologica Scandinavica,* 1972, in press. (a)

Pappenheimer, J. R., Heisey, S. R., Jordan, E. F., & Downer, J. de C. Perfusion of the cerebral ventricular system in unanesthetized goats. *American Journal of Physiology,* 1962, **203**, 763–774.

Peck, J. W., & Novin, D. Evidence that osmoreceptors mediating drinking in rabbits are in the lateral preoptic area. *Journal of Comparative and Physiological Psychology,* 1971, **74**, 134–147.

Verney, E. B. The antidiuretic hormone and the factors which determine its release. *Proceedings of the Royal Society of London,* 1947, **135 B**, 25–106.

PART II:
MECHANISMS OF MOTIVATION
AND NONHOMEOSTATIC THIRST

3
HYPOTHALAMIC LIMBIC MECHANISMS IN THE CONTROL OF WATER INTAKE[1]

Gordon J. Mogenson[2]
University of Western Ontario

Water is essential to life, and it is not surprising that complex neural and neuroendocrine mechanisms have evolved for the regulation of water balance. It is now well established that lesions of the lateral hypothalamus cause adipsia and lesions of the septum cause polydipsia. On the other hand, electrical stimulation of the lateral hypothalamus elicits drinking, and stimulation of the septum suppresses drinking (Table 1). These observations indicate that both the lateral hypothalamus and the septum have an important role in the control of water intake, the former having a facilitatory effect and the latter an inhibitory influence on drinking behavior. Other areas of the limbic system, such as the amygdala, and the hippocampus as well as the midbrain have also been implicated in thirst. This chapter is concerned with the role of these structures in the control of water intake and in particular with trying to understand something of the mechanisms involved when drinking is elicited by electrical stimulation of the brain.

THE HYPOTHALAMUS

Elicited Drinking

Strong and persistent drinking has been elicited by electrical stimulation of the hypothalamus in the rat (Greer, 1955; Mogenson & Stevenson, 1966, 1967)

[1] Research support was provided by a grant from the Medical Research Council of Canada and by a grant from the National Research Council of Canada.
[2] The assistance of Miss B. Box and Miss B. Woodside with the illustrations and of Miss Anne Baxter with the typing of the manuscript is gratefully acknowledged. Miss Box also provided valuable advice in the preparation of the manuscript.

TABLE 1

Water Drinking: Effects of Lesioning versus Electrical Stimulation of Lateral
Hypothalamus and Septum

Brain site		Lesions		Electrical stimulation
	Effect[a]	Reference	Effect[a]	Reference
Lateral hypothalamus	↓	Anand & Brobeck, 1951 Teitelbaum & Stellar, 1954 Montemurro & Stevenson, 1957 Morrison & Mayer, 1957 Teitelbaum & Epstein, 1962	↑	Andersson & McCann, 1955 Greer, 1955 N. E. Miller, 1960 Mogenson & Stevenson, 1966
Septum	↑	Harvey & Hunt, 1965 Lubar, Schaefer & Wells, 1969 Wishart & Mogenson, 1970b	↓	Asdourian, 1962 Mabry & Peeler, 1968 Wishart & Mogenson, 1970a

[a]↑ = increase; ↓ = decrease.

and in the goat (Andersson & McCann, 1955; Andersson & Wyrwicka, 1957). In these earlier studies the stimulated sites were in a region of the lateral hypothalamus between the fornix and the mamillothalamic tract, usually just dorsolateral to the fornix (Figure 1a).

The stimulating electrodes (Figure 1b), insulated except at the tips, are positioned accurately in the brain using the stereotaxic technique and attached permanently to the skull. Following recovery from the surgical procedure, electrical stimulation is administered to the unanesthetized, freely moving animal (Figure 1c). Some animals are induced to drink the equivalent of their 24-hour intake in an hour or less, and during 10- or 12-hour periods of intermittent stimulation animals have ingested quantities of water which approach their body weight (Figure 1d).

Since the water intake elicited by hypothalamic stimulation is in excess of need and apparently is not initiated by primary thirst or homeostatic signals, it is sometimes designated nonregulatory drinking. At the same time it is frequently assumed that the hypothalamic stimulation is activating neural integrative systems that subserve regulatory drinking in response to homeostatic deficits. However, this is merely an assumption—not proven; rats drink in several circumstances and for a number of reasons, not always in response to deficits of body water. The central stimulation might also activate neural mechanisms which mediate nonregulatory signals for drinking.

There are numerous examples that animals apparently do not always use the homeostatic mechanisms perfected during millions of years of biological evolution. This is often overlooked by investigators working with the rat. The results of drinking elicited by electrical (Robinson & Mishkin, 1968) and chemical (Sharpe & Myers, 1969) stimulation "suggest that the neural control system for water intake in the monkey may lie principally in the telencephalon rather than in the diencephalon [Sharpe & Myers, 1969, p. 306] ." As the nervous system becomes more complex, with increased capacity for perceptual and memory functions, it seems that neural systems have developed which enable the animal to ingest water before a water deficit has occurred (Fitzsimons, 1972). Unfortunately, there has been little attention given to the possibility that electrical stimulation (and lesions) which alter water intake, do so by influencing systems that mediate such cognitive functions.

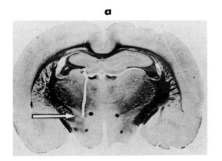
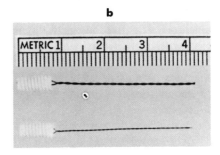

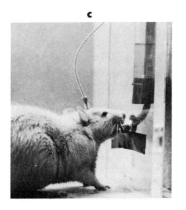
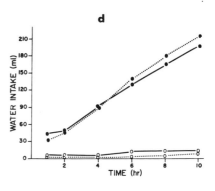

FIG. 1. (*a*) Photomicrograph of a coronal section of the rat brain showing the track of an electrode from which drinking was elicited by electrical stimulation. The electrode tip, shown with an arrow, is in the ventral portion of the zona incerta. (*b*) Electrodes used for chronic brain stimulation. The electrode shown at the top and used in most of the earlier studies, is made of stainless steel wires that are 250 μ in diameter. The electrode shown at the bottom and made of wire that is 100 μ in diameter, has been used for more discrete stimulation in recent studies. (*c*) A rat induced by the brain stimulation to drink water. (*d*) The cumulative intake of water (*closed circles*) by two rats being stimulated (10 seconds on, 10 seconds off) for 10 hours. Control intakes when no stimulation was presented are shown by *open circles*. (From experiments by Mogenson, Gentil, & Stevenson, 1971.)

Characteristics of Elicited Drinking and Other Elicited Behaviors

Elicited drinking behavior shares many of the characteristics of other external, goal-directed responses produced by hypothalamic stimulation. They have been reviewed recently by Roberts (1970) and include:

Exaggerated intensity of response. The elicited behavior is very intense, especially when the stimulation activates the focus or more responsive regions of the system (Doty, 1969).

Multiple behavioral responses. Other responses besides drinking, both behavioral (e.g., feeding, gnawing) and visceral (e.g., heart rate, blood pressure, gastrointestinal motility) are elicited by electrical stimulation of the lateral hypothalamus. Since the stimulating electrodes are usually relatively large, more than one response is frequently elicited from the same electrode site. The basis of the multiple responses seems to be the histological complexity of this region. Fibers pass rostrally and caudally in the medial forebrain bundle and medially and laterally to the ventromedial hypothalamus and globus pallidus.

Dependence on environmental stimuli. Hypothalamic stimulation is likely to induce exploratory behavior in the absence of appropriate environmental stimuli. The elicited behavior becomes goal-directed when specific stimuli are present (e.g., the animal approaches and drinks water). It appears that the hypothalamic stimulation does not directly activate motor systems but rather sensory-motor integrative mechanisms; "it enhances the capacity of the object stimuli to elicit the responses [Roberts, 1970, p. 178]."

Habit transfer with normal drive states. Electrical stimulation of the hypothalamus of sated goats was shown by Andersson and Wyrwicka (1957) to initiate a conditioned response that the animals had learned previously while water-deprived. Results of this sort suggest that "some centrally induced motivational states possess habit-eliciting capacities similar to the natural motivational states that they resemble, possibly through similar cue properties or possibly through a more direct access to habit storage mechanisms [Roberts, 1970, p. 181]."

The performance of goal-directed behaviors elicited by hypothalamic stimulation is positively reinforcing. Electrode sites from which drinking (Mogenson & Stevenson, 1966) and feeding (Hoebel & Teitelbaum, 1962; Margules & Olds, 1962) and other goal-directed behaviors (Glickman & Schiff, 1967) are elicited are very potent for self-stimulation. This represents an added complication when studying the neural mechanisms for such behaviors, since they might occur because of incentive motivational and reward properties of the stimulation as well as being induced by the stimulation.

Mechanisms of Elicited Drinking

It has frequently been assumed that the lateral hypothalamus integrates thirst and hunger signals (Anand & Brobeck, 1951; Stellar, 1960; Stevenson, 1969)

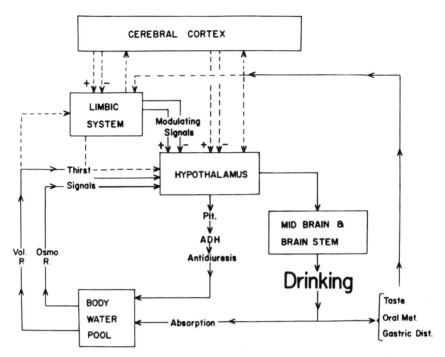

FIG. 2. This diagram illustrates a widely accepted model which assumes that the primary thirst (hyperosmolarity, hypovolemia, thermal) and modulatory (smell, taste, familiar stimuli, etc.) signals are integrated by the lateral hypothalamus before command signals are transmitted to the midbrain and brainstem. Limbic forebrain structures which seem to have a role in mediating the modulatory signals have connections to both the lateral hypothalamus and midbrain. It is possible, however, that primary and modulatory signals are merely conducted through the hypothalamus by "fibers of passage" for integration elsewhere. Furthermore, there is some evidence to suggest that there are multiple pathways and perhaps multiple integrative mechanisms for the primary and modulatory signals.

and exerts facilitatory influences on motor circuits that control drinking and feeding (Figure 2). Rats recovered from the adipsia which follows lesions of the lateral hypothalamus ("recovered laterals") do not respond to thirst signals produced by the administration of hypertonic saline or polyethylene glycol (Epstein, 1971). Since lesions and sections rostral to the proposed integrative region also cause adipsia, it has been suggested that thirst signals pass caudally to the lateral hypothalamus (Stevenson, 1969), perhaps from osmoreceptors (Blass & Epstein, 1971; Peck & Novin, 1971) or from neurons sensitive to angiotensin located in the preoptic region (Epstein, Fitzsimons, & Rolls, 1970). According to this model, drinking in response to electrical stimulation of the lateral hypothalamus is due to the activation of the integrative mechanism for thirst signals or to the activation of fibers to it from thirst receptors.

The critical output from the hypothalamic integrative sites appears to be to the midbrain (Figure 2), which is considered by some investigators to contain motor elements for ingestive and other behaviors (Glickman & Schiff, 1967;

Roberts, 1970). This suggestion is supported by the following evidence: (*a*) Electrical stimulation of the lateral hypothalamus has been reported to produce evoked potentials in the area of Tsai and in the midbrain tegmentum ventrolateral to the central gray (Wyrwicka & Doty, 1966). (*b*) Degenerating fibers have been traced from drinking and feeding sites in the lateral hypothalamus to the midbrain (Huang & Mogenson, 1972). (*c*) Lesions of the midbrain cause adipsia and aphagia (Parker & Feldman, 1967; Lyon, Halpern, & Mintz, 1968). (*d*) Lesions in the posterior hypothalamus, placed between stimulating electrodes in the hypothalamus that elicited feeding and the midbrain, suppressed elicited feeding; but lesions rostral and lateral to the stimulating electrodes had no effect (Bergquist, 1970). Thus, as shown in Figure 2, it appears that the primary thirst and modulatory signals are integrated in the hypothalamus, which sends command signals to the midbrain for the organization and execution of drinking and feeding behaviors.

Although this model of hypothalamic midbrain mechanisms in ingestive behaviors is widely accepted, two other possibilities should be mentioned. The first alternative is that the critical events for the initiation of drinking occur in limbic forebrain structures such as the amygdala and septum, and the fibers that transmit the relevant signals pass through the hypothalamus to the midbrain. According to this view, drinking is elicited by electrical stimulation of these "fibers of passage" in the lateral hypothalamus, with the important integrative events taking place in the midbrain or elsewhere. This proposal cannot be excluded since the septum, hippocampus, amygdala, and other forebrain structures have been implicated in ingestive behaviors (Fonberg, 1971; Grossman, 1968; Harvey & Hunt, 1965; Pizzi & Lorens, 1967; Robinson & Mishkin, 1968). Since electrical stimulation can have disruptive effects on the temporal and spatial patterning of nerve impulses at an integrative site in the immediate vicinity of the electrode (Doty, 1969), the activation of "fibers of passage" from these forebrain structures is more likely to produce relatively normal effects where these fibers terminate. Furthermore, there is evidence from experiments in which the hypothalamus has been isolated that drinking can still occur (Ellison & Flynn, 1968). This observation is consistent with the view that the activation of midbrain ingestive circuits can be initiated by extrahypothalamic structures.

The other alternative is that signals for the initiation of drinking come from extrahypothalamic structures as well as the hypothalamus. As suggested below these signals may be modulatory rather than primary, and this information could be first processed in the hypothalamus or exert direct influences on the midbrain.

Finally, it should be noted that although the model illustrated in Figure 2 emphasizes caudally directed connections, the hypothalamus and midbrain also have rostral connections with limbic forebrain structures. A number of investigators (e.g., Grossman, 1968; Morgane, 1969) have suggested these rostral connections may be important in ingestive and other goal-directed behaviors.

Recently Ungerstedt (1971) has reported that lesions of a nigrostriatal dopamine pathway using localized intracerebral injections of 6-hydroxydopamine cause adipsia and aphagia. However, he does not think the lesions specifically disrupt drinking and feeding. He suggests that this pathway is more likely concerned with controlling "a general arousal or drive level that is necessary for performing a number of activities, where eating and drinking deficits are noticed only because they are easily measured by the observer and disastrous to the animal [Ungerstedt, 1971, p. 116]." Oltmans and Harvey (1972) made electrolytic lesions in this nigrostriatal pathway and also observed adipsia and aphagia as well as reduced levels of catecholamines in telencephalic tissue samples which included the caudate nucleus and putamen.

The Stability of Elicited Drinking and the Specificity of Neural Systems

Feeding, gnawing, and other behaviors as well as drinking are frequently elicited from the same electrode site. Furthermore, some animals that are initially induced by this brain stimulation to feed, subsequently are induced to drink when stimulated in the absence of food (Figure 3a); and some animals that are initially induced to drink, later are induced to feed when stimulated with water removed (Mogenson, 1971; Mogenson & Morgan, 1967; Valenstein, Cox, & Kakolewski, 1968; Milgram, Devor, & Server, 1971; Wayner, 1970; Wise, 1968). The occurrence of multiple responses suggests that the neuronal systems for drinking and feeding partially overlap in the hypothalamus, a view which is supported by the effects of hypothalamic lesions on water and food intakes (Montemurro & Stevenson, 1957; Teitelbaum & Epstein, 1962). However, the modification of elicited behavior by removing the initially preferred goal object has been considered a challenge to the popular hypothesis that drinking and feeding are subserved by specific neural systems whose focus is in the hypothalamus. As an alternative Valenstein et al. (1968) have suggested that the brain stimulation produces an aroused or motivated state, the specificity and goal directedness of the behavior being determined by the environmental stimuli available.

A detailed discussion of the specificity issue is beyond the scope of this article; it has been dealt with elsewhere (Caggiula, 1969; Mogenson, 1971; Roberts, 1969, 1970). It should be recognized, however, that their suggestions are part of a more general issue concerning the specificity of drive and satiety mechanisms (Grossman, 1966; Hebb, 1955; Morgane, 1969) and, in the wider biological sense, the specificity of physiological regulatory mechanisms (Adolph, 1959). In addition, I would like to suggest that the elicitation of multiple behaviors or the elicitation of a new behavior by changing goal objects in the environment is not necessarily incompatible with the hypothesis that specific neuronal systems subserve drinking, feeding, and other behaviors. There is some evidence that these neural systems which subserve drinking and feeding behaviors, while partially overlapping in the hypothalamus, are functionally distinct.

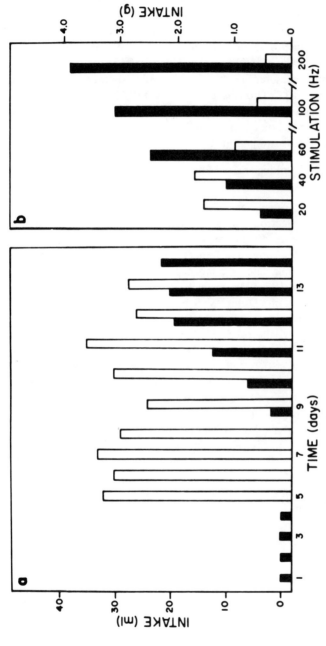

FIG. 3. (*a*) Change in behavior elicited by hypothalamic stimulation when goal objects are manipulated. Water intake elicited by hypothalamic stimulation is shown by *solid bars*, and food intake (condensed milk) elicited by the stimulation is shown by *open bars*. This rat was initially (days 1 to 8) induced to feed only; but after 6 days (days 9 to 14) during which food was removed for the first half of each session, the amount of elicited drinking gradually increased. (After Mogenson & Morgan, 1967.) (*b*) This graph illustrates the effect of varying the frequency of stimulation (0.4-msec pulses, 50 to 125 μA) from the same electrode site in the hypothalamus on elicited feeding (*open bars*) and drinking (*closed bars*). Feeding was the stronger response to hypothalamic stimulation when the lower frequencies were used. With higher frequencies of stimulation the volume of water intake increased and the quantity of food intake decreased. (For further details, see Mogenson, Gentil, & Stevenson, 1971.)

1. (*a*) Drinking only or feeding only has been elicited by electrical stimulation of the hypothalamus in some animals, and a second behavior is not elicited when the initially preferred goal object is removed (Mogenson, 1971). (*b*) The occurrence of only drinking or feeding is more readily obtained using stimulating electrodes with smaller tips (Figure 1*b*).

2. Elicited feeding occurs immediately in some animals when the water is removed, although only drinking was elicited initially by the hypothalamic stimulation (Mogenson, 1971, rat no. 16). This observation suggests that both systems were being activated from the beginning but one more strongly than the other.

3. When electrical stimulation of a hypothalamic site elicits both drinking and feeding using a stimulation frequency of 60 Hz, lowering the frequency to 30 or 40 Hz results in feeding becoming the dominant response, and raising the frequency to 100 Hz results in drinking becoming the dominant response (Figure 3*b*).

4. Severe adipsia with no or only transient aphagia has been observed in a few animals following lesions of the lateral hypothalamus (Montemurro & Stevenson, 1957), and the recovery of water intake following lesions of this area is typically slower and less complete than the recovery of food intake (Teitelbaum & Epstein, 1962).

5. Drinking is elicited by the local application of carbachol, a cholinergic compound, and feeding is elicited by the local application of noradrenalin (Grossman, 1962).

6. In an extensive study in which behaviors were elicited by electrical stimulation of many brain sites in the monkey, Robinson and Mishkin (1968) conclude that "the food intake and water intake systems are separable anatomically. The distribution of the two sets of points are quite different ... [p. 360]."

External stimuli are important for goal-directed behaviors such as those observed in the water-deprived animal or in the animal which seeks water when its brain is stimulated (Mogenson & Kaplinsky, 1970; Mogenson & Morgan, 1967; Phillips & Mogenson, 1968). Since drinking and other motivated behaviors depend on the presence and interaction of appropriate external stimuli with an activated state, usually produced by internal signals (Bindra, 1969), it is not surprising that the behavior elicited by brain stimulation changes following certain critical changes in the external environment. However, we need to determine the neural events that occur during this interaction. In the meantime, our working hypothesis is that water-seeking and food-seeking behaviors are represented by neural events that are partially distinctive. Accordingly, with the stimulation of certain sites, especially with fine electrodes, it has been possible to elicit one or the other of these behaviors (Huang & Mogenson, 1972; Olds, Allan, & Briese, 1971).

THE LIMBIC SYSTEM

Drinking, feeding, and other behaviors that contribute to homeostasis and the well-being of the animal are influenced by lesions and stimulation of limbic forebrain structures. These structures are interconnected with one another and with the hypothalamus, and the complexity of the anatomical relationships has made it difficult to gain an understanding of the role of limbic structures in the control of water intake and other physiological and behavioral responses.

Forebrain limbic structures receive visceral and somatic afferents (Green & Machne, 1955; Machne & Segundo, 1956) and appear to be involved in the feedback control of several hormones (Lincoln, 1967; Lincoln & Cross, 1967). They also receive inputs from exteroceptors (Creutzfeldt, Bell, & Adey, 1963; Gloor, 1955; Norgren, 1970) and have reciprocal connections with the cerebral cortex (Gloor, 1955; Nauta, 1971). The limbic system is thus in a position to integrate information from both the internal environment and the external environment (MacLean, 1969) and to influence the visceral and behavioral responses as the animal responds and adapts to changing circumstances.

The connections of limbic structures with the hypothalamus, via the medial forebrain bundle, fornix, stria terminalis, and other pathways, enable the limbic system to influence the homeostatic mechanisms traditionally associated with the hypothalamus. Stimulation of the amygdala, hippocampus and septum, and other limbic structures has been shown to facilitate or inhibit neurons in the hypothalamus (Dafny & Feldman, 1969; Murphy, Dreifuss, & Gloor, 1968; Miller & Mogenson, 1971; Oomura, Ooyama, Yamamoto, Naka, Kobayashi, & Ono, 1967) as well as to facilitate or inhibit many responses under the control of the hypothalamus (Egger & Flynn, 1967; Stuart, Kawamura, & Hemingway, 1961; Sibole, Miller, & Mogenson, 1971; Siegel & Skog, 1970).

The Septum and Water Intake

Following large lesions of the septum of rats which destroy most of the medial and lateral septum, water intake is increased by 25 to 50% within 2 or 3 days (Figure 4a). Polydipsia has also been obtained following more discrete lesions (Figure 4c), but the locus of the essential neural tissue has been uncertain (Carey, 1968; Lubar, Schaefer, & Wells, 1969). Recently, Huang and Mogenson (1972) confirmed that small lesions increased water intake and studied the connections of these sites with the hypothalamus.

Electrical stimulation of the septum has been shown to reduce water intake in rats. The lap rate of animals which are drinking after a period of water deprivation decreases gradually with septal stimulation (Figure 4b and d), suggesting that the septum plays some role in the cessation of drinking. The septal stimulation could directly inhibit the lateral hypothalamus or have an indirect influence on it, perhaps by activating the inhibitory interneurons described by Murphy and Renaud (1969).

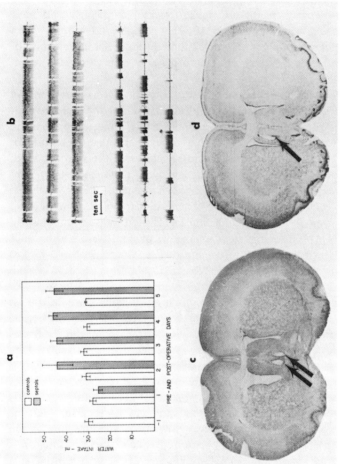

FIG. 4. (*a*) Average daily water intake in eight rats with large septal lesions (*cross-hatched bars*) compared to the daily intake of eight sham-operated rats (*open bars*). (*b*) Drinking after being water-deprived for 23 hours (*top*) and under similar conditions (*bottom*) when the septum was being stimulated. (For further details, see Wishart & Mogenson, 1970b.) (*c*) An example of small bilateral lesions of the septum that caused polydipsia in the rat. (From Wishart, 1970.) (*d*) The site of electrical stimulation of the septum in one of the rats in which water intake was reduced. (Used by permission of Physiology & Behavior. Wishart & Mogenson, 1970, **5**, 1399-1404.)

129

The effects of lesions and stimulation of the septum on water intake are similar to the effects of lesions and stimulation of the ventromedial hypothalamus on food intake. They suggest by analogy that the septum may be part of a satiety system for the control of drinking behavior. There has been some reluctance, however, to postulate an anatomically defined satiety system for thirst. The cessation of drinking could result merely from the disappearance of dipsogenic signals as water is ingested (Corbit, 1969). The consequences of large intakes of water, such as the nonregulatory drinking of highly palatable solutions (Valenstein, Cox, & Kakolewski, 1967) or schedule-induced polydipsia (Falk, 1961), are not as serious as excessive intake of food. Since the output of urine is readily increased, a shutoff mechanism may not be necessary to protect the animal from excessive intake.

Two other suggestions may be made in regard to the effects of lesions and stimulation of the septum on water intake. The first is that the septum might play some role in short-term satiety, perhaps by integrating oropharyngeal, metering signals (Wishart & Mogenson, 1970a). The other is that the septum, or fibers funneled through it from other limbic structures or the frontal cortex, exert a tonic inhibitory influence on hypothalamic and midbrain systems. This latter proposal is consistent with the observations that septal stimulation inhibits many autonomic responses (Kaada, 1951) and somatomotor responses and causes behavioral arrest in freely moving animals (G. J. Mogenson, unpublished observations, 1967). It is also consistent with views of investigators who doubt that there are specific satiety systems (Grossman, 1966; Morgane, 1969, p. 828) or who question the discreteness of physiological regulatory systems in general (Adolph, 1959).

Some clues about the influence of the septum on drinking behavior and on other functions of the hypothalamus have come from electrophysiological experiments. We have made extracellular recordings from neurons in the lateral hypothalamus. The firing rate of many of these neurons was facilitated by stimulation of the septum (Figure 5a). This was unexpected in view of the earlier hypothesis that the septum exerts a tonic inhibitory effect on the hypothalamus and midbrain. However, the firing rate of other neurons was inhibited, and it was subsequently observed that the effect of septal stimulation depended upon the baseline firing rate of the hypothalamic neuron. When the hypothalamic neuron was discharging at a slow rate, septal stimulation speeded up its firing rate; when it was discharging at a fast rate, septal stimulation decreased the firing rate (Figure 5b and c). If the activity of hypothalamic neurons was altered by peripheral stimulation such as stimulation of the olfactory bulb, then presentation of septal stimulation altered the activity in the opposite direction (see Miller & Mogenson, 1971, Fig. 9).

It has been shown that there are two pathways by which these effects of septal stimulation on hypothalamic neurons are mediated. The fibers of the precommissural fornix exert a facilitatory effect, and the fibers of the stria terminalis an inhibitory effect (Miller & Mogenson, 1972). The pathway which

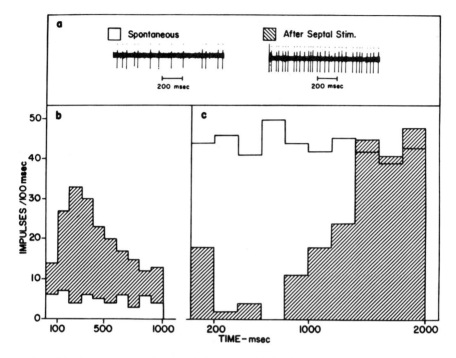

FIG. 5. (*a*) Action potentials recorded extracellularly from a neuron in the lateral hypothalamus of the rat. Following electrical stimulation of the septum (*right*) this neuron discharged at a faster rate. (*b*) Frequency histograms showing facilitatory effects of stimulating the septum when the baseline firing rate of the hypothalamic neuron is slow. The ordinate is the total number of impulses per 100 msec in each address of the histogram for 15 trials. (*c*) Frequency histograms showing inhibitory effects of stimulating the septum when the baseline firing rate of the hypothalamic neuron is fast. (After Miller & Mogenson, 1971.)

has the dominant influence on hypothalamic neurons at any particular time appears to depend on the discharge rate of hypothalamic neurons, which in turn depends on the inputs which are impinging on them (Miller & Mogenson, 1971, 1972). From these observations it has been suggested that the septum acts as a stabilizer of hypothalamic activity, exerting either a facilitatory or inhibitory bias as a function of the discharge rate of the neurons of the system.

The results of these electrophysiological experiments suggested that the septum may facilitate as well as inhibit drinking. As a test of this possibility we have stimulated the septum of animals in which drinking was elicited by hypothalamic stimulation. An electrode was first implanted in the lateral hypothalamus and those animals selected that were induced by stimulation to drink water. A second operation was then performed, and a stimulating electrode was positioned in the septum while recording evoked potentials from the lateral hypothalamic electrode. This was to ensure a functional connection between the septal site stimulated and the hypothalamic site from which drinking was elicited. A week later, trains of pulses were presented to both the septum and the hypothalamus, with each pulse to the septum preceding each pulse to the hypothalamus by 5 msec. As anticipated from the electrophysiological experiments, septal stimulation both facilitated and inhibited elicited drinking (Sibole, 1971; Sibole et al., 1971).

These effects of septal stimulation appeared to depend on the site of stimulation. With stimulation of the mediodorsal septum, in the region of the dorsal fornix fibers, elicited drinking was facilitated, whereas inhibition occurred with stimulation of the ventrolateral septum in the region of the bed nucleus of the stria terminalis. The evoked potentials recorded from the hypothalamic electrode differed for these two regions of the septum (Figure 6). Stimulation of the mediodorsal septum elicited an evoked potential in the lateral hypothalamus with a latency of 10 to 14 msec, whereas stimulation of the ventrolateral region in the vicinity of the bed nucleus of the stria terminalis elicited a response with the opposite polarity and a latency of 18 to 23 msec. Discrete lesions of the pathways attenuated the evoked potentials, providing additional evidence that these responses are mediated via the fornix and the stria terminalis (Miller & Mogenson, 1972).

An additional series of five animals was prepared with two septal electrodes, one positioned in the dorsomedial region and one in the ventrolateral region while recording the characteristic evoked potentials from an electrode in the hypothalamus from which drinking had been elicited (Figure 7a). Typical results

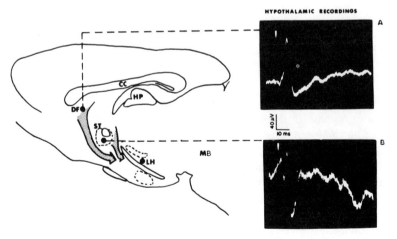

FIG. 6. Evoked potentials recorded from an electrode in the lateral hypothalamus from which drinking had been elicited by electrical stimulation. The 10 to 14 msec evoked potential shown in the upper panel (*A*) was produced when the mediodorsal septum, in the region of the precommissural fornix fibers, was stimulated. The 18 to 23 msec evoked potential shown in the lower panel (*B*) was produced when the ventrolateral septum, in the region of the bed nucleus of the stria terminalis, was stimulated. (With the collaboration of W. Sibole.)

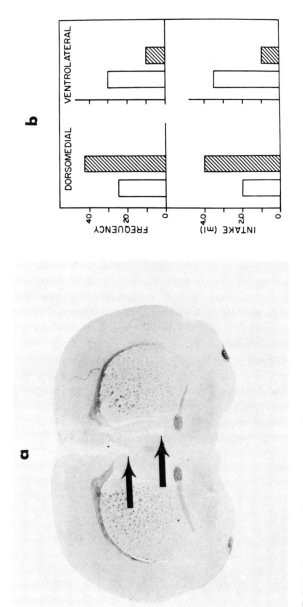

FIG. 7. Two sites of stimulation of the septum in the same animal are shown by arrows. The *upper arrow* indicates the electrode placement in the mediodorsal septum from which there was facilitation of the drinking elicited by hypothalamic stimulation. The *lower arrow* indicates the electrode placement in the basolateral septum from which there was suppression of the elicited drinking. (With the collaboration of W. Sibole.)

obtained from one of the animals are shown in Figure 7*b*. They confirm the earlier observation that stimulation of the dorsomedial region facilitates drinking elicited by hypothalamic stimulation, while stimulation of the ventrolateral region inhibits the elicited drinking.

What signals are being mediated by these pathways which influence elicited drinking behavior? There is no evidence that they are concerned with primary thirst signals, but it is possible that they mediate certain modulatory signals which influence ingestive behaviors. Since the fibers of the stria terminalis and fornix originate in the amygdala and hippocampus, the modulatory signals may come from those structures. This hypothesis will now be considered.

The Amygdala

Since suppression of elicited drinking was produced by stimulation of the bed nucleus of the stria terminalis (Sibole et al., 1971), which receives fiber projections from the amygdala, it is possible that the inhibitory effects originate in the amygdala. Recently, White and Fisher (1969) reported that the suppression of feeding, produced by stimulation of the amygdala was eliminated when the stria terminalis was severed. Experiments conducted in our laboratory have shown that stimulation of the stria terminalis produced an evoked potential which was similar to, but of longer latency than, that obtained when the ventrolateral septum was stimulated. This evoked potential was markedly attenuated following lesions of the ventrolateral septum, which included the bed nucleus of the stria terminalis (Figure 8). Thus it appears that septal stimulation which inhibited elicited drinking may have been firing fibers of the stria terminalis which have their origin in the amygdala.

Recently we have placed electrodes in the amygdala to see what effect stimulation there has on drinking elicited by hypothalamic stimulation (Figure 9). The procedures were similar to those described by Sibole et al. (1971). As expected, water intake was suppressed in six of the eight rats. However, in one animal stimulation of the amygdala increased the induced drinking. These results suggest that the effects of the amygdala on water intake may be both facilitatory and inhibitory.

There is other evidence that the amygdala is involved in the control of ingestive behaviors (Fonberg, 1969; Lewinska, 1968; Morgane, 1962; Robinson & Mishkin, 1968), but its precise role is still uncertain. It seems unlikely that it integrates signals from water and energy deficits, in parallel with the hypothalamus (Epstein, 1971; Stevenson, 1967), but rather it seems likely that it has modulatory influences on these hypothalamic sites (Gloor, 1960; Grossman, 1964; Russell, 1966). Grossman and Russell observed that the application of carbachol, a cholinergic compound, to the amygdala did not initiate drinking in satiated rats but increased water intake in deprived animals. These observations suggest that once the hypothalamic drinking system is activated, stimulation of the amygdala modulates this activity to further increase water intake. Olfactory, taste, and other external stimuli are known to influence

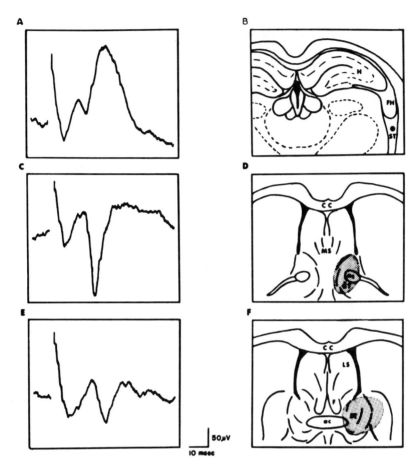

FIG. 8. Evoked potentials (*A*) recorded in the hypothalamus to stimulation of the stria terminalis (*B*) are similar to those obtained with stimulation of the septum in the region of the bed nucleus of the stria terminalis (for comparison, see Miller & Mogenson, 1972, Fig. 3-3), except they have a somewhat longer latency. This evoked potential is attenuated (*C* and *E*) by lesions of the septum (*D* and *F*), and the attenuation is greater when the lesion is placed in the more posterior part of the septum destroying the bed nucleus of the stria terminalis. These observations suggest that the fibers mediating the inhibitory effect on elicited drinking might not be of septal origin but "fibers of passage" from the amygdala to the hypothalamus. (Used by permission of Experimental Neurology. Miller & Mogenson, 1972, **34**, 229-243.)

ingestive behaviors, and there is evidence that the amygdala is involved in mediating these signals. Lewinska (1968) has reported that stimulation of the amygdala has olfactory effects; food is sniffed with obvious satisfaction. On the other hand, stimulation of the other sites of the amygdala produced an aversion to food.

It may be assumed that protopathic aspects of olfactory stimuli, just like protopathic aspects of gustatory stimuli, are represented in the amygdala and their role is to control the food intake along with the taste stimuli. Accordingly, by the stimulation of individual points in the facilitatory hunger center the olfactory units representing the attractive aspects of the smell of food are activated and hence the animals sniff the food with obvious satisfaction, thus increasing their hunger drive. On the contrary, the stimulation of some points in the inhibitory hunger center produced a distinct aversive response to the food sniffed [Lewinska, 1968, p. 32].

Another possibility is that the amygdala is concerned with short-term satiety. Milner (1966) points out that the amygdala receives inputs from chewing and swallowing as well as from taste and smell, and has suggested that it might monitor drinking and feeding.

Some cells of the amygdala have the peculiarity that, if they are stimulated for a time, they become more and more sensitive and finally continue to fire for long periods of time with no further input. One theory as to the role of the amygdaloid nuclei in eating is that they "clock up" the amount of chewing and taste stimulation

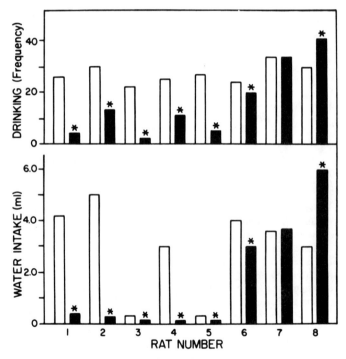

FIG. 9. The frequency of drinking (in 60 presentations) and the volume of water intake in response to hypothalamic stimulation (50-Hz, 1-msec pulses, 75 to 125 μA) for eight rats are shown by *open bars*. A pulse of stimulation to the amygdala (1 msec, 50 μA) 5 msec before each pulse to the hypothalamus reduced the frequency of drinking and the volume of water intake in six of the animals as shown by *filled bars*. (With the collaboration of W. Sibole.)

of the mouth and throat, and, when it reaches a critical total, they fire and thus shut off the feeding system.[3] They continue to fire until after food has been digested and has produced an increase in the sugar content of the blood. It is also possible that the amygdala are especially sensitive to the input from inedible or bad-tasting substances in the mouth, causing the feeding system to shut off immediately [Milner, 1966, p. 243].

The Hippocampus

As indicated earlier the facilitation of elicited drinking from electrical stimulation of the mediodorsal septum might have been due to the activation of fornix fibers which originate in the hippocampus. This suggestion was supported by the observation that stimulation of the hippocampus caused an evoked potential similar in form to, but of somewhat longer latency than, that produced by stimulation of the mediodorsal septum. Furthermore, when this region of the septum was lesioned, the evoked response was markedly attenuated (Miller & Mogenson, 1972, Fig. 6).

The first indication that the hippocampus might have a facilitatory influence on drinking behavior was provided by chemical stimulation experiments. Fisher and Coury (1962) showed that the local application of carbachol to the hippocampus increased water intake in rats. A facilitatory influence of the hippocampus is also suggested by the observation that discharge rates of hippocampal neurons are increased just before water is made available when rats have been trained to anticipate water (Olds, Mink, & Best, 1969).

Several years ago Nauta (1962, p. 518), from histological evidence, proposed that the hippocampus and amygdala could exert effects on hypothalamic functions that are mutually antagonistic. Our results which show that stimulation of pathways from the hippocampus and amygdala (the fornix and the stria terminalis) have opposite effects on elicited drinking are consistent with this suggestion.

SUMMARY AND CONCLUSIONS

1. Electrical stimulation of certain regions of the brain, particularly in the region of the lateral hypothalamus and zona incerta, elicits strong and persistent drinking behavior in the rat.

2. (a) As a working hypothesis, in line with the classical model of the role of the hypothalamus in ingestive behaviors, it is assumed that an integrative mechanism is being activated which subserves primary regulatory signals as well as modulatory signals. (b) Alternatively the stimulation may be activating "fibers of passage" which transmit such signals for integration in the midbrain or elsewhere.

---

[3] Author's note: Sham drinking in water-deprived dogs results in temporary satiety (Towbin, 1949), and Adolph (1950) has suggested that an oral-pharyngeal metering mechanism terminates the drinking. The amygdala could also play a role in the oral metering of water intake. G.J.M.

3. The hypothalamic integrative mechanism is influenced by limbic forebrain structures. (*a*) Water intake is altered by electrical stimulation and lesions of the septum and amygdala. (*b*) With the combined use of electrophysiological and behavioral techniques it has been shown that facilitatory and inhibitory effects on elicited drinking are mediated by the fornix and stria terminalis, two important pathways from limbic forebrain to hypothalamus. (*c*) It seems unlikely that these pathways, and the limbic structures from which they originate, mediate primary thirst signals. There is some evidence that they subserve modulatory signals such as taste, smell, and past experience.

4. Discrete lesions of "drinking and feeding sites" in the hypothalamus and zona incerta result in degeneration of fibers to the midbrain, and lesions between the hypothalamus and midbrain disrupt ingestive behaviors elicited by hypothalamic stimulation. This evidence suggests that the hypothalamic integrative system for thirst projects to the midbrain to influence the reflex patterns for ingestive behaviors.

REFERENCES

Adolph, E. F. Thirst and its inhibition in the stomach. *American Journal of Physiology,* 1950, **161**, 374–386.

Adolph, E. F. How specific are physiological regulations? *Perspectives in Biology and Medicine,* 1959, **3**, 55–69.

Anand, B. K., & Brobeck, J. R. Hypothalamic control of food intake in rats and cats. *Yale Journal of Biology and Medicine,* 1951, **24**, 123–140.

Andersson, B., & McCann, S. M. A further study of polydipsia evoked by hypothalamic stimulation in the goat. *Acta Physiologica Scandinavica,* 1955, **33**, 333–346.

Andersson, B., & Wyrwicka, W. The elicitation of a drinking motor conditioned reaction by electrical stimulation of the "drinking area" in the goat. *Acta Physiologica Scandinavica,* 1957, **41**, 194–198.

Asdourian, D. Interaction effects of intracranial stimulation with rewarding and aversive solutions. *Journal of Comparative and Physiological Psychology,* 1962, **55**, 685–690.

Bergquist, E. H. Output pathways of hypothalamic mechanisms for sexual, aggressive and other motivated behaviors in opossum. *Journal of Comparative and Physiological Psychology,* 1970, **70**, 389–398.

Bindra, D. The inter-related mechanisms of reinforcement and motivation, and the nature of their influence on response. In W. J. Arnold & D. Levine (Eds.), *Nebraska Symposium on Motivation.* Lincoln: University of Nebraska Press, 1969. Pp. 1–33.

Blass, E. M., & Epstein, A. N. A lateral preoptic osmosensitive zone for thirst in the rat. *Journal of Comparative and Physiological Psychology,* 1971, **76**, 378–394.

Caggiula, A. R. Stability of behavior produced by electrical stimulation of the rat hypothalamus. *Brain, Behaviour and Evolution,* 1969, **2**, 343–358.

Carey, R. J. A further localization of inhibitory deficits resulting from septal ablation. *Physiology and Behavior,* 1968, **3**, 645–649.

Corbit, J. D. Osmotic thirst: Theoretical and experimental analysis. *Journal of Comparative and Physiological Psychology,* 1969, **67**, 3–14.

Creutzfeldt, O. D., Bell, F. R., & Adey, W. R. The activity of neurons in the amygdala of the cat following afferent stimulation. In W. Bargmann & J. P. Schade (Eds.), *The rhinencephalon and related structures. Progress in brain research.* Amsterdam: Elsevier, 1963, **3**, 31–49.

Dafny, N., & Feldman, S. Effects of stimulating reticular formation, hippocampus and septum on single cells in the posterior hypothalamus. *Electroencephalography and Clinical Neurophysiology,* 1969, **26**, 570–587.

Doty, R. W. Electrical stimulation of the brain in behavioral context. *Annual Review of Psychology,* 1969, **20**, 289–320.

Egger, M. D., & Flynn, J. P. Further studies on the effects of amygdaloid stimulation and ablation on hypothalamically elicited attack behavior in cats. In W. R. Adey & T. Tokizane (Eds.), *Structure and function of the limbic system. Progress in brain research.* Amsterdam: Elsevier, 1967, **27**, 165–182.

Ellison, G. D., & Flynn, J. P. Organized aggressive behavior in cats after surgical isolation of the hypothalamus. *Archives Italiennes de Biologie (Pisa),* 1968, **106**, 1–20.

Epstein, A. N. The lateral hypothalamic syndrome: Its implications for the physiological psychology of hunger and thirst. In E. Stellar & J. M. Sprague (Eds.), *Progress in physiological psychology.* Vol. 4. New York: Academic Press, 1971.

Epstein, A. N., Fitzsimons, J. T., & Rolls, B. J. Drinking induced by injection of angiotensin into the brain of the rat. *Journal of Physiology (London),* 1970, **210**, 457–474.

Falk, J. L. Production of polydipsia in normal rats by an intermittent food schedule. *Science,* 1961, **133**, 195–196.

Fisher, A. E., & Coury, J. N. Cholinergic tracing of a central neural circuit underlying the thirst drive. *Science,* 1962, **138**, 691–693.

Fitzsimons, J. T. Thirst. *Physiological Reviews,* 1972, **52**, 468–561.

Fonberg, E. The role of the hypothalamus and amygdala in food intake, alimentary motivation and emotional reactions. *Acta Biologiae Experimentalis (Warsaw),* 1969, **29**, 335–358.

Fonberg, E. Hyperphagia produced by lateral amygdalar lesions in dogs. *Acta Neurobiologiciae Experimentalis,* 1971, **31**, 19–32.

Glickman, S. E., & Schiff, B. B. A biological theory of reinforcement. *Psychological Reviews,* 1967, **74**, 81–109.

Gloor, P. Electrophysiological studies on the connections of the amygdaloid nucleus in the cat. Part II. The electrophysiological properties of the amygdaloid projection system. *Electroencephalography and Clinical Neurophysiology,* 1955, 7, 242–264.

Gloor, P. The amygdala. In J. Field, H. W. Magoun, & V. E. Hall (Eds.), *Handbook of Physiology.* Sec. 1. *Neurophysiology.* Vol. 2. Baltimore: Williams & Wilkins, 1960. Pp. 1395–1420.

Green, J. D., & Machne, X. Unit activity of rabbit hippocampus. *American Journal of Physiology,* 1955, **181**, 219–224.

Greer, M. A. Suggestive evidence of a primary "drinking center" in hypothalamus of rat. *Proceedings of the Society of Experimental Biology (New York),* 1955, 89, 59–62.

Grossman, S. P. Direct adrenergic and cholinergic stimulation of hypothalamic mechanisms. *American Journal of Physiology,* 1962, **202**, 872–882.

Grossman, S. P. Behavioral effects of chemical stimulation of the ventral amygdala. *Journal of Comparative and Physiological Psychology,* 1964, **57**, 29–36.

Grossman, S. P. The VMH: A center for affective reactions, satiety, or both? *Physiology and Behavior,* 1966, **1**, 1–10.

Grossman, S. P. Hypothalamic and limbic influences on food intake. *Federation Proceedings,* 1968, **27**, 1349–1360.

Harvey, J. A., & Hunt, H. F. Effect of septal lesions on thirst in the rat as indicated by water consumption and operant responding for water reward. *Journal of Comparative and Physiological Psychology,* 1965, **59**, 49–56.

Hebb, D. O. Drives and the C.N.S. (Conceptual Nervous System). *Psychological Reviews,* 1955, **62**, 243–254.

Hoebel, B. G., & Teitelbaum, P. Hypothalamic control of feeding and self-stimulation. *Science,* 1962, **135**, 375–377.

Huang, Y. H., & Mogenson, G. J. Neural pathways mediating drinking and feeding in rats. *Experimental Neurology*, 1972, **37**, 269–286.

Kaada, B. R. Somatomotor, autonomic and electrocorticographic responses to electrical stimulation of "rhinencephalic" and other structures in primates, cat and dog: A study of response from the limbic subcallosal, orbital insula, pyriform and temporal cortex, hippocampus, fornix and amygdala. *Acta Physiologica Scandinavica*, 1951, **24**, 1–285.

Lewinska, M. K. Inhibition and facilitation of alimentary behavior elicited by stimulation of the amygdala in the cat. *Acta Biologiae Experimentalis (Warsaw)*, 1968, **28**, 23–34.

Lincoln, D. W. Unit activity in the hypothalamus, septum and preoptic area of the rat: Characteristics of spontaneous activity and the effect of oestrogen. *Journal of Endocrinology*, 1967, **37**, 127–189.

Lincoln, D. W., & Cross, B. A. Effect of oestrogen on the responsiveness of neurons in the hypothalamus, septum and preoptic area of rats with induced persistent oestrus. *Journal of Endocrinology*, 1967, **37**, 191–203.

Lubar, J. F., Schaefer, C. F., & Wells, D. J. The role of the septal area in the regulation of water intake in associated motivational behavior. *Annals of the New York Academy of Sciences*, 1969, **157**, 875–893.

Lyon, M., Halpern, N. M., & Mintz, E. Y. The significance of the mesencephalon for coordinated feeding behavior. *Acta Neurologica Scandinavica*, 1968, **24**, 323–346.

Mabry, P. D., & Peeler, D. F. Response rate for food and water in the rat as a function of noncontingent, reinforcing septal stimulation. *Psychonomic Science*, 1968, **13**, 51–52.

Machne, X., & Segundo, J. P. Unitary responses to afferent valleys in amygdaloid complex. *Journal of Neurophysiology*, 1956, **19**, 232–240.

Maclean, P. D. The internal-external bonds of the memory process. *Journal of Nervous and Mental Disease*, 1969, **149**, 40–47.

Margules, D. L., & Olds, J. Identical "feeding" and "rewarding" systems in the lateral hypothalamus of rats. *Science*, 1962, **135**, 374–375.

Milgram, N. W., Devor, M., & Server, A. C. Spontaneous changes in waves induced by electrical stimulation of the lateral hypothalamus in rats. *Journal of Comparative and Physiological Psychology*, 1971, **75**, 491–499.

Miller, J. J., & Mogenson, G. J. Effect of septal stimulation on lateral hypothalamic unit activity in the rat. *Brain Research*, 1971, **32**, 125–142.

Miller, J. J., & Mogenson, G. J. Projections of the septum to the lateral hypothalamus. *Experimental Neurology*, 1972, **34**, 229–243.

Miller, N. E. Motivational effects of brain stimulation and drugs. *Federation Proceedings*, 1960, **19**, 846–854.

Milner, P. M. The role of the brain in motivation. In B. M. Foss (Ed.), *New Horizons in Psychology*. Baltimore: Penguin, 1966. Pp. 237–252.

Mogenson, G. J. Stability and modification of consummatory behavior elicited by electrical stimulation of the hypothalamus. *Physiology and Behavior*, 1971, **6**, 255–260.

Mogenson, G. J., Gentil, C. G., & Stevenson, J. A. F. Feeding and drinking elicited by low and high frequencies of hypothalamic stimulation. *Brain Research*, 1971, **33**, 127–137.

Mogenson, G. J., & Kaplinsky, M. Brain self-stimulation and mechanisms of reinforcement. *Learning and Motivation*, 1970, **1**(2), 186–198.

Mogenson, G. J., & Morgan, C. W. Effects of induced drinking on self-stimulation of the lateral hypothalamus. *Experimental Brain Research*, 1967, **3**, 111–116.

Mogenson, G. J., & Stevenson, J. A. F. Drinking and self-stimulation with electrical stimulation of the lateral hypothalamus. *Physiology and Behavior*, 1966, **1**, 251–254.

Mogenson, G. J., & Stevenson, J. A. F. Drinking induced by electrical stimulation of the lateral hypothalamus. *Experimental Neurology*, 1967, **17**, 119–127.

Montemurro, D. G., & Stevenson, J. A. F. Adipsia produced by hypothalamic lesions in the rat. *Canadian Journal of Biochemistry and Physiology*, 1957, **35**, 31–37.

Morgane, P. J. Amygdalar stimulation effects on instrumental alimentary and avoidance reactions in rats. In *XXII International Congress of Physiological Sciences* (Abstracts of Communications). Amsterdam: Exerpta Medica Foundation, 1962, No. 363.

Morgane, P. J. The function of the limbic and rhinic forebrain–limbic midbrain systems and reticular formation in the regulation of food and water intake. *Annals of the New York Academy of Sciences,* 1969, **157,** 806-848.

Morrison, S. D., & Mayer, J. Adipsia and aphagia in rats after subthalamic lesions. *American Journal of Physiology,* 1957, **191,** 248-254.

Murphy, J. T., Dreifuss, J. J., & Gloor, P. Topographical differences in the response of single hypothalamic neurons to limbic stimulation. *American Journal of Physiology,* 1968, **214,** 1443-1453.

Murphy, J. T., & Renaud, L. P. Mechanisms of inhibition in the ventromedial nucleus of the hypothalamus. *Journal of Neurophysiology,* 1969, **32,** 85-102.

Nauta, W. J. H. Neural associations of the amygdaloid complex in the monkey. *Brain,* 1962, **85,** 505-520.

Nauta, W. J. H. The problem of the frontal lobe: A reinterpretation. *Journal of Psychiatric Research,* 1971, **8,** 167-187.

Norgren, R. Gustatory responses in the hypothalamus. *Brain Research,* 1970, **21,** 63-77.

Olds, J., Allan, S., & Briese, E. Differentiation of hypothalamic drive in reward centers. *American Journal of Physiology,* 1971, **221,** 368-375.

Olds, J., Mink, W. D., & Best, P. J. Single unit patterns during anticipatory behavior. *Electroencephalography and Clinical Neurophysiology,* 1969, **26,** 144-158.

Oltmans, G. A., & Harvey, J. A. LH syndrome and brain catecholamine levels after lesions of the nigrostriatal bundle. *Physiology and Behavior,* 1972, **8,** 69-78.

Oomura, Y., Ooyama, H., Yamamoto, T., Naka, F., Kobayashi, N. & Ono, T. Neuronal mechanisms of feeding. In W. R. Adey & T. Tokizane (Eds.), *Structure and Function of the Limbic System. Progress in Brain Research.* Amsterdam: Elsevier, 1967, **27,** 1-33.

Parker, W., & Feldman, S. Effect of mesencephalic lesions on feeding behavior in rats. *Experimental Neurology,* 1967, **17,** 313-326.

Peck, J. W., & Novin, D. Evidence that osmoreceptors mediating drinking in rabbits are in the lateral preoptic area. *Journal of Comparative and Physiological Psychology,* 1971, **74,** 134-147.

Phillips, A. G., & Mogenson, G. J. Effects of taste on self-stimulation and induced drinking. *Journal of Comparative and Physiological Psychology,* 1968, **66,** 654-660.

Pizzi, W. J., & Lorens, S. A. Effects of lesions of the amygdala-hippocampo-septal system on food and water intake in the rat. *Psychonomic Science,* 1967, **7,** 187-188.

Roberts, W. W. Are hypothalamic motivational mechanisms functionally and anatomically specific? *Brain, Behaviour and Evolution,* 1969, **2,** 317-342.

Roberts, W. W. Hypothalamic mechanisms for motivational and species-typical behavior. In R. E. Whalen (Ed.), *The Neural Control of Behavior.* New York: Academic Press, 1970. Pp. 175-207.

Robinson, B. W., & Mishkin, M. Alimentary responses to forebrain stimulation in monkeys. *Experimental Brain Research,* 1968, **4,** 330-366.

Russell, R. W. *Frontiers in physiological psychology.* New York: Academic Press, 1966.

Sharpe, L. G., & Myers, R. D. Feeding and drinking following stimulation of the diencephalon of the monkey with amines and other substances. *Experimental Brain Research,* 1969, **8,** 295-310.

Sibole, W. Septal-hypothalamic interactions in the control of water intake. Unpublished masters thesis, University of Western Ontario, 1971.

Sibole, W., Miller, J. J., & Mogenson, G. J. Effects of septal stimulation on drinking elicited by electrical stimulation of the lateral hypothalamus. *Experimental Neurology,* 1971, **32,** 466-477.

Siegel, A., & Skog, D. Effects of electrical stimulation of the septum upon attack behavior elicited from the hypothalamus in the cat. *Brain Research*, 1970, **23**, 371–380.

Stellar, E. Drive and motivation. In J. Field (Ed.), *Handbook of Physiology*. Sec. 1. *Neurophysiology*. Vol. 3. Baltimore: Williams & Wilkins, 1960. Pp. 1501–1527.

Stevenson, J. A. F. Central mechanisms controlling water intake. In C. F. Code (Ed.), *Handbook of Physiology*. Sec. 6. *Alimentary Canal*. Vol. 1. *Food and Water Intake*. Washington: American Physiological Society, 1967. Pp. 173–190.

Stevenson, J. A. F. Neural control of food and water intake. In W. Haymaker, E. Anderson, & W. J. H. Nauta (Eds.), *The Hypothalamus*. Springfield: Charles C Thomas, 1969. Pp. 524–621.

Stuart, D. G., Kawamura, Y., & Hemingway, A. Activation and suppression of shivering during septal and hypothalamic stimulation. *Experimental Neurology*, 1961, **4**, 485–506.

Teitelbaum, P., & Epstein, A. N. The lateral hypothalamic syndrome: Recovery of feeding and drinking after lateral hypothalamic lesions. *Psychological Review*, 1962, **69**, 74–90.

Teitelbaum, P., & Stellar, E. Recovery from the failure to eat produced by hypothalamic lesions. *Science*, 1954, **120**, 894–895.

Towbin, E. J. Gastric distention as a factor in the satiation of thirst in eosphagostomized dogs. *American Journal of Physiology*, 1949, **159**, 533–541.

Ungerstedt, U. Adipsia and aphagia after 6-hydroxydopamine induced degeneration of the nigro-striatal dopamine system. *Acta Physiologica Scandinavica*, 1971, Supplement 367, 95–122.

Valenstein, E. S., Cox, V. C., & Kakolewski, J. W. Polydipsia elicited by the synergistic action of a saccharine and glucose solution. *Science*, 1967, **157**, 552–554.

Valenstein, E. S., Cox, V. C., & Kakolewski, J. W. Modification of motivated behavior elicited by electrical stimulation of the hypothalamus. *Science*, 1968, **159**, 1119–1121.

Wayner, M. J. Motor control functions of the lateral hypothalamus and adjunctive behavior. *Physiology and Behavior*, 1970, **5**, 1319–1325.

White, N. M., & Fisher, A. E. Relationship between amygdala and hypothalamus in the control of eating behavior. *Physiology and Behavior*, 1969, **4**, 199–205.

Wise, R. A. Hypothalamic motivation system: Fixed or plastic neural circuitis? *Science*, 1968, **162**, 377–379.

Wishart, T. B. The role of the septum in water intake and satiety mechanisms. Unpublished doctoral dissertation, University of Western Ontario, 1970.

Wishart, T. B., & Mogenson, G. J. Effects of food deprivation on water intake in rats with septal lesions. *Physiology and Behavior*, 1970, **5**, 1481–1486. (a)

Wishart, T. B., & Mogenson, G. J. Reduction of water intake by electrical stimulation of the septal region of the rat brain. *Physiology and Behavior*, 1970, **5**, 1399–1404. (b)

Wyrwicka, W., & Doty, R. W. Feeding induced in cats by electrical stimulation of the brain stem. *Experimental Brain Research*, 1966, **1**, 152–160.

DISCUSSION: ON THE USE OF ELECTRICAL STIMULATION TO STUDY HYPOTHALAMIC STRUCTURE AND FUNCTION[1]

Philip Teitelbaum
University of Pennsylvania

A scientific experiment is like cutting a diamond. We contemplate a puzzling phenomenon from all sides before deciding on a particular angle of approach to it. We devise an experimental method to achieve that angle, and using it, we strike the phenomenon. If the angle is good, we highlight certain facets, certain important variables in the phenomenon, thus revealing a gem of truth and beauty.

But like cut diamonds, all experiments are oversimplifications. A different angle of approach would have produced another gem, perhaps of equal beauty, but yielding a truth of different shape. That is why scientists apply as many methods as possible to the same phenomenon, to try to decide which oversimplified version of the truth is the best one to be content with for the time being.

In the course of time, one method is often adopted as the best angle of approach to a given phenomenon. When that happens, it becomes a scientific paradigm; earlier approaches are generally abandoned, and scientists train their students in the use of that method (Kuhn, 1962). The oversimplifications inherent in it are often forgotten, as everyone comes to accept this angle of approach as the most natural. Perhaps that is why Pavlov once said, "If you want new ideas you should read old books".[2]

Eventually, however, as a common method is applied in ever varied circumstances, it begins to yield truths of bizarre shapes, that violate our

[1] This work was supported by NSF Grants GB–8050X and GB–33440 and by USPHS Grant NS–05937.
[2] Pavlov's remark was quoted to me some years ago by the late Georg von Békésy. I have not found its published source.

standards of simple beauty. These are scientific paradoxes that force us to draw back and reexamine the basic oversimplifications inherent in our method that we have long ignored.

Such a paradox in our view of the structure and function of the brain has been highlighted by the work in recent years on the hypothalamus by Valenstein, Cox, and Kakolewski (1968b, 1969, 1970). They point out that there exists a widespread acceptance of the idea that in the brain there are specific neural circuits underlying all forms of behavior. For instance, in the hypothalamus, electrical stimulation can elicit motivated behavior characteristic of hunger. An otherwise sated rat stimulated through implanted electrodes in the hypothalamus will eat large quantities of food, and if this is done every day, it will greatly overeat and even become obese (Steinbaum & Miller, 1965). Such an animal will learn a new operant or perform a previously learned one (e.g., running a maze or pressing a bar to get food) during stimulation, thus supporting the idea that this is truly motivated behavior, not merely some kind of motor automatism (such as chewing) where the ingestion of food is an accidental by-product of the behavior, rather than a desired outcome (Coons, Levak, & Miller, 1965; Miller, 1960; Mendelson & Chorover, 1965). The same is true of thirst (Andersson & Wyrwicka, 1957) and other species-typical behaviors (Roberts, 1970).

Furthermore, based on a long history of successful mapping of the brain by electrical stimulation, people speak of relatively discrete anatomically separate systems that mediate various kinds of behavior. It is common, for example, to think of the lateral hypothalamus as a region involved in hunger and the regulation of food intake.

However, on careful review of the earlier functional maps of the hypothalamus based on electrical stimulation, Valenstein et al. (1970) pointed out that there was impressive overlap of the anatomical sites yielding different behaviors. Therefore it is difficult to justify the impression given by many observers, who had restricted their observations to one behavior, that there were discrete areas associated with a specific behavior. Furthermore, Valenstein, Cox, and Kakolewski (1968b; 1969) have found that if ample opportunity is provided, the behavior elicited by hypothalamic stimulation is subject to change without any modification of stimulation parameters. For example, if a rat ate in response to stimulation, removal of food from his cage resulted in a few hours or days in the gradual emergence of another behavior such as drinking or woodgnawing. When the food was again inserted into the test chamber, the new behavior was elicited as frequently as eating. Therefore, the animal's learning experience during the stimulation plays an important role in determining which behavior is electrically evoked from the tissue. Indeed, rather than discrete areas associated with different specific behaviors, perhaps one should think of a single plastic system, whose response to electrical stimulation depends on the learning experience during the time the animal is being stimulated (Wise, 1968).

Such a challenge to established scientific opinion in an active field does not long go without reply. Dr. Mogenson (whose chapter in this book offers me the occasion to discuss some of these issues) has ably summarized a good deal of the evidence from his own work and that of others which is relevant. Other comprehensive reviews (Caggiula, 1969; Roberts, 1969, 1970) have also done so. As they point out, evidence can be marshalled to support the view: (*a*) that these results can be explained as threshold changes in multiple systems subjected to electrical stimulation (Wise, 1968, 1969; Milgram, Devor, & Server, 1971); (*b*) that food and water intake exert specific and homeostatically appropriate modulation over the neural systems involved in electrically elicited feeding and drinking (Devor, Wise, Milgram, & Hoebel, 1970); (*c*) that by judicious selection of the frequency of the electrical stimulus (20–40 cycles/sec for feeding, 100–200 cycles/sec for drinking) one can selectively activate specific integrative systems involved in water and energy deficit (Mogenson, Gentil, & Stevenson, 1971); (*d*) that by using electrodes of very small diameter, with currents just at the behavioral threshold, a much clearer separation of eating and drinking can be achieved (Olds, Allan, & Briese, 1971; Mogenson, this volume); (*e*) cholinergic stimulation of the lateral hypothalamus reliably elicits drinking but inhibits hunger, whereas adrenergic stimulation at that site evokes eating while inhibiting thirst (Grossman, 1962); and (*f*) there is less plasticity and more evidence for anatomical specificity, particularly in species other than the rat, than is warranted to support Valenstein, Cox, and Kakolewski's views (Roberts, 1969; Woodworth, 1971).

From studies of brain damage, it is also clear that there must be a great deal of inborn specificity of neural circuitry in the brain. Localized lesions in a given area of the brain will lead to a characteristic loss of function. For instance, appropriate lateral hypothalamic damage in a rat will lead to aphagia and adipsia, with a course of recovery so typical it is called the lateral hypothalamic syndrome (Anand & Brobeck, 1951; Teitelbaum & Epstein, 1962).

In general, to be useful, a map must be simple. Thus, many early maps of cortical control of movement or of subcortical control of autonomic function were carried out using animals under deep anesthesia. An anesthetic is a great simplifier. It eliminates the activity of many cells highly sensitive to it, thus yielding maps of relatively discrete areas related to different behavioral functions. Such geographical maps of the brain are useful to help scientists locate areas and systems of interest for further research exploration. But they are often greatly oversimplified, as became apparent when it was possible to explore the effects of brain stimulation through chronically implanted electrodes in unanesthetized waking animals. This was achieved by W. R. Hess (1932), whose monograph on his methods of brain stimulation remains a classic that still serves as a valuable reminder of the enormous complexities involved in this method of correlating brain structure and function. From his work on the cat diencephalon, it is clear that systems controlling autonomic functions and instinctive activities are closely interdigitated in the hypothalamus (Hess, 1954).

One can simplify the unanesthetized brain by restricting the behaviors it can manifest. Thus, as Valenstein, Cox, and Kakolewski (1970) correctly point out, many modern studies of rat behavior in response to electrical brain stimulation are greatly oversimplified, because they merely observe the behavior of an isolated animal in a bare living cage (equipped only with food pellets and a water bottle) where the behavior patterns elicited are often difficult to interpret meaningfully, i.e., in the context of a normal animal in a natural setting. Such maps may be useful within a given behavioral function (where, for instance, a scientist may be interested in the brain sites whose stimulation can evoke food intake), but as Valenstein (1969) points out, there may be too much overlap for such maps to be very useful when several systems are being considered simultaneously.

The situation is further complicated by the fact that an electrical stimulus is a very indiscriminate one (Hess, 1932; Holst & St. Paul, 1960; Roberts, 1969). Many different behavior patterns can be activated from a given electrode in the brain with only slight differences in threshold over a wide range of stimulus frequencies. Thus, as shown in Figure 1 (from Holst & St. Paul), when stimulating the diencephalon of the chicken with sinusoidal current, several behaviors (calling to food, clucking, and looking about with jerky head movements in all directions or with motionless head and neck) could all be elicited at very similar voltages over a frequency range from 25 to 200 cycles per second. Furthermore, as shown in Figure 2 (also from Holst & St. Paul), slight

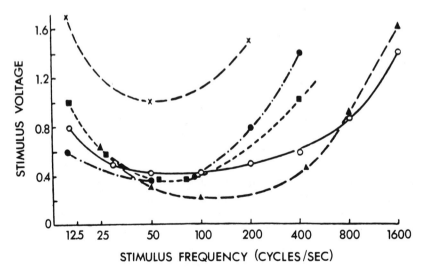

FIG. 1. Examples of the dependence of the necessary stimulus voltage (threshold voltage) on the stimulus frequency. (Sinusoidal alternating current. Reactions: X and ▲, clucking; ●, looking about [Aufmerken] with jerky head movements in all directions; ○, calling to food; ■, watching out [Sichern] with extended neck and motionless head.) Note that several behaviors can be elicited at very similar voltages over a broad frequency range (25-200 cycles per second). (Used by permission of Dalliere, Tindall, & Cox Ltd.)

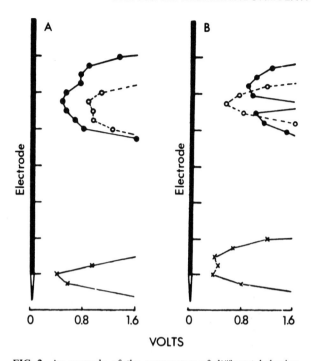

FIG. 2. An example of the appearance of different behavior patterns as the electrode moves deeper. The horizontal markings along the electrode path designate millimeter intervals. The horizontal distance of the points from the electrode indicates the threshold voltage. The reactions are: •, looking about [Aufmerken] ; ○, turning to the left; X, fleeing downwards; in A, the electrode was moved downwards; in B, about 30 minutes later, it was withdrawn upwards along the same path. Note that distinct behaviors with different thresholds can often be evoked from the same point in the brain. (Used by permission of Dalliere, Tindall, & Cox Ltd.)

differences in the depth or rostral placement of an electrode tip could change the behavior evoked from one pattern to another.

In my opinion, the evidence is thus overwhelmingly in support of the view that fixed, inborn, specific motivational systems exist in the brain and that they are anatomically closely interdigitated in the diencephalon. How then can we explain the very clear phenomenon demonstrated by Valenstein, Cox, and Kakolewski (1968b), that the behavioral outcome of brain stimulation can depend on the learning experience during that stimulation?

At this point, it may be useful to turn the question around: Given that multiple specific behavior patterns are being activated from anatomically intermeshed structures by an extremely indiscriminate electrical stimulus, how does the nervous system manage to respond with only one behavior pattern at a time? In other words, by what mechanisms can the nervous system exaggerate its

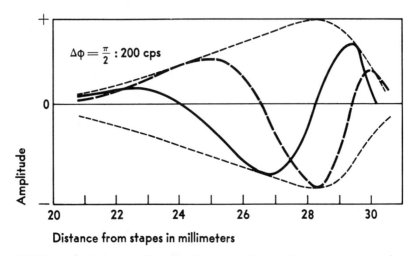

FIG. 3. A traveling wave along the human basilar membrane at two successive instants (*heavy solid and broken lines*), and the envelope formed by the positive and negative waves as they move up the cochlea (*lighter broken lines*). (From Békésy, 1967 and used by permission of the Journal of the Acoustical Society of America.)

own simplicity, thus leading us to believe that simple maps are appropriate to describe it? This is the problem of dominance, revealed in phenomena common to all of the nervous system. Sherrington (1906) dealt with it in his analysis of reflex integration. Where many stimuli clamor for reflex response, how does one reflex dominate and overcome all the others?

An identical problem arises in hearing. The mechanical vibrations of sound waves are transmitted from the ear drum to the fluid-filled cochlea in the inner ear. The receptors for hearing are the sensitive hair cells which lie along the basilar membrane in the cochlea. Precise measurements of the vibration pattern of the basilar membrane by Békésy have proven that the ear mechanically generates in the cochlea a traveling wave whose place of peak amplitude along the basilar membrane varies with the frequency of the sound (see Figure 3). High tones cause the stiff narrow segment of the basilar membrane near the oval window to vibrate, whereas low tones cause a vibration in the wider, more flexible part of the basilar membrane further away. But the traveling wave is so broad in shape that the amounts of excitation generated all along the broad peak could not possibly produce the fine tuning required to account for our precise discrimination of pitch. In other words, receptors corresponding to many different sensations of pitch are excited almost equally along a wide region of the basilar membrane by any sound, yet we hear only one pitch.

Similar phenomena occur in skin sensations. Using a giant model of the cochlea (Figure 4) that faithfully reproduced enlarged versions of the traveling waves in the ear, Békésy showed that localization on the skin of the arm was remarkably precise (see Figure 5), despite the wide area of the arm being stimulated. These phenomena clearly demonstrated that there must be some kind of inhibitory sharpening performed by the nervous system in response to the broad, mechanical traveling-wave stimulus.

The basic principle of frequency discrimination by sharpening is shown more clearly by another of Békésy's models (Figure 6), which uses a different form of vibration. A box is constructed with five holes spaced 2 cm apart. In each hole, a tiny piston can vibrate at a given frequency and amplitude independently of the other pistons. As shown, they are set to vibrate at 20, 40, 80, 160, and 320 cycles per second. The skin of the subject's forearm is pressed firmly against the upper surface of the box, and the amplitude of each piston is adjusted so that they feel equally intense—that is, equally loud—in their vibration. Each of them

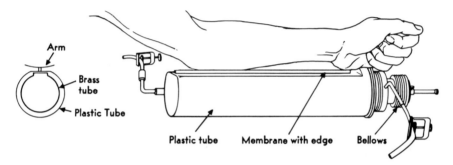

FIG. 4. Plastic tube model of the cochlea with the skin of the arm as the stimulated surface. (Adapted from Békésy, 1967.)

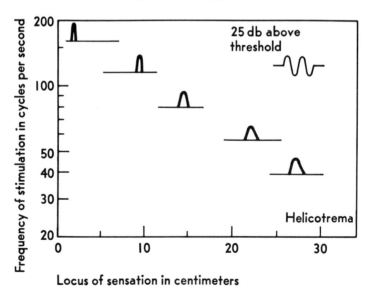

FIG. 5. The perceived extent of the sensation produced by the cochlea model on the skin of the arm as a function of frequency for a pulse of two waves. (From Békésy, 1967 and used by permission of the Journal of the Acoustical Society of America.)

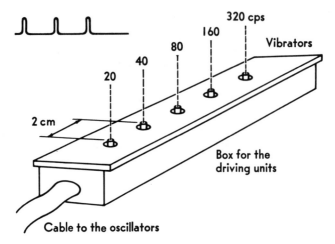

FIG. 6. A series of vibrators operating at different frequencies, used in the study of inhibitory interaction on the skin of the arm. (From Békésy, 1967 and used by permission of the Journal of the Acoustical Society of America.)

can be identified by its place and its frequency when it alone is vibrating. What does the arm feel when all of them vibrate simultaneously? As shown in Figure 7, when their amplitude is equal, the arm feels only the one in the middle—80 cycles per second. The others are not felt at all. They do contribute to the intensity felt in the middle, because when they are turned off, the 80-cycle vibration provided by the middle vibrator feels much less intense. But when all the others vibrate with it, their frequencies and location on the skin are completely inhibited. The touch receptors on the skin are connected to the nervous system by nerve fibers running into the spinal cord. Many side branches interconnect these fibers by a lateral plexus, similar to the horizontal interconnections of the retina. Therefore, principles of spatial summation and inhibition can operate in the skin as they do in the eye. There is clearly a summation because the sensation felt in the middle when all vibrators are on is increased. The difference in peak amplitude of stimulation, created by spatial summation, enables the central area to inhibit the areas on either side. We can demonstrate this easily: If we increase the intensity of any one of the vibrators—for instance, 40 cycles per second—so that it is stronger than the rest, the sensation jumps immediately to that point and the only frequency now felt is 40 cycles, not 80. The ear does the same thing—the effect of the peak amplitude of the traveling wave on the basilar membrane is to inhibit the sensation of stimulation around it, thus sharpening localization on the basilar membrane, and thereby sharpening the frequency discrimination of sound. As shown in Figure 8, a slight gradient is sharpened by lateral inhibition and central summation. Békésy called this process "funneling." It is analogous to the generation of Mach bands by mutual inhibition.

From Békésy's beautiful example, we see that many of the same principles of nervous function operate in skin, ear, and eye. In my opinion, very similar phenomena are occurring during electrical stimulation of the hypothalamus. Mechanisms of sharpening and funneling between mutually inhibitory systems allow the indiscriminate electrical stimulus to evoke only one kind of behavior by inhibiting competing systems. One system can have an advantage, either by anatomical proximity (Roberts, 1969; Olds et al., 1971), by sensitivity to frequency of stimulation (Mogenson et al., 1971), by differential motivational tuning through selective activation by prior food or water deprivation (Devor et al., 1970), by the physical stimuli in the environment (Flynn, 1967; Valenstein, 1969; Roberts, 1969, 1970), and by the animal's past experience (Valenstein, 1971; Wise, 1969; Roberts, 1969).

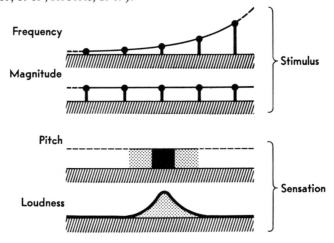

FIG. 7. A representation of the sensory effects of presenting five vibrations to the skin simultaneously, with frequency varying in the manner indicated in the preceding figure. (From Békésy, 1967 and used by permission of the Journal of the Acoustical Society of America.)

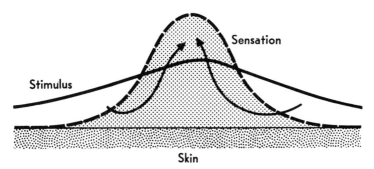

FIG. 8. An illustration of "funneling" on the skin. The stimulus gradient is sharpened by central summation and lateral inhibition. (From Békésy, 1967 and used by permission of the Journal of the Acoustical Society of America.)

It is perfectly clear that motivational systems can be modified by learning. In virtually every recorded example, a motivational and species-typical behavior evoked by electrical stimulation is reinforcing—i.e., the animal will perform an operant for the opportunity to engage in that act (Hoebel & Teitelbaum, 1962; Roberts, 1969, 1970; Valenstein, 1970). This is probably true of all normally aroused instinctive motivated approach behavior as well. Indeed, we can best be certain that a motivational state exists when the animal will perform an operant to obtain the desired outcome (Teitelbaum, 1966). Perhaps, in a system capable of learning, the strengthening of an electrically elicited response through learning may also be subject to inhibitory sharpening. What Valenstein (1971) calls "channeling" may be Békésy's "funneling" in a system that can be permanently modified by experience. The principles of inhibitory sharpening and funneling may be one way we can reconcile Valenstein, Cox, and Kakolewski's demonstration of plasticity of response to electrical stimulation with the evidence showing that there are anatomically specific but overlapping inborn motivational systems in the hypothalamus.

We are still a long way from understanding all the complexities of the nervous system's response to electrical stimulation. I believe we are hindered by our acceptance of the technique as a scientific paradigm. We assume that the behavior elicited by hypothalamic stimulation is normal motivated behavior, i.e., affected by all of the variables that govern normal adult rat behavior. After all, a rat can perform a previously learned task to get food during stimulation as he would when normally hungry (Miller, 1960). But sometimes the behavior evoked by stimulation is rather puzzling (Valenstein et al., 1969; Roberts, 1969). For instance, Valenstein, Cox, and Kakolewski (1968a) have shown that a rat drinking water in response to hypothalamic stimulation will continue licking at an empty tube or even at the air where the tube used to be. Similarly, a rat eating in response to hypothalamic stimulation will not switch to a more familiar and palatable food when it is offered, though when eating under a normal (food-deprivation–induced) hunger, it switches with alacrity. It is thus more stimulus-bound, more compulsive, more stereotyped in its eating than normal. A few years ago, Carol Garten Basbaum and I (unpublished data) observed a similar aberration. We were using lateral hypothalamic stimulation through bilaterally damaged tissue in the attempt to facilitate recovery of eating in aphagic rats. In such an aphagic rat, we could elicit vigorous eating during stimulation if the food pellet were held up to the animal's mouth, but it totally ignored the food on the cage floor only an inch further away. Many of the abnormalities resulting from lateral hypothalamic damage may be understood as more reflexive, more infantile, less encephalized forms of the same behavior (Teitelbaum, 1971). Under some circumstances, perhaps normal tissue is similarly de-encephalized by electrical stimulation. Similarly, the compulsive licking at an empty water tube or even the air where the tube used to be that can be seen in amphetamine-dosed animals drinking to avoid shock (Teitelbaum & Derks, 1958) may be a similar instance of such reflexive, less encephalized behavior.

As Valenstein and his coworkers point out (1968a), it may indeed be appropriate here to recall Neal Miller's (1961) admonition that it is necessary to employ different tasks in evaluating motivational states. To this I would add that we should now scale those tasks in terms of the level of encephalization of behavior required. When that has been accomplished, we may find that the paradoxes of today have become the diagnostic indicators of tomorrow.

REFERENCES

Anand, B. K., & Brobeck, J. R. Hypothalamic control of food intake in rats and cats. *Yale Journal of Biology and Medicine,* 1951, **24**, 123–140.

Andersson, B., & Wyrwicka, W. The elicitation of a drinking motor conditioned reaction by electrical stimulation of the hypothalamic drinking area in the goat. *Acta Physiologica Scandinavica,* 1957, **41**, 194–198.

Békésy, G. v. *Sensory inhibition.* Princeton, N. J.: Princeton University Press, 1967.

Caggiula, A. R. Stability of behavior produced by electrical stimulation of the rat hypothalamus. *Brain, Behavior and Evolution,* 1969, **2**, 343–358.

Coons, E. E., Levak, M., & Miller, N. E. Lateral hypothalamus: Learning of food-seeking response motivated by electrical stimulation. *Science,* 1965, **150**, 1320–1321.

Devor, M., Wise, R. A., Milgram, N. W., & Hoebel, B. G. Physiological control of hypothalamically elicited feeding and drinking. *Journal of Comparative and Physiological Psychology,* 1970, **73**, 226–232.

Flynn, J. P. The neural basis of aggression in cats. In D. C. Glass (Ed.), *Neurophysiology and emotion.* New York: Rockefeller University Press and Russell Sage Foundation, 1967. Pp. 40–60.

Grossman, S. P. Direct adrenergic and cholinergic stimulation of hypothalamic mechanisms. *American Journal of Physiology,* 1962, **202**, 872–882.

Hess, W. R. *Die Methodik der lokalisierten Reizung und Ausschaltung subkortikaler Hirnabschnitte.* Leipzig: G. Thieme Verlag, 1932.

Hess, W. R. *Diencephalon: Autonomic and extrapyramidal functions.* New York: Grune & Stratton, 1954.

Hoebel, B. G., & Teitelbaum, P. Hypothalamic control of feeding and self-stimulation. *Science,* 1962, **135**, 375–377.

Holst, E. v., & St. Paul, U. v. Vom Wirkungsgefüge der Triebe. *Naturwissenschaften,* 1960, **47**, 409–422. (On the functional organisation of drives. Trans. by J. E. Burchard, Jr. *Animal Behavior,* 1963, **11**, 1–20.)

Kuhn, T. S. *The structure of scientific revolutions.* Chicago: University of Chicago Press, 1962.

Mendelson, J., & Chorover, S. L. Lateral hypothalamic stimulation in satiated rats: T-maze learning for food. *Science,* 1965, **149**, 559–561.

Milgram, N. W., Devor, M., & Server, A. C. Spontaneous changes in behaviors induced by electrical stimulation of the lateral hypothalamus in rats. *Journal of Comparative and Physiological Psychology,* 1971, **75**, 491–499.

Miller, N. E. Motivational effects of brain stimulation and drugs. *Federation Proceedings,* 1960, **19**, 846–854.

Miller, N. E. Analytical studies of drive and reward. *American Psychologist,* 1961, **16**, 739–754.

Mogenson, G. J., Gentil, C. G., & Stevenson, J. A. F. Feeding and drinking elicited by low and high frequencies of hypothalamic stimulation. *Brain Research,* 1971, **33**, 127–137.

Olds, J., Allan, W. S., & Briese, E. Differentiation of hypothalamic drive and reward centers. *American Journal of Physiology,* 1971, **221**, 368–375.

Roberts, W. W. Are hypothalamic motivational mechanisms functionally and anatomically specific? *Brain, Behaviour and Evolution,* 1969, **2**, 317–342.

Roberts, W. W. Hypothalamic mechanisms for motivational and species-typical behavior. In R. E. Whalen (Ed.), *The neural control of behavior.* New York: Academic Press, 1970. Pp. 175–207.

Sherrington, C. S. The integrative action of the nervous system. New Haven, Conn.: Yale University Press, 1906. Issued as a Yale Paperbound, Forge Village, Mass., Murray Printing, 1961.

Steinbaum, E. A., & Miller, N. E. Obesity from eating elicited by daily stimulation of hypothalamus. *American Journal of Physiology,* 1965, **208**, 1–5.

Teitelbaum, P. The use of operant methods in the assessment and control of motivation states. In W. K. Honig (Ed.), *Operant behavior: Areas of research and application.* New York: Appleton-Century-Crofts, 1966. Pp. 565–608.

Teitelbaum, P. The encephalization of hunger. In E. Stellar & J. M. Sprague (Eds.), *Progress in physiological psychology.* Vol. 4. New York: Academic Press, 1971.

Teitelbaum, P., & Derks, P. The effect of amphetamine on forced drinking in the rat. *Journal of Comparative and Physiological Psychology,* 1958, **51**, 801–810.

Teitelbaum, P., & Epstein, A. N. The lateral hypothalamic syndrome: Recovery of feeding and drinking after lateral hypothalamic lesions. *Psychological Review,* 1962, **69**, 74–90.

Valenstein, E. S. Behavior elicited by hypothalamic stimulation. *Brain, Behavior and Evolution,* 1969, **2**, 295–316.

Valenstein, E. S. Channeling of responses elicited by hypothalamic stimulation. *Journal of Psychiatric Research,* 1971, **8**, 335–344.

Valenstein, E. S., Cox, V. C., & Kakolewski, J. W. The motivation underlying eating elicited by lateral hypothalamic stimulation. *Physiology and Behavior,* 1968, **3**, 969–971. (a)

Valenstein, E. S., Cox, V. C., & Kakolewski, J. W. Modification of motivated behavior elicited by electrical stimulation of the hypothalamus. *Science,* 1968, **159**, 1119–1121. (b)

Valenstein, E. S., Cox, V. C., & Kakolewski, J. W. The hypothalamus and motivated behavior. In J. Tapp (Ed.), *Reinforcement.* New York: Academic Press, 1969.

Valenstein, E. S., Cox, V. C., & Kakolewski, J. W. Reexamination of the role of the hypothalamus in motivation. *Psychological Review,* 1970, **77**, 16–31.

Wise, R. A. Hypothalamic motivational systems: Fixed or plastic neural circuits? *Science,* 1968, **162**, 377–379.

Wise, R. A. Plasticity of hypothalamic motivational systems. *Science,* 1969, **165**, 929–930.

Woodworth, C. H. Attack elicited in rats by electrical stimulation of the lateral hypothalamus. *Physiology and Behavior,* 1971, **6**, 345–353.

INVITED COMMENT: ELECTRICAL STIMULATION AND HYPOTHALAMIC FUNCTION: HISTORICAL PERSPECTIVE

Elliot S. Valenstein
University of Michigan

Although it was not possible for me to attend the AAAS meeting on which this volume is based, the editors of this work on thirst have been most considerate in offering me the opportunity to make a brief reply to the comments on work from my laboratory contained in the chapters by Drs. Mogenson and Teitelbaum. After considering several strategies in forming my reply, I elected to use as a point of departure the statement Dr. Teitelbaum attributed to Pavlov that "if you want new ideas you should read old books." I have become convinced that a review of the historical developments in this field is necessary to gain the perspective required to evaluate present theories and even experimental data.

It will be recalled that when W. R. Hess began his classic studies on stimulation of the cat's diencephalon, his main emphasis was on the regulation of autonomic ("vegetative") and extrapyramidal motor functions. Following in the tradition of Karplus and Kreidl, Hess described the hypothalamic sites at which it was possible to elicit changes in pupillary functions, respiration, blood pressure, panting, salivation, and similar responses known to be regulated by autonomic activity. He also described such motor responses as lowering, raising, or rotation of the head, turning of the body, and various movements of the extremities. In the course of his investigations, Hess noted that stimulation could evoke aggressive behavior and voracious eating (bulimia), and he gradually came to the conclusion that stimulation could evoke changes in "mood and drives."

Probably because his main interest was in anatomical organization rather than behavior analysis, Hess provided only observational evidence of the presumed changes in drive state and motivation. It was not surprising, however, that others would be interested in following up these observations with experimentation that was directed by their own theoretical orientation. It was obvious to many that if hypothalamic stimulation could be shown to evoke natural motivational states, the theoretical and practical implications of this phenomenon would be considerable. Neal Miller, for example, has been very explicit about his own motivation in initiating brain stimulation studies. He approached the subject of hypothalamic stimulation and elicited behavior from the vantage point of a drive-reduction learning theorist and hoped that it would be possible to directly study the physiological counterpart of the major construct of that theory. On reflecting on his interest in hypothalamic stimulation in the early 1950s, Miller has written:

> If I could find an area of the brain where electrical stimulation has the other properties of normal hunger, would the sudden termination of that stimulation function as a reward? If I could find such an area, perhaps recording from it would provide a way of measuring hunger which would allow me to see the effects of a small nibble of food that is large enough to serve as a reward, but not large enough to produce complete satiation. Would such a nibble produce a prompt, appreciable reduction in hunger, as demanded by the drive-reduction hypothesis? [Miller, 1973]

It is certain that the above quotation does not represent Miller's current thinking on this problem, but it does provide a historical example of the emphasis that was placed on a search for the similarities between eating and drinking elicited by hypothalamic stimulation and the same behaviors when they were known to be motivated by hunger and thirst. Similarities were searched for and found, but dissimilarities were deemphasized and overlooked. The most convincing similarity reported was that stimulation-elicited eating was motivated behavior. Like hungry animals, satiated animals receiving hypothalamic stimulation would perform some learned response (Coons, Levak, & Miller, 1965) and overcome such adversities as quinine additives (Tenen & Miller, 1964) and electrified grids to obtain food (Morgane, 1961). The fact that the eating and drinking elicited by hypothalamic stimulation was motivated and not simply reflexive was considered compelling evidence that hunger and thirst were involved.

Once it was accepted that stimulation evoked hunger, other evidence that seemed consistent with this view was often accepted uncritically. I have not been allotted sufficient space to develop the arguments, but raising some questions may help to lay the groundwork for discussion at some other time. Consider the following: (a) From the fact that food consumption elicited by electrical stimulation of the lateral hypothalamus (ESLH) produced a compensatory decrease in normal food intake throughout the rest of the day, it was concluded that "this adds yet another similarity to the effects of ESLH and those of normal hunger [Steinbaum & Miller, 1965, p. 5]." Actually these results contribute little to the understanding of the motivation underlying elicited eating. They demonstrate only that the postingestional consequences of food intake are similar regardless of the cause of the eating. (b) The demonstration that food or water deprivation or ingestion can modify the facility of an electric stimulus to elicit eating or drinking is claimed to provide support for "the idea that hypothalamic stimulation can trigger neural substrates which regulate

normal feeding and drinking (Devor, Wise, Milgram, & Hoebel, 1970, p. 23)."
Although it may be useful to know that elicited eating and drinking can be
influenced by hunger and thirst, there is no logical reason for concluding that
hunger and thirst mechanisms were responsible for the evocation of the
behavior. (c) A great amount of weight has been given to the observations that
self-stimulation rate obtained from electrodes said to be in the "lateral
hypothalamic feeding area" (but not shown to elicit eating or drinking) can be
modified by manipulations known to influence normal ingestion patterns
(Hoebel, 1969). The significance of these observations is considerably diminished, however, when it is noted that self-stimulation obtained from areas not
considered part of the circuitry controlling ingestion is also modified by many of
the same manipulations. Adequate experimental controls providing data on
self-stimulation changes in nonfeeding areas where comparable self-stimulation
performance can be obtained have not been provided.

The general acceptance of the view that hypothalamic stimulation elicited
eating and drinking by evoking hunger and thirst resulted in a selective
perception of some of the pioneering work in this field. Although Hess is
consistently mentioned as having produced *bulimia* by hypothalamic stimulation, it sometimes seems that he is not read as often as he is cited. Describing the
behavior elicited by a given hypothalamic electrode, Hess (1957) had written:

> Stimulation here produces bulimia. If the animal has previously taken neither milk
> nor meat, it now devours or drinks greedily. *As a matter of fact, the animal may even
> take into its mouth or gnaw on objects that are unsuitable as food, such as forceps,
> keys, or sticks* [p. 25, italics added].

Similarly, while Greer (1955) is frequently cited as having discovered a discrete
"drinking center" in the rat, it is generally overlooked that in the only case
reported, the stimulus was delivered between two asymmetrically positioned,
bilateral hypothalamic electrodes. It should be obvious that there is little
justification for concluding very much about anatomical location. Furthermore,
the similarity between Greer's description of the behavior of the stimulated rat
and Hess' description of the elicited bulimia has apparently not been noted. In
both cases, there is ample reason for questioning interpretations based
exclusively on the assumption of hunger and thirst:

> Stimulation of the animal began 24 hours after the electrodes were implanted. It was
> immediately apparent that the animal was under great compulsion to perform violent
> "licking" activity when a current was passed between the hypothalamic electrodes. In
> response to stimulaton, it would stand on its hind legs and run vigorously around the
> glass enclosed circular cage, licking wildly at the glass wall. This behavior would cease
> immediately upon shutting off the current. If the voltage were slowly increased,
> licking would gradually become more vigorous.
>
> With stimulation continuing by timer control, the reaction of the animal changed
> during the first night. The water bottle containing 200 ml was found completely
> empty at 9 A.M. even though it had been filled at 6 P.M. the previous evening. It was
> now found that stimulation would result in violent drinking activity. The non-specific
> licking response had been lost. As soon as the current was turned on, the animal

would jump for the water bottle and continue to drink avidly until the switch was turned off. If the water bottle was removed and the current then turned on, the rat would go back to its 'licking' behavior of the previous day, but would immediately transfer it to drinking behavior when the water bottle was replaced [Greer, 1955, pp. 60–61].

Our own studies have stressed another interpretation of the behavior elicited by stimulation and have been reviewed in several articles (Valenstein, 1969, 1970; Valenstein, Cox, & Kakolewski, 1970). In brief, it has been shown that: (a) the hypothalamic sites from which eating and drinking can be obtained are much more widespread than previously suggested (Cox & Valenstein, 1969a); (b) the eating and drinking elicited by stimulation differs in many significant ways from the same behavior when motivated by hunger and thirst (Valenstein, Cox, & Kakolewski, 1968; Valenstein, Kakolewski, & Cox, 1968); (c) most hypothalamic electrodes elicit several behaviors if sufficient opportunity is offered (see review articles); (d) many of the behaviors evoked by hypothalamic stimulation can better be understood by an analysis of the prepotent responses of the species (Phillips, Cox, Kakolewski, & Valenstein, 1969) and the individual animal (Valenstein, 1969; Panksepp, 1971; Wise, 1971) rather than by assuming underlying motivational states such as hunger and thirst.

In spite of frequent statements to the contrary, I have *never* implied that all hypothalamic stimulation evokes one common plastic system. Such a position would be blatantly absurd. What has been stated is that "hypothalamic stimulation at different regions may activate several different states, but these states are not sufficiently designated to preclude response substitution or to justify the application of terms that imply specific drive states [Valenstein, 1969, p. 313]." If testing is appropriately arranged, animals can demonstrate that they are able to distinguish between hunger and thirst. It follows that this ability must be reflected in distinctive neural activity. Whether such specific motivational states can be duplicated by electrical stimulation of discrete hypothalamic sites is another question.

One criticism of our work that frequently comes up was originally raised by Wise (1968) and is mentioned in the contributions of Mogenson and Teitelbaum to this volume. It concerns the implications of our finding, which has been confirmed a number of times subsequently, that hypothalamic electrodes commonly elicit several behaviors at the same current intensity. As some of the elicited behaviors are observed only after a prolonged period of stimulation, it appeared that some modification in the consequences of stimulation may have taken place. Wise (1968) maintained that the emergence of additional elicited behaviors in our experiments could be explained by "fixed neural circuits, functionally isolated from each other," but with different thresholds. He observed that the current threshold for eliciting a behavior declined over time, presumably as a result of repeated stimulation. If it was assumed that we stimulated at intensities below the threshold for one of the behaviors, that behavior would not be observed until the threshold of its neural circuit had been sufficiently lowered. In other words, Wise argued that nothing had been changed except for a lowering of the threshold—had we used higher currents to begin with, we would have observed all the behaviors during our initial stimulation. Subsequently, we demonstrated that this was not the case, as even if the current was raised to the maximal tolerable level, the second behavior was often not seen (Cox & Valenstein, 1969b). In such cases the behavior only gradually emerged, a phenomenon recently confirmed by Mogenson (1971). It appears that Wise (1971) also has had to modify his original hypothesis as a result of his recent work with movable electrodes. It has been found that electrodes moved in 0.5-mm steps continue to elicit the same behaviors over a range of hypothalamic sites, but threshold changes occur only following stimulation at the first site. Apparently, it is not the direct effect of stimulation on the neural tissue surrounding the electrode tip which produces the threshold change, but rather some factor such as a developing tendency of the animal to respond in a particular way that is important.

The examples of the gradual emergence of additional behavior elicited by the stimulation and the evidence that the execution of those behaviors can become reinforcing may be extremely important. Figure 1 illustrates in detail the gradual emergence and strengthening of elicited drinking which was not seen at all initially during prolonged stimulation bouts with either food and water present, or even with only water present—the competing food having been removed. I have called this process "channeling" of responses elicited by hypothalamic stimulation (Valenstein, 1971). These observations have led to the speculation that under certain conditions (unfortunately not yet understood) an association can be established between mechanisms underlying reinforcement and the neural substrate for built-in responses. This established linkage between reinforcement and certain classes of responses produces a tendency to repeat these responses whenever similar emotional states are involved, and this process may form the basis of acquired stereotypical and compulsive behaviors.

My own belief at present is that the behavior elicited by hypothalamic stimulation will be misinterpreted if it is assumed that it is motivated by natural drive states. The elicited behaviors have only a very remote relationship to the homeostatic regulation of tissue needs. It is well known that eating and drinking may occur under many circumstances when there is no need for food or water. This point is illustrated by our investigation of object carrying controlled by hypothalamic stimulation (Phillips et al., 1969). Under conditions in which the stimulation was always delivered on one side of the test chamber and turned off when the other side was entered, rats picked up objects when stimulated and carried them to the opposite side, where they were dropped when stimulation was terminated. It was demonstrated that: (a) the object carrying could be elicited by stimulation at all hypothalamic sites that supported good self-stimulation performance; (b) the elicited object carrying was reinforcing over and above any reinforcement produced by the stimulation alone; (c) the object carrying was elicited only in those species and under those conditions in which

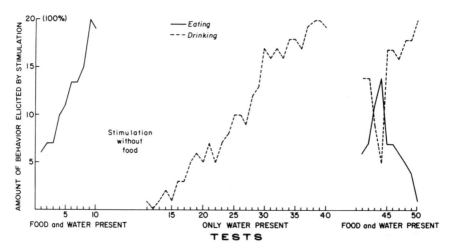

FIG. 1. An example of the gradual emergence of drinking elicited by hypothalamic stimulation. Initially, when food and water were both present, the animal displayed eating in response to stimulation with increasing reliability over the course of the 10 tests. No drinking at all was observed during these tests. Following a prolonged period of intermittent stimulation with only water present, the animal started to lick the drinking tube occasionally during stimulation periods. At this point, the animal was given 40 tests with only water present. It can be seen that during these tests, drinking came to be elicited with increasing realiability. Ten additional tests with food and water present revealed that the stimulation now elicited drinking more reliably than eating. (Stimulation intensity was constant for all tests. Each test consisted of twenty, 20-second stimulation periods. It was possible for the stimulation to elicit both eating and drinking during a single period.)

this behavior normally was prepotent. For example, rats normally carry objects only in one direction—toward their home site; stimulation only elicits carrying of objects when it is turned on and off regularly at the same place in the test chamber. Had we used only edible objects, we might have concluded that the stimulation had elicited hoarding behavior motivated by hunger; if pups had been used instead of inanimate objects, we might have been misled into speaking of retrieving of pups and maternal behavior. The elicitation of object carrying cannot be considered evidence for the activation of hunger or a maternal drive. Object carrying is a basic response unit that can be studied separately from biological need states. This type of analysis makes it evident that even eating and drinking may occur without involvement of the physiological mechanisms underlying the regulation of bodily needs for nutrients and fluids. At least some eating and drinking as well as object carrying, foot thumping, preening, head scratching, ear pulling, and other "reinforcing" behaviors of this type may have to be examined in a context that is quite different from the traditional.

REFERENCES

Coons, E. E., Levak, M., & Miller, N. E. Lateral hypothalamus: Learning of food-seeking response motivated by electrical stimulation. *Science,* 1965, **150**, 1320–1321.

Cox, V. C., & Valenstein, E. S. Distribution of hypothalamic sites yielding stimulus-bound behavior. *Brain, Behavior and Evolution,* 1969, **2**, 359–376. (a)

Cox, V. C., & Valenstein, E. S. Effects of stimulation intensity on behavior elicited by hypothalamic stimulation. *Journal of Comparative and Physiological Psychology,* 1969, **69**, 730–733. (b)

Devor, M., Wise, R. A., Milgram, N. W., & Hoebel, B. G. Physiological control of hypothalamically elicited feeding and drinking. *Journal of Comparative and Physiological Psychology,* 1970, **73**, 226–232.

Greer, M. A. Suggestive evidence of a primary "drinking center" in hypothalamus of rat. *Proceedings of the Society of Experimental Biology* (New York), 1955, **89**, 59–62.

Hess, W. R. *The functional organization of the diencephalon.* New York: Grune & Stratton, 1957.

Hoebel, B. G. Feeding and self-stimulation. In P. J. Morgane (Ed.), Neural Regulation of Food and Water Intake. *Annals of the New York Academy of Science,* 1969, **157**, (2) 758–778.

Miller, N. E. Learning motivated by electrical stimulation of the brain: A commentary. In E. S. Valenstein (Ed.), *Brain stimulation and motivation.* Glenview, Ill.: Scott, Foresman & Co., 1973, in press.

Mogenson, G. J. Stability and modification of consummatory behavior elicited by electrical stimulation of the hypothalamus. *Physiology and Behavior,* 1971, **6**, 255–260.

Morgane, P. J. Distinct "feeding" and "hunger" motivating systems in the lateral hypothalamus of the rat. *Science,* 1961, **133**, 887–888.

Panksepp, J. Aggression elicited by electrical stimulation of the hypothalamus in albino rats. *Physiology and Behavior,* 1971, **6**, 321–329.

Phillips, A. G., Cox, V. C., Kakolewski, J. W., & Valenstein, E. S. Object carrying by rats: An approach to the behavior produced by stimulation. *Science,* 1969, **166**, 903–905.

Steinbaum, E. A., & Miller, N. E. Obesity from eating elicited by daily stimulation of hypothalamus. *American Journal of Physiology,* 1965, **208**, 1–5.

Tenen, S. S., & Miller, N. E. Strength of electrical stimulation of lateral hypothalamus, food deprivation, and tolerance for quinine in food. *Journal of Comparative and Physiological Psychology,* 1964, **58**, 55–62.

Valenstein, E. S. Behavior elicited by hypothalamic stimulation: A prepotency hypothesis. *Brain, Behavior and Evolution,* 1969, **2**, 295–316.

Valenstein, E. S. Stability and plasticity of motivation systems. In F. O. Schmitt (Ed.), *The neurosciences: Second study program.* New York: Rockefeller University Press, 1970. Pp. 207–217.

Valenstein, E. S. Channeling of responses elicited by hypothalamic stimulation. *Journal of Psychiatric Research,* 1971, **8**, 335–344.

Valenstein, E. S., Cox, V. C., & Kakolewski, J. W. The motivation underlying eating elicited by lateral hypothalamic stimulation. *Physiology and Behavior,* 1968, **3**, 969–971.

Valenstein, E. S., Cox, V. C., & Kakolewski, J. W. Reexamination of the role of the hypothalamus in motivation. *Psychological Review,* 1970, **77**, 16–31.

Valenstein, E. S., Kakolewski, J. W., & Cox, V. C. A comparison of stimulus-bound drinking and drinking induced by water deprivation. *Communications in Behavioral Biology,* 1968, **2**, 227–233.

Wise, R. A. Hypothalamic motivational systems: Fixed or plastic neural circuits? *Science,* 1968, **162**, 377–379.

Wise, R. A. Individual differences in effects of hypothalamic stimulation: The role of stimulation locus. *Physiology and Behavior,* 1971, **6**, 569–572.

4
NONHOMEOSTATIC
CONTROLS OF DRINKING[1]

Harry R. Kissileff [2]
University of Pennsylvania

INTRODUCTION AND DEFINITIONS

The major emphasis of most previous studies of thirst (cf. A. V. Wolf, 1958; Wayner, 1964; Fitzsimons, this volume) has been on drinking of water as the major means for repletion of body fluids to assist in maintenance of their relative constancy of volume and concentration. This view of thirst and drinking fails to account for drinking under a variety of conditions and is therefore incomplete. A more comprehensive picture emerges when drinking is considered as the behavioral outcome of both homeostatic and nonhomeostatic influences. After considering several nonhomeostatic controls along with their neural mechanisms, I will propose a definition of thirst as the major homeostatic control of drinking and show that it operates through a different neural substrate than do the nonhomeostatic controls. In order to avoid confusion over the meanings of the technical terms, they are now defined.

Drinking

Drinking is most generally defined as "the act of taking into the mouth and swallowing liquids."[3] However, there are three qualifications which are often

[1] The experimental data reported here were supported at various times by grants NB 03496 (NIH to Alan N. Epstein), GB4198X (NSF to Carl Pfaffmann), and a Biomedical Sciences Support Grant from the University of Pennsylvania to the author.

[2] The author wishes to thank Emil Becker for assistance in collecting some of the data reported on the intragastric self-injection experiments and Natalie Marchalonis for assistance in preparing the manuscript.

[3] Definition adapted from *Webster's New World Dictionary,* College edition, 1956, Cleveland, Ohio: World Publishing Co. "Drink: v.t. to take (liquid) into the mouth and swallow it."

used to distinguish eating from drinking which restrict the foregoing definition: the type of liquid ingested, the antecedent state (deprivation of food or water), and the motor acts of ingestion. In man, for instance, soup is a liquid considered as eaten because it is taken with a spoon, rather than from a vessel directly. In rats and other mammals the distinction is less clear because the motor acts of ingestion are identical for water and liquid foods. The question becomes even more complicated in animals which have selectively recovered hunger and not thirst after lateral hypothalamic brain damage.

Since this book is devoted to thirst, and the liquid which most generally satisfies it is water, I will restrict my use of the term "drinking" to the object "water" unless explicitly stated to the contrary. The self-injection of fluids into the stomach has been used to study the effects of removal of specific stimuli on the ingestive process (Epstein, 1967a; Kissileff, 1972), but I shall not refer to this type of ingestion as drinking, either, although I will describe evidence from such experiments which have implications for the control of drinking.

Drinking can be considered quantitatively as the output of a system which can be specified completely by time of onset, time of termination, and rate of ingestion X time during its occurrence. These three parameters are in turn controlled by variables arising from within or outside the animal. Examples of these variables which I shall refer to as *controls of drinking* are changes in blood composition (Adolph, 1967; Fitzsimons, 1971), stimulus quality of the drinking fluid (Epstein, 1967b; Mook, 1969) and endogenous rhythms (Oatley, 1971; Zucker, 1970), to name a few. These controls of drinking can be divided both by neural mechanism and by physiological consequences into two broad classes, homeostatic and nonhomeostatic.

Homeostatic Controls of Drinking

Homeostatic (Cannon, 1929) controls of drinking are those variables which operate to initiate, terminate, or change the rate of drinking in response to change in the cellular or extracellular fluid compartments (collectively referred to as imbalances in body water) so that any disturbance in these compartments is relieved. The second and fourth sections of the book are devoted to homeostatic controls and their neural mechanisms. Hence further discussion of homeostatic controls in this chapter will be restricted to their articulation with the nonhomeostatic controls which are defined next.

Nonhomeostatic Controls of Drinking

Nonhomeostatic controls of drinking are those variables which either are insensitive to imbalances in the body water or operate heedless of the state of body water. In discussing nonhomeostatic controls of drinking 10 years ago, John Falk (1961) cited some examples in which drinking was influenced by factors not related to the state of water balance of the animal. He discussed: (*a*) changes in amount drunk produced by changes in palatability of the fluid; (*b*) a phenomenon of psychogenic adipsia in which a rat preferred electrical brain stimulation to drinking even though severely dehydrated; and (c) psychogenic polydipsia, which is excessive drinking by rats forced to eat small quantities of food intermittently after reduction to 80% body weight. Psychogenic adipsia can be excluded from the present discussion because it is more closely related to the relative reinforcing effects of water and brain stimulation than to nonhomeostatic controls of drinking. This leaves psychogenic polydipsia and palatability changes as two major examples of nonhomeostatic controls of drinking.

To these may be added five other examples. (a) First there is prandial drinking, which is drinking of small drafts taken alternately with small morsels of food in a meal (Teitelbaum & Epstein, 1962; Kissileff, 1969b). (b) Drinking independent of body water imbalance can also be produced by providing an additional reinforcer for drinking. In such a case the animal must drink in order to avoid or terminate shock (Williams & Teitelbaum, 1956), or in order to obtain another reward such as food (Morrison, 1967). (c) Effort required to obtain water (Miller, 1967) is another nonhomeostatic control, although we do not know which parameters of drinking it influences. (d) Endogenous circadian rhythms have been implicated in the control of drinking, but it is not yet certain that they have a direct effect on drinking or that their influence is nonhomeostatic (cf. section on "Nonhomeostatic Control of Nocturnal Drinking," below). (e) Finally, as discussed by Mogenson (this volume), electrical brain stimulation produces drinking independent of needs for water. As he suggests, this drinking is probably related to activation of neural elements of the homeostatic controls of drinking and represents direct stimulation of the mechanisms which normally respond to body water imbalances. I will, therefore, not treat it further.

The remainder of this chapter will describe some of the above examples more fully, and, where possible, an indication of the separation of neural mechanisms for homeostatic and nonhomeostatic drinking will be given.

PSYCHOGENIC POLYDIPSIA

The Phenomenon

When a rat which has been reduced to 80% body weight by food restriction is given 45-mg pellets of food on a spaced-reward schedule with water freely available, the rat drinks excessively. For example, in a 3.17-hour session a typical rat drank 92.5 ml, or 3.43 times its preexperimental, 24-hr water intake (Falk, 1969). John Falk, who first reported the phenomenon (Falk, 1961), termed it psychogenic polydipsia. Both Falk (1969) and later Chapman (1969) showed that once established, psychogenic polydipsia is not under homeostatic control since it cannot be suppressed by concurrent or preloading of water intragastrically. However, Chapman showed that a state of water lack was necessary for the learning of psychogenic polydipsia, and that its learning could be blocked by preloading with water. This effect, however, depends not on the fact that the animals are no longer thirsty, but on their failure to associate drinking and eating. If they are preloaded and also forced to drink in order to obtain their food, drinking becomes excessive (Chapman, 1969). Therefore, neither the learning nor the maintenance of psychogenic polydipsia is under homeostatic control.

The Dry-Mouth Interpretation

However, psychogenic polydipsia can be blocked by injection of water into the mouth (Chapman, 1969) and disappears with liquid food reinforcement (Stein, 1964; Stricker & Adair, 1966). This could be interpreted to mean that a dry mouth is somehow responsible for the psychogenic polydipsia (Teitelbaum, 1966). The following arguments indicate that it is not. As will be discussed shortly, the dry-mouth animal is, par excellence, the animal without saliva (salivaless) produced either by extirpation of the three major salivary glands (salivarectomy—Epstein, Spector, Samman, & Goldblum, 1964) or by ligation of their ducts (desalivation—Vance, 1965). The salivaless rat drinks in a pattern which is qualitatively similar to that seen in psychogenic polydipsia. In both phenomena the rat takes small drafts of water immediately after small pellets of food (prandial drinking). These phenomena are also similar in that the salivaless rat does not reduce its water intake when hydrated intragastrically, but does so when water is injected into the mouth while eating (Kissileff, 1969c). However, three facts indicate that the mechanism of psychogenic polydipsia is different from that of prandial drinking in salivaless rats. First, the amounts of oral water necessary to suppress psychogenic polydipsia approximate the amounts the animal actually drinks (Chapman, 1969). On the other hand, prandial drinking in salivaless rats disappears when only 30 to 40% of the amount drunk is injected and prandial drinking is replaced by regulatory drinking (Kissileff, 1969c). Second, desalivate rats do not learn psychogenic polydipsia any faster than normals (Chapman, 1969). If there were a common mechanism, immediate or at least rapid transfer would have been expected. Finally, atropine sulfate in a dose as high as 15 mg/kg leaves prandial drinking unaffected in desalivate rats (Blass & Chapman, 1971), but in a dose of 9 mg/kg it reduces water intake of psychogenic polydipsia by 63% while only reducing food intake by 6% (Burks & Fisher, 1970). Given these differences between psychogenic polydipsia and prandial drinking of salivaless rats, a dry mouth explanation of psychogenic polydipsia is clearly unsatisfactory.

The Frustration Interpretation

The common denominator in all experiments on psychogenic polydipsia is the necessity for high degrees of both hunger and thwarting of eating. This combination results in behavior which could be interpreted as frustration (Miller & Stevenson, 1936). McFarland (1965) has shown that frustration can lead to displacement. Falk (1969) has suggested that the thwarting of eating by spaced presentation of pellets to a hungry rat results in excessive drinking as stable displacement activity. There are two problems with this interpretation. First, as recognized by Falk (1969), the excessive amount of drinking cannot be accounted for by this explanation since displacement activities are usually incomplete, low in intensity, and poorly oriented. Secondly, while placing psychogenic polydipsia into a behavior category is useful for classifying behavior, it is not very satisfactory as an explanation of the mechanism of the phenomenon. It classifies a mystery as an enigma.

A Neurochemical Interpretation

The following proposals, while as incomplete and speculative as previous ones, may at least indicate where further work would be fruitful. Frustration is considered to be an emotional response and therefore undoubtedly involves the autonomic nervous and limbic systems (Maclean, 1949). Psychogenic poly-dipsia may therefore be a response to increased levels of transmitter substances, accumulating in the limbic system during the experience of frustration. Whether drinking would be facilitated by any kind of frustrating situation remains to be determined. Certainly some drinking in man (alcoholism) can be related to the experience of frustration. Perhaps psychogenic polydipsia is a form of addiction for the frustrated, hungry rat.

Frustration as the underlying motive for psychogenic polydipsia can account for a number of the observed facts. Frustration and psychogenic polydipsia are both reduced whenever primary motivation (e.g., hunger) is reduced. Psycho-genic polydipsia was reduced or disappeared entirely when the animal's body weight was allowed to return to normal (Falk, 1961). Psychogenic polydipsia is also reduced whenever thwarting is reduced—for example, by increasing the reinforcement density or increasing its palatability. Falk (1967) showed that psychogenic polydipsia was greatly reduced when more than 45 mg of dry food per reinforcement was given, and also when the reinforcement was made more palatable by substituting sugar pellets for lab chow pellets as the reinforcer. Similarly, liquid reinforcers seem to be less thwarting than dry ones, considering that equal polydipsia was elicited by 45-mg reinforcements of dry food and only 22-mg reinforcements of liquid (Falk, 1967).

Furthermore, the act of drinking itself undoubtedly activates many of the neural systems concerned with the affect normally provided by eating (e.g., the feel of the food in the mouth, proprioception from swallowing), so that drinking may be a substitute for eating, which in this situation reduces frustration but not hunger. Injection of water into the mouth may also reduce the frustration by providing the same affects, and hence it reduces the excessive drinking. Drugs such as pentobarbital, metamphetamine, and atropine, which have little effect on normal eating or drinking, are capable of reducing or abolishing psychogenic polydipsia (Falk, 1964; Burks & Fisher, 1970). Whether these same drugs also reduce frustration in other situations remains to be determined. Finally, consideration of the diffuse cholinergic drinking system, its beautiful overlap

with the Papez circuit (Fisher & Coury, 1964), and the large suppressant effect
of atropine on psychogenic polydipsia (Burks & Fisher, 1970) compared with its
much smaller effect on regulatory drinking (Blass & Chapman, 1971), all suggest
that acetylcholine may play a greater role in emotionally driven drinking than in
drinking driven by thirst. In any case, a frustration hypothesis of psychogenic
polydipsia and the possible transmitters involved, should lead to some new
experiments in what is quantitatively the biggest and least understood
phenomenon in drinking behavior.

OROPHARYNGEAL SENSATIONS EXCLUDING
TASTE

Types of Sensations

Sensations arising from the oropharyngeal cavity as a result of drinking can
modulate drinking behavior. These sensations can be categorized as taste,
thermal, and tactile. There are also the perceptions of dryness and wetness which
will be treated in the section on prandial drinking. Taste alone will be considered
in the next section. In this section we will examine some of the effects of
removing the oropharyngeal stimulation derived from the fluid during ingestion
by using rats, each chronically implanted with an intragastric tube and trained to
hydrate itself by pressing a lever to inject water directly into its own stomach
(Epstein, 1960, 1967a; Kissileff, 1972). At the end of the section we will
consider the reasons for classifying oropharyngeal sensations as nonhomeostatic
controls of drinking.

To understand the oropharyngeal contribution to drinking, it is important to
recognize that the sensory qualities of the fluid both control the amount taken
in a draft and influence the initiation of subsequent bouts of drinking.
Operationally these two aspects of drinking can be measured by examining the
influence of the variables on the size of drafts and the number of drafts taken in
a day. The effect of oropharyngeal stimulation on the subsequent ingestion of
water can be seen by observing the pattern of ingestion when the act of drinking
is removed from the ingestive process.

Intragastric Self-Injection

Rats were fitted with intragastric tubes and trained to ingest their daily water
orally at first, and then intragastrically by pressing a lever for water delivery (cf.
legend, Table 1). An event recorder registered the occurrence of each
reinforcement. When the amount of water delivered intragastrically with each
lever press was fixed at 2 ml (slightly more than the size of the average oral
draft), the number of drafts decreased from its oral baseline (Table 1). This
means that in the absence of oropharyngeal feedback from feeling and
swallowing the ingested water, the animal is less likely to return to the lever. In
two of the five animals, the reduction in number of drafts was compensated for

TABLE 1

Daily Number of Drafts and Water Intake

Rat	Oral				Intragastric					
...	4	3	2	1	1	2	3	4	5	6

Number of drafts

Rat	Oral				Intragastric					
17	...	23	22	29	15	10	11	7	4	...
18	...	16	27	50	11	8	10	6	10	4
46*	...	...	13	18	7	7	11	6	11	8
51*	37	24	22	26	22	17	10	12	18	15
55*	...	...	16	22	11	10	9	9	7	4

Water intake (ml)

Rat	Oral				Intragastric					
17	...	30	29	27	55	28	29	22.5	17.5	...
18	...	15	25	33	27	23	30	17.5	30	13
46	...	...	24	27	44	23	23	26	37	37
51	45	47	44	50	60	40	30	32	55	35
55	...	...	31	37	40	25	25	27	23	28

Note.—Each rat was housed individually in a chamber equipped with a lever and water delivery system. Every fifth lever press was rewarded with a 0.125-ml water reward in 7.5 seconds (i.e., FR-5) for oral consumption. A draft was defined as a bout of drinking greater than one reinforcement and separated from other reinforcements by at least 5 minutes. After shaping to FR-5 orally, rats were maintained on that schedule for 2 to 5 days and then switched to intragastric reinforcement of 2 ml per reward by connecting the lead from the pump to the rat's chronically implanted intragastric tube rather than to the spout in the chamber. At the same time the reward schedule was changed to CRF (one reward per lever press). Three of the five rats were deprived of water overnight on the day before they were switched to intragastric reward (indicated by *).

by an increase in draft size when the animal did press the lever. In the rest, there was a reduction in total water intake.

Although the above confirms Epstein's (1960) original findings that the constancy of daily water intake is maintained in the absence of oropharyngeal feedbacks, acute and chronic challenges to body water regulation are met by less vigorous behavioral response in the absence of oropharyngeal feedbacks than in their presence. For example, of three rats acutely depleted of cellular water by intraperitoneal saline injection, only one responded by pressing the lever for intragastric water within 6 hours, and its response was attenuated by 50% compared with a subsequent test when drinking by mouth (Table 2). Both of the rats which failed had been maintaining body weight on intragastric water reinforcement for the previous 4 to 6 weeks before these tests were made. Because of

TABLE 2

Drinking and Intragastric Self-Injection Following Acute Cellular Dehydration

Rat	I.P. Load[a]												I.G. Load[b]											
	Amount drunk[c]						Amount self-injected[d]						Amount drunk						Amount self-injected					
	Control[e]			Test[f]			Control			Test			Control			Test			Control			Test		
	M	(R)	N	M	(R)	N	M	(R)	N	M	(R)	N	M	(R)	N	M	(R)	N	M	(R)	N	M	(R)	N
IGPR - 51	8.5	(4–11)	4	19	...	1	2	(0–5)	6	9	...	1	...	...	...	...	...	...	5.5	(0–8)	4	14	...	1
IGPR - 44	...	...	...	...	...	...	...	...	...	...	...	...	10	(10–11)	3	34	...	1	0	...	5	3.6	(0–7)	3
IGPR - 46	...	...	...	...	...	...	0	...	3	0	...	2	...	...	...	...	...	...	...	...	...	...	...	...
IGS - 1	...	...	...	...	...	...	...	...	...	...	...	...	.25	(0–1)	4	11	(11–11)	2	...	...	...	...	...	...
IGPR - 4	...	...	...	...	...	...	...	...	...	...	...	...	...	...	...	...	...	...	1.6	(0–3.5)	4	9.6	(7–14.5)	3

Note.—M = mean; N = number of tests; R = range of tests. All amounts are expressed in milliliters.
[a] IP Load—the rat was injected intraperitoneally with 1% of its body weight of a 1 molar sodium chloride solution (about 3 ml for most rats).
[b] IG Load—the rat received 4 ml of 10% sodium chloride solution either injected through a chronically implanted intragastric tube or by gavage.
[c] Amount drunk refers to water freely drunk (no operant required).
[d] Intragastric self-injection—the animal was previously trained to press a lever once for a 1-ml intragastric injection of water through a chronically implanted intragastric tube.
[e] Control is the water intake during a 5-hour test period with no load.
[f] Test indicates the water intake during the same 5-hour period on a different day following a load.

other tests, the rat which did respond had been on the intragastric reward schedule for 10 weeks. Although these results should be duplicated under more uniform conditions of prior experience, they strongly suggest that oropharyngeal afferents play a significant role in facilitating the response to water imbalance.

An example of the deficient response to chronic challenge to body water regulation is the reduced water intake seen in rats working for intragastric water when given a milk diet containing 5% sodium chloride as their sole source of food for 2 to 3 days. In all three animals in which this experiment was performed, intragastric water intakes were 25 to 66% of their oral water intakes on the diet (Table 3).

TABLE 3

Water and Food Intakes During Chronic Cellular Dehydration

Rat	Drinking[a]				Intragastric self-injection[b]			
	Standard diet[c]		High-salt diet[d]		Standard diet		High-salt diet	
	M(ml) (R)	N[e]	M(ml) (R)	N	M(ml) (R)	N	M(ml) (R)	N
Water intake								
IGPR - 51	23.5 (13–45)	3,4	72 (55–85)	3	6 (2–8)	3,3	51 (44–49)	3
IGPR - 44	15.6 (8–26)	3,5	83.7 (74–95)	3	7 (0–18)	2,2	55 (46–64)	2
IGPR - 46	20.7 (16–25)	3,6	61.3 (43–77)	3	2 (0–5)	5,1	19 (3–27)	3
Food intake								
IGPR - 51	41.5 (37–46)	3,3	24 (18–27)	3	46 (42–50)	3,3	21 (20–23)	3
IGPR - 44	45.6 (32–51)	3,5	29.3 (25–32)	3	29.25 (20–35)	2,2	25.5 (21–30)	2
IGPR - 46	38.5 (33–45)	3,3	12.3 (5–17)	3	41.5 (25–61)	5,1	7.3 (0–13)	3

[a]Rat drank water freely (no operants required).

[b]Rat was previously trained to press a lever once for a 1-ml injection of water through a chronically implanted intragastric tube.

[c]Diet consisted of 3 parts Borden's sweetened condensed milk (Magnolia brand) to 1 part water by volume. The diet was freely available ad libitum.

[d]Diet consisted of 3 parts Borden's sweetened condensed milk to 1 part of 20% (w/v) sodium chloride solution by volume, and was therefore equivalent to the standard diet plus 5% sodium chloride (w/v).

[e]On standard diet, N is the number of days before, and after (separated by commas), being fed the high-salt diet. On the high-salt diet, N is the number of days on high-salt diet. R is the pooled range on standard diet. The experiment was conducted in each condition (drinking and IG self-injection) for 3 to 5 days on standard diet, followed by 2 to 3 days on high-salt diet, followed by 1 to 3 days on standard diet.

Do these findings mean that oropharyngeal feedbacks are part of the homeostatic system controlling body water economy? Not necessarily. It seems that only the magnitude or frequency of response and not its absolute presence or absence is modulated by oropharyngeal controls. Apparent absence of the occurrence of a response may be overcome by training. As will be seen later, when homeostatic mechanisms for drinking are eliminated by lateral hypothalamic brain damage, drinking recovers but is controlled entirely by oropharyngeal sensations without reference to homeostasis. Thus although oropharyngeal (nonhomeostatic) controls interact with homeostatic controls, there is good reason for treating them separately and considering the nonhomeostatic controls as modulators of drinking in the same sense that Adolph and colleagues (Adolph, Barker, & Hoy, 1954) used the term, that is, as controls which are appended to the regulatory responses but are not essential components of them.

Interaction Between Homeostatic and Nonhomeostatic Controls

These results on the facilitatory effects of oropharyngeal stimulation suggest a hypothesis in which oropharyngeal nonhomeostatic controls interact with homeostatic to lead to thirst in the following way: An imbalance of body water sets up a state of excitation in the central nervous system (Stellar, 1954) proportional to the deficit for large deficits (Adolph, 1939) which persists until drinking is terminated by inhibitory stimuli arising from the digestive tract and rehydration of the tissues (homeostatic control) (Holmes & Montgomery, 1960), provided an oropharyngeal expectation and affect (nonhomeostatic control) have been met. Oropharyngeal sensations involved in drinking water are conceived of as nonhomeostatic psychic energizers which control drinking by maintaining facilitation. Alternatively, oropharyngeal stimulation can inhibit the drinking response. Bitter tastes and extremes of temperature are examples of this type of inhibition. Regulation is accomplished by adjusting the level of inhibitory signals needed to terminate drinking, to the level of imbalance. This can be seen from the experiment of Adolph (1950) in which drinking was almost completely suppressed by gastric loads of water equal to the water deficit.

This hypothesis can account for a large number of facts concerning both homeostatic and nonhomeostatic controls of drinking. The ideas of expectation and affect have been introduced to account for the fact that ingestion continues in the absence of the act of drinking as mentioned above, but the reduced frequency in initiation of lever pressing indicates that the expectation and reward value of the reinforcer have changed. Indeed, on the first day that an animal is switched from drinking to intragastric self-injection, its intake is far larger than normal, and the first bout of drinking is usually prolonged (Table 1). The expectation for water is high at first, and when it is not satisfied, lever pressing persists as in extinction. However, after several days the expectation for oral water is low, and lever pressing occurs with a pattern of reduced frequency of drafts.

Miller, Sampliner, and Woodrow (1957) showed that less water is drunk following 15 minutes of drinking, than following 15 minutes of intragastric injection of the same amount as that drunk. This could be explained as a failure of the oropharyngeal expectation to have been met, following a state of thirst. The persistence of drinking following esophagostomy (Bellows, 1939) indicates the fundamental nature of facilitation by oropharyngeal stimuli associated with drinking in water lack and the necessity of postingestive stimuli for relatively sustained inhibition of drinking.

Finally, when rats are automatically hydrated with water via stomach tube with a continuous flow, they drink substantial quantities of water, even if given the amount they normally drink (Fitzsimons, 1971). This drinking, however, is much reduced by giving water with meals, but it is still necessary to give at least 20% more than that ordinarily drunk to achieve complete suppression of drinking with intragastrically administered water (Kissileff, 1969c). The reason for this finding is that intragastrically administered water meets water needs but does not satisfy oropharyngeal expectations associated with body water deficits. One would predict from this that the amount of suppression during such infusions ought to be related to the number of times an expectancy (i.e., a state of water imbalance in which water need exceeds rate of intragastric administration) for water develops. In accord with this, it has been found that the reduction of intake with intragastric loads is related to a decrease in the number of drafts but not to a change in their size, as the amount of water loaded increases (Figure 1).

The Minimum-Draft Concept

A working hypothesis to account for these data is that the onset of drinking is triggered at a certain threshold of cellular and extracellular dehydration (see Oatley, this volume, for discussion of the threshold issue). Only when this threshold is reached does the animal develop an oral expectation for water and begin to seek it. Termination of drinking when water is found is set to a fixed minimum of about 0.5 to 1.0 ml (100 to 300 licks), probably by neural mechanisms residing in the hypothalamus, but can be modified upward by increasing water requirements or absence of satiety signals. Therefore if the animal's need for water is properly anticipated by the experimental loading procedure, it should be possible to completely suppress drinking without oral hydration. On the other hand, if dehydration occurs, the oral expectation will develop and it will be impossible to completely satisfy the animal without oropharyngeal stimulation. It has been repeatedly demonstrated (cf. Adolph, 1950; Miller et al., 1957) that placing a volume of water in the stomach equivalent to the amount that would have been drunk after a deficit, is not sufficient to fully satisfy thirst. The prediction of the present hypothesis is that drinking can be prevented if deficits are not allowed to occur.

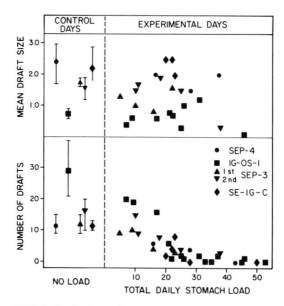

FIG. 1. Draft size and number as a function of water loaded during meals of dry food. Each rat was fitted with a chronically implanted intragastric tube for water injection and was trained to press a lever once for a single 45-mg pellet. On control days (*left side*) no water was injected. On experimental days water was injected with each pellet delivered. Each point shows the total injected in a single day and the mean draft size (*top*) and number of drafts for that day.

Although there is apparently a minimum draft under conditions of normal ad libitum drinking which may be fixed by neural mechanisms, the minimum draft size is not so rigidly fixed as to be incapable of reduction. During prandial drinking (cf. below), draft sizes average 0.2 ml and rarely exceed 0.5 ml (Kissileff, 1969b). Perhaps the latency required for prandial drinking to develop may be due to the relative rigidity of the minimum draft size which can be modified only by higher brain control. The control of tidal volume in respiration is an obvious parallel. Tidal volume is usually at a minimum for each breath and is increased to meet needs for additional oxygen consumption or carbon dioxide loss. It is controlled primarily by periodic activity of inspiratory neurons in the medulla (Wang & Ngai, 1964), but can be reduced, presumably by the intervention of more anterior neural systems, such as during panting which requires hypothalamic control (Teague & Ranson, 1936).

Thermal Sensations as the Basis of Reinforcement

The sensory basis for the oropharyngeal expectation of the thirsty animal has yet to be identified, but recent experiments indicate that it may be thermal. The amount of licking at an air stream which cools the tongue by evaporation is proportional to length of water deprivation (Oatley & Dickinson, 1970), and water deprivation enhances the reward value of licking at a cool metal surface (Mendelson & Chillag, 1970). Licking at both air streams and metal surfaces drops to low levels or disappears when the animal is in water balance or when the metal is heated to body temperature (Mendelson & Chillag, 1970). Finally, desalivation, which prevents the evaporative cooling of licking at air streams, reduces the air licking to low levels (Chillag & Mendelson, 1969; Mendelson, Zec, & Chillag, 1972). In experiments reported here on intragastric self-injection, rats which seem to learn most quickly to maintain high intakes during intragastric self-injection, also were observed to lick the lever or metal side of the chamber while pressing, which, being at room temperature, undoubtedly cooled the tongue. Similar observations during intragastric feeding have been reported by Snowdon (1969) and Holman (1969). Holman has even suggested that the intragastric reinforcing effects in earlier studies (Epstein & Teitelbaum, 1962) were produced "by the enhancement of temperature cues resulting from intragastric injections rather than by the injections alone. [Holman, 1969, p. 441]." He was referring to the cooling of nasopharyngeal membranes by passage through the tube of fluid at or below room temperature. Thermal sensations may therefore play an important role in oropharyngeal reinforcement. They are probably not, however, the exclusive basis for oropharyngeal reinforcement in the absence of taste and smell of the fluid.

Consummatory Responses as the Basis for Reinforcement

Careful examination of Holman's results suggests another conclusion. He reported that three out of five rats were unable to maintain lever pressing for intragastric food reward when the diet was heated to 40° C. and that those which did maintain responding did so mainly by chewing the lever. One possible reason that Holman did not have 100% success is that the temperature used was hot and may have been aversive in passage through the nasopharynx and esophagus. It is more significant in Holman's experiment that two animals did continue to work for intragastric reinforcement even when it was warmed than that three animals did not. The conclusion to draw is that the acts of licking, chewing, and swallowing when associated with the entrance of fluid into the stomach constitute the essentials of reinforcement to the hungry or thirsty animal.

TASTE

References to the role of taste sensations as nonhomeostatic modulators of drinking which neither initiate nor terminate it, but instead increase or decrease the amounts drunk in response to a given arousal (Adolph, 1967; Adolph et al., 1954), are numerous in the literature (cf. Pfaffmann, 1969; Epstein, 1967b).

Other workers have emphasized the view that taste is part of a homeostatic system controlling intake in response to specific deficits (cf. Stricker, this volume; Richter, 1942; G. Wolf, 1969). Finally, some (e.g., Young, 1955; Pfaffmann, 1960, 1969) have proposed that tastes can have hedonic value capable of arousing drinking in the need-free animal. This section will be devoted to a brief survey of the mechanisms by which taste alone and in combination with postingestional factors controls intake in the need-free animal. "Need-free" means "maintained on an unrestricted ad libitum diet that is fully adequate nutritionally [Young, 1967, p. 355]."

The classic method for studying the influence of taste on fluid intake is Richter's (1936) two-bottle 24-hour test. The animal is given water in one tube and a solution in another. After 24 hours, intakes are measured. To control for side preferences, the position of the water and taste solution are reversed periodically (Bare, 1949). The so-called preference-aversion curves generated by plotting intake against concentration generally take an inverted U-shape form for palatable solutions. To understand how intake is controlled by taste in these tests, we must consider four kinds of experiments.

First the experiments of Young (Young & Falk, 1956; Young & Greene, 1953) have shown that taste can direct choices in a preference situation. He used short-term tests in which the influence of postingestional factors was minimized. The animal was allowed only brief samples of the two fluids in a series of discrete trials where the choice of a solution or water was recorded when the animal had committed itself to a few seconds of uninterrupted drinking (Young & Greene, 1953) or contact with the fluid (Young & Falk, 1956). In this brief-exposure situation, nonthirsty rats selected dilute saline solutions when the solutions were below the isotonic level, and selected water more often than the solutions when the concentrations were above isotonic. In the case of sweet substances, selection of the sweet substance at all concentrations predominated over water, and more sweet was chosen in preference to less sweet.

Second, in order to explain the reduction of intake of sugar solutions above the isotonic concentration, it is necessary to consider the effects of postingestional factors. McCleary (1953), Stellar, Hyman, and Samet (1954), and later Mook (1963) showed that intake of tasted solutions was powerfully modified by postingestional osmotic factors, in that intake of concentrated solutions was enhanced by placing dilute solutions or water in the stomach, but was reduced by placing concentrated solutions in the stomach. The intake of dilute (i.e., less than isotonic) solutions was oppositely affected: concentrated solutions in the stomach enhanced intake, but dilute solutions depressed intake.

Third, when the oropharyngeal receptors are bypassed, using the intragastric self-injection technique, the preferences disappear (Borer, 1968). In the original study, aversions also disappeared. However, subsequently I (Kissileff, 1969a) found that aversion could be shown using the intragastric self-injection technique, if the positions of the levers were kept fixed rather than being

18-HR ACCESS INTRAGASTRIC

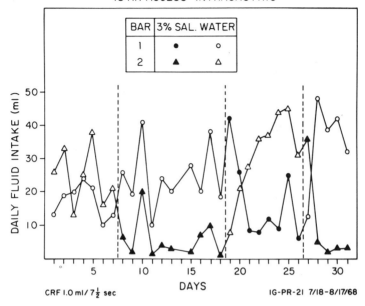

CRF 1.0 ml/ 7½ sec   DAYS   IG-PR-21 7/18-8/17/68

FIG. 2. Aversion to 3% sodium chloride by rat ingesting untasted fluids. Each point shows the daily intake of fluid as a result of pressing the lever for an intragastric injection of 1.0 ml/7½ sec. The key at the top indicates whether pressing a given lever delivered water or saline.

switched each day. These data are shown in Figure 2. After an initial period during which either lever produced water, 3% (*w/v*) saline was delivered intragastrically (see day 8) when the animal pressed the formerly preferred lever (#1). A clear-cut aversion was shown and the animal reversed its preference on each subsequent occasion when the position of the levers delivering water and saline were switched. Note, however, that except for the first occasion, 2 or 3 days were required before the reversal occurred. In contrast, two animals pressing for oral delivery showed reversals the first day, each time the positions were reversed. When the solutions were in the preferred range, and even as high as 2%, Borer's results were replicated. This experiment further illustrates the importance of taste in directing choice and controlling intake of dilute solutions. When stimulation of oropharyngeal receptors is removed from the ingestive process, preferences are not expressed, but intake can still be suppressed by postingestive factors associated with ingestion of concentrated solutions.

Fourth, direct examination of the pattern of intake of the two solutions in a 2-bottle 24-hour test reveals important information about the interaction between taste and homeostatic controls. The first study on this problem (Chiang & Wilson, 1963) showed that the rats drank more saline (0.8%) than water both by taking larger drafts and by choosing the saline tube more often (i.e., more drafts of saline than water). They suggested that the data on the number of

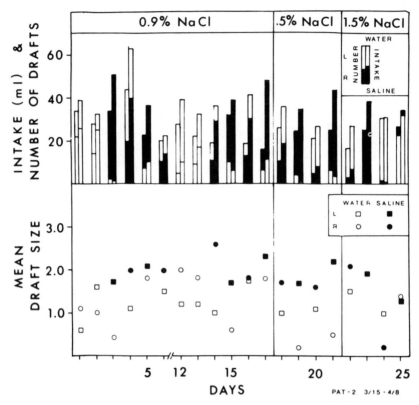

FIG. 3. Fluid intake, number of drafts, and mean draft size during 2-bottle, 24-hour preference test in one rat. The vertical extent (not cumulative) of each bar indicates the 24-hour measurement. In the top portion, the *left-hand bars* indicate number of drafts, and the *right-hand bars* indicate intake. The *top* portion is from the left-hand tube, the *bottom* from right. *Filled symbols* indicate saline; *open* ones, water. Drinking (contact with drinkometer) and feeding (eatometer) were recorded continuously. Drafts were defined as 1 minute without drinking or interruption of drinking by feeding.

drafts were consistent with the hypothesis that random selection occurred, and that if the rat selected water it would switch to saline, but if it selected saline it would continue drinking. The increased draft size is readily explained by Mook's postingestive hypothesis, (Mook & Kozub, 1968) based on single-bottle 24-hour tests: saline is less hydrating than water. When the animal encounters the saline tube, it is likely to drink more than when it encounters water because saline satisfies the animal's thirst less rapidly than does water. My own analysis of drinking patterns of rats given various concentrations of saline and water in a 2-bottle 24-hour test confirms Chiang and Wilson's findings of an increased draft size when saline is drunk, but indicates that their interpretation of overall preference is incorrect. Switching from water to saline or saline to water never occurred. Once a rat finished drinking from either tube, it did not drink again from either tube for periods ranging from 20 minutes to several hours (depending on the time of day). In addition, it was found with only two exceptions out of 16 days shown in Figure 3, that the total number of drafts when saline was present was no greater than the number of drafts when water was present in both tubes. This finding means that the taste of the saline alone is not sufficient to elicit more frequent drinking.

In view of the above, the following explanation is proposed for the increased intake of dilute saline in the 2-bottle 24-hour test. The rat becomes thirsty through cellular or extracellular dehydration. It then drinks from one of the tubes. If it drinks from a tube containing saline, it will drink more for the same deficit than from a tube containing water. By initially selecting the tubes at random, it learns within a few trials (perhaps on the first trial that it encounters the saline tube) what is in each tube. Thereafter, its choices are directed by memory of the taste and position of the preferred tube. In short, imbalance in body water arouses the urge to drink, previous experience and taste direct the selection of a drinking tube, and postingestional factors in combination with taste and water deficit (actual or effective) determine how long drinking will continue.

It should be noted that these data do not support the proposition (Young, 1955; Pfaffmann, 1960) that taste alone or recollection of a pleasant taste is a sufficient condition for arousing drinking. If it were, a larger total number of drafts would have been expected. One possible way of further confirming this would be to determine the relative effectiveness of intragastrically administered water in suppressing saline, as opposed to water drinking. The role of taste in drinking therefore appears to be a modulator as Adolph (1967) has proposed, and in combination with learning, a selector.

The most dramatic interaction of learning and taste in controlling drinking is shown by the recent work on specific aversions produced by poisoning (cf. Revusky & Garcia, 1970; Rozin & Kalat, 1971). In the basic phenomenon, a rat drinking a solution with a taste distinctly different from its usual fare that is thereafter made ill by X-irradiation, or by a toxic injection, will avoid that fluid or those fluids with a similar taste on subsequent occasions. As few as four licks provide the animal with sufficient information to completely inhibit drinking of a solution associated with the poisoning (Halpern & Tapper, 1971), providing, incidentally, another example of how higher neural controls can override the minimal draft.

NONHOMEOSTATIC CONTROL OF
NOCTURNAL DRINKING

The influence of ambient illumination on drinking is another control which appears on the surface to be nonhomeostatic, since it produces no obvious alteration in body fluid balance. This may be erroneous, as the following analysis of this phenomenon and its manipulation will show. Rats drink relatively more water during the dark than during the light phase of a dark-light cycle when kept with food and water available ad libitum (Siegel & Stuckey, 1947; Young & Richey, 1952). There are at least three non–mutually exclusive explanations for this phenomenon, each of which has both homeostatic and nonhomeostatic determinants. First, the increased nocturnal drinking could be due to increased nocturnal food intake (Siegel & Stuckey, 1947). Secondly, it could be due to endogenous circadian activity of the nervous system. Third, it may be due to release from the inhibitory influence of light.

Increased Nocturnal Drinking Caused by Increased Eating

A high correlation between food and water intake has been observed under a variety of conditions in rats (Siegel & Stuckey, 1947; Strominger, 1947; Cizek & Nocenti, 1965). Furthermore, feeding and drinking occur within close temporal relationship to one another. For example, rats drink 73% of their total daily water intake within 10 minutes before or after eating (Kissileff, 1969b). Since rats eat more during the dark phase of a dark-light cycle (Le Magnen & Tallon, 1966), the increased nocturnal drinking could be the result of the association of a given amount of drinking with a given amount of eating.

Fitzsimons (1971) has pointed out several possible reasons for this association. First, the animal anticipates water deficits caused by the food before they occur and drinks to prevent their occurrence. This is therefore a nonhomeostatic control. As evidence for this, Fitzsimons and Le Magnen (1969) found a delay in the reassociation of drinking with meals following a change in diet from high carbohydrate to high protein, suggesting that the rat uses oral cues provided by the diet to anticipate its hydrational needs as a result of the dehydration experienced while eating the diet in previous meals. Further supporting this notion is the finding of Oatley and Toates (1969) that hydrational changes following feeding lag behind drinking.

There is also ample evidence for a homeostatic mechanism of food-associated drinking operating in the following way. Drinking which follows feeding is due to temporary dehydration resulting from digestive secretions (Gregersen, 1932). Novin (1962) has shown, using conductivity measurement (increased ion concentration) as a correlate of dehydration, that dehydration has a rapid onset following feeding which I later found (Kissileff, 1969b) to correlate perfectly with the times of onset of drinking following feeding. Furthermore, drinking is suppressed, in proportion to the volume injected, by water injected intragastrically with meals (Kissileff, 1969c). Drinking which precedes feeding may be the result of disinhibition of feeding by hydration (Kakolewski & Deaux, 1970). Additional support linking nocturnal drinking to feeding is the experiment of Zucker (1970). He found that water intake during the dark phase (usually 85% of total daily intake when food and water were available ad libitum) dropped to only 10% of total intake when rats were fed two meals a day during the middle portion of the light phase.

It appears, then, that both anticipatory, nonhomeostatic mechanisms and homeostatic mechanisms are involved in food-associated drinking. It is not possible at present to account for Fitzsimons and Le Magnen's (1969) findings of delayed reassociation of feeding and drinking on the basis of a homeostatic hypothesis. On the other hand, metabolic changes in response to changes in feeding habits are not without precedent. Tepperman and Tepperman (1969) have shown increased lipogenesis following large meals. Perhaps a metabolic change will be discovered which could also be the basis for the delayed reassociation between feeding and drinking. Likewise the discrepancy between Novin's (1962) findings and those of Oatley and Toates (1969) needs to be reconciled. On the other hand, a homeostatic explanation for normal food-associated drinking appears well grounded and does not require additional assumptions about anticipation of deficits. It may be important to know, however, with what time course the adjustment to intragastric water loading occurs. At the present time, the most accurate statement we can make about nocturnal water intake related to feeding is that there are definitely homeostatic mechanisms contributing to it and probably nonhomeostatic anticipatory mechanisms as well.

Controls of Drinking When the Feeding Schedule Is Altered

Although increased food intake at night is a sufficient reason for increased drinking at that time, it is clearly not the only mechanism which can enhance nocturnal drinking.

The following experiments on the persistence of nocturnal drinking with changes in feeding schedule indicate that a factor other than the dehydrating effect of the food can control drinking. Oatley (1971) has shown that when food is eaten in meals evenly spaced throughout the 24-hour period, intakes are still considerably higher at night. Furthermore, when rats were fed a liquid diet for only 12 hours a day during either the light or the dark phase, they continued drinking during the dark phase when food was withheld from them (Table 4). There are several possible interpretations of the preceding results.

Increased hunger as a cause of increased drinking. First, water may serve as a substitute for food for the deprived rat. This has not been considered very seriously in the past because rats generally drink less rather than more when deprived of food (Verplanck & Hayes, 1953). However, it must be recalled that in those studies the rats were eating dry food. If we stop to consider that the rat has a minimum basal requirement for water which is augmented by dry food and partially satisfied by liquid foods, then it is reasonable to expect that water intake would fall when the dry food was withheld. On the other hand, if the liquid food had sufficient water in it to meet the temporary needs of digestion, withholding of that food should not reduce water intake, but would augment it, if water serves as a substitute for food.

Diurnal rhythms. Oatley (1971) has suggested that drinking is controlled by an independent (presumably neural) programmer which has a marked circadian

TABLE 4

Light-Dark Water Intakes Before, During, and After 12-Hour Food Restriction

Rat	Before Restriction			During Restriction			After Restriction		
	Light	Dark	N	Light	Dark	N	Light	Dark	N
Fed During Dark									
P - 2	1.7	9.2	9	2.9	10.5	18	3.4	10.3	9
	(0–6)	(0–17)		(1–7)	(4–25)		(0–9)	(4–23)	
P - 3	0.7	7.2	9	2.16	6.9	19	1.4	8.0	9
	(0–3)	(5–13)		(0–6)	(4–13)		(0–3)	(6–12)	
LC - 10	1.0	7.6	5	4.0	7.5	2	3.0	7.0	5
	(0–2)	(5–12)		(4–4)	(5–10)		(2–5)	(5–10)	
LC - 11	0.8	6.8	5	3.7	5.7	3	2.4	7.6	5
	(0–2)	(5–12)		(2–8)	(6–9)		(1–4)	(6–9)	
Fed During Light									
LC - 9	1.2	6.4	5	1.8	5.3	4	3.0	4.4	5
	(1–2)	(5–8)		(1–2)	(5–6)		(1–4)	(3–5)	
LC - 12	2.5	4.8	4	2.6	11.3	3	3.0	6.0	3
	(2–3)	(4–7)		(2–3)	(7–14)		(4–10)	(1–8)	
DAY - 1	...[a]	...		7.3	10.22	16	2.15	9.4	14
				(5–12)	(4–17)		(1–4)	(7–13)	
DAY - 2	...	...		8.6	8.07	16	4.3	6.8	14
				(5–19)	(4–21)		(2–6)	(3–11)	

Note.–Rats were kept on a liquid diet (3 parts Borden's sweetened condensed milk to 1 part water by volume, supplemented with vitamins and minerals [Kissileff, 1972]) for the number of days shown under column headed N "Before Restriction." They were then restricted to 12 hours access to food during either dark (columns headed "Fed During Dark") or light (columns headed "Fed During Light") for the number of days shown under column headed N "During Restriction." Following this, they were returned to ad libitum feeding again for the number of days shown under column headed N "After Restriction." Water was always available ad libitum and the 12-hour light, 12-hour dark cycle was maintained automatically. (From Kissileff, Becker, & Marchalonis, unpublished data, 1972). Mean intakes are expressed in ml. Numbers in ( ) are ranges of intake in ml.

[a]Data on water intake not collected before food restriction.

rhythm. According to this mechanism, drinking under ad libitum conditions is controlled not by needs for water but by the presumed programmer. This mechanism therefore also accounts for the persistence of increased drinking and maintenance of normal drinking patterns when food is presented in evenly spaced meals (Oatley, 1971). In further support of such a hypothesis is the finding that water intakes following cellular dehydration induced at various times of the day were equal except at 4:00 P.M., when they were higher, although the author attaches no particular significance to this exception (Oatley, 1967). Since other stimuli to thirst produce drinking in proportion to their magnitude (Adolph et al., 1954) and are additive (Fitzsimons & Oatley, 1968; Blass & Fitzsimons, 1970) while diurnal influences neither have additive effects with other stimuli nor vary in magnitude throughout the day, they appear to be nonhomeostatic.

There are a number of difficulties with Oatley's hypothesis. First, the persistence of normal drinking patterns during evenly spaced meals is simply not borne out by the data presented. Examination of Oatley's Figure 8 presented (see p. 216) indicates that, rather than continuing to occur at approximately the same time as it had during ad libitum feeding, drinking occurs in much smaller drafts with shorter pauses between them. This indicates that although the animal may be programmed to drink more water during the night, its drinking is not programmed into individual drafts, ready to be played out at set times. Second, the hypothesis fails to account for the proportional reduction of water intake when water is injected systemically with meals (Kissileff, 1969c). Third, the fact that more drinking occurred in response to loads given at 4:00 P.M., while dismissed by the author as unimportant, could be an indication that a diurnal factor related to homeostasis (the animal may have gone longest without drinking at this time) could account for the results. In summary, a diurnal rhythm of drinking does not account satisfactorily for increased nocturnal drinking.

Light inhibits drinking. A third explanation for the persistence of nocturnal drinking, even when the feeding schedule is altered, is that light itself is an active inhibitor of drinking. Such inhibition could occur directly through neural pathways controlling the release of transmitter substances active in inhibiting thirst. Rats certainly drink less when placed under continuous illumination (Zucker, 1970), but the mechanism remains obscure. Finally, the change in illumination from light to dark (or dark to light) could be a cue which synchronizes a drinking rhythm with a particular time of day (a Zeitgeber in the circadian sense). However, considering the difficulties confronting a diurnal theory as discussed above, this possibility would seem remote at present, and should not be taken seriously until it can be shown that simpler explanations cannot be ruled out.

Homeostatic controls of nocturnal drinking in the absence of food. I have just leveled rather strong criticisms at all the nonhomeostatic hypotheses for nocturnal drinking. Homeostasis is one of physiology's most unifying principles, and it could operate here also in the following manner. Rats are more active at night (Richter, 1922) and therefore generate more heat than when they are sleeping (Abrams & Hammel, 1965) during the light phase. Since heat is lost in the rat primarily by evaporative cooling through grooming, water is also lost. The rat, therefore, has a greater water requirement at night, and drinks more, whether food is present or not, scheduled in meals or not. It has already been shown how food-associated drinking is homeostatically controlled, and the above explanation accounts for increased nocturnal drinking when food is not present. It also accounts for the effect of light on drinking since light inhibits activity. The ideas are, however, only hypothetical and require vigorous testing.

In support of a thermoregulatory account of nocturnal drinking, it has been shown by Hainsworth and colleagues that at elevated core temperature, loss of saliva makes a vital contribution to thermoregulation (Hainsworth, 1968), and produces extracellular water loss which results in drinking (Hainsworth, Stricker, & Epstein, 1968). Ritter and Epstein (1972) have shown that at neutral ambients, saliva lost in grooming accounts for 32% of total evaporative water loss, and therefore makes a significant contribution to water economy of the rat. Grooming is of course more frequent during the dark hours of increased activity and would, in itself, result in an increased water requirement without regard to thermoregulation. It remains to be shown that the causal chain of events is increased activity, rise in the body temperature, grooming.

Hierarchies of Control

While a nonhomeostatic theory of ad libitum nocturnal drinking does not appear necessary at present, it is important to recognize that such a mechanism might be necessary under other conditions (for example, under brain damage). It should, therefore, be recalled that drinking is controlled, not by one factor, but by many (Adolph et al., 1954). Whether these factors operate simultaneously or sequentially remains to be determined. Consideration of the structure of the nervous system and the principle of dominance would lead us to expect that sequential hierarchical control is most likely. Therefore homeostatic controls are the normal operating condition, but these can be replaced by nonhomeostatic controls when the homeostatic controls are destroyed (e.g., by lateral hypothalamic lesions), when they are undeveloped, or, when normal homeostatic controls of one system override those of another (need for food resulting in excessive water intake). We shall consider these issues now.

PRANDIAL DRINKING

Description of the Phenomenon

Prandial drinking is a behavior pattern in which eating of small quantities of food and drinking of small quantities of water occur alternately in rapid succession. It was originally described by Teitelbaum and Epstein (1962) in the recovered lateral rat. Prandial drinking was then thought to be a recovery of a normal component of thirst (Epstein & Teitelbaum, 1964). However, subsequent work has indicated that it is not normal, because it is never seen in naive adult rats (Kissileff, 1969b), and it is not thirst, because it can occur in fully hydrated and even overhydrated rats (Kissileff, 1969c).

My initial experiments in prandial drinking were concerned with recording spontaneous ingestion patterns in normal rats and in rats recovered from lateral hypothalamic lesions. It was found that the normal rat ate and drank in clearly separated bouts (Figure 4, top). Although drinking occurred closely associated in

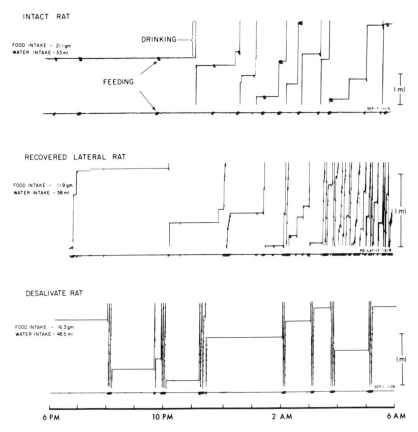

FIG. 4. Ingestion patterns of intact rat (*top*), recovered lateral rat (*middle*), and desalivate rat (*bottom*). Drinking is shown by upward movement of the upper pen (stepped by contacts with fluid through drinkometer). The 1-ml scales at right were obtained by dividing total upward excursion of the pen by the day's total water intake. Feeding is shown by a hatch mark on the upper and lower traces for each pellet obtained. Blocks of hatch marks run together and constitute a meal. Prandial drinking is readily seen on middle and lower traces by alternation of short upward moving vertical lines and hatch marks. (Taken from Kissileff, 1969b. Reproduced by permission of the American Psychological Association.)

time with feeding, it clearly occurred shortly before or after each meal and not during the meal. The drinking of the recovered lateral rat contrasted sharply with that of the normal. Each meal consisted of an alternating sequence of ingestion of small quantities of food and small drafts of water (Figure 4, middle). Since the recovered lateral rat did not drink in response to imbalances in body water, Teitelbaum and Epstein (1962) suggested that its drinking was controlled by mouth factors involved in eating dry food. This hypothesis was confirmed by my subsequent experiments with Epstein (Kissileff & Epstein, 1969).

Analysis of Controlling Mechanism

First we demonstrated that recovered lateral rats which would not respond normally to other stimuli to drinking increased their water intakes, if their mouths were dried by removal of the three salivary glands or ligation of their ducts (Figure 5).

Oral hydration. Kissileff (1969c) next showed that injecting small quantities of water through a chronically implanted cheek fistula, while the animals were eating dry food, completely abolished prandial drinking in the recovered lateral rat. The same quantity of water injected directly into the stomach, while the animal ate the same food, was without effect (Figure 6). In fact, even administration of several times the animal's daily water ration failed to reduce the animal's intake by more than a few milliliters, which could be attributed to incipient water intoxication or discomfort. It was thus clear that both increases and decreases in the dryness of the mouth led to appropriate changes in water intake in the recovered lateral rat; but imbalances in body water, either of excess or deficit, had no effect on the animal's drinking.

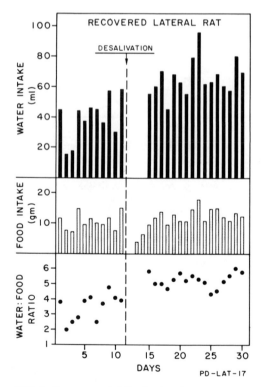

FIG. 5. Sequence of daily food and water intakes and water: food ratios of a recovered lateral rat before and after desalivation. (Kissileff, 1966).

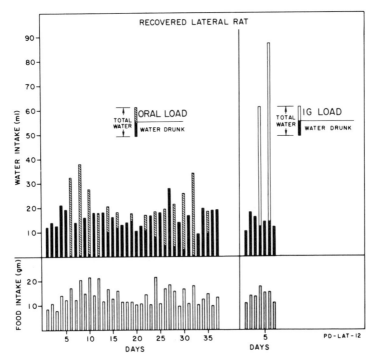

FIG. 6. Food and water intakes during a sequence of control (no water injected) days and experimental (water injected either into mouth or stomach with each pellet delivered) days in a single recovered lateral rat. Note that food intake was somewhat elevated by the loads, while water intake was suppressed in proportion to oral load but unaffected by gastric loads. (Taken from Kissileff, 1969c. Reproduced by permission of the American Psychological Association.)

Oral desiccation. Dehydration of the mouth by salivary reduction in the neurologically normal animal results in a pattern of prandial drinking qualitatively similar to that seen in the recovered lateral rat (Figure 4, bottom). It is tempting to speculate that the prandial drinking in the recovered lateral rat is the result of the animal's inability to secrete sufficient saliva during meals to easily swallow dry food. In support of this proposition is Hainsworth's and Epstein's (1966) finding that recovered laterals are unable to increase salivary production in the heat. More interesting than the parallel of prandial drinking in the neurologically normal desalivate rat is the similarity of its controlling mechanisms. Prandial drinking in desalivate rats is abolished by injections into the mouth while they are eating, but is unaffected by injections directly into the stomach while they are eating. Thus in both the neurologically normal desalivate and the recovered lateral, prandial drinking is controlled by oropharyngeal sensations and not requirements for body water (Kissileff, 1969c). These results are summarized in Figure 7.

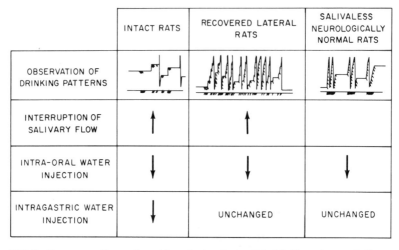

	INTACT RATS	RECOVERED LATERAL RATS	SALIVALESS NEUROLOGICALLY NORMAL RATS
OBSERVATION OF DRINKING PATTERNS			
INTERRUPTION OF SALIVARY FLOW	↑	↑	
INTRA-ORAL WATER INJECTION	↓	↓	↓
INTRAGASTRIC WATER INJECTION	↓	UNCHANGED	UNCHANGED

FIG. 7. Summary of experimental analysis of prandial drinking. Arrows indicate direction of change in water intake. (Taken from Kissileff, 1969c. Reproduced by permission of the American Psychological Association.)

Prandial Versus Food-Associated Drinking

Recall now the sharp difference between prandial drinking of recovered lateral and desalivate rats and the food-associated drinking of the normal rat. Prandial drinking is controlled by oropharyngeal sensations. Is the sharp difference in drinking pattern the result of a difference in the control mechanism? The next experiment indicates that it is. In normal animals, hydration via intragastric injection during feeding results in precisely the same reduction of water intake as does oral hydration (Figure 8). Therefore, water intake associated with feeding is clearly controlled in normal rats by factors related to water balance and not by oropharyngeal sensations.

There is an important contrast here with the results of Fitzsimons in which intragastric injections had a much smaller effect on drinking when given continuously throughout the day. Calculations based on his data (Fitzsimons, 1971, p. 184) indicate a reduction in drinking of only 0.4 ml for each milliliter infused, whereas in my experiments a reduction of 0.9 ml/ml infused was more common. Fitzsimons has used his data to argue that normal drinking is not related to thirst. This, however, would only follow if the animal had a constant need for water. But the stress on body water needs induced by eating dry foods results in periodic increase in the need for water (Gregersen, 1932) which, since water can not be stored, would not be met by a continuous injection. My results indicate that natural drinking associated with feeding, which accounts for 73% of the total intake on the average, is controlled by thirst and that when the water is administered in accordance with the animal's needs, its intake is reduced precisely in proportion to the load.

Origin of Prandial Drinking

Having shown that prandial drinking is not a normal component of thirst, it is logical to ask by what mechanism it arises following lateral hypothalamic lesions or desalivation. One possibility is that it is a built-in or previously acquired behavior which is suppressed by the presence of regulatory drinking. Another is that it is a behavior pattern acquired in response to a newly experienced set of sensations. In order to test the innate versus acquired hypothesis, the development of prandial drinking was observed in adult rats after desalivation or while they recovered from lateral hypothalamic lesions. If prandial drinking is acquired rather than the expression of a built-in mechanism, suppressed by regulatory controls, then prandial drinking will be acquired gradually rather than appearing abruptly. It was found that prandial drinking appeared gradually in both recovering lateral and desalivate rats (Kissileff, 1969b; 1971). In desalivates it gradually replaced large-draft drinking which occurred shortly before or after meals (Figure 9). In recovering lateral lesioned rats it appeared while the animals were passing into Stage IV (Figure 10); i.e., they would not maintain their weights on water but would accept it in small quantities. In these animals

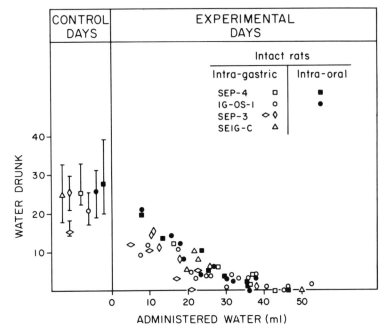

FIG. 8. Water intake as a function of water administered either intraorally or intragastrically through chronically implanted tubes in intact rats. Rat was trained to press a lever once for each 45-mg pellet of food. Each pellet delivery also resulted in a small injection of water. The points show the total drunk from an inverted graduate and the total injected for a single experimental day. Points and lines at the left are the no-load control days.

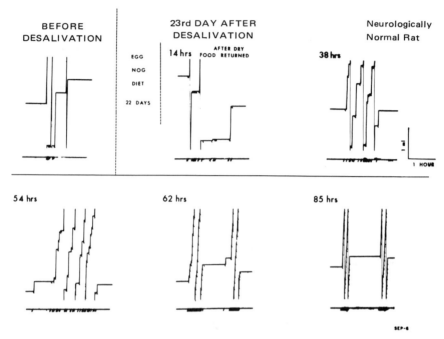

FIG. 9. Development of prandial drinking in a neurologically normal rat after desalivation. Each block shows a selection of a continuous record of the ingestion pattern. The rat was maintained on a liquid diet to prevent artifactual development of prandial drinking as a result of surgical trauma. Feeding and drinking are indicated as described in Figure 4. (Taken from Kissileff, 1969b. Reproduced by permission of the American Psychological Association.)

prandial drinking developed while the animals drank saccharin solutions with their meals. Between-meal drinking of saccharin was gradually replaced by prandial-style saccharin drinking. Although Stage III recovering lateral rats will treat saccharin solutions as foods when food-deprived (Teitelbaum & Epstein, 1962), they also treat them as lubricating fluids when eating dry food (Kissileff, 1971).

This raised the interesting question of whether the animal is eating or drinking the saccharin. It is of course difficult to answer this question in a rat in which eating and drinking of liquids utilize the same consumatory acts. However, in the chicken, Lepkovsky, Furuta, Sharon, and Snapir (1971) have shown that following lateral hypothalamic lesions, chickens which recover feeding and drinking never drink like normal chickens but peck at the water in the style of eating. It would thus appear that, in the chicken, prandial drinking is really part of the eating response. If one is willing to generalize from chickens to rats, it would seem that prandial drinking is actually a component of the feeding response and clearly its function is to facilitate the swallowing of dry food.

The gradual development of prandial drinking suggests that it is learned in response to a new set of sensations and is not simply released fully developed by

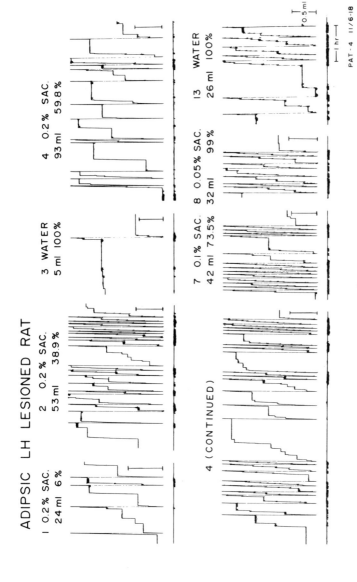

ADIPSIC LH LESIONED RAT

FIG. 10. Development of prandial drinking in rat recovering from lateral hypothalamic lesions. Each block is a section from a continuous record of the ingestion pattern. The number at the left of each section indicates the day of testing following access to dry food after the lesion. The type of fluid available is shown at the top of each record. Feeding and drinking are indicated as described in Figure 4. (Taken from Kissileff, 1971. Reproduced by permission of the American Psychological Association.)

the appropriate stimuli. However, recent experiments of Teitelbaum and collaborators (Teitelbaum, Cheng, & Rozin, 1969a, 1969b; Cheng, Rozin, & Teitelbaum, 1971) have shown that the entire lateral hypothalamic syndrome, including prandial drinking, is paralleled by development in immature rats whose development has been retarded by starvation or thyroidectomy. If this is the case, prandial drinking must be the relearning of a juvenile pattern lost after maturity. To determine whether prandial drinking occurred in normally developing rats, and to study its acquistion, feeding and drinking patterns were recorded continuously in weanling rats whose mothers were fed a liquid diet from the pups' fourteenth day of life (Kissileff, 1971). The animals were separated from their mothers at various ages from 16 to 22 days and kept on the liquid diet. At various ages beginning with 21 days they were abruptly switched from liquid to dry food.

Prandial drinking developed only in pups placed on dry food and water for the first time in their lives between 21 (the earliest age studied this way) and 35 days (Figure 11). Beyond 35 days prandial drinking did not appear. When it did, its development was always gradual, and intakes always slightly exceeded those of rats which were not drinking prandially at the same age. Thus, even in the

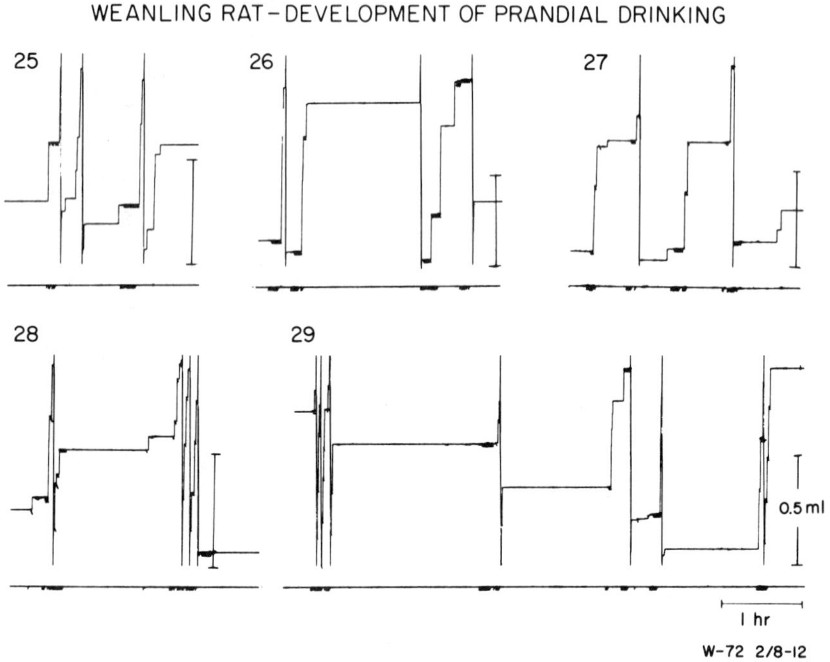

WEANLING RAT–DEVELOPMENT OF PRANDIAL DRINKING

FIG. 11. Development of prandial drinking in a weanling rat. Each block shows a section from an otherwise continuous record for the day of age numbered at the upper left. A scale at the right of each section indicates the pen excursion equivalent to 0.5 ml for that day. Feeding and drinking are indicated as described in Figure 4. (Taken from Kissileff, 1971. Reproduced by permission of the American Psychological Association.)

weanling, prandial drinking is learned. It is not due to maturation, since animals placed on dry food at various ages did not show a progressive increase with age in the percentage of prandial drinking on the first day with dry food and water. Either the mechanism of prandial drinking is different in adult rats from that in infants, or it is lost during maturation. Further experiments will be needed to distinguish between the alternatives. For the present we may conclude that prandial drinking is learned in response to the difficulties in swallowing, experienced by adult rats whose salivary production has been impaired (Vance, 1965; Epstein, 1971), and by the infant rats which may be dysphagic because of immature salivary function (Jacoby & Leeson, 1959; Schneyer & Schneyer, 1961).

To summarize this section, prandial drinking is an entirely different drinking pattern from normal food-associated drinking. It occurs in weanling desalivate and recovered lateral rats. It is learned in response to sensations of dryness of the mouth and difficulty in swallowing. Its controlling factors, therefore, do not control drinking of normal adult rats whose drinking is controlled by imbalances in body water.

A DEFINITION OF THIRST

Imbalances in body water create a state of excitation in the central nervous system (or alternatively, disinhibit an inhibitory state) which results in the seeking and the ingestion of water. This "central motive state" has been overwhelmingly equated with the meaning of thirst by physiological psychologists since the 1940s (Lashley, 1938; Morgan, 1943; Stellar, 1954).

How do these results fit with the idea of Cannon (1929) that thirst is a sensation of dryness in the mouth produced by reduction of salivary flow during states of dehydration? If this were the normal mechanism of thirst, removal of saliva ought to augment drinking. However, we have seen that polydipsia occurs only after prandial drinking has been learned. As I just indicated, if the salivary glands were a normal link in the chain of events producing drinking, learning of prandial drinking would be unnecessary. At the present time our experiments do not support a dry-mouth theory of thirst in the normal rat, but do indicate that the dry-mouth in combination with difficulty in swallowing is part of the hierarchy of controls of drinking. Conversely, lesions of the lateral hypothalamus abolish drinking in response to all conditions save difficulty in swallowing due to a dry mouth. The recovered lateral thus appears to be an animal which drinks without thirst. Of course, it may be questioned whether this is an adequate description of thirst.

What are the alternatives? One is to dismiss this definition as too restrictive, and thus to admit prandial drinking into the class of behaviors controlled by thirst. However, since there is clearly a different mechanism controlling prandial drinking than that which controls other food-associated drinking, placing them both in the same category would simply perpetuate the confusion I am trying to dispel. Another alternative is to broaden the term thirst to apply to any antecedent state, physiological, sensory, or neurological, which precedes drinking, but to qualify each as to type—thus, hypovolemic thirst, osmotic thirst, or dry-mouth thirst. Another would be to maintain the old distinction between true and false thirst on the basis of whether a water need or imbalance existed. The reason I have not admitted prandial drinking into the category of behaviors controlled by thirst is that it is clearly a case of what H. Wettendorff (cited in A. V. Wolf, 1958) meant by false thirst, that is, drinking without need for water. But this is really a contradiction, since if it is false it cannot be thirst and must therefore be something else.

If nothing else, I think I have made it clear that drinking can be controlled by factors other than those arising from imbalances in body water. In the interests of simplicity, a state of thirst should be inferred only when drinking follows states of body water imbalance. Drinking which is not controlled by states of body water can be called "nonhomeostatic drinking," and its mechanism can be further specified by the type of nonhomeostatic control involved: taste, oropharyngeal, anticipatory, or schedule-induced.

REFERENCES

Abrams, R., & Hammel, H. T. Cyclic variations in hypothalamic temperature in unanesthetized rats. *American Journal of Physiology,* 1965, **208,** 698–702.

Adolph, E. F. Measurements of water drinking in dogs. *American Journal of Physiology,* 1939, **125,** 75–86.

Adolph, E. F. Thirst and its inhibition in the stomach. *American Journal of Physiology,* 1950, **161,** 374–386.

Adolph, E. F. Regulation of water intake in relation to body water content. In C. F. Code (Ed.), *Handbook of physiology.* Section 6. *Alimentary canal.* Vol. 1. Washington, D. C.: American Physiological Society, 1967. Pp. 163–171.

Adolph, E. F., Barker, J. P., & Hoy, P. A. Multiple factors in thirst. *American Journal of Physiology,* 1954, **178,** 538–562.

Bare, J. K. Specific hunger for sodium chloride in normal and adrenalectomized white rats. *Journal of Comparative and Physiological Psychology,* 1949, **42,** 242–253.

Bellows, R. T. Time factors in water drinking in dogs. *American Journal of Physiology,* 1939, **125,** 87–97.

Blass, E. M., & Chapman, H. W. An evaluation of the contribution of cholinergic mechanism to thirst. *Physiology and Behavior,* 1971, 7, 679–686.

Blass, E. M., & Fitzsimons, J. T. Additivity of effect and interection of a cellular and an extracellular stimulus of drinking. *Journal of Comparative and Physiological Psychology,* 1970, **70,** 200–205.

Borer, K. T. Disappearance of preferences and aversions for sapid solutions in rats ingesting untasted fluids. *Journal of Comparative and Physiological Psychology,* 1968, **65,** 213–221.

Burks, C. D., & Fisher, A. E. Anticholinergic blockade of schedule induced polydipsia. *Physiology and Behavior,* 1970, **5,** 635–640.

Cannon, W. B. Organization for physiological homeostasis. *Physiological Reviews,* 1929, 9, 399–431.

Chapman, H. W. Oropharyngeal determinants of non-regulatory drinking in the rat. Unpublished doctoral dissertation, University of Pennsylvania, 1969.

Cheng, M., Rozin, P., & Teitelbaum, P. Starvation retards development of food and water regulations. *Journal of Comparative and Physiological Psychology,* 1971, 76, 206–218.

Chiang, H., & Wilson, W. Some tests of the diluted-water hypothesis of saline consumption in rats. *Journal of Comparative and Physiological Psychology,* 1963, 56, 660–665.

Chillag, D., & Mendelson, J. Air licking in desalivate rats. *American Zoologist,* 1969, 4, 1059.

Cizek, L. J., & Nocenti, M. R. Relationship between water and food ingestion in the rat. *American Journal of Physiology,* 1965, 208, 615–620.

Epstein, A. N. Water intake without the act of drinking. *Science,* 1960, 131, 497–498.

Epstein, A. N. Feeding without oropharyngeal sensations. In M. R. Kare & O. Maller (Eds.), *The chemical senses and nutrition.* Baltimore: Johns Hopkins Press, 1967. Pp. 263–280. (a)

Epstein, A. N. Oropharyngeal factors in feeding and drinking. In C. F. Code (Ed.), *Handbook of physiology.* Section 6. *Alimentary canal.* Vol. 1. Washington, D. C.: American Physiological Society, 1967. Pp. 197–218. (b)

Epstein, A. N. The lateral hypothalamic syndrome: Its implications for the physiological psychology of hunger and thirst. In E. Stellar & J. M. Sprague (Eds.), *Progress in physiological psychology.* New York: Academic Press, 1971. Pp. 263–317.

Epstein, A. N., Spector, D., Samman, A., & Goldblum, C. Exaggerated prandial drinking in the rat without salivary glands. *Nature,* 1964, 201, 1342–1343.

Epstein, A. N., & Teitelbaum, P. Regulation of food intake in the absence of taste, smell, and other oropharyngeal sensations. *Journal of Comparative and Physiological Psychology,* 1962, 55, 753–759.

Epstein, A. N., & Teitelbaum, P. Severe and persistent deficits in thirst in rats with lateral hypothalamic damage. In M. J. Wayner (Ed.), *Thirst.* New York: Pergamon Press, 1964. Pp. 395–406.

Falk, J. L. The behavioral regulation of water and electrolyte balance. Nebraska Symposium on Motivation, 1961, 9, 1–33.

Falk, J. L. Studies on schedule-induced polydipsia. In M. J. Wayner (Ed.), *Thirst.* New York: Pergamon Press, 1964. Pp. 95–116.

Falk, J. L. Control of schedule-induced polydipsia: Type, size, and spacing of meals. *Journal of Experimental Analysis of Behavior,* 1967, 10, 199–206.

Falk, J. L. Conditions producing psychogenic polydipsia in animals. *Annals of the New York Academy of Sciences,* 1969, 157, 569–593.

Fisher, A. E., & Coury, J. N. Chemical tracing of neural pathways mediating the thirst drive. In M. J. Wayner (Ed.), *Thirst.* New York: Pergamon Press, 1964. Pp. 515–529.

Fitzsimons, J. T. The physiology of thirst: A review of the extraneural aspects of the mechanisms of drinking. In E. Stellar & J. M. Sprague (Eds.), *Progress in physiological psychology.* Vol. 4. New York: Academic Press, 1971. Pp. 119–201.

Fitzimons, J. T., & Le Magnen, J. Eating as a regulatory control of drinking in the rat. *Journal of Comparative and Physiological Psychology,* 1969, 67, 273–283.

Fitzsimons, J. T., & Oatley, K. Additivity of stimuli for drinking in rats. *Journal of Comparative and Physiological Psychology,* 1968, 66, 450–455.

Gregersen, M. I. Studies on regulation of water intake. II: Conditions affecting daily water intake of dogs as registered continuously by a potometer. *American Journal of Physiology,* 1932, 102, 344–349.

Hainsworth, F. R. Evaporative water loss from rats in the heat. *American Journal of Physiology,* 1968, 214, 979–982.

Hainsworth, F. R., & Epstein, A. N. Severe impairment of heat-induced saliva spreading in rats recovered from lateral hypothalamic lesions. *Science,* 1966, 153, 1255–1257.

Hainsworth, F. R., Stricker, E. M., & Epstein, A. N. Water metabolism of rats in the heat: Dehydration and drinking. *American Journal of Physiology,* 1968, 214, 983–989.

Halpern, B. P., & Tapper, D. N. Taste stimuli: Quality coding and time. *Science,* 1971, **171,** 1256–1258.

Holman, G. Intragastric reinforcement effect. *Journal of Comparative and Physiological Psychology,* 1969, **69,** 432–441.

Holmes, J. H., & Montgomery, V. Relation of route of administration and types of fluid to satisfaction of thirst in the dog. *American Journal of Physiology,* 1960, **199,** 907–911.

Jacoby, F., & Leeson, C. R. Postnatal development of the rat submaxillary gland. *Journal of Anatomy,* 1959, **93,** 201–216.

Kakolewski, J. W., & Deaux, E. Initiation of eating as a function of ingestion of hypoosmotic solutions. *American Journal of Physiology,* 1970, **218,** 590–595.

Kissileff, H. R. *Control of water intake in the rat recovered from lateral hypothalamic lesions.* (Doctoral dissertation, University of Pennsylvania) Ann Arbor, Mich.: University Microfilms, 1966, No. 67–7848.

Kissileff, H. R. Aversion for hypertonic saline solution by rats ingesting untasted fluids. In C. Pfaffmann (Ed.), *Olfaction and taste III.* New York: Rockefeller University Press, 1969. Pp. 615. (a)

Kissileff, H. R. Food-associated drinking in the rat. *Journal of Comparative and Physiological Psychology,* 1969, **67,** 284–300. (b)

Kissileff, H. R. Oropharyngeal control of prandial drinking. *Journal of Comparative and Physiological Psychology,* 1969, **67,** 309–319. (c)

Kissileff, H. R. Acquisition of prandial drinking in weanling rats and in rats recovering from lateral hypothalamic lesions. *Journal of Comparative and Physiological Psychology,* 1971, **77,** 97–109.

Kissileff, H. R. Manipulation of the oral and gastric environments. In R. D. Myers (Ed.), *Methods in psychobiology.* Vol. 2. New York: Academic Press, 1972, in press.

Kissileff, H. R., & Epstein, A. N. Exaggerated prandial drinking in the recovered lateral rat without saliva. *Journal of Comparative and Physiological Psychology,* 1969, **67,** 301–308.

Lashley, K. S. An experimental analysis of instinctive behavior. *Psychological Review,* 1938, **45,** 445–471.

Le Magnen, J., & Tallon, S. La périodicité spontanée de la prise d'aliments ad libitum du rat blanc. *Journal de Physiologie (Paris),* 1966, **58,** 323–349.

Lepkovsky, S., Furuta, E. M., Sharon, I. M., & Snapir, N. Thirst and behavior in adipsic chickens with hypothalamic lesions before and after intravenous injections of hypertonic sodium chloride solutions. *Physiology and Behavior,* 1971, **6,** 477–480.

McCleary, R. A. Taste: Post-ingestion factors in specific hunger theory. *Journal of Comparative and Physiological Psychology,* 1953, **46,** 411–421.

McFarland, D. J. Hunger, thirst, and displacement pecking in the Barbary dove. *Animal Behavior,* 1965, **13,** 293–300.

Maclean, P. D. Psychosomatic disease and the "visceral brain": Recent developments bearing on the Papez theory of emotion. *Psychosomatic Medicine,* 1949, **11,** 338–353.

Mendelson, J., & Chillag, D. Tongue cooling: A new reward for thirsty rodents. *Science,* 1970, **170,** 1418–1421.

Mendelson, J., Zec, R., & Chillag, D. Effects of desalivation on drinking and air licking induced by water deprivation and hypertonic saline injections. *Journal of Comparative and Physiological Psychology,* 1972, **80,** 30–42.

Miller, N. E. Behavioral and physiological techniques: Rationale and experimental designs for combining their use. In C. F. Code (Ed.), *Handbook of physiology.* Section 6. *Alimentary canal.* Vol. 1. Washington, D. C.: American Physiological Society, 1967. Pp. 51–61.

Miller, N. E., Sampliner, R. I., & Woodrow, P. Thirst reducing effects of water by stomach fistula vs. water by mouth measured by both a consummatory and an instrumental response. *Journal of Comparative and Physiological Psychology,* 1957, **50,** 1–5.

Miller, N. E., & Stevenson, S. S. Agitated behavior of rats during experimental extinction and a curve for spontaneous recovery. *Journal of Comparative Psychology,* 1936, **21**, 205–231.

Mook, D. G. Oral and post-ingestional determinants of the intake of various solutions in rats with esophageal fistulas. *Journal of Comparative and Physiological Psychology,* 1963, **56**, 645–659.

Mook, D. G. Some determinants of preference and aversion in the rat. *Annals of the New York Academy of Sciences,* 1969, **157**, 1158–1175.

Mook, D. G., & Kozub, F. J. Control of sodium chloride intake in the nondeprived rat. *Journal of Comparative and Physiological Psychology,* 1968, **66**, 105–109.

Morgan, C. T. *Physiological psychology.* (1st. ed.) New York: McGraw-Hill, 1943.

Morrison, R. Behavioral response patterns to salt stimuli in the rat. *Canadian Journal of Psychology/Revue Canadienne de Psychologie,* 1967, **21**, 141–152.

Novin, D. The relation between electrical conductivity of brain tissue and thirst in the rat. *Journal of Comparative and Physiological Psychology.,* 1962, **55**, 145.

Oatley, K. Drinking in response to salt injections at different times of day. *Psychonomic Science,* 1967, **9**, 439–440.

Oatley, K. Dissociation of the circadian drinking pattern from eating. *Nature,* 1971, **229**, 494–496.

Oatley, K., & Dickinson, A. Air drinking and the measurement of thirst. *Animal Behavior,* 1970, **18**, 259–265.

Oatley, K., & Toates, F. M. The passage of food through the gut of rats and its uptake of fluid. *Psychonomic Science,* 1969, **16**, 225–226.

Pfaffmann, C. The pleasures of sensation. *Psychological Review,* 1960, **67**, 253–268.

Pfaffmann, C. Taste preference and reinforcement. In J. Tapp (Ed.), *Reinforcement and Behavior.* New York: Academic Press, 1969. Pp. 215–241.

Revusky, S. H., & Garcia, J. Learned associations over long delays. In C. H. Bower & J. T. Spence (Eds.), *The psychology of learning and motivation: Advances in research and theory IV.* New York: Academic Press, 1970.

Richter, C. P. A behavioristic study of activity of the rat. *Comparative Psychological Monographs,* 1922, **1**(2).

Richter, C. P. Increased salt appetite in adrenalectomized rats. *American Journal of Physiology,* 1936, **115**, 155–161.

Richter, C. P. Total self-regulatory functions. *Harvey Lectures,* 1942, **38**, 63–101.

Ritter, R. C., & Epstein, A. N. Groomed saliva: A major component of evaporative water loss in the rat. *American Zoologist,* 1972, **12**(403), xxxiii.

Rozin, P., & Kalat, J. W. Specific hungers and poison avoidance as adaptive specialization of learning. *Psychological Review.* 1971, **78**, 459–480.

Schneyer, C. A., & Schneyer, L. H. Secretion by salivary glands deficient in acini. *American Journal of Physiology,* 1961, **201**, 939–942.

Siegel, P. S., & Stuckey, H. L. The diurnal course of water and food intake in the normal mature rat. *Journal of Comparative and Physiological Psychology,* 1947, **40**, 365–370.

Snowdon, C. T. Motivation, regulation, and the control of meal parameters with oral and intragastric feeding. *Journal of Comparative and Physiological Psychology,* 1969, **69**, 91–100.

Stein, L. Excessive drinking in the rat: Superstition or thirst? *Journal of Comparative and Physiological Psychology,* 1964, **58**, 237–242.

Stellar, E. The physiology of motivation. *Psychological Review,* 1954, **61**, 5–22.

Stellar, E., Hyman, R., & Samet, S. Gastric factors controlling water and salt-solution drinking. *Journal of Comparative and Physiological Psychology,* 1954, **47**, 220–226.

Stricker, E. M., & Adair, E. R. Body fluid balance, taste, and post-prandial factors in schedule-induced polydipsia. *Journal of Comparative and Physiological Psychology,* 1966, **62**, 449–454.

Strominger, J. F. The relation between water intake and food intake in normal rats and rats with hypothalamic hyperphagia. *Yale Journal of Biology and Medicine,* 1947, **49,** 279–288.

Teague, R. S., & Ranson, S. W. The role of the anterior hypothalamus in temperature regulation. *American Journal of Physiology,* 1936, **117,** 562–570.

Teitelbaum, P. The use of operant methods in the assessment and control of motivational states. In W. K. Honig (Ed.), *Operant behavior: Areas of research and application.* New York: Meredith, 1966. Pp. 565–608.

Teitelbaum, P., Cheng, M., & Rozin, P. Development of feeding parallels its recovery after lateral hypothalamic damage. *Journal of Comparative and Physiological Psychology,* 1969, **67,** 430–441. (a)

Teitelbaum, P., Cheng, M., & Rozin, P. Stages of recovery and development of lateral hypothalamic control of food and water intake. *Annals of the New York Academy of Sciences,* 1969, **157,** 849–860. (b)

Teitelbaum, P., & Epstein, A. N. The lateral hypothalamic syndrome: Recovery of feeding and drinking after lateral hypothalamic lesions. *Psychological Review,* 1962, **69,** 74–90.

Tepperman, J., & Tepperman, W. M. Adaptive hyperlipogenesis – late 1964 model. *Annals of the New York Academy of Sciences,* 1965, **131,** 404–411.

Vance, W. B. Observations on the role of salivary secretion in the regulation of food and fluid intake in the white rat. *Psychological Monographs,* 1965, **79**(5, Whole No. 598).

Verplanck, W. S., & Hayes, J. R. Eating and drinking as a function of maintenance schedule. *Journal of Comparative and Physiological Psychology,* 1953, **46,** 327–333.

Wang, S. C., & Ngai, S. H. General organization of central respiratory mechanisms. In W. O. Fenn & H. Rahn (Eds.), *Handbook of physiology.* Section 3. *Respiration.* Vol. 1. Washington, D.C.: American Physiological Society, 1964. Pp. 487–505.

Wayner, M. J. (Ed.) *Thirst.* New York: Pergamon Press, 1964.

Williams, D. R., & Teitelbaum, P. Control of drinking behavior by means of an operant conditioning technique. *Science,* 1956, **124,** 1294.

Wolf, A. V. *Thirst, physiology of the urge to drink and problems of water lack.* Springfield, Ill.: Charles C. Thomas, 1958.

Wolf, G. Innate mechanisms for regulation of sodium intake. In C. Pfaffmann (Ed.), *Olfaction and taste III.* New York: Rockefeller University Press, 1969. Pp. 548–553.

Young, P. T. The role of hedonic processes in motivation. *Nebraska Symposium on Motivation,* 1955, **3,** 193–238.

Young, P. T. Palatability: The hedonic response to foodstuffs. In C. F. Code (Ed.), *Handbook of physiology.* Section 6. *Alimentary Canal.* Vol. 1. Washington, D. C.: American Physiology Society, 1967. Pp. 353–366.

Young, P. T., & Falk, J. L. The relative acceptability of sodium chloride as a function of concentration and water need. *Journal of Comparative and Physiological Psychology,* 1956, **49,** 569–575.

Young, P. T., & Greene, J. T. Quantity of food ingested as a measure of relative acceptability. *Journal of Comparative and Physiological Psychology,* 1953, **46,** 288–294.

Young, P. T., & Richey, H. W. Diurnal drinking patterns in the rat. *Journal of Comparative and Physiological Psychology,* 1952, **45,** 80–89.

Zucker, I. Light-dark rhythms in rat eating and drinking behavior. *Physiology and Behavior,* 1970, **6,** 115–126.

5
SIMULATION AND
THEORY OF THIRST

Keith Oatley[1]
University of Sussex

The aim of brain research is to be able to explain behavior and mental processes in terms of the workings of the nervous system. Mechanisms of thirst have been, and continue to be, of interest because of the role our grasp of them has in this larger scheme. It is therefore germane to relate work that has taken place in the growth of our knowledge about thirst to more general understandings of how the brain produces behavior, to the issues of how purposeful motivation is controlled as well as to the specific topic of how an animal controls its water balance. Also, since our understandings of the brain are theories about how its mechanisms work, I will concentrate upon formal (or formalizable) accounts, and suggest that adequate theories of thirst or indeed any other behavior or mental process can conveniently be expressed in terms of a computer simulation or some equivalent system which combines both the rigor and the flexibility of the computer program.

SIMULATION AS THEORY IN BRAIN RESEARCH

The human brain is said to contain 10^{10} to 10^{11} neurones, each of which may make some 10^3 connections. So far as our present understanding of

[1] This paper was written while I was visiting The Department of Psychology, University of Toronto, and I am grateful to Dr. G. E. Macdonald and the members of that department for their hospitality. Much of the experimental and computational work was carried out under grants from the Medical Research Council and Science Research Council, and I am particularly indebted to Dr. F. M. Toates, who collaborated in this work and commented on the manuscript. I am also grateful to Dr. D. A. Booth, who also made helpful criticisms of the manuscript.

neurophysiology is correct, the capacities of these neurones are of transmission of information along specific axons, the performance of operations similar to addition (summed excitation) and subtraction (summed inhibition) on postsynaptic membranes, and multiplicative operations in processes such as presynaptic inhibition. It is not unreasonable to suppose that the whole of behavior can be based on such relatively simple operations, since computer behavior comparable to that of people, e.g., understanding and answering questions in English (Winograd, 1971, 1972), can be based on the concatenation of logical operations which, although different in detail from those of the brain, are just as simple. Complex patterns of behavior are therefore shaped by the pattern and sequence of interconnections of basic elements, not so much by properties of these elements as such.

The notion that behavior is dependent upon rather simple logical switching operations in the brain was, of course, introduced by Descartes (e.g., 1664). He gave the first account of a mechanism that could actually produce behavior, and in its negligibly altered modern version, stimulus-response theory, the idea still continues. Descartes described behavior as being produced by stimuli affecting receptor surfaces in such a way as to pull on little strings. These strings ran inside tubular nerves to the brain, where they opened valves to allow fluid which had been pumped up by the heart into ventricular reservoirs to run through the tubular nerves and inflate muscles appropriate for responding to the stimulus. A particularly nice touch is the way in which the fluid functions both hydraulically to produce movement and as a lubricant for the strings which constitute the afferent nerves.

Hunger and thirst are among the events giving rise to appropriate behavior that Descartes (1649) mentions as being accounted for by his scheme. The reflex idea has turned out to be hopelessly inadequate as a general explanation, and this is amply demonstrated by perceptual and motor equivalence (e.g., Lashley, 1942) and indeed by many other facts. But the idea that the basic processes of the brain are relatively simple logical operations we cannot replace. We should not replace the demonstration implicit in Descartes' arguments that a theory of how the brain works should be capable of being expressed as a model (he used as a model the mechanism of hydraulically operated garden statues). Nor should we neglect the implication that such models should actually work under their own steam, themselves producing something corresponding to behavior.

One can usefully set up two criteria for the acceptability of theories of brain mechanisms: (a) a proposed model must, by means of its own workings (or manipulation of formally specified rules) and without the substitution of human judgment for such processes, be able to produce something corresponding to behavior, and (b) the model must actually use and exhibit the principles that make behavior possible. Many proposals, including those illustrated with arrows and boxes labeled "short-term memory," "satiety center," or suchlike, fail to meet the first criterion. They may exhibit a ground plan for the production of some aspect of behavior, but they do not always exactly specify either what information flows along an arrow or what operation a box performs upon it. Since the operations of the components are not specified (often for the good reason that they are not yet specifiable), the model cannot by means of its own operation produce any output at all, let alone behavior. It is only by people allowing their mental processes to substitute for mechanism in the propositions of the model that such accounts are of value. In psychology it is sometimes precisely the nature of these mental processes that the model is supposed to explain. For example, if a psychological model contained a box marked "analyze," this could not enable the model actually to work on its own, because it would not relate to any exact specification of the process of analyzing. Block diagrams are only adequate theories if each block is specified in terms of precise rules for producing its output from its input.

Clearly Descartes' model of how the brain works satisfies this first criterion: stimulus-response machines can interact with the environment and produce behavior. However, except possibly for explaining certain behavior in insects, such as the way moths avoid bats by detecting their ultrasonic squeaks and emitting one of two response patterns according to their intensity (Roeder, 1964), and perhaps certain behavior patterns in higher animals controlled by closely specified sign stimuli (Tinbergen, 1951), it is not clear that the stimulus-response formulation goes very far. It often fails to meet the second criterion. For instance, if I said that I had constructed a computer model to explain the homeostatic control of drinking, and this turned out to be a program in which I had stored a set of drinking curves determined from experiments where rats had been deprived of water for various intervals and the computer was programmed to select the appropriate recorded output in response to inputs like "24 hours deprivation," nobody would be very impressed. Though the mechanism itself would produce behavior under its own steam, it would utilize no principle that makes that kind of behavior possible in animals. Another slightly more subtle example is the kind of learning curve that can be produced from an equation which represents the drawing of balls from an urn. Though curves which correspond to the probability of response may be produced, it is not clear what corresponds to anything going on inside a rat, and few people would assert that drawing balls from an urn is a learning process. Rather the changing probability of some aspect of behavior when an animal learns, presumably derives from his acquisition of successively more appropriate representations of what his environment is like. The probability of a response changes as a consequence, but if we are to understand that behavior, we must understand what the animal's representations of the world might be like.

This brings us to the core of the problem. Craik (1943) argued that in order to explain behavior, we must suppose that the brain constructs models of the world, i.e., represents those aspects of the environment which are relevant to success in some ecological niche or in reaching some goal. This ability of the brain to simulate the workings of the environment allows it to predict and control the outcome of its own actions and external events. Craik's hypothesis also suggests one avenue of relevant research in psychology: first determine which aspects of the environment are relevant to some piece of behavior, then produce a formal representation or simulation of how those aspects of the environment are interrelated. Because the brain too has to model these same features of the environment, the artificial simulation can be regarded as a possible competence model of what the brain must know to produce the given behavior. One can then determine empirically how far the artificial simulation is a good theory of how the brain operates in this instance, by comparing the behavior which it can generate with that of the real animal.

One reason why the idea of models, simulations, or representations is such a powerful one is that, as well as evidently being necessary for behavior, simulation is also the forte of the computer. What makes simulation possible is the fact that underlying many physical events which are quite different in superficial form, there are basic principles which are the same. Familiar examples of this are the way a map represents a geographical area, by a mixture of semiarbitrary symbolism and the fact that distance and direction are common to both, or the way electric circuits in which the principal components are capacitors, resistors, and inductors can represent mechanical systems made up of masses, dashpots, and springs. Both the electrical and mechanical components exhibit the same processes of storage and dissipation of energy and for this reason obey similar differential equations, which are of course yet other representations. More apposite in this context is the fact that logical processes can be representational, by making the arguments of logical operators correspond to the existence of defined states, and the operators themselves correspond to relationships between these states. The logical operations can be hydraulic, as in Descartes' scheme, optical, mechanical, electromechanical, electronic, or presumably, electrochemical as in the brain. It is precisely the fact that informational processes are independent of their embodiment that makes simulation of the environment possible, and it makes our simulation of the brain not only possible, but appropriate to one of the brain's own principal functions.

The computer is therefore a useful vehicle for theories of the brain not just because it works on the basis of rather simple logical operations, nor only because it is a mechanism that can produce behavior. Nor is it useful just because the computer is the only machine we have with the versatility and complexity to act as a theory of the vastly versatile and complex brain. It is useful principally because by means of it we can grapple with the same problems of representation that the brain does. By having at least two examples of how some behavior is produced (say a real brain and a computer), we may more easily identify common principles which make the behavior possible. This identification of course would be our individual understanding of the process—yet another representation.

THIRST AND THEORIES OF MOTIVATION

It was not before the principles underlying homeostasis were recognized that thirst motivation began to be understood. Clearly an animal motivated by thirst behaves purposefully. His behavior is directed to certain goals, he acts in a certain way until he finds water and then drinks some appropriate quantity of it. Without the notion of an internal representation many of the reasons for this would remain obscure, not just in detail but in principle, and the problem of purpose would remain logically insoluble. The argument against teleology used to run: purpose implies a state in the future affecting events in the present, but causality requires precisely the opposite temporal sequence. Therefore either purposeful behavior is produced without causation, or if it is produced causally then it is not really purposeful. The set of nonsense resulting from this syllogism (which includes assertions of some philosophers that a priori it is impossible to give a physical account of mental processes) is avoided by the simple notion that the brain can model the environment. If the brain can represent the world, it can represent an ideal state of the world which does not at present exist. It can compare that representation with the present state and use the difference to drive behavior towards a state where the difference no longer exists. This is what we mean by purposefulness, and the mechanism of a feedback control system in a straightforward and physical way demonstrates the principle that makes it possible. Dry-mouth theories of thirst depended implicitly on this notion, with the feedback of water reaching the mouth to remove the stimulus. However the idea was empirically unsound, as well as failing explicitly to illuminate the nature of brain mechanisms producing motivated behavior. The formulation of Grindley (1927), who supposed that a special group of neurones activated by need states was responsible for energizing behavior, and of Hull (1951), who similarly hypothesized drive as a neural state dependent on physiological inbalances, were altogether clearer. Furthermore, such ideas meshed well with the notion of central receptors of fluid inbalance which was introduced by Gilman's (1937) discovery of drinking dependent on effective osmotic pressure and hence cellular shrinkage. Subsequently the hypothesis that motivated behavior is based on homeostasis has been taken up by many authors, e.g., Hebb (1955) and Deutsch (1960). What makes such theories potentially capable of explaining motivation (although not necessarily correct) is the idea of a neural representation of an aspect of the internal environment working within the structure of a feedback control system. Deutsch illustrates this clearly (see Figure 1*a*). What is involved in thirst is a nonadapting receptor sensitive to some aspect of body fluid change. Most receptors adapt: they respond to the difference between what is now and what just has been, i.e., to a rate of change. Nonadapting receptors must compare the present state with some internal standard or representation. The operation therefore corresponds closely to the comparison of an aspect of the controlled environment with a reference value or set point (see Figure 1*b*). Furthermore, Fitzsimons (1963) has shown that osmoreceptors controlling drinking do not adapt.

Comparison of a body fluid parameter with a reference value in a feedback system is most appropriately expressed in terms of a control model, since control theory not only gives an understanding of how regulation is achieved,

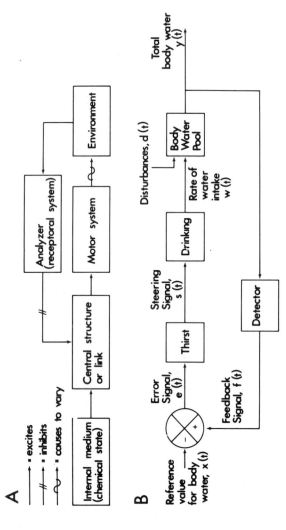

FIG. 1. (a) Deutsch's (1960) general model of a mechanism of need, and (b) a homeostat with a similar structure for regulating drinking. (Used by permission of University of Chicago Press.)

but also gives a means for simulation of actual systems. With the idea of a control system one can not only understand homeostasis but also give the theory a formal basis in, for instance, a computer program. This formalization allows the criteria (outlined above) of producing behavior and embodying necessary principles to be met, and stimulates a useful interplay between theory and empirical findings.

SIMULATION OF BODY FLUID HOMEOSTASIS

A model of thirst and water balance was proposed by Oatley (1967a) and simulated on a digital computer by Toates and Oatley (1970). The simulation (which is specifically of the water balance system of the rat) embodies the principles necessary for homeostasis. It also captures many of the other issues that have been important in thirst (see elsewhere in this volume, and particularly the chapters by Blass, Fitzsimons, and Stricker). The simulation is indeed a quantitative understanding of dynamic physiological processes which contribute to thirst.

Within this particular simulation is embodied the notion of multiple factors in thirst (cf. Adolph, Barker, & Hoy, 1954; Stellar, 1954), though in the simulation we have had to state very precisely the role and modes of interaction of each factor. The model contains both a simulation of osmotic exchange in the body fluids, and the brain's measurement of osmolality by comparison of cellular size with an idealized representation. It also displays measurement of hypovolemia (Fitzsimons, 1961a) and the addition of osmotic and hypovolemic stimuli (Oatley, 1964; Fitzsimons & Oatley, 1968; Fitzsimons, 1969) which represents the fact that water contained in two compartments is exchanged quantitatively between them. Further, it contains an account of relevant renal and alimentary processes.

To explain how our understanding of physiological processes is simulated, I will consider part of the program that deals with osmotic passage of water across the cell membranes. Referring to Figure 2 (which illustrates a small part of the simulation by Toates & Oatley, 1970), one sees in the diagram arrows which represent signals, round symbols with crosses in them which represent addition according to the signs given, and a number of boxes which represent other operations on incoming signals. Figure 2 is in the formal notation of block diagrams and transfer functions. Such diagrams are helpful for the purposes of explanation, since as well as being formal representations, they display the layout of the system in an intuitively appealing way. The actual working simulation, however, is a digital computer program (available from the authors on request).

In Figure 2 the top left-hand summing symbol adds together rates of flow of water into and out of the extracellular compartment (losses in this model are simply negative rates of flow). The output from the summing unit is the net flow, and this signal points to a box containing the transfer function $1/s$, which is Laplace notation for the mathematical operation of integration. Now

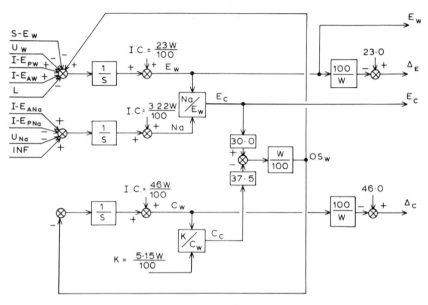

FIG. 2. Diagram illustrating the part of the simulation by Toates & Oatley (1970) dealing with exchanges of water between the body fluid compartments. (Used by permission of Pergamon Press Ltd.)

integration of a rate of flow produces a volume, so the output of that box is the net total gain or loss of extracellular water. To this is added the volume of extracellular water at the beginning of the run, known as an initial condition (I.C.) which in this case is taken to be *23 ml* for each 100 grams body weight. (This is taken to approximate Fitzsimons' [1961b] measurements where he found total body water of rats to be 69 ml per 100 grams body weight and inulin space to be about one third of that value.) The signal at this point represents extracellular water at any time. Immediately below the calculation of extracellular water in the diagram are similar operations for extracellular sodium. Dividing the quantity of sodium by the volume of water (the operation performed by the box marked Na/E_w) gives the extracellular sodium concentration (E_c) and similar operations shown below in Figure 2 calculate the cellular concentration of potassium (C_c).

Our physiological understanding of osmotic exchange is that it is dependent on the osmotic gradient. This means that the rate of flow of water across cell membranes is proportional to the osmotic concentration difference. Thus in the simulation the signals for sodium and potassium concentrations are multiplied by constants (30.0 and 37.5) whose ratio converts the chemical concentrations of the principal cations into effective osmotic concentrations, and one signal is subtracted from the other to give the gradient. This results in a signal proportional to the osmotic concentration difference, which after multiplication by a factor $W/100$ to scale it for the rat's weight, gives the rate of flow to be added to one compartment and, of course, subtracted from the other. The

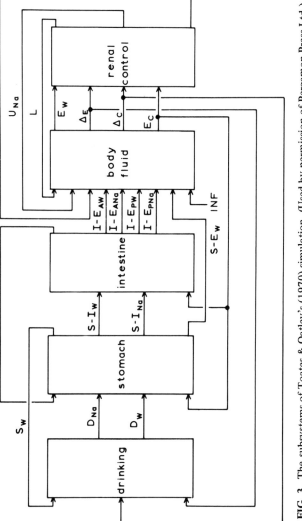

FIG. 3. The subsystems of Toates & Oatley's (1970) simulation. (Used by permission of Pergamon Press Ltd.)

absolute values of the constants (30.0 and 37.5) give the value of the proportionality of osmotic flow to concentration difference, and this value was fitted carefully to published data for osmotic exchange rates across the cellular membrane. The operations of plasma volume receptors and osmoreceptors are shown as comparisons with ideal extracellular and cellular volumes made by summing units on the right of Figure 2.

Two points may need emphasizing: First, what is expressed in the simulation is precisely and only what we understand about the physiological working of the system. What is not understood, i.e., cannot be expressed as a very precise hypothesis, cannot go in. Secondly, parameter values are fitted only to component processes in the system, and are thereafter not altered. The relationships of the five subsystems of the model are shown in Figure 3, and these subsystems are described in detail elsewhere.

Because the simulation represents a physiological understanding and has no arbitrarily adjustable parameters, it is not an exercise in curve fitting, or a network of insubstantial intervening variables. It displays the logical consequences of our understanding of component processes arranged in a particular structure. Unaided, the human brain is not good at comprehending the operation of even such a relatively simple interacting dynamic system as the body fluids.

The simulation has been tested for overall responses (e.g., drinking, urinary output, etc.) in a number of ways. Figure 4 shows responses of computer and rat for an intravenous injection of sodium chloride. We have also tested other standard manipulations of thirst such as deprivation of water and extracellular depletion, as well as less standard ones such as sinusoidally varying rates of salt

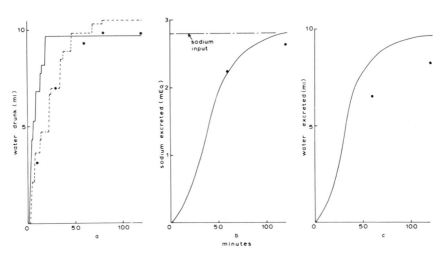

FIG. 4. Drinking and urinary responses of simulation and rat to an intravenous injection of NaCl: (——— computer simulation; - - - typical experimental result; ● mean experimental result. (From Toates & Oatley, 1970. Used by permission of Pergamon Press Ltd.)

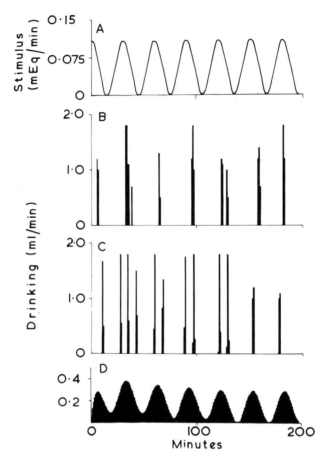

FIG. 5. Drinking responses of computer and rat to a sinusoidally varying rate of infusion of NaCl: *A*, input rate; *B*, drinking rate of a typical rat; *C*, simulated drinking rate; *D*, simulation without threshold at twice the scale. (From Oatley & Toates, 1971. Used by permission of Macmillan (Journals) Ltd.)

infusion (Oatley & Toates, 1971; see Figure 5). Mismatches between data from rats and the output from the computer are construed not as an invitation to twiddle parameters, but as indications of something not included or not understood. For instance, the fact that in Figure 5 the computer's drinking response to each cycle of the input infusion is less bunched than that of the rat indicates an omission. This seems likely to be a positive feedback incentive process, keeping the rat's attention on drinking once he has started, and such processes have been deduced by McFarland & McFarland (1968) for drinking in doves, by Le Magnen (1968) for feeding in rats, and by Wiepkema (1971) for feeding in mice. The idea should also be compared with Snowdon's (1969) suggestion that oropharyngeal sensations facilitate feeding and with Kissileff's (this volume) that they facilitate drinking. For drinking in rats however, we do not have sufficient data to insert a quantitatively appropriate component in our model until some further experiments have been completed.

The model has also been used to investigate the results of nephrectomy, intragastric infusions, sham drinking, and suchlike (K. Oatley & F. M. Toates, in preparation). Bloodless operations of this type are easy to do on the computer, and since the model is a formal expression of our understanding, it acts as a powerful tool in disclosing gaps in our knowledge, suggesting experiments, sharpening up hypotheses, and even resolving disputes in the literature. For instance, we have used it to investigate Corbit's (1969) suggestion that there is no threshold for osmotic drinking. We simply removed the threshold from the model. The drinking pattern that the computer produced in response to sinusoidal infusions of salt was entirely uncharacteristic of any rat (see Oatley & Toates, 1971; and the bottom record of Figure 5). This strongly suggests that in the undisturbed rat there is a threshold, and that Corbit's (1969) result can be explained by supposing that the act of picking the rat up and injecting it can initiate drinking. (We have observed in experiments with continuous recording of ad-lib intake that even slightly disturbing a rat usually initiated a drink and sometimes a meal.) With the type of threshold with hysteresis that we postulate (Toates & Oatley, 1970), one can suppose that once drinking has started for any reason (including disturbance), the rat continues to drink until it reaches zero deficit. The amount consumed might reflect even such small changes in body fluids as were used by Corbit. The concept of a thirst threshold here differs from the notion of a threshold in psychophysics, where it represents the problem of detecting signal from noise. The functions for thirst thresholds do not show characteristics of typical psychophysical judgments, and in any case the threshold in thirst probably serves the quite different function of being part of the system that allows the animal to divide its time among incompatible activities.

The structure of the basic control system of drinking can best be seen in an informal diagram such as Figure 6, where the relationships of the components of the system are made clear, as are the processes of comparison of fluid volumes with internalized standards. Figure 7 displays in the formal notation of block diagrams the part of the system representing neural operations on body fluid measurements and feedback signals. From these two diagrams (Figures 6 and 7) another aspect of the brain's ability to make and deploy models emerges. In a simple control system the representation held in the brain allows comparison with a feedback signal, and this enables purposive behavior characteristic of a regulator to be produced. The significance of the short-term feedback loops is that the role of representations must be extended to make behavior not simply purposeful but appropriate. The short-term feedback signals from mouth and throat allow the brain to subtract from the measured water deficit a quantity proportional to the amount of water entering the mouth and filling the stomach, thus bridging the time delay of absorption from the gut. These signals produce a satiety which anticipates restoration of the deficit that initiated thirst. However,

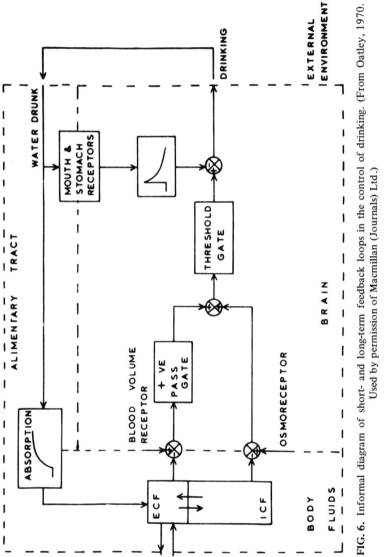

FIG. 6. Informal diagram of short- and long-term feedback loops in the control of drinking. (From Oatley, 1970. Used by permission of Macmillan (Journals) Ltd.)

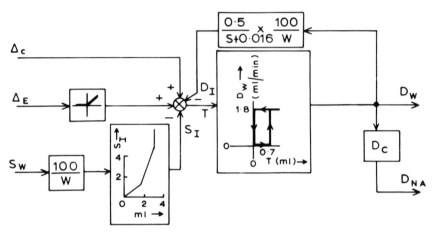

FIG. 7. Diagram illustrating the part of the simulation of Toates & Oatley (1970) dealing with drinking. (Used by permission of Pergamon Press Ltd.)

for this short-term feedback to work it would be no good merely subtracting a quantity proportional to the amount of water swallowed. In the case of feedback from mouth and throat at least, the signals have to be operated upon by a process which reflects the time course of absorption. So if absorption from the gut is roughly exponential, then short-term satiety signals need to decay exponentially with the same time constant. (This is shown diagramatically in Figure 6, and in Laplace notation as a transfer function for mouth and throat signals in Figure 7; stomach distension signals will undergo decay in any case.) At any time, the sum of preabsorptive and absorptive consequences will reflect the amount drunk in a given bout. Thus the significance of the finding that when animals sham-drink they achieve only temporary satiety (e.g., Bellows, 1939) is that a temporary effect is just what is needed to bridge absorptive delay, and that the shape of the decay function in the effect of mouth and throat signals is achieved by a presumably neural process which models the time course of absorption.

NONHOMEOSTATIC PROCESSES

Essential though formal expression of homeostatic processes in thirst is, it still does not go far enough, because as Falk (1961) pointed out, not all drinking can be explained by homeostatic principles. Schedule-induced polydipsia in which hungry rats receiving small quantities of food at intervals longer than they leave when eating freely still has no completely satisfactory explanation. Probably the behavior is overdetermined. Drinking during starvation seems to be released from its normal tight control (Oatley & Tonge, 1969), and dryness of the mouth, drinking becoming superstitiously linked to presentation of food, and frustration-induced displacement activity may all be involved. An indication of the role of displacement is that rats trained without water to press a bar for food pellets on a continuously reinforced schedule drank significantly more when water was presented in extinction, than controls who were not trained to press (Panksepp, Toates, & Oatley, 1972). The existence of such behavior patterns, clearly motivated, but equally clearly nonhomeostatic, is certainly a challenge; but there are yet other types of nonhomeostatic drinking behavior, and these may be more revealing of general principles at the present stage.

Consider, for instance, the timing of water drunk with ad-lib meals. On the basis of experiments in which the normal diet of rats was changed to one requiring a larger amount of water to be drunk with it, Fitzsimons and Le Magnen (1969) argued that learning plays a role in the timing of food-associated drinking. Though on the switch to the new diet total water intake adjusted almost immediately, not until 2 to 3 days later did meal-associated drinking return to its normal, apparently anticipatory, temporal relationship with meals. Probably this is another example of a specialized mechanism of alimentary learning. Garcia and Ervin (1968), for example, have shown the existence of a special mode of associating tastes and smells of consumed substances with their delayed absorptive consequences. One attractive explanation, though not the only one possible (see Revusky & Garcia, 1970), is that learning in part involves the appreciation of causal relationships in the environment. In learning about the outside world, events closely contiguous in time are likely to define the set of most important causal connections. Hence our competence model for that kind of learning copes only with events in close temporal contiguity. For things eaten and drunk, however, causality takes longer, and this may be reflected in a special mechanism which represents this delay in alimentary causal relationships in order to allow associations to be made over long intervals. Again, the problem can be attacked by supposing that the brain in some sense represents or models processes outside the brain which are of importance to behavior, and in the case of drinking this results in being able to anticipate deficits. The idea that special learning mechanisms adjust the timing (and perhaps the quantity) of drinking is as yet largely uninvestigated, but it is now clear that specialized learning mechanisms, reflecting powerful innate determinants of what can be learned and how certain events are construed, are at work in many types of behavior (e.g., see Shettleworth, 1971, for an excellent review). Investigation of thirst may have an important place in understanding how innate competence models for representing processes in the world constrain what is learned.

In this well-adjusted temporal relationship between ad-lib drinking and eating, it is clear that although anticipation serves the purposes of integrated homeostasis, a mechanism that programs drinking to occur before the onset of a water deficit cannot be accounted for in terms of a simple homeostatic regulator of the kind indicated in Figure 1b or Figure 6. There are in fact several other aspects of drinking that cannot be accounted for by homeostasis (see Kissileff, this volume). But even apart from empirical findings that some drinking which serves purposes of regulation, as well as all the drinking which does not, occurs other than as a response to deficits, there is another clear reason for the shortcoming. In representing only a single aspect of the environment, a homeostat can only account qualitatively for a single binary decision. This is all right for deciding whether to drink or not, but both Hull (1951) and Deutsch (1960) assume that before an animal learns anything, a homeostat is also sufficient to account for appetitive activity. Deutsch rather gives the game away (see Figure 1) by specifying that a deficit produces the operation "causes to vary," but the system cannot specify what the variations are. The idea that this problem can be circumvented by supposing that animals emit responses randomly until reinforced is contradicted by a great deal of ethological evidence (e.g., see Tinbergen, 1951; Lorenz, 1969). Typically, animals pursue well-defined species-specific strategies appropriate to their ecological problems (Oatley, 1970). In other words, appetitive behavior involves choice among more than two alternatives, and it cannot be accounted for by the degrees of freedom allowed by a mechanism that controls with respect to a single aspect of the environment.

Rather we have to extend the idea of a representation of the world beyond its role as part of a feedback system detecting deficit, to that of a model of the characteristics of the environment which is predicative and embedded, as it were, in a structure of feed-forward. The knowledge an animal has of the real world needs to be organized within a model in the brain which informs the addressing of the world. One of the major problems of psychology is how such representations of the world operate and how learning improves them. Although we understand more than we did, we are not very far ahead with being able to specify what an animal's representations are like. There is, however, one example of a small aspect of the animal's models of its world that we are beginning to understand, and that concerns the topic of circadian rhythms.

CIRCADIAN RHYTHMS

Animals typically exhibit circadian rhythms of physiological and behavioral processes, and these are part of a genetically determined strategy fitting the animals to their particular ecological niche. Thus an animal which depends heavily on photopic vision will operate well in daylight and be disadvantaged at night. Its motivational mechanisms have to suit this fact, and the alternating sequence of sleeping and waking exhibits just such a fit. However, it is no good having a mechanism which simply detects light in order to initiate and maintain the active phase. An animal sleeping in a dark hole would never know that day had come. Instead the animal needs a model of the rotation of the earth, or perhaps more prosaically, a working model of the alternation of light and darkness which itself exhibits daily oscillations and will keep in time with the rotation of the earth to predict day and night. This is precisely the role of mechanisms giving rise to circadian rhythms, and incidently also of artificial clocks. The characteristics of ad-lib drinking in rats provide a very good example of such a rhythm. Rats subjected to a 12 hour light–12 hour dark schedule typically take about 80% of their total water intake at night. (The occasional rat may take as much as 100% at night.) The rhythm continues under conditions of constant darkness, though it drifts out of phase with the solar day, indicating that lighting is the major synchronizing signal. With phase shifts of the lighting conditions, for instance, reversal of day and night, the phase of the drinking rhythm shifts over a period of a week or 10 days to become resynchronized (K. Oatley & L. Hoad, in preparation).

One might imagine, and there is strong suggestive evidence (Oatley, 1967b), that the circadian drinking rhythm can be accounted for on homeostatic grounds by being linked with other variables such as eating, urinary excretion, sleep, etc., which exhibit rhythmicity. Apparently also, the time of day as such does not affect the rat's drinking response to an osmotic stimulus (Oatley, 1967c). On closer examination it turns out not to be the case that the drinking is only dependent on other interacting systems. For instance, Fitzsimons (1971) showed the rhythm of drinking in rats to· continue unchanged following nephrectomy. Also rats continue to drink during the night when infused with either water (Fitzsimons, 1957) or liquid food (Fitzsimons, 1971) at a constant rate via a stomach tube. Furthermore, by delivering meals to slightly hungry rats at fixed intervals of 1 or 2.4 hours over periods of many days, Oatley (1971) has shown that the drinking rhythm is secondary neither to eating nor, since the animals came and ate each meal within seconds of its presentation, to sleep. Figure 8 illustrates an example of the eating and drinking of one rat from these experiments. In the first few days following a period of habituation to the apparatus, it exhibited the usual pattern with the majority of eating and drinking taking place in discrete bouts at night. Notice how the activity period preceded the moment of lights-off: this type of anticipation is not untypical of circadian mechanisms. On day 7 there started a 24-hour period of food deprivation; but the rhythm of drinking, including its fine pattern of bouts, continued virtually undisturbed. On day 8, meals (each consisting of 30 of the 54-mg pellets the animal was eating under the ad-lib regime) started to be delivered automatically into the food magazine every 2.4 hours. These meals were always eaten promptly, but although eating was now equal during day and night, no substantial change of the amount or proportion of water drunk at night occurred in rats subjected to 1- or 2.4-hour meal schedules. Although a small tendency towards more but smaller bouts of drinking (perhaps a result of frustration) may be seen under conditions of scheduled meals in Figure 8, the basic pattern of predominance of drinking in the night, and (for this rat) a pause of about 2 hours in the middle of the night, remained more or less unchanged from the pattern that obtained when the animal chose its own mealtimes. Also the timing of bouts of drinking was not readjusted to coincide with eating, with the result that a fall in the probability of drinking within 16 minutes of a meal occurred. This is entirely consonant with the findings of Fitzsimons & Le Magnen (1969),

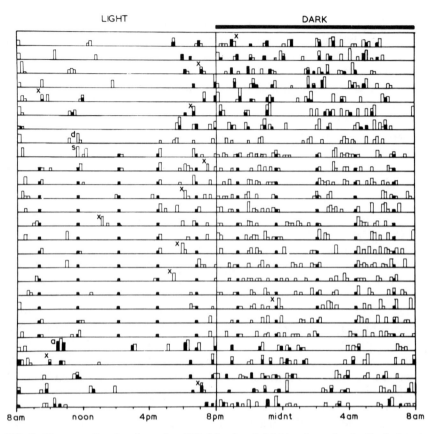

FIG. 8. Histogram showing the eating (*filled bars*) and drinking (*open bars*) of a single rat. Each row represents a single day, with a cycle of light 0800h to 2000h to 0800h. The rat ate and drank ad lib up to *d*, was deprived of food at that point, began a schedule of 1.6-gram meals every 2.4 hours at *s*, and returned to ad lib food at *a*. (Used by permission of Macmillan (Journals) Ltd.)

who fed rats two large meals in the daytime and found that 50% of drinking still took place at night, but apparently not consonant with those of Zucker (1971). He repeated Fitzsimons and Le Magnen's experiment of giving two meals during the light period, but found that when these meals were around midday, nighttime drinking dropped to only 15% of the total after 4 days on this schedule. He argued that Fitzsimons and Le Magnen found substantial drinking at night only because the second meal immediately preceded darkness, but this cannot explain all the results. It certainly is the case that animals fed only once or twice a day come eventually to reduce nocturnal water consumption, but the transition from ad-lib eating is complicated. On the first day of food deprivation, rats exhibit a relative polydipsia (Morrison, 1968): that is to say, they drink in excess of need, and excrete a large volume of dilute urine. This corresponds with a continued pattern of drinking (see Figure 8), mostly at night. This maintained noctural drinking was also found by Zucker (1971) on the first day of deprivation in his group of animals that were to be fed two meals in the middle of each day. On the next 2 or 3 days of continued food deprivation or of a schedule of one or two periods of feeding, drinking becomes associated in time with the scheduled eating period as well as declining to the usual level of correlation of water with food. This series of changes has been observed by a number of experimenters including Fitzsimons and Le Magnen (1969), F. M. Toates and K. Oatley (in preparation), and Zucker (1971). Evidently the schedule of meals every 1 or 2.4 hours following an initial 24 hours of food deprivation in Oatley's (1971) experiment avoids the abolition of nocturnal drinking, in a way that schedules with one or two large meals per day do not always succeed in doing. It will be interesting to increase intermeal interval in such schedules to find the point at which the ad-lib pattern and the circadian rhythm break down.

Oatley's (1971) result needs to be compared with Kissileff's (1969) finding that intragastric injection of water by the experimenter following rats' normal meals reduced their voluntary drinking. When the intragastric loads were a fraction of voluntary intake, drinking was reduced in a more or less compensatory fashion with the number of bouts but not their average size being reduced. This seems to indicate that what the ad-lib drinking controller programs is not the motor activity of drinking as such, but thirst which can be reduced by water that does not pass through the mouth. The finding that bouts stay the same size may be attributable to the threshold with hysteresis (see p. 210). Kissileff's finding that loading with 20% more than the normal water intake was necessary to suppress drinking completely, may reflect the relative weightings for the values of gastric and oropharyngeal feedback, and indeed the simulation of Toates and Oatley (1970) predicts that this manipulation would fall short of precise compensation, because gastric feedback alone is worth (in the model) only 90% of the postabsorptive value of water consumed. It is also a possibility that the values of the weightings for oral and gastric feedback signals may be subject to modification by learning, in which case intragastic injection accompanying voluntary drinking may itself modify the value of the various signals.

It would be interesting to measure changes in body fluid parameters, e.g., osmolality, in experiments such as that of Oatley (1971), particularly in view of Deaux, Sato, and Kakolewski's (1970) result that with rats on a schedule of food deprivation that were given 1½ grams of food every 15 minutes for 2 hours per day, the food intake was quickly followed by increased osmolality. Kakolewski and Deaux (1970) also propose that osmolality changes control the onset of meals; by lowering osmotic pressure, drinking disinhibits feeding. This group might account for the association between meals and drinking by supposing that the drinking that anticipates meals reduces tonicity of a hypertonic state, whereas drinking following meals is a response to hypertonicity. Meal-associated drinking is in other words dependent only on cellular shrinkage. Formidable difficulties accompany this explanation. In the first place, it depends upon the finding of an increase in osmolality of much shorter latency following a meal than that found previously (cf. Novin, 1962; Oatley & Toates, 1969); secondly, it cannot account for the finding of Oatley (1971) that the probability of drinking in association with regularly scheduled meals was substantially lower than with self-initiated meals; and thirdly, there is the whole host of phenomena associated with the circadian rhythmicity of drinking, e. g., the difference in the food-to-water ratio between night and day (e.g., K. Oatley & L. Hoad, in preparation) that osmolality arguments can not begin to address.

Intake of food is known to be the largest single factor determining water drunk, and yet, making food intake constant had no effect on the circadian drinking rhythm. One is forced to conclude that the thirst was not caused by deficits, but by a device that models the alternation of night and day, and generates a detailed program of motivation to drink, appropriate for a small nocturnal scavenger. Such a mechanism has the advantage both in elegance and (presumably) in survival value and pleasantness for the animal of not relying on deficits which have already occurred and may get worse, but of preventing deficits from occurring. If the mechanism helps to predict water needs, albeit in quite a simple way, it may be that in the wild, rats need to fall back on the homeostatic mechanisms only in emergency.

Processes underlying biological rhythms (see, e.g., Oatley & Goodwin, 1971) are relevant to the argument here. Systems capable of giving rise to all the phenomena of biological rhythms are well known in engineering as nonlinear oscillators. This class of oscillators includes all those which produce periodic phenomena that can not be described by linear differential equations. Rather, a nonlinear oscillator is described in terms of a nonlinear equation, and the waveform of its output is not sinusoidal. Time-base waveforms of oscilloscopes, bank balances in checking accounts, the series of impulses in an axon when a constant current is applied, and the menstrual cycle are all examples of nonlinear oscillations.

The first observations of the interesting phenomena associated with nonlinear oscillators were made by Huygens in 1665. He found that two clocks which when apart and hanging on separate walls, kept slightly different time from one another, would come to keep exactly the same time as each other when suspended close together from the same beam. Evidently very weak mechanical interactions were capable of mutually synchronizing the two clocks, and further experimentation and theoretical analysis (see, e.g., Minorsky, 1962) has demonstrated that this so-called entrainment is a perfectly general property of nonlinear oscillators. A nonlinear oscillator subjected to even very weak periodic stimulation near the oscillator's own natural frequency or a harmonic of it, will tend to entrain with the input oscillation. It is from this property that the phenomena of biological rhythms emerge. Circadian oscillations of physiological processes entrain with what might be a relatively weak hormonal or neural signal arising ultimately from photoreceptors, and because of their interactions, they also entrain with one another.

The probable explanation of the experiment in which drinking patterns were dissociated from eating (Oatley, 1971; and see Figure 8) is that in part eating and drinking are controlled by independent mechanisms, each of which produces a rather standard schedule of bouts of intake (cf. also Kavanau & Rischer, 1968). This finer grain output is superimposed upon a slower daily oscillation. In the normal course of events, both the bouts and the daily rhythm of eating and drinking are entrained upon one another, partly because of the normal interactions of feeding and drinking, though apparently in the finer grain behavior also with some learned anticipatory phase adjustment so that drinking tends to precede water deficits as discussed above. If one of the patterns of intake is smoothed out, the other continues more or less as before. There exist therefore motivational mechanisms of a nonhomeostatic kind whose function is to model periodicities of the environment, and whose properties allow them to predict those periodicities, keep physiological processes in time with them, and act as means of maintaining interlocking time relationships between related physiological processes.

In the same way that control theory can give a formal explanation of the principles of feedback that make homeostasis possible, the theory of nonlinear oscillators gives an explanation of the anticipatory (feed-forward) mechanisms capable of modeling periodicities in the environment.

We are still running a series of experiments to determine the characteristics of the circadian oscillation underlying drinking, and have yet to discover how nonhomeostatic ad-lib drinking fits together with the homeostatic aspect we understand better. With the simulation that we have built we can investigate whether the oscillations (both circadian and of higher frequency) can conceivably arise from the operation of a system of the kind we have specified, whether the circadian process feeds into or modulates the activity of the homeostatic controller in some way, or whether it is necessary to postulate a control system, e.g., an adaptive controller, of a more sophisticated order which will oscillate in one mode and will act as a regulator in another. Without formal accounts or models of homeostasis, circadian oscillation, and so on, it would be difficult to formulate these questions properly and impossible to answer them.

CONCLUSION

The simulation even with all the circulatory processes and the more detailed account of renal mechanisms which we have recently added (F. M. Toates & K. Oatley, in preparation), the interactions with food intake, temperature control, and circadian oscillations on which we are still working, will still be limited to explaining only some aspects of drinking. The more difficult and important problems of appetitive aspects of thirst it will leave largely untouched. But even in its present state the role of the simulation as a formal theory of neural and physiological processes is amply fulfilled. For instance, compare with the diagram of Figure 7, which represents some of the minimal neural operations necessary to control drinking, the older notions such as "satiety center" which do not themselves explain how satiety is produced but act as shorthand descriptions of the behavior they are supposed to account for. No collection of such descriptive terms is capable of itself producing behavior, any more than a collection of labels of terms like "take-off," "glide," etc., would be capable of constituting a model airplane. It seems clear that what we need in brain research is more understanding of the principles that make particular kinds of behavior possible. These principles can then guide direct manipulations of nervous tissue. When one understands the need for an osmoreceptor in a system controlling water balance, then is the time to look for it (just the strategy followed by Verney, 1947; Jewell & Verney, 1957; see also Blass, this volume). When we understand that extracellular signals must reach the brain, the effects of intracranial angiotensin (Epstein, Fitzsimons, & Rolls, 1970) acquire significance. Compare this with the relative lack of insight about how the mechanisms responsible for controlling drinking work that has been afforded by experiments on central stimulation with carbachol. When we understand the additivity of cellular and extracellular stimuli, then lesions that dissociate the two (Blass & Epstein, 1971) make sense.

Thus on the one hand understanding (by insight, invention, and empirical investigation) of the mechanisms that are logically necessary for behavior is usually a prerequisite for a physiological understanding of the brain or for the interpretation of experiments on brain tissue. On the other hand, the computer program that I have been discussing represents simply a formal statement of those logical operations and their interactions which are necessary for behavior, and necessary for our own understanding of the problem. Furthermore, the understanding that we already have indicates that these processes are sufficiently complex to make it inescapable that our further comprehension and successful investigation of whole systems, though perhaps not of component processes, is expressed formally using some such vehicle as the computer program. Armed with sufficiently powerful theoretical understandings, we will know what to look for in the physiology, and will be able to recognize it when we see it. Since, furthermore, in thirst we have a grasp of at least some of the principles that allow the whole system to work, and can construct detailed simulations, one may predict that thirst will continue to be important for the more general understanding of the brain: if in thirst we can understand some principles, we will be in a good position to see how these are worked out in neural practice.

SUMMARY

Models which act as theories of how brain mechanisms produce behavior should display principles which make the behavior possible. Computer simulations have this property, and can in particular embody the notion that the brain itself models or represents characteristics of the environment with which it deals. The explanation of homeostatic drinking depends on the idea of a feedback control system which represents an ideal state of the body fluids. This and other aspects of the water balance system have been simulated in such a way as to embody in a computer program a precise understanding of the component processes of the system and the ways in which they interact. The simulation has been tested for overall responses and predicts homeostatic drinking of rats in response to a variety of manipulations with fair precision. The homeostatic model cannot account for all drinking, though, and the circadian rhythm of ad-lib drinking provides an example of motivation that is dependent on a model of the characteristics of the environment which is deployed not in the feedback mode so that deficits can be corrected, but in a feed-forward mode so that they can be anticipated. Homeostatic control of drinking may thus be an emergency mechanism. Simulation of the homeostatic and ad-lib mechanisms of drinking will allow us to understand how these major features of drinking are related, but still will leave appetitive aspects of thirst unexplained. Prospects are hopeful for further understanding of brain mechanisms via the study of thirst, but as the extent of our understanding of the system increases, the role of a formal theory becomes even more important.

REFERENCES

Adolph, E. F., Barker, J. P., & Hoy, P. A. Multiple factors in thirst. *American Journal of Physiology*, 1954, **178**, 538–562.

Bellows, R. T. Time factors in water drinking in dogs. *American Journal of Physiology*, 1939, **125**, 87–97.

Blass, E. M., & Epstein, A. N. A lateral preoptic osmosensitive zone for thirst in the rat. *Journal of Comparative and Physiological Psychology*, 1971, **76**, 378–394.

Corbit, J. D. Osmotic thirst: Theoretical and experimental analysis. *Journal of Comparative and Physiological Psychology*, 1969, **67**, 2–14.

Craik, K. J. W. *The nature of explanation*. Cambridge: Cambridge University Press, 1943.

Deaux, E., Sato, E., & Kakolewski, J. W. Emergence of systemic cues evoking food-associated drinking. *Physiology and Behaviour*, 1970, **5**, 1177–1179.

Descartes, R. L'homme. In *Oevres de Descartes*. Volume 11. Paris: C. Adam & P. Tannery, 1909. Pp. 119–202. (Originally published: Paris, 1664.)

Descartes, R. Les passions de l'ame. In *Oevres de Descartes*. Volume 11. Paris: C. Adam & P. Tannery. Pp. 327–488. (Originally published: Amsterdam, 1649.)

Deutsch, J. A. *The structural basis of behaviour*. Cambridge: Cambridge University Press, 1960.

Epstein, A. N., Fitzsimons, J. T., & Rolls (née Simons), B. J. Drinking induced by injection of angiotensin into the brain of the rat. *Journal of Physiology*, 1970, **210**, 457–474.

Falk, J. L. The behavioural regulation of water-electrolyte balance. *Nebraska Symposium on Motivation*, 1961, **9**, 1–32.

Fitzsimons, J. T. Normal drinking in rats. *Journal of Physiology*, 1957, **138**, 39P.

Fitzsimons, J. T. Drinking by nephrectomised rats injected with various substances. *Journal of Physiology*, 1961, **155**, 563–579. (a)

Fitzsimons, J. T. Drinking in rats depleted of body fluid without increase in osmotic pressure. *Journal of Physiology*, 1961, **159**, 297–309. (b)

Fitzsimons, J. T. The effects of slow infusions of hypertonic solutions on drinking and drinking thresholds in rats. *Journal of Physiology*, 1963, **167**, 344–354.

Fitzsimons, J. T. Effect of nephrectomy on the additivity of certain stimuli of drinking in the rat. *Journal of Comparative and Physiological Psychology*, 1969, **68**, 308–314.

Fitzsimons, J. T. The physiology of thirst: A review of the extraneural aspects of the mechanisms of drinking. *Progress in Physiological Psychology,* 1971, **4**, 119-201.

Fitzsimons, J. T., & Le Magnen, J. Eating as a regulatory control of drinking in the rat. *Journal of Comparative and Physiological Psychology,* 1969, 67, 273-283.

Fitzsimons, J. T., & Oatley, K. Additivity of stimuli for drinking in rats. *Journal of Comparative and Physiological Psychology,* 1968, **66**, 450-455.

Garcia, J., & Ervin, R. R. Gustatory visceral and telereceptor cutaneous conditioning–adaptation in external and internal milieus. *Communications in Behavioural Biology,* 1968 (Part A), **1**, 389-415.

Gilman, A. The relation between blood osmotic pressure, fluid distribution and voluntary water intake. *American Journal of Physiology,* 1937, **120**, 323-328.

Grindley, G. C. The neural basis of purposive activity. *British Journal of Psychology,* 1927, **18**, 168-188.

Hebb, D. O. Drives and the C.N.S. (Conceptual Nervous System). *Psychological Review,* 1955, **62**, 243-254.

Hull, C. L. *Essentials of behaviour.* New Haven: Yale University Press, 1951.

Huygens, C. Sympathie des horloges. In Société Hollandaise des Sciences (Ed.), *Oeuvres completes de Christian Huygens.* Vol. 17. La Haye: Nijhoff, 1932. Pp. 183-186. (Originally published: 1665.)

Jewell, P. A., & Verney, E. B. An experimental attempt to determine the site of the neurohypophysical osmoreceptors in the dog. *Philosophical Transactions, Series B,* 1957, **240**, 197-324.

Kakolewski, J. W., & Deaux, E. Initiation of eating as a function of ingestion of hypoosmotic solutions. *American Journal of Physiology,* 1970, **218**, 590-595.

Kavanau, J. L., & Rischer, C. E. Program clocks in small mammals. *Science,* 1968, **161**, 1256-1259.

Kissileff, H. R. Oropharyngeal control of prandial drinking. *Journal of Comparative and Physiological Psychology,* 1969, **67**, 309-319.

Lashley, K. S. The problem of cerebral organization in vision. *Biological Symposia,* 1942, **7**, 301-322.

Le Magnen, J. The eating rate as related to deprivation and palatability. Paper presented at the Third International Conference on the Regulation of Food and Water Intake, Haverford, Pa., 1968.

Lorenz, K. Z. Innate bases of learning. In K. H. Pribram (Ed.), *On the biology of learning.* New York: Harcourt, Brace & World, 1969.

McFarland, D. J., & McFarland, F. J. Dynamic analysis of an avian drinking response. *Medical and Biological Engineering,* 1968, **6**, 659-668.

Minorsky, N. *Nonlinear Oscillations.* Princeton, N.J.: Van Nostrand, 1962.

Morrison, S. D. The regulation of water intake by rats deprived of food. *Physiology and Behavior,* 1968, **3**, 75-81.

Novin, D. The relation between electrical conductivity of brain tissue and thirst in the rat. *Journal of Comparative and Physiological Psychology,* 1962, **55**, 145-154.

Oatley, K. Changes in blood volume and osmotic pressure in the production of thirst. *Nature,* 1964, **202**, 1341-1342.

Oatley, K. A control model of the physiological basis of thirst. *Medical and Biological Engineering,* 1967, **5**, 225-237. (a)

Oatley, K. Diurnal influences on postdeprivational drinking in rats. *Journal of Comparative and Physiological Psychology,* 1967, **64**, 183-185. (b)

Oatley, K. Drinking in response to salt injections at different times of day. *Psychonomic Science,* 1967, **9**, 439-440. (c)

Oatley, K. Brain mechanisms and motivation. *Nature,* 1970, **225**, 797-801.

Oatley, K. Dissociation of the circadian drinking pattern from eating. *Nature,* 1971, **229**, 494-496.

Oatley, K., & Goodwin, B. C. The explanation and investigation of biological rhythms. In W. P. Colquhoun (Ed.), *Biological rhythms and human performance.* London: Academic Press, 1971.

Oatley, K., & Toates, F. M. The passage of food through the gut of rats and its uptake of fluid. *Psychonomic Science,* 1969, **16**, 225-226.

Oatley, K., & Toates, F. M. Frequency analysis of the thirst control system. *Nature,* 1971, **232**, 562-654.

Oatley, K., & Tonge, D. A. The effect of hunger on water intake in rats. *Quarterly Journal of Experimental Psychology,* 1969, **21**, 162-171.

Panksepp, J., Toates, F. M., & Oatley, K. Extinction induced drinking in hungry rats. *Animal Behaviour,* 1972, in press.

Revusky, S. H., & Garcia, J. Learned associations over long delay. *The Psychology of Learning and Motivation,* 1970, **4**, 1-84.

Roeder, K. D. Aspects of the noctuid tympanic nerve response having significance in the avoidance of bats. *Journal of Insect Physiology,* 1964, **10**, 529-546.

Shettleworth, S. Constraints on learning. *Advances in the Study of Animal Behaviour,* 1971, **4**, in press.

Snowdon, C. T. Motivation, regulation and the control of meal parameters with oral and intragastric feeding in rats. *Journal of Comparative and Physiological Psychology,* 1969, **69**, 91-100.

Stellar, E. The physiology of motivation. *Psychological Review,* 1954, **61**, 5-22.

Tinbergen, N. *The study of instinct.* Oxford: Oxford University Press, 1951.

Toates, F. M., & Oatley, K. Computer simulation of thirst and water balance. *Medical and Biological Engineering,* 1970, 8, 71-87.

Verney, E. B. The antidiuretic hormone and the factors which determine its release. *Proceedings of the Royal Society (London), Series B,* 1947, **135**, 25-106.

Wiepkema, P. A. Positive feedbacks at work during feeding. *Behaviour,* 1971, **39**, 266-273.

Winograd, T. Procedures as a representation for data in a computer program for understanding natural language. Doctoral dissertation, Massachusetts Institute of Technology (Department of Mathematics Rep. AI TR-17), 1971.

Winograd, T. Understanding natural language. *Cognitive Psychology,* 1972, 3, 1-191.

Zucker, I. Light-dark rhythms in rat eating and drinking behavior. *Physiology and Behavior,* 1971, **6**, 115-126.

INVITED COMMENT:
COMMENTS ON
DR. KISSILEFF'S CHAPTER

John L. Falk
Rutgers University

About a dozen years ago, it was considered heretical to hold that fluid intake could be determined in any important way by nonhomeostatic variables. Homeostatic mechanisms might be deceived, it was thought, by gustatory factors or pathological processes. The physiological or behavioral outcomes were nonetheless viewed as reactions of homeostatic mechanisms. These reactions took the theoretical forms of normal responses to deceptive signals or disordered reactions to normal signals. For example, the overresponse to a nonnutritive, sweet solution would be explained away as a normal response to a stimulus deceptively signaling calories. The decades of research by P. T. Young (1948, 1949, 1967) and others showing that the high acceptability of and preference for such solutions was not primarily a function of caloric deprivation was bypassed by a vague appeal to the "survival value" of sweet-tasting solutions. Harry Kissileff has done us all a valuable service by gathering together for review research which seriously questions the adequacy of regulatory homeostatic notions as an acceptable account of the phenomena of fluid intake.

States of frank fluid depletion or at least osmotic imbalance had been assumed to generate signals leading to more or less appropriate repletion behavior. The realization that not only can huge fluid intakes result from the nonhomeostatic variables imbedded in the schedule-induced polydipsia situation, but also that day-to-day fluid regulation probably is accomplished in the absence of true depletion signals has shaken faith in the generality of homeostatic theory. In his recent review, Fitzsimons (1972) has distinguished between primary and secondary drinking. Primary drinking results from "a relative or an absolute lack of body water in one or other fluid compartment of the body," [p. 476] while secondary drinking comprises intake arising from a host of other situations including oropharyngeal stimuli, feeding schedules, direct CNS stimulation, and handling. Secondary drinking "is the normal way whereby water is introduced into the body . . . not by an existing need for water." [p. 477]. Primary drinking is viewed as an emergency response rather than a day-to-day regulatory mechanism. The various stimuli that are in current research use by many of us (e.g., water deprivation, osmotic loading, hyperoncotic stimuli, sodium depletion) have significance in the elucidation of emergency mechanisms rather than for the analysis of normal water balance. It is slightly ironic that the host of variables Fitzsimons lists under the rubric of secondary drinking includes many pathological and "unnatural" stimulating conditions as well as those assumed to control normal, daily fluid regulation, while primary drinking, produced by variables of long-standing familiarity to physiologists, is, from the regulatory standpoint, metaphysiological. According to the Fitzsimons classification, then, primary drinking occurs only under unusual, stress situations, with daily fluid regulation occurring in relative independence of the mechanisms of fluid homeostatic control.

One hopes that those few investigators who have fought over several years for the recognition of the importance of nonhomeostatic determinants of fluid intake have not somehow won a too crushing and demoralizing victory. There is a danger that those stimuli producing alterations in the locus or composition of body water will now be considered irrelevant to real, that is, daily regulatory, drinking. The continuing, hard lesson to be learned is that one set of variables producing fluid intake cannot be "more relevant" than some other set. As dipsologists, our interest in factors controlling fluid intake should remain universal. Those factors exerting strong control over fluid intake should exert strong quality control over our theoretical notions concerning ingestive phenomena. It would be most unfortunate if we began to play off "natural" versus "unnatural" stimuli to drinking, just as I think it was stultifying to do it for homeostatic at the expense of nonhomeostatic determinants. What is considered an interesting phenomenon from one viewpoint can be denigrated as a pathological process if it spells trouble for someone's theoretical presumptions; one man's fact is another individual's artifact.

In a less general mode, I would like to comment on some aspects of Dr. Kissileff's treatment of schedule-induced polydipsia. In addition to the evidence against the dry-mouth interpretation he presents, there are several additional difficulties which could be listed (Falk, 1969, pp. 582 ff. and 590 ff.). An important one is the finding that a reinforcing agent one-third water by weight (SKF liquid monkey diet) when substituted for the standard Noyes pellets on a variable-interval 1-minute schedule produced polydipsia in rats when the portion magnitude was adjusted to 22 mg (Falk, 1967).

Dr. Kissileff's frustration interpretation of schedule-induced polydipsia is a valiant try but contains serious difficulties.

Attempts to use notions such as "frustration" as explanations of behavior are problematic in that they are vernacular terms referring to inner causal entities.

Rather than unifying disparate sets of observations the way the term "gravity" unifies data in, for example, ballistics, tidal movements, and celestial mechanics, "frustration" results in explaining away behavioral phenomena as opposed to giving accounts of them which produce predictive statements.

Dr. Kissileff suggests that I have classified a mystery (schedule-induced polydipsia) as an enigma (displacement behavior). Not really. First, polydipsia is a mystery only if one is a true believer in the adequacy of the explanatory capacity of homeostatic theory. Since certainly neither of us is a believer, polydipsia should be no more mysterious than other fluid intake phenomena; they are all at least medium mysterious. Actually, we know a fair amount about the major determinants of polydipsia (feeding intermittencies, portion magnitudes, type of food, deprivation-produced weight level). Second, classifying polydipsia as a species of displacement behavior was not meant to provide an explanation. What I hoped to accomplish was to point out that various displacement activities described by ethologists and schedule-induced phenomena (polydipsia, pica, aggression, and escape) seemed to be controlled by similar classes of environmental determinants (Falk, 1969, 1971). At present, this should function more as an experimental challenge than as a tour de force in theory construction.

The evidence cited to support the frustration theory is rather equivocal. While it is true that increasing reinforcement density decreases polydipsia, so does decreasing the density beyond a certain point (Falk, 1969) which should increase frustration further. The decreased polydipsia found when sucrose or glucose pellets were substituted for standard Noyes food pellets can hardly be attributed to an increased palatability decreasing frustration. While the animals were not given a choice between the sugar and the standard pellets, I would guess that a whole meal of sugar might be a less satisfactory gustatory experience than one involving the more nutritionally balanced pellet.

The equal polydipsic level produced by 45-mg laboratory rat food pellets and 22-mg SFK liquid diet was probably due to their approximately equal efficacy in holding the animals' weights at the 80% level at the portion magnitudes used (45 mg and 22 mg), rather than to any differential thwarting effect of the diets.

It is claimed that the polydipsia reduces frustration, but not hunger. If frustration decreases, so should the subsequent drinking.

Dr. Kissileff correctly points out that several drugs have been shown to reduce the level of polydipsia. This shows that the phenomenon is sensitive to the administration of various drugs, not that it is frustration-based. The drug effects demonstrated thus far do not allow us to make any pharmacological statement concerning the basis of polydipsia.

In his last paragraph, Dr. Kissileff points out that "a state of thirst should be inferred only when drinking follows states of body water imbalance." This is an important point, for it means that we cannot infer the activation of intake mechanisms congruent with those serving "primary drinking" (Fitzsimons, 1972) if there is no concomitant change in the state of body water (Falk, 1969, pp. 586–587). For example, electrical or chemical stimulation of the brain may or may not activate intake mechanisms having anything in common with those operating in primary or secondary drinking resulting from other stimuli. Response topography has never been a reliable guide to the identification of the variables controlling behavior. Drinking and daily fluid regulation apparently can occur without the mediation of "thirst". The activation of exaggerated drinking by food schedule, lesion, or chemical or electrical means is no certain guide that the elusive "thirst" state is in any sense present.

REFERENCES

Falk, J. L. Control of schedule-induced polydipsia: Type, size, and spacing of meals. *Journal of the Experimental Analysis of Behavior,* 1967, **10**, 199–206.

Falk, J. L. Conditions producing psychogenic polydipsia in animals. *Annals of the New York Academy of Sciences,* 1969, **157**, 569–593.

Falk, J. L. The nature and determinants of adjunctive behavior. *Physiology and Behavior,* 1971, **6**, 577–588.

Fitzsimons, J. T. Thirst. *Physiological Reviews,* 1972, **52**, 468–561.

Young, P. T. Appetite, palatability, and feeding habit: A critical review. *Psychological Bulletin,* 1948, **45**, 289–320.

Young, P. T. Food-seeking drive, affective process, and learning. *Psychological Review,* 1949, **56**, 98–121.

Young, P. T. Palatability: The hedonic response to foodstuffs. In C. F. Code (Ed.), *Handbook of Physiology.* Section 6. *Alimentary Canal.* Vol. 1. Washington, D. C.: American Physiological Society, 1967. Pp. 353–366.

PART III: NEUROPHARMACOLOGY OF THIRST

INTRODUCTION: NEUROPHARMACOLOGY OF THIRST[1]

Gerard P. Smith

Cornell University Medical College—Westchester Division

The ghost of Gall haunts Neuropsychology. As Professor Young (1970) recently pointed out, all studies which attempt to correlate a neurological parameter with a behavioral parameter share Gall's intuition: there is neural localization of psychological function. Contemporary studies differ from phrenology by their methodological rigor, not by their intellectual penetration. Modern interpretations of localization of function remain unsatisfactory because each interpretation assumes what it seeks—the rules of the relationship of brain to behavior.

But great problems stimulate. It is clear that it was the failure of lesions or electrical stimulation of lateral hypothalamus to *selectively* affect feeding or drinking which led Grossman (1962) to inject adrenergic and cholinergic agents directly into lateral hypothalamus. The stimulation of feeding by norepinephrine and epinephrine, and the stimulation of drinking by cholinergic drugs injected through the same cannula into the same site, were interpreted to mean that synapses in the neural networks for feeding and drinking behavior located in the lateral hypothalamus were differentiated by the nature of their chemical transmitter ("chemical coding"—Miller, 1965). Grossman's results, and Fisher and Coury's (1962) delineation of a "cholinergic circuit" for drinking, provoked an enormous amount of interesting work which is assessed in the following chapters.

[1] Preparation of this chapter and the research reported here were supported in part by N.I.H. Grant NS08402. The author is a career development awardee of the National Institute of Neurological Disease and Stroke (7-K04-NS38601).

During the recent decade of exploitation of the intracerebral injection technique, there have been two major advances in neuropharmacology which are just beginning to nourish the analysis of thirst.

The first of these advances was the description of the neuroanatomy of monoamine and cholinergic neurons in the rat brain (Shute & Lewis, 1963; Dahlström & Fuxe, 1964). Although these neurons are classified into four types by the chemical transmitters they synthesize, store, and release (serotonergic, dopaminergic, noradrenergic, and cholinergic), they have much in common (see also Figure 1 in the chapter by Harvey):

1. Most of them originate in the brainstem.

2. Almost all of their axons course cephalad.

3. Their axons diverge widely to terminate throughout the limbic system and cerebral cortex.

4. These neurons are confined to the central nervous system—they are interneurons.

Knowing the course and terminations of these neurons will strengthen the neuropharmacological investigation of drinking behavior in two ways:

First, it will be possible to determine if the transmitter that affects drinking when injected, is also present in terminals at the injection site. Such a correlation will favor a physiological interpretation of the results of injection. Used in this way, histochemistry is a control.

Second, it will be possible to systematically inject exogenous transmitter at the terminal sites of these ascending systems to test for effects on drinking behavior. Here histochemistry is a guide.

The second advance was the discovery that 6-hydroxydopamine (6-OHDA) caused the selective degeneration of noradrenergic and dopaminergic neurons in the peripheral and central nervous systems (Thoenen & Tranzer, 1968; Ungerstedt, 1968). The selective destruction depends on the fact that 6-OHDA satisfies the structural requirements for active uptake by the catecholaminergic neurons. In this way 6-OHDA achieves much higher concentration inside catecholaminergic neurons than in other neurons which it apparently penetrates by diffusion only. The higher concentration of 6-OHDA destroys the catecholaminergic neuron by an unknown mechanism. This agent is beginning to contribute to the neuropharmacological investigation of thirst, particularly when it is injected directly into the brain.

Ungerstedt (1968) was the first to use stereotactic injections of 6-OHDA into specified neural sites. With this technique Ungerstedt (1971a) produced prolonged adipsia (and aphagia) by injecting 6-OHDA at several sites along the dopaminergic nigrostriatal pathway. If adipsic rats were maintained by tube feeding, they gradually recovered the ability to eat dry food and drink water. Ungerstedt thought that the pattern of recovery was similar to that described by Teitelbaum and Epstein (1962) as characteristic of the lateral hypothalamic syndrome, but he did not perform the necessary behavioral analysis. Since one of the effective injection sites was the far-lateral hypothalamus where large electrolytic lesions produce the lateral hypothalamic syndrome, Ungerstedt suggested that damage of the nigrostriatal dopaminergic pathway was the necessary and sufficient lesion responsible for the lateral hypothalamic syndrome.

We (Smith, Strohmayer, & Reis, 1972) extended these observations by making stereotactic injections of 6-OHDA at three sites along the medial forebrain bundle in the lateral hypothalamus: (a) the anterior injection site was at the level of the caudal edge of the optic chiasm (A7.0, RL2.0, and H8.0 down from the dural surface according to the atlas of DeGroot [1959], all distances in millimeters); (b) the middle injection site was at the level of the middle of the ventromedial nucleus (A6.0, RL2.0, and H8.0 down); (c) the posterior injection site was at the level of the posterior portion of the dorsomedial and ventromedial nuclei (A5.0, RL2.0, and H8.0 down).

Injections of 6-OHDA (6.5μg/μl, 4μl at each site bilaterally; see Smith et al., 1972, for details) produced adipsia and aphagia in 26 of 29 rats (see Table 1). The adipsia was prolonged, often lasting for weeks. The adipsia was profound. It resisted the dipsogenic action of hypertonic saline (1 M NaCl, 1% body weight, ip) or isoproterenol (0.33 mg/kg, sc). The production of adipsia required the presence of 6-OHDA in the injection fluid. Injections of vehicle solutions (ascorbic acid in distilled water, 0.4 or 0.8μg/μl) which were isovolumetric, of similar pH, and hypotonic in comparison to 6-OHDA injections did not produce adipsia consistently (2 of 20 rats were adipsic for 1 or 2 days, as shown in Table 1).

The production of adipsia also required injections into the lateral hypothalamus. Identical injections of 6-OHDA made 1.0 to 1.25 mm medial to the lateral injection sites (RL0.75 or 1.0 mm) did not produce adipsia (see Table

TABLE 1

Adipsia after 6-OHDA at Anterior, Middle, and
Posterior Hypothalamic Sites

Injection sites	Dose of 6-OHDA (μg)	Number of rats	Percent adipsic	Median duration (days)
Lateral hypothalamus	26	29	90	21.0
Lateral hypothalamus	vehicle	20	10	0
Medial hypothalamus	26	8	0	0

Note.—6-OHDA (26μg of base in 4μl vehicle solution) was injected into each of three sites bilaterally in the lateral or medial hypothalamus. Injections of 6-OHDA into the lateral hypothalamus produced adipsia, but medial injections did not. Identical injections of vehicle solution alone (0.4 or 0.8 μg ascorbic acid per microliter of distilled water) into the lateral hypothalamus produced trivial effects on drinking behavior.

1). This regional specificity is impressive and unexpected in view of the large injection volumes (4μl/site), but it was a consistent observation (see below).

The effectiveness of lateral injections depends upon perfusion of hypothalamic tissue and not upon the perfusion of overlying structures by 6-OHDA coming up the cannula track. Identical injections of 6-OHDA 0.5 to 2.0 mm below the dural surface overlying the lateral injection sites did not produce significant adipsia (1 of 8 rats was adipsic for 1 day).

Bilateral injections of 6-OHDA at the anterior site alone also produced significant adipsia in 6 of 9 rats (see Table 2). Identical injections of vehicle at this anterior site did not produce adipsia, and medial injections of 6-OHDA were also not effective (Table 2). The duration of the adipsia produced by anterior injections was shorter than the duration of adipsia produced by the combination of anterior, middle, and posterior injections (compare Tables 1 and 2). Because anterior injection sites were 1 mm anterior to the place where the dopaminergic nigrostriatal pathway leaves the lateral hypothalamus to course toward the caudate, adipsia after anterior injections was not likely to be the result of damage to the nigrostriatal pathway.

To measure the extent of catecholaminergic damage after injections of 6-OHDA, we made anterior or triple injections in another series of rats and killed them by cervical dislocation at 72 hours, a time when adipsia was present in anterior- or triple-injected animals. Lateral injections of 6-OHDA at anterior, middle, and posterior sites which produced a prolonged adipsia, decreased the concentration of norepinephrine in the hypothalamus and of dopamine in the caudate (see Table 3). Lateral injections of 6-OHDA at anterior sites alone which produced a shorter period of adipsia decreased hypothalamic norepinephrine, but anterior injections did not decrease the concentration of dopamine in the caudate. We interpret the lack of a significant decrease of caudate dopamine to mean that the nigrostriatal dopaminergic pathway was not significantly damaged by the injections of 6-OHDA made 1 mm anterior (A7.0) to the point where the

TABLE 2

Adipsia after 6-OHDA at Anterior Hypothalamic Site

Injection sites	Dose of 6-OHDA (μg)	Number of rats	Percent adipsic	Median duration (days)
Lateral	26	9	67	7
Lateral	vehicle	8	0	0
Medial	26	12	0	0

Note.—6-OHDA (26μg of base in 4μl vehicle solution) was injected bilaterally into the anterolateral or anteromedial hypothalamus. Lateral injections of 6-OHDA produced adipsia, but medial injections of 6-OHDA did not. Identical injections of vehicle solution into the lateral sites did not affect drinking behavior.

TABLE 3

Effects of 6-OHDA on Thirst and Brain Catecholamines

Injection sites	Adipsia	Hypothalamic NE (% of control)	Caudate DA (% of control)
Lateral hypothalamus:			
Anterior, middle, & posterior	++	45 ± 8^a	49 ± 2^a
Anterior	+	58 ± 4^a	82 ± 15^b
Medial hypothalamus:			
Anterior, middle, & posterior	0	46 ± 5^a	60 ± 7^a
Anterior	0	69 ± 10^b	94 ± 9^b

Note.–The concentration of hypothalamic norepinephrine and of caudate dopamine 72 hours after triple or single injections of 6-OHDA into the lateral or medial hypothalamus. + indicates adipsia of shorter duration than ++. 0 indicates the absence of adipsia. Note that adipsia can occur without a significant decrease of caudate dopamine (anterior-lateral hypothalamic injection site). Note also that hypothalamic norepinephrine and caudate dopamine can decrease significantly without producing adipsia (triple injections in medial hypothalamus). Catecholamines were assayed by the technique of Euler and Lishajko (1961).

[a]Significant difference from control ($p < 0.05$).

[b]Difference from control was not significant.

nigrostriatal pathway left the lateral hypothalamus (A6.0). Thus, damage of the dopaminergic nigrostriatal pathway was neither necessary nor sufficient for the adipsia that occurred after anterolateral hypothalamic injections of 6-OHDA.

Although triple injections along the medial hypothalamus did not produce adipsia, such injections decreased hypothalamic norepinephrine and caudate dopamine (Table 3). Medial injections at the anterior site only did not change caudate dopamine, but did reduce hypothalamic norepinephrine. Although the reduction in hypothalamic norepinephrine was not significant, the reduction was considerable. We are repeating these measures in another series of experiments to determine more clearly the magnitude of the decrease of hypothalamic norepinephrine after medial injections. The larger decrease of hypothalamic norepinephrine after lateral anterior injections than after medial anterior injections is consistent with the production of adipsia by *lateral,* but not *medial,* anterior injections, if the adipsia is the result of lateral hypothalamic catecholaminergic damage.

Such a correlation between the production of adipsia and the decrease of hypothalamic norepinephrine cannot be made from a comparison of the data from lateral and medial triple injections (see Table 3). It is possible that the greater loss of caudate dopamine after lateral triple injections is the differentiating factor, but this is not likely because the results of anterior injections only demonstrated that decrease of caudate dopamine was not necessary for the production of adipsia (Table 3).

We are testing two hypotheses which are consistent with the results of the lateral and medial triple injections. The first hypothesis is that there are two pools of catecholaminergic axons and terminals which are differentially affected by the lateral or medial injections and that it is damage of the lateral pool which produces adipsia. Such an explanation would account for our results. It would also account for the failure of intraventricular or intracisternal injections of 6-OHDA to produce adipsia (Bloom, Algeri, Groppetti, Revuelta, & Costa, 1969; Breese & Traylor, 1972; Uretsky & Iversen, 1970). Such injections would damage lateral catecholaminergic neurons least because the diffusion distance from the third ventricle to the lateral hypothalamus is longer than the diffusion distance to the medial hypothalamus (Fuxe & Ungerstedt, 1968). Recent reports (Zigmond & Stricker, 1972; Fibiger, Lonsbury, Cooper, & Lytle, 1972) of the successful production of aphagia and adipsia after intraventricular or intracisternal 6-OHDA when 6-OHDA was preceded by a monoamine oxidase inhibitor are also consistent with lateral hypothalamic specificity, because the monoamine oxidase inhibition would increase the effective concentration gradient of 6-OHDA from medial to lateral and thus produce more lateral catecholaminergic damage. Direct evidence for lateral and medial catecholaminergic pools may come from fluorescent histochemical analysis of catecholaminergic damage after lateral or medial injections. Such studies are in progress in our laboratory.

A second hypothesis consistent with the results of lateral and medial triple injections is that the lateral injections produce adipsia because lateral injections damage noncatecholaminergic neural elements which are necessary for thirst. In this view, the dissociation of adipsia from significant catecholaminergic damage seen after medial injections demonstrates that the correlation of loss of catecholamine with adipsia after lateral injections is not a causal relationship. There is no doubt that direct injections into brain tissue produce *some* nonspecific damage. Estimates of the damage observed by light microscopy vary from Ungerstedt's (1971b) report of small areas of cell loss and glial infiltration of greatest diameter of 0.2 to 0.3 mm, to the large, necrotic areas observed by Poirier, Langelier, Roberge, Boucher, & Kitsikis, (1972). Preliminary analysis of our own material by light microscopy confirms Ungerstedt's results. Furthermore, in our material, there appears to be little difference in the damage observed after 6-OHDA injections compared to the damage observed after vehicle injections. Vehicle injections at lateral sites, however, did not produce adipsia (see Tables 1 and 2).

Although the transmitters for most of the neural tissue in the medial forebrain bundle have not been identified, ascending serotonergic and cholinergic fibers are represented there and probably undergo some damage after 6-OHDA injections. There is indirect evidence, however, for dismissing serotonergic or cholinergic damage as the cause of adipsia after lateral hypothalamic injections of 6-OHDA. The evidence against the importance of serotonergic damage comes from three experiments: First, Harvey (this volume, Table 4) reports that the decrease of striatal and nonstriatal serotonin does not correlate well with the defect of non–food-related drinking observed after electrolytic lesions of the medial forebrain bundle. Second, Harvey and Lints (1971) reported that the decreased concentration of telencephalic serotonin produced by electrolytic lesions of the medial forebrain bundle was correlated with a decreased jump threshold. Jump threshold, however, has not decreased in any of our rats after triple or single injections of 6-OHDA into the medial forebrain bundle (Levin & Smith, 1972). Third, Coscina, Grant, Balagura, & Grossman, (1972) lesioned the midbrain raphe nuclei which are the major sources of the ascending serotonergic fibers in the medial forebrain bundle and observed a transient hyperdipsia instead of adipsia.

The case against cholinergic damage is less secure, but, at least after septal lesions, a decreased concentration of whole brain acetylcholine correlated with hyperdipsia, not adipsia (Sorensen & Harvey, 1971; Harvey, this volume).

If the weight of present evidence favors the view that lateral hypothalamic catecholaminergic axons are important neural mechanisms in thirst, what is their function? Doctor Setler (this volume) underlines the paradox of profound adipsia after catecholaminergic damage and the weak dipsogenic power of catecholamines injected into hypothalamus when peripheral actions produced by diffusion are excluded (Fisher, this volume). The solution to the paradox may be that the catecholaminergic neurons sensitize other elements (receptors, inter-' neurons, effectors) of the neurological network for thirst, but catecholaminergic neurons do not command the neural system. Thus, when endogenous catecholamine neurons are present and active in the conscious rat, local injections of exogenous catecholamine have little effect on thirst. But when endogenous catecholamine neurons are eliminated by 6-OHDA, the neural network for thirst becomes insensitive to local stimulation with angiotensin (Setler, this volume) or to stimulation by cellular dehydration, systemic isoproterenol, or water deprivation (see Smith, et al., 1972). This type of sensitizing function is logically identical with the "permissive action" of adrenal corticosteroids and may be similar to what Fisher (this volume) has in mind for angiotensin, and it is consistent with the widespread distribution of the central catecholaminergic terminals. It is also consistent with the assortment of functional defects we have observed after lateral, but not medial, hypothalamic injections of 6-OHDA. Besides adipsia and aphagia, the defects include the loss of visual placing (Sechzer, Ervin, & Smith, 1972), failure to acquire a one-way, active avoidance response (Levin & Smith, 1972), decreased anorexia, excitement, and stereotypy after systemic d-amphetamine (Ervin & Smith, 1973), and decreased movement in an open-field test (Young & G. P. Smith, 1973). Central catecholamine neurons must tie into numerous networks with a variety of behavioral expressions. At many loci, catecholaminergic synapses may sensitize, but at some sites they may command. One command function for catecholaminergic synapses is suggested by the powerful feeding effect of hypothalamic injections of norepinephrine observed in the sated rat. At this stage of the neuropharmacological analysis of catecholaminergic function in thirst, the distinction between sensitizing and command synapses may be useful in two ways: First, they are the terminology of a preliminary analysis, and current analytic understanding is very preliminary. Second, they emphasize that the behavioral effect of a specific synaptic transmitter is specified by the position of the synapse in the neural network that manages the behavioral system. Thus, specified sites within neural networks for thirst or other behaviors are chemically coded by the transmitter(s) released at the site, but the neural networks for behavioral systems are defined by complex interneuronal connections within the network that cannot be expected to employ a single transmitter substance throughout. In his authoritative presentation, Fisher (this volume) emphasizes the collapse of one of the extended models of chemical coding—the cholinergic circuit for thirst. Current suggestions of dopaminergic or noradrenergic thirst (see chapters by Fisher, Harvey, and Setler, this volume) are best understood as statements about the relative potency of a transmitter to influence thirst at *one* site in the neural network. When discussion proceeds on this basis, we are not likely to forget the architectural complexity (much of it still unknown) of the neural network we are manipulating pharmacologically.

If appreciation of neurological architecture is important in the neuro-pharmacological analysis of thirst, respect for the behavioral details of drinking is essential. Fisher (this volume) reminds us that it is not enough to specify stimuli and measure the volume of water consumed. The nature of the drinking fluids offered significantly affects the pattern and volume consumed. Such results disclose dimensions of the neurological network for thirst which invite analysis.

Of greater importance for the development of current neurological knowledge of thirst was the meticulous behavioral analysis of the effect of lateral hypothalamic electrolytic lesions first described by Teitelbaum and Epstein (1962) and recently reviewed by Epstein (1971). The lateral hypothalamic syndrome is dominated by permanent deficits of thirst. This accounts to a great extent for the fixed sequence of incomplete recovery. The deficits in thirst are so severe that the typical recovered lateral hypothalamic rat only drinks when it eats. (This specific form of prandial drinking is discussed in detail by Kissileff in this volume). With this careful behavioral description available, it is unfortunate that recent lesion experiments on the neuropharmacology of thirst have used the term lateral hypothalamic syndrome for rats that have been adipsic, without demonstrating the characteristic deficits of drinking behavior (see Ungerstedt, 1971a). There is more involved here than semantics because we have observed that recovery from profound and prolonged adipsia produced by our lateral, triple injections of 6-OHDA is more complete than the recovery characteristic of the lateral hypothalamic syndrome (see Table 4). After 6-OHDA, the recovery of drinking parallels the recovery of feeding. The extreme form of prandial drinking which characterizes the recovered lateral rat, however, is not present after 6-OHDA. Rats recovered from 6-OHDA eat dry pellets without water and drink water without food (Table 4). Such rats do not show aversive behavior towards

TABLE 4

Behavioral Differences of Rats Recovered
from Lateral Hypothalamic Lesions or 6-OHDA

Drinking behavior	Electrolytic lesion	6-OHDA injection
Drink water without food	No	Yes
Drink after NaCl or isoproterenol	No	Yes
Eat dry food without drinking	No	Yes
Prandial drinking	Yes	No

Note.—The characteristics of drinking behavior of rats recovered from the lateral hypothalamic electrolytic lesions are those described by Teitelbaum and Epstein (1962). The characteristics of rats recovered from triple injections of 6-OHDA along with the lateral hypothalamus are from our observations.

water at any time and are not more sensitive than normal to quinine adulteration of drinking water. There do not appear to be permanent deficits of thirst after 6-OHDA, although drinking to hypertonic saline or isoproterenol may be absent for 1 to 2 months.

These behavioral differences in rats recovered from 6-OHDA injections along the medial forebrain bundle demonstrate that these rats do not have the lateral hypothalamic syndrome. The behavioral differences also suggest biological differences in the recovery process. It may be relevant that 6-OHDA lesions of spinal catecholaminergic axons permit a much greater catecholaminergic regeneration than transections of the cord with scissors (Nygren, Olson, & Seiger, 1971). Whatever the biological basis of the difference in recovery of drinking after lateral lesions or 6-OHDA damage, the behavioral data are fundamental to the experimental search.

From our results and those of others which receive intelligent and imaginative scrutiny by Fisher, Setler, and Harvey in the following chapters, a strategy of neuropharmacological investigation emerges. The strategy is to manipulate the function of chemically specified interneurons at explicit loci in the brain and to measure the effects on drinking behavior. Current manipulations vary from microinjections of agonists and antagonists to measuring the neurochemical results of electrolytic or 6-OHDA lesions. Interpretation of the relationship observed between transmitter manipulation and drinking behavior must allow for the distortion of the neurochemical network which the experimental manipulations produced. Given the variety of techniques and the numerous and widespread synaptic sites at which a single transmitter is released, we should expect to discover more than one relationship between a transmitter and thirst. The pace of the neuropharmacological analysis of thirst will depend on our ability to use these relationships to uncover the design for drinking which lies in the brain.

REFERENCES

Bloom, F. E., Algeri, S., Groppetti, A., Revuelta, A., & Costa, E. Lesions of central norepinephrine terminals with 6OH-Dopamine: Biochemistry and fine structure. *Science,* 1969, **166**, 1284–1286.

Breese, G. R., & Traylor, T. D. Developmental characteristics of brain catecholamines and tyrosine hydroxylase in the rat: Effects of 6-hydroxydopamine. *British Journal of Pharmacology,* 1972, **44**, 210–222.

Coscina, D. V., Grant, L. D., Balagura, S., & Grossman, S. P. Hyperdipsia after serotonin-depleting midbrain lesions. *Nature New Biology,* 1972, **235**, 63–64.

Dahlström, A., & Fuxe, K. Evidence for the existence of monoamine-containing neurons in the central nervous system. *Acta Physiologica Scandinavica,* 1964, **62**, Supplement 232.

DeGroot, J. The rat forebrain in stereotaxic coordinates. *Transactions of the Royal Netherland Academy of Science,* 1959, **52**, 1–31.

Epstein, A. N. The lateral hypothalamic syndrome: Its implications for the physiological psychology of hunger and thirst. In E. Stellar and J. M. Sprague (Eds.), *Progress in Physiological Psychology.* New York: Academic Press, 1971. Pp. 263–317.

Ervin, G. N., & Smith, G. P. Decreased anorexia, excitement and stereotypy to amphetamine after lateral hypothalamic 6-OHDA injections. *Federation Proceedings,* 1973, in press.

Euler, U. S. von, & Lishajko, F. Improved technique for the fluorometric estimation of catecholamines. *Acta Physiologica Scandinavica,* 1961, **51**, 348–355.

Fibiger, H. C., Lonsbury, B., Cooper, H. P., & Lytle, L. D. Early behavioural effects of intraventricular administration of 6-hydroxydopamine in rat. *Nature New Biology,* 1972, **236**, 209–211.

Fisher, A. E., & Coury, J. N. Cholinergic tracing of a central neural circuit underlying the thirst drive. *Science,* 1962, **138**, 691–693.

Fuxe, K., & Ungerstedt, U. Histochemical studies on the distribution of catecholamines and 5-hydroxytryptamine after intraventricular injections. *Histochemie,* 1968, **13**, 16–28.

Grossman, S. P. Direct adrenergic and cholinergic stimulation of hypothalamic mechanisms. *American Journal of Physiology,* 1962, **202**, 872–882.

Harvey, J. A., & Lints, C. E. Lesions in the medial forebrain bundle: Relationship between pain sensitivity and telencephalic content of serotonin. *Journal of Comparative and Physiological Psychology,* 1971, **74**, 28–36.

Levin, B. E., & Smith, G. P. Impaired learning of active avoidance response in rats after lateral hypothalamic injection of 6-hydroxydopamine. *Neurology,* 1972, **22**, 433. (Abstract)

Miller, N. E. Chemical coding of behavior in the brain. *Science,* 1965, **148**, 328–338.

Nygren, L. G., Olson, L., & Seiger, A. Regeneration of monoamine-containing axons in the developing and adult spinal cord of the rat following intraspinal 6-OH-dopamine injections or transections. *Histochemie,* 1971, **28**, 1–15.

Poirier, L. J., Langelier, P., Roberge, A., Boucher, R., & Kitsikis, A. Nonspecific histopathological changes induced by the intracerebral injection of 6-hydroxy-dopamine (6-OH-DA). *Journal of the Neurological Sciences,* 1972, **16**, 401–416.

Sechzer, J. A., Ervin, G. N., & Smith, G. P. Suppression of the visual placing response by 6-hydroxydopamine: Restoration with amphetamine. *Program of the Society for Neuroscience,* 1972, Abstract 12.7.

Shute, C. C. D., & Lewis, P. R. Cholinesterase-containing systems of the brain of the rat. *Nature,* 1963, **199**, 1160–1164.

Smith, G. P., Strohmayer, A. J., & Reis, D. J. Effect of lateral hypothalamic injections of 6-hydroxy-dopamine on food and water intake in rats. *Nature New Biology,* 1972, **235**, 27–29.

Sorensen, J. P., Jr., & Harvey, J. A. Decreased brain acetylcholine after septal lesions in rats: Correlation with thirst. *Physiology and Behavior,* 1971, **6**, 723–725.

Teitelbaum, P., & Epstein, A. N. The lateral hypothalamic syndrome: Recovery of feeding and drinking after lateral hypothalamic lesions. *Psychological Review,* 1962, **69,** 74–90.

Thoenen, H., & Tranzer, J. P. Chemical sympathectomy by selective destruction of adrenergic nerve endings with 6-hydroxy-dopamine. *Naunyn-Schmiedebergs Archiv für Pharmakologie und Experimentelle Pathologie,* 1968, **261,** 271–288.

Ungerstedt, U. 6-hydroxy-dopamine induced degeneration of central monoamine neurons. *European Journal of Pharmacology,* 1968, **5,** 107–110.

Ungerstedt, U. Adipsia and aphagia after 6-hydroxy-dopamine induced degeneration of the nigro-striatal dopamine system. *Acta Physiologica Scandinavica,* 1971, Supplement 367, 95–122. (a)

Ungerstedt, U. Histochemical studies on the effect of intracerebral and intraventricular injections of 6-hydroxydopamine on monoamine neurons in the rat brain. In T. Malmfors and H. Thoenen (Eds.), *6-hydroxydopamine and catecholamine neurons.* New York: Elsevier, 1971. Pp. 101–127. (b)

Uretsky, N. J., & Iversen, L. L. Effects of 6-hydroxydopamine on catecholamine-containing neurones in the rat brain. *Journal of Neurochemistry,* 1970, **17,** 269–278.

Young, R. M., & Smith, G. P. Rats do not explore an open field but are active in home cages after hypothalamic injections of 6-hydroxydopamine. Program of the Society for Neurosciences, 1973, in press.

Young, R. M. *Mind, brain and adaptation in the nineteenth century.* London: Oxford University Press, 1970.

Zigmond, M. J., & Stricker, E. M. Deficits in feeding behavior after intraventricular injection of 6-hydroxydopamine in rats. *Science,* 1972, **177,** 1211–1214.

6

RELATIONSHIPS BETWEEN CHOLINERGIC AND OTHER DIPSOGENS IN THE CENTRAL MEDIATION OF THIRST[1]

Alan E. Fisher[2]
University of Pittsburgh

INTRODUCTION AND OVERVIEW

During the recently completed decade we experienced a period of evolutionary, if not revolutionary, change in the study of the central regulation of thirst. With the full emergence of techniques for linking aspects of brain chemistry, as well as peripheral physiology, to specific behaviors, there was even hope that a meaningful theoretical order could be imposed on thirst-related data, possibly involving a measure of understanding and, conceivably, enlightenment. It was during the 1960s as well that we saw the emergence of cholinergic agents and those drugs that influence cholinergic nerve transmission as popular and even crucial tools for research on the central regulation of thirst.

One contribution I can make to this volume is to provide a resume of the evidence linking brain cholinergic activity to thirst and, where possible, to integrate such data with that deriving from other more recently implicated central dipsogens such as angiotensin and isoproterenol. The early literature on the cholinergic elicitation of thirst is too well documented to bear detailed repetition here. The high points would include: (*a*) Grossman's (1960) decade-opening report that thirst could be elicited by application of a cholinergic drug to the rat's hypothalamus and could be partially suppressed by systemic or

[1] Research reported in this paper was supported in part by National Institute of Mental Health Grant MH-1951.

[2] Collaborators on the research reported here include Seymour Antelman, Martin Block, James Buggy, Thomas Clifford, Ronald Giardina, Theodore Green, Kim Johnson, Edward Matta, Edward Redgate and James Tarter. Particular thanks are also due to Alan Epstein and Edward Stricker for their helpful editorial suggestions and to Claudia Kraft for the care and extra time she gave to the preparation of the manuscript.

hypothalamic application of anticholinergic drugs; (*b*) our own reports (Fisher & Coury, 1962, 1964; Fisher, 1964, 1969) that many parts of the limbic system and diencephalon are positive cholinergic drinking sites and that these sites might represent a central cholinergic substrate for thirst; (*c*) Stein and Seifter's (1962) report that muscarine, but not nicotine, has central dipsogenic properties, thus linking the effects of central cholinergic stimulation more directly to transmitter actions and to a specific type of receptor site; and (*d*) our own report, still not fully interpretable, that anticholinergics could totally block cholinergic drinking, even if the cholinergic and anticholinergic agents were applied to positive sites on opposite sides of the brain (Levitt & Fisher, 1966).

As the 1960s drew to a close, however, it was becoming apparent that a cholinergically induced paralysis (of thought) was setting in, and that new chemicals, as well as concepts, were necessary if our high hopes were to be realized. For example, at least three lines of evidence now make it unreasonable to hypothesize that acetylcholine is *the* central transmitter for thirst. First, and most important, the central dipsogenic properties of cholinergic agents are highly species-specific, working admirably in the rat, but not at all in many other animals, including cat and monkey. The closest we have come to discovering a possible link between cholinergics and thirst in other mammals occurred during a recent study with monkeys in which carbachol potentiated the drinking response to angiotensin (M. L. Block & A. E. Fisher, unpublished data, 1972). Second, a series of studies (including some recent and as yet unpublished ones to be reported here) have made it evident that the only type of thirst that can be completely blocked by nontoxic doses of anticholinergic drugs is cholinergic thirst itself. And finally, it is becoming evident that agents that block the action of dopamine or beta-adrenergic agents are more effective than anticholinergics in attenuating some forms of thirst. Thus, although individual problems and discrepancies could be explained away, the sum total of evidence now makes it appear highly unlikely that either thirst or a major component of thirst will be found to be mediated entirely by cholinergic neurons.

As the limitations of the cholinergic hypothesis have become clearer, rival theoretical models and candidates for thirst-related central transmitter action have quickly, and perhaps sometimes too quickly, been thrust to center stage. We seem now to have entered a decade that promises revolutionary rather than evolutionary change, with all the excitement, renewed prospects, and chaos that usually accompany rapid conceptual shifts. The terms listed in Table 1 include three classes of transmitter substances and at least one hormone (angiotensin) that have now been tentatively linked to the central facilitation of thirst. Table 1 should also serve as a reminder that we still have not resolved fully all problems concerning the identification of the primary stimuli for thirst, whether or how separate systems interact, how thirst for ion-containing fluids is regulated centrally, and whether such regulation is mediated independently of thirst for water.

Of the five "primary stimulus" candidates spanning the top of Table 1, cellular dehydration can be given the cleanest bill of health. Clearly, here is a "primary stimulus" that has developed firm support, although some may still

TABLE 1

Some Thirst Variables for the Insatiable 1970s

Possible primary stimuli for thirst				
Cellular dehydration (of osmoreceptor neurons)	Cellular Na^+ increase (in thirst-related neurons)	Hypovolemia	Hypotension	Temperature increase

Possible thirst-related transmitter substances			
Cholinergics	Dopaminergics	Beta-adrenergics	Others?

Hormones implicated in the regulation of fluid-electrolyte balance
Angiotensin Aldosterone ADH

question where and how such effects are mediated. However, most of us in the field now accept as highly probable the tenet that partial dehydration (or shrinkage) of special monitoring neurons within the brain initiates a chain of events culminating in the thirst-related behavior of a wide variety of animals.

The only recent challenge to the cellular dehydration theory relates to the second of the possible primary stimuli listed in Table 1. Andersson and Eriksson (1971) are proposing that differential entry of Na^+ into thirst-related neurons may be the crucial variable rather than cellular dehydration. It is far too early to assess the predictive or staying power of this late entry, but it will be of interest to see whether cellular dehydration is, in its turn, forced into the state of retirement to which it once relegated "hypertonicity." If so, we should be a giant step closer to a belief in at least *one* generalization, that none of our tenets can ever be considered either safe or sacred.

Hypovolemia is nearly as respected a primary thirst stimulus candidate as is cellular dehydration, but some nagging questions still arise. First, the animal's actual need is to ingest materials isotonic with body fluids, not water alone, and the animal's behavior during many hypovolemic states accurately reflects this need. Typically, such animals accept only small quantities of water but will ingest large quantities of isotonic saline if it is provided. They will also select a "mix" of hypertonic and hypotonic fluids that approaches isotonicity (see Stricker, this volume). These facts alone lead one to question the extent of congruity of the mechanisms supporting osmotic and hypovolemic thirst, and to doubt whether they will fit within the same conceptual framework. Stricker's hypothesis that hypovolemia activates a separate and distinct primary thirst mechanism, independent either of osmoreceptors or of the actions of angiotensin, is an eminently reasonable one. The crucial evidence in favor of this position appears to be that (*a*) no change in *effective* osmolarity has been recorded during hypovolemia, and that (*b*) the water ingestion and at least part of the enhanced response to isotonic saline which attends the hypovolemic state induced by PG (polyethylene glycol) survives nephrectomy—a condition which deprives the animal of the major peripheral source of angiotensin. Nevertheless, it is perhaps too early to scrap all alternatives to Stricker's suggestion that hypovolemic thirst is independent of cellular dehydration or of angiotensin levels. At least one investigator (Almli, 1970) has reported that a transient state of hypertonicity can be demonstrated at the point in time when hypovolemic animals begin to ingest water. The author is to be commended for placing a much-needed emphasis on the importance of taking physiological measures at the time that the drinking behavior under investigation is initiated. However, my colleague Edward Stricker makes the telling point that Almli's measure of total osmolarity is not relevant to the assessment of cellular dehydration and that a demonstration of a change in *effective* osmolarity would be necessary to implicate osmoreceptor stimulation in the water ingestion that attends hypovolemia. Although it is true that there is no evidence for a change in effective osmolarity (relative to fluid exchange in peripheral tissue) following a hypertonic challenge such as PG, there is a rise in plasma urea concentration (Stricker, 1971a). Since the blood-brain barrier would retard the passage both of urea and of PG macromolecules, there could be a subtle but selective shift of water from the brain or CSF to the periphery, and a resultant dehydration of brain cells.

In relation to the independence or the partial or complete congruity of hypovolemic and angiotensin-induced thirst, we are faced with the intriguing fact that some extracellular thirst stimuli (PG, gum acacia, formalin) continue to elicit drinking in nephrectomized animals, while others (caval ligation, renal artery or abdominal aortic constriction or isoproterenol) do not (Fitzsimons, 1972). Since the first group of stimuli listed have in common the fact that they produce a definite plasma volume decrease rather than the simulated decrease typical of stimuli in the second group, Stricker's argument in favor of two separate extracellular thirst systems seems reasonable. However, we also must consider the alternate possibility that the first group of stimuli are providing a more efficient, rather than a different or a differently directed, feedback to the brain, and are somewhat less dependent than the second group of stimuli on any enhancing actions of angiotensin formed in the periphery.

In any event, the recent discovery of a separate and complete renin-angiotensin system in brain (Ganten, Minnich, Granger, Hayduk, Brecht, Barbeau, Boucher, & Genest, 1971) certainly reopens the question of a possible involvement of angiotensin in hypovolemic thirst. Although the functions of the brain angiotensin system are unknown, Stricker's (this volume) new finding that PG treatment increases plasma renin-angiotensin levels dramatically should alert us to the need to investigate the effect of such treatments on the formation of brain-based angiotensin before concluding that angiotensin plays no role in the mediation of hypovolemic thirst.

To summarize, I do not believe we have as yet entirely ruled out the possible involvement of osmoreceptors—or of other functionally related downstream neurons in the water ingestion which attends hypovolemia. Some face validity may still remain for the hypothesis that cellular dehydration and/or activation of neurons within a network linked directly to brain osmoreceptors may be the only *primary* (unlearned) signal for the seeking and acceptance of dilute, neutral-tasting fluids such as water. The thirst most uniquely linked to the arousal of a volemic mechanism would then be understood as a selective search for an isotonic mix of materials or a selective rejection of hypotonic solutions unless a separate source of Na^+-containing material was available.

It is of interest that "increased temperature" (see Table 1) lost much ground as a major primary stimulus for thirst following the demonstration that the water ingestion linked previously to increases in temperature could be attributed more readily to a concomitant intravascular dehydration (Hainsworth, Stricker, & Epstein, 1968). Recently, this issue has been raised again (Grace & Stevenson, 1971) by a study in which temperature and tonicity variables were carefully separated. However, the amount of drinking attributable to the temperature variable appears to be too small to suggest that temperature change plays a major or primary role in the regulation of water intake, at least in the rat (possible species differences could be an important qualifier, considering the cholinergic data).

Some of these points may seem more devilish than worth advocating, but since we have suddenly entered an era of overabundance of postulated central thirst systems and relevant variables, it will not hurt us to pause to test the limits of parsimony, and to proceed toward further proliferation of variables and systems with caution. In any event, it behooves me to demonstrate as best I can that acetylcholine is not the only dipsogenic stimulus marooned in troubled, muddied, or brackish waters.

Which brings me to the primary stimulus candidate in Table 1 that is the most difficult to assess. In considering the drinking associated with hypotension (regarding agents such as angiotensin or isoproterenol), we must contrast two approaches or theories.

First, there is the angiotensin model (see Fitzsimons, 1970) in which release of renin from the kidney (triggered by, among other things, certain hypotensive and hypovolemic states, and mediated, at least in part, via excitation of peripheral beta-adrenergic receptor sites) leads to angiotensin formation in the plasma and a subsequent thirst-inducing action on brain tissue.

Since it has been demonstrated that angiotensin is an effective central as well as peripheral dipsogen (Epstein, Fitzsimons, & Simons, 1969), the main problems for the theory are (a) to demonstrate conclusively that angiotensin can reach the brain, (b) to elucidate its mechanism(s) of action, and (c) to determine what, if any, role the separate brain angiotensin system plays in thirst.

Second, we must consider the central beta-adrenergic thirst system hypothesis, based in part on the initial evidence and suggestions of Lehr, Mallow, and

Krukowski (1967), and on the recent central data and more complete theoretical formulation by Leibowitz (1971a, 1971b). Since the latter part of this chapter will take a detailed look at our own experimental evidence bearing on this theory, I will comment only briefly here. In general, the role of hypotension per se as a *direct* and/or independent central stimulus for thirst remains unclear at this time because: (*a*) it is difficult to separate out the states of hypotension and hypovolemia, as well as the involvement or noninvolvement of angiotensin in particular instances; (*b*) some methods for producing hypotension do not produce drinking, and it appears essential that the stimulus either have beta-adrenergic properties or cause a severe or simulated drop in the circulatory input to the kidneys; and (*c*) the beta-adrenergic agents (such as isoproterenol) which induce both a hypotensive state and drinking behavior may well exert their primary effects in or on the periphery with resultant release of angiotensin. To this point in time, at least, no one has reported inducing central isoproterenol drinking reliably at dosage levels at or below the effective peripheral dose.

SOME RECENT CHOLINERGIC DATA AND SOME RELATIONSHIPS TO OTHER THIRST STATES

Within my own laboratory, we have been building from a premise stated earlier—that it has been some time since it was sensible to hold to a strictly cholinergic central theory of thirst, even for the rat. On the other hand, suggestions that the cholinergic elicitation of drinking is an artifact, or is unrelated to natural thirst, appear equally untenable. I intend to illustrate several of these points in some detail with examples from recent studies.

There have been several reports (Gandelman, Panksepp, & Trowill, 1968; Franklin & Quartermain, 1970) suggesting that the state induced by central cholinergic stimulation is unlike natural thirst. In one such report (Gandelman et al., 1968), cholinergically stimulated animals were shown to prefer sucrose solution to water, whereas water-deprived animals preferred plain water. Kim Johnson and I attempted to replicate and extend such findings, but have come to quite opposite conclusions. Essentially, we find the more detailed the analysis, the less significant the differences between cholinergically stimulated and deprived animals appear to be (Johnson & Fisher, 1973a). Figure 1 indicates that in our laboratory, both water-deprived and cholinergically stimulated animals show a typical initial burst of sucrose drinking, and the total amount of sucrose ingested (7 to 10 cc) is remarkably constant across all conditions tested (11-, 23-, and 47-hour deprivation, plus cholinergic stimulation). The amount of water ingested in addition to sucrose is seen to be a function of the level of deprivation (or by inference, of the strength of drive of cholinergically stimulated animals), with water intake surpassing sucrose intake only for the 47-hour deprived animals, and then only during the latter part of the test period. The data for cholinergically stimulated animals (Figure 1*d*) appear, in general, to place them somewhere between the 11- and 23-hour deprived groups, although

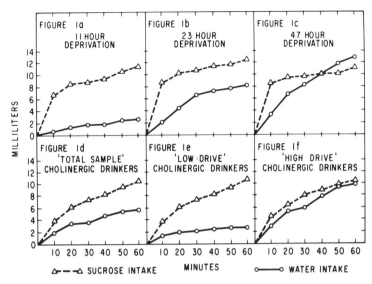

FIG. 1. Cumulative water and 25% sucrose solution intakes during the hour following 11, 23, and 47 hours of water deprivation, or following cholinergic stimulation (crystalline carbachol, 3- to 12-μg dosage range) in a limbic or diencephalic site (N/condition = 12).

their initial burst of sucrose ingestion is lower, rather than higher, than that shown by deprived animals. Figure 1e and f illustrates the outcome of splitting the sample of cholinergic drinking into "low-drive" cholinergic drinkers (< 8 cc water in a one hour, one bottle test) and "high-drive" cholinergic drinkers (> 15 cc water in a one hour, one bottle test). Here, we find that the "low-drive" cholinergic drinkers perform very much like the 11-hour deprived animals, while the "high-drive" cholinergic drinkers generate preference curves which appear to fall between those of 23- and 47-hour deprived animals.

Thus, we find a strong resemblance in the fluid preferences shown following natural thirst and cholinergic stimulation, with the degree or intensity of the effect of the cholinergic stimulation being a strong determining factor. It is paradoxical, considering the results obtained by Gandelman and his colleagues (1968), that the only major difference we see between cholinergic drinkers and water-deprived animals is a less intense and immediate ingestion of sucrose on the part of the cholinergically stimulated animals. We believe that this difference relates to the fact that the motivation to drink builds up gradually in the cholinergically stimulated animal, while the "drive to drink" of the deprived animals is maximal at the onset of the test. Partial, but indirect, confirmation for this idea has come from another study we have done (Johnson & Fisher, 1973b) in which the response of cholinergically stimulated and water-deprived animals to aversive (quinine) solutions was studied. Here, we did find a marked difference between 23-hour deprived and cholinergically stimulated animals, in that the latter would tolerate significantly less quinine in the water even though the groups were equated on amount of water consumed during a standard hour test.

However, on analyzing our methods and data carefully, we came to the realization that the cholinergically stimulated animals were probably at a distinct disadvantage. We were using a method in which the animal's score depended on the number of receptacles he would drink from when each new one made available to him contained, in sequence, an increment in percent quinine. Such tests last only a few minutes, so time since cholinergic stimulation could be a significant variable if the motivation to drink after such stimulation is increasing over time. We therefore ran a second series of tests in which cholinergically stimulated animals (matched for water ingestion with 23-hour deprived animals) were introduced to the quinine test 10 and 25 minutes after cholinergic stimulation. Under these conditions, although there was a significant difference between the scores of 23-hour deprived and 10-minute delay cholinergic animals, there was no difference between the scores of the deprived animals and the 25-minute delay cholinergic animals. Consequently, we have reached the conclusion that the reported major differences between cholinergic and natural thirst are more artifactual than real, or at least are explicable on grounds other than that a state independent of or unrelated to natural thirst is being induced.

Although such data lead us to emphasize similarities rather than differences between cholinergic and natural thirst, still another fluid preference study from our laboratory (J. Buggy, unpublished data, 1972) has pinpointed a potentially important difference between the effects of cholinergic and angiotensin brain stimulation. Animals were implanted with preoptic or septal brain cannulae, and given separate pretests with angiotensin and carbachol. When a rat tested positive to both drugs at a single site, it was placed in a cage providing continual access to both isotonic saline and water. Several weeks later the animals were run through a test sequence involving 3 angiotensin doses (10, 100, and 1000 ng) and 3 carbachol doses (.25, 1, and 25 μg) given in random order and separated by at least 2 days. Because the long test sequence could produce or encompass marked baseline change, results were analyzed in terms of the change in percentage of isotonic saline intake between the hour following a drug injection and the immediately preceding control day. Table 2 gives a summary of the test results on 16 animals.

It is important to keep in mind that the tests were carried out on sated, or at least nondeprived, animals. Under these conditions, cholinergic stimulation clearly shifted the animal's preference toward water and, in addition, over 70% of the total fluid consumed during the hour after cholinergic stimulation was from the water burette. In contrast, angiotensin (at all three dose levels) shifted the animals' preference strongly toward

TABLE 2

Percent Isotonic Saline Drunk (Relative to Water) Under
Baseline, Central Angiotensin, or Central Carbachol
Stimulation Conditions

Stimulation	Dose	23-hour baseline, % saline	1-hour postdrug, % saline
Angiotensin[a]	10 ng	47	68
	100 ng	43	81
	1,000 ng	39	73
Carbachol[b]	.25μg	50	26
	1μg	56	33
	2.5μg	57	27

[a]Over all doses of angiotensin, animals drank an average of 16 ml of which 74% was saline and 26% water.

[b]Over all doses of carbachol, animals drank an average of 13.5 ml of which 29% was saline and 71% was water.

isotonic saline, and 74% of the total fluid consumed was from the saline burette.[3] Of even more interest, we have new evidence that in a water–1.8% saline choice situation, animals given angiotensin drink a higher proportion of 1.8% saline than they do under baseline or deprivation conditions.

Other investigators have thus far failed to find such differences (see Fitzsimons, 1970), so replication (and caution) are necessary, but most work along these lines has stressed single-bottle tests, and more concentrated saline solutions. It may well be the case that animals in water and sodium balance do not respond to central angiotensin stimulation with an appetite for high concentrations of saline, but do show an enhanced preference for solutions close to isotonicity. Under natural conditions, this might manifest itself as a choice of a mix of available fluids and foodstuffs that approach isotonicity. Such a response makes good biological sense, since angiotensin is released primarily in response to cues signaling a *volume* regulatory problem, not a cellular dehydration problem. Clearly, it would be adaptive for such an animal to ingest a fluid or a total mix as close to body fluid tonicity as possible. As has been indicated (see Stricker, this volume), animals with real or simulated volume regulatory problems do show a marked preference for isotonic saline and refuse to ingest even normal amounts of water following an initial period in which some water is accepted. Although evidence for a strong Na^+ appetite (the

---

[3] It is possible that only one of these conditions involves a significant preference shift, since we do not have (and it is difficult to devise a way to obtain) baseline control data that are strictly comparable with our stimulation data. Nevertheless, the odds favor the validity of a dual shift in preference. Not only were the ad-lib data completely unlike the results obtained under either drug, but control data obtained during hour tests following 11 and 22 hours of water deprivation did not indicate a level of preference for either water or saline that was comparable to that observed under either carbachol or angiotensin.

overcoming of an aversion for hypertonic Na^+ solutions) does not become evident until 6 to 10 hours after the onset of hypovolemia, an enhanced intake of isotonic saline occurs rapidly and may correspond to the heightened preference for isotonic saline that we have seen after central angiotensin.

If the preference shifts we have seen are valid and meaningful, why has angiotensin proven such a remarkably effective dipsogen in studies where only water was available to the subjects? If angiotensin's chief and only function was to signal that a hypovolemic and/or hypotensive state existed, then one might expect to obtain rather limited fluid ingestion following central angiotensin stimulation unless isotonic saline was available. Nevertheless, such animals accept water readily and often in quantities that make it unlikely (though still worth testing) that even larger volumes of isotonic saline would be ingested. What, then, are the probable mechanisms of action of angiotensin, assuming that it does manage to pass from the peripheral circulation into brain or CSF? The most parsimonious hypothesis might be that angiotensin can act as an emergency signal to further sensitize several different functional systems in the brain, and that the *outcome* of its actions is only predictable in reference to the animal's physiological state at the time. Thus, angiotensin might act to sensitize osmoreceptors or functionally related neurons as well as nerve cells or systems which would have the more complex task of monitoring a "mixed" input of water and electrolytes. The integrated outcome would depend on the functioning of additional cues and factors—rather than on any unitary function of angiotensin. If this model has a virtue, it is that several predictions can be made that would be readily testable. Thus, a salt-loaded animal given central angiotensin should show an *enhanced* rate of water intake even with isotonic saline available, while an animal challenged with a real or simulated volume loss plus central angiotensin should show an even more pronounced isotonic saline preference (and rate of intake) than the normal animal we have already studied (or the hypovolemic nephrectomized animal without angiotensin). Finally, a sodium-depleted animal protected from hypovolemia should show an enhanced efficiency in selecting a hypertonic stimulus after central angiotensin, although available evidence suggests that this is a delayed and probably indirect action of angiotensin mediated, at least in part, by release of aldosterone. In any event, the theory predicts that the efficiency with which the animal would resolve its particular problem would be enhanced by the angiotensin release.

What is being suggested is that angiotensin essentially catalogues and integrates the function of several mechanisms related to fluid balance, at least under emergency conditions. The "fluid-balanced" animals that we and others have tested with central angiotensin accept *either* isotonic saline or water (or a relatively isotonic mix of water and electrolytes), at least momentarily, because there is a neural facilitation (or partial suppression of inhibition) within two or more families of neurons. Fluid preferences or preference shifts would only be evident in situations in which the animal was given access to water as well as to other solutions or sources of electrolytes. Whether angiotensin-related shifts in preference are mediated via strictly central events, via changes in peripheral receptors, or via changes in the rewarding and/or the aversive characteristics of certain classes of external stimuli is not fathomable at this time. We intend to explore this fascinating question further.

In summary, it seems to be the case that most cellular (osmoregulatory) challenges produce a significant increase in water consumption (relative to isotonic or hypertonic saline), while extracellular (hypovolemic, hypotensive) challenges usually produce a marked increase in isotonic saline consumption (while briefly increasing, inhibiting, or failing to affect water intake, depending on method and duration of testing) (i.e., Smith & Stricker, 1969; Stricker, 1971a). Since the increment or shift in preference following such treatments takes 15 to 90 minutes to develop (the effects of extracellular challenges requiring the longer times), it has been proposed that postingestional factors or learned discriminations based on the effectiveness of a solution in meeting physiological needs are operating (Mook, 1969; Smith & Stricker, 1969).

However, if we are correct that brain injections of carbachol and angiotensin can produce rapid and opposite shifts in the percentages of water and isotonic saline ingested by animals in normal fluid balance, then the data may indicate that: (a) central cholinergic stimulation is selectively (or more effectively) activating a cellular rather than an extracellular component of thirst; (b) central angiotensin (under conditions of normal fluid-electrolyte balance) is exerting a greater facilitatory effect on an extracellular thirst component (although my position favors involvement of cellular components as well, since sated animals given angiotensin accept water readily if this is all that is offered and also show a facilitation of salt-induced water ingestion) (Fitzsimons & Simons, 1969); and (c) postingestional factors or discrimination learning may not be as significant a factor in regulating these preference shifts as the timing of hormonal actions which can increase the probability that such shifts will occur. These could include time for sufficient endogenous angiotensin to penetrate to appropriate brain tissue, time for an initial action of angiotensin on neurons mediating a water preference to lead to water ingestion and overhydration of the monitor-neurons, and time for a separate action of angiotensin on neurons which initiate or enhance a preference for Na^+-containing materials.

In any event, the effects of centrally injected angiotensin on fluid ingestion typically occur within seconds, and our data suggest that a rapid enhancement of isotonic saline intake is demonstrable if rats are provided a choice of water and saline, and that the converse is true for cholinergic stimulation. It would be nice to be able to accept the fact that nephrectomy eliminates Na^+ appetite (Fitzsimons & Stricker, 1971) as additional evidence that angiotensin plays a key role in mediating shifting water-Na^+ preferences. However, it is evident that the problem of assessing the part played by the kidney or by the byproducts of its actions (including renin-angiotensin and urea) in Na^+ appetite is exceedingly complex and unresolved, (Stricker, this volume).

A PHARMACOLOGICAL APPROACH TO THE INVESTIGATION OF CHOLINERGIC AND OTHER THIRST-RELATED STATES

During the past year, a major attempt has been made in our laboratory to assess the worth of a pharmacological approach to the study of the central regulation of thirst. As I have already indicated, a general cholinergic model for thirst cannot handle the data we ourselves have generated, let alone that of others.

Our secondary hypothesis has been that it might be possible to differentiate separate components within an overall fluid-electrolyte regulatory system that utilize specific transmitters or are selectively influenced by hormones. Put another way, we are testing the relative value of pharmacological agents (in contrast, for example, to a brain lesion approach) in separating out unitary components of thirst. If the brain is organized such that separate components utilize single or at least different sets of transmitters, then the approach could prove to be a powerful one. If, on the other hand, there is considerable overlap in the utilization of transmitters by separate parts of an overall thirst system, the approach would be of little value beyond the initial demonstration of such overlap.

In earlier work on this problem, Martin Block and I had tested the extent to which natural (deprivation) thirst was blocked by doses of centrally administered anticholinergics that totally abolished cholinergic drinking (Block & Fisher, 1970). As Table 3a indicates, we found evidence for only a partial blockade. The percentage of water intake suppressed, relative to controls,

TABLE 3a

Water Intake of Water-Deprived Animals Given Central Stimulation

Stimulation	N	1-hour water intake, cc (means)
6-hour deprived		
Dextrose	7	8.9
Methyl atropine	7	3.1^a (–66%)
Empty cannula	6	9.0
Sodium nitrate	7	8.5
23-hour deprived		
Dextrose	3	20.9
Methyl atropine	4	14.5^b (–30%)

[a]Significant at .1 level.
[b]Significant at .01 level.

TABLE 3*b*

Water Intake of Saline-Injected Animals
Given Central Stimulation

Drug or placebo	N	1-hour water intake, cc (means)
Dextrose	11	13.5
Methyl atropine	11	6.5[a] (−48%)
Dextrose	3	13.0
Dybenzyline	3	12.3

[a]Significant at .01 level.

decreased with increasing deprivation (from 66% blockade after 6 hours of deprivation to 30% blockade at 23 hours of deprivation). However, it may be worth noting that the actual amount of the decrease (5.9 cc at 6 hours and 6.4 cc at 23 hours) was remarkably constant. Since natural thirst could involve a number of functional components of a thirst system, we took this as suggestive evidence that we might be having our major effect on a single component. Our next step was to challenge animals with a hypertonic stimulus, and to determine the effectiveness of anticholinergics in blocking cell dehydration drinking. Table 3*b* indicates that we again obtained only a partial blockade (48%), and that the average decrease in intake (7.0 cc) was of the same order as that seen in the deprivation study. Let me say in passing that we do have dose-response data indicating that higher doses of central anticholinergics do not give an increasingly effective blockade of either natural or cell dehydration thirst.

More recently, Ronald Giardina and I (Giardina & Fisher, 1971) have tested the effectiveness of centrally administered anticholinergics in blocking drinking induced by central injections of angiotensin and isoproterenol. The atropine and the dipsogens were applied at the same locus. Here, as Figure 2 indicates, the results are more clear-cut. Although the anticholinergic stimulus was predictably effective in blocking cholinergic drinking, no suppression whatever of angiotensin or isoproterenol drinking was evident. Thus, there is no evidence that the immediate actions of these dipsogens involve cholinergic components.

However, this does not necessarily mean that cholinergic components are not involved in some aspect of such drinking, since they might be making their contribution at other neural levels than the one directly stimulated. In fact, we have observed a partial blockade of *both* isoproterenol and angiotensin drinking when anticholinergics are injected peripherally at dosage levels (3 to 6 mg/kg) which have no effect on ingestion of moist food. At this point, Block and I initiated a series of experiments to test the effects of peripheral and central administration of selective blocking agents on a wide range of dipsogenic challenges. These should be viewed as pilot studies, requiring further validation, but designed primarily to test the overall efficacy of the pharmacological approach. The first problem was of course to select the pharmacological agents

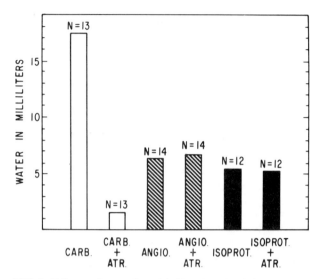

FIG. 2. Effects of central anticholinergic stimulation on carbachol-, angiotensin-, and isoproterenol-induced drinking during a 1-hour postinjection test. All compounds were applied to lateral septal tissue via a permanently implanted brain cannula. The doses of crystals delivered to the brain site were as follows: carbachol, 5 to 10 μg; atropine sulfate, 15 to 20 μg; atropine methyl nitrate, 15 to 20 μg; angiotensin II, 15 to 20 μg; and *DL*-isoproterenol HCl, 15 to 20 μg. When anticholinergics were used, they were introduced to the brain site 10 minutes prior to a previously positive drug.

(and the dipsogenic challenges) that might best match up with separate components of thirst.

During the meetings of the International Conference on the Regulation of Food and Water Intake held in Cambridge, England, in the summer of 1971, Fitzsimons reported that haloperidol, a selective dopaminergic blocker at low dosages, suppressed angiotensin drinking but spared cholinergic drinking. He also suggested that dopamine might be involved in the mediation of extracellular thirst. At the same time, one of my graduate students was obtaining evidence which also appeared to link dopamine to drinking. Martin Block (unpublished data, 1971) had found that dopamine itself had no demonstrable effect when injected into brain (possibly due to uptake by a variety of catecholamine nerve terminals, to metabolic breakdown, or to conversion to NE). But, when he tried apomorphine chloride stabilized with ascorbic acid, he obtained evidence that this selective activator of dopamine receptor sites increased drinking when injected (6 to 20 μg) into certain hypothalamic areas. The latencies were long (an average of 23 minutes), and the drinking response averaged only 4 to 5 cc, but the response was significantly above control values. Peripheral injection of equivalent amounts of the substance had no effect on drinking behavior, so the effect appeared to be centrally mediated. I should say, however, that since Block has left the laboratory for postdoctoral work, we have had no success in replicating this apomorphine effect in new series of animals, although we have been successful with two of the survivors of his original study. Under the circumstances, I would prefer to downplay our somewhat scanty evidence for a central facilitatory effect of dopamine on drinking until the data are more conclusive.

In any event, the Fitzsimons and Block data were instrumental in our choice of haloperidol as our other major blocking agent. In designing these preliminary screening studies, Block and I decided to do a large number of pilot experiments with small *N*s and to utilize a range of drug dosages. Our aim was to select those variables deserving more detailed study and to determine whether the technique of pharmacological intervention was at all suited to the problems at hand. We are quite aware that more controls are needed to insure that differences in motivational or physiological states are not acting as artifacts in these studies. I will also tip my hand and say that I still have not been able to reach a firm conclusion regarding the relative merits of the pharmacological approach to this problem area.

With that as a preamble, let me briefly summarize some of the methods utilized and major results obtained. In the peripheral work, animals were challenged in separate tests with 2 cc SC of a 2 M NaCl solution (cellular dehydration), 11 hours of water deprivation, 22 hours of water deprivation, 5 cc SC of 30% PG solution (hypovolemic stimulus), or .04 mg/kg SC isoproterenol (hypotensive or beta-adrenergic stimulus). With the exception of the 22-hour deprivation condition, the mean amounts of water ingested following each of these treatments (but without blocking agents) did not differ significantly, so there was at least a rough equilibration of motivational levels. Also, since there are marked differences in latency to drink following many of these treatments, as well as differences in latency of drug action, blocking agents were not introduced, nor was water provided prior to an appropriate point within the latency period for a given treatment. Three separate peripheral dosages of the anticholinergic drug scopolamine HCl were given (.1, .5 and 1 mg/kg), as well as three dosages of haloperidol (.02, .08, .17 mg/kg). Ultimately, the data for the highest dose of haloperidol were discounted entirely, since at that dosage both drinking and eating behavior (as well as self-stimulation behavior and activity level) were attenuated severely. In some experiments, intermediate doses of scopolamine and haloperidol were also administered simultaneously to determine whether effects were additive. Isotonic saline controls were run for each drug condition, and the percent changes in response between the placebo and the drug conditions were obtained.

Table 4 is an example of the detailed data from one of the experiments from this study, and Table 5 gives an overview of the more interesting results for intermediate dosage levels across all treatments.

TABLE 4

Deprivation-Induced Drinking[a]: Effects of Neuropharmacological Blocking Agents

Group[b]	Drug	Dose, mg/kg	N	$\bar{X}$ HOH intake (+SE) in cc	
				1 hour	Change from placebo, %
1	Isotonic saline	(placebo)	4	16.1 ± .8	
	Haloperidol	.02		16.4 ± 2.1	+ 2
2	Isotonic saline	(placebo)	4	19.8 ± 1.3	
	Haloperidol	.08		9.6 ± 1.6*	−52
3	Isotonic saline	(placebo)	4	15.8 ± 2.9	
	Haloperidol	.17		2.8 ± .9*	−82
4	Isotonic saline	(placebo)	4	16.4 ± 1.5	
	Scopolamine HCl	.1		14.3 ± .6	−10
5	Isotonic saline	(placebo)	4	16.0 ± 1.2	
	Scopolamine HCl	.5		10.1 ± .9*	−37
6	Isotonic saline	(placebo)	4	18.5 ± 1.5	
	Scopolamine HCl	1.0		8.9 ± 1.0*	−52
7[c]	Isotonic saline	(placebo)	7	19.1 ± 1.7	
	Haloperidol	.08		4.7 ± 1.4*	−76
	+Scopolamine HC1	.5			

[a] 22 hours of water deprivation; food available ad lib.
[b] Groups 1–3: SC injections of placebo or drug 1 hour before test. Groups 4–6: IP injections of placebo or drug 1/2 hour before test.
[c] Placebo injections 1 hour and 1/2 hour before drinking test; drugs given 1 hour and 1/2 hour (as above) before test.
*Significantly different from placebo intake at .05 level; one-tailed t test for paired observations.

The Ns per treatment ranged from 4 to 7 and, as mentioned previously the baseline water intake control values for all treatments except 22-hour water deprivation were roughly equivalent, ranging from a mean intake of 8.0 cc (±1.1 cc) for isoproterenol-induced drinking to a mean of 11.2 cc (±1.7 cc) for hypovolemic (PG) drinking. The interesting contrasts in the summary table are between conditions that emphasize hypertonic or hypovolemic-hypotensive challenges. Thus, for cellular dehydration drinking and 11 hours of water deprivation (conditions that should emphasize an osmotic rather than a volemic component of thirst), the combined effects of anticholinergic and antidopaminergic actions were not additive. Following hypovolemic (PG) or hypotensive (isoproterenol) challenges, however, the combined effects of scopolamine and haloperidol *were* additive, and virtually all drinking was blocked. Following the 22-hour water-deprivation challenge, the only condition tested which would surely involve both osmotic and volemic components of thirst, a partial additive effect of the two blocking agents was observable.

In order to determine the relative specificity of drug action at the dosages utilized, we also measured the effects of these blocking agents on eating induced by 22 hours of food deprivation and by 750 mg/kg injections of 2-deoxy-D-glucose. As summarized in Table 5, the doses of scopolamine and haloperidol that were effective in attenuating thirst had no significant effect on the intake of a moist food. Scopolamine (but not haloperidol) depressed the intake of dry food, but this can be attributed to the peripheral inhibitory actions of

TABLE 5

Summary of the Effects of a Selected Peripheral Dose of Scopolamine and Haloperidol, Singly and in Combination, on Drinking and Eating Induced by a Variety of Manipulations

Condition	Drug	Dose mg/kg	% changes in water intake (from placebo or vehicle control)
Salt-induced drinking	Scopolamine	.5	−58
	Haloperidol	.08	−62
	Scopolamine +Haloperidol	.5/ .08	−62
Deprivation-induced drinking−11 hours	Scopolamine	.5	−75
	Haloperidol	.08	−51
	Scopolamine +Haloperidol	.5/ .08	−79
Hypovolemic (PG) drinking	Scopolamine	.5	−45
	Haloperidol	.02	−35
	Scopolamine +Haloperidol	.5/ .02	−96
Isoproterenol drinking	Scopolamine	.5	−46
	Haloperidol	.08	−75
	Scopolamine +Haloperidol	.5/ .08	−95
Deprivation-induced drinking−22 hours	Scopolamine	.5	−37
	Haloperidol	.08	−52
	Scopolamine +Haloperidol	.5/ .08	−76

Condition	Drug	Dose mg/kg	% change in food intake
Deprivation-induced eating−22 hours	Scopolamine	.5	−63 (dry food)
	Haloperidol	.08	− 7 (dry food)
	Scopolamine	.5	− 9 (wet mash)
	Haloperidol	.08	− 8 (wet mash)
	Scopolamine +Haloperidol	.5/ .08	− 4 (wet mash)
2-deoxy-D-glucose-induced eating	Scopolamine	.5	− 6 (wet mash)
	Haloperidol	.08	+ 6 (wet mash)
	Scopolamine +Haloperidol	.5/ .08	− 8 (wet mash)

scopolamine on saliva secretion, since the same dose of scopolamine had no effect on the intake of wet mash.

The hypotheses that emerge from this study are that: (a) the central system which responds to osmotic (cellular) challenges probably contains some components that are neither cholinergic nor dopaminergic; (b) the system or systems responding to extracellular challenges cannot function if denied access to both dopaminergic and cholinergic transmitter substances; (c) the effects of these doses of haloperidol and scopolamine on thirst are relatively specific, since eating behavior was not attenuated by either single or combined dosages of these blocking agents; and (d) it appears highly unlikely that *any* of the major components of thirst utilize or are entirely dependent upon a single transmitter substance.

Point (d) is discouraging, but it is not very surprising when one considers the many levels of function and control that are necessary for mediating the complex of behaviors involved in seeking, selecting, and ingesting fluids. What *is* perhaps surprising is the lack of evidence for a single final common path that would be dependent on the availability of a particular transmitter. However, since the drugs given peripherally partially blocked all forms of thirst, the results could mean that there is only one neural substrate mediating water ingestion. On the other hand, methodology must be assessed carefully, since peripherally delivered drugs may fail to achieve an optimal concentration at key sites within the CNS and drug side effects could also be confounding factors. These problems can be circumvented in part by making some assumptions concerning the possible locations of crucial CNS sites of drug action and then applying blocking agents directly to them.

We have done some preliminary work with this approach, but so far the results are very similar to those obtained with peripherally administered drugs. Thus, when 5 μg of scopolamine or haloperidol was injected bilaterally in selected brain sites (see Figure 3) of 22-hour deprived animals, partial blockades were obtained which were similar in magnitude to those obtained following the intermediate peripheral dosages of these drugs. Several other points are of interest. For lateral preoptic placements (see Figure 3), only scopolamine had a significant effect on water ingestion (63% blockade), which provides support for the idea that cholinergic portions of an osmo-related thirst component may have massive representation there. For the two other brain areas tested, both dopaminergic and cholinergic blocking agents were roughly equivalent in their blocking actions, suggesting that relevant dopaminergic and cholinergic receptor sites are perhaps to be found in or near these regions.

We are going on to determine the effects of localized central application of haloperidol and scopolamine (plus vehicle and local anesthetic controls) on the water intake following peripheral challenges such as polyethylene glycol, hypertonic saline, and isoproterenol. These data are not yet complete, but it is clear that we have yet to demonstrate a complete blockade of a real or imagined unitary component of thirst with one particular blocking agent—at least without

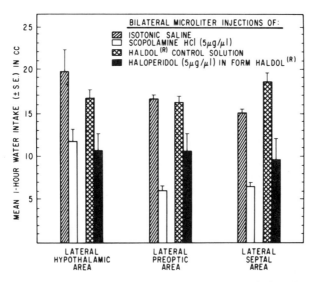

FIG. 3. Effects of bilateral central injections of anticholinergic, antidopaminergic, and control substances on the water ingestion induced by 22 hours of water deprivation. All drugs were given in a 1-μl volume 15 minutes prior to the start of the 1-hour drinking test.

incurring drastic side effects. Consequently, although some of our results with selective blocking agents appear promising, I do not feel that our rather major investment has as yet paid adequate dividends.

We do intend to make additional efforts in order to insure a full testing of the limits of such a pharmacological approach. It may well be the case, however, that we are asking the wrong questions or dealing with chemical codes that are too complex, even within a given subsystem, to be comprehensible or resolvable by the techniques at hand. Unfortunately, a more microanalysis, at this stage in our program would almost certainly lose touch with the behavioral link that is so vital to those who believe it is essential that some of us approach these problems as psychobiologists, rather than as neurophysiologists or brain biochemists. I do continue to have faith that some of the major breakthoughs on the horizon will require and be sustained by the less molecular, considerably less efficient, but perhaps ultimately more rewarding attempts to link brain organization and function to behavior.

AN ANALYSIS OF THE BETA-ADRENERGIC
ELICITATION OF THIRST

The most direct challenge (other than its own failings) to the cholinergic theory of thirst has come from the work linking beta-adrenergic transmitter action with drinking behavior. Lehr et al. (1967) were the first to report that systemic injections of isoproterenol, a beta-adrenergic agent, induced thirst in the rat, and were also the first to suggest that thirst-related central neurons might be involved. Later, Leibowitz (1971a, 1971b) provided evidence that beta-adrenergic stimulation of the hypothalamus facilitated drinking, while alpha-adrenergic stimulation (or beta-blocking agents) inhibited thirst. She also developed a complex theoretical model, based on anatomical and pharmacological data, which proposed that the facilitation and inhibition of both eating and drinking were reciprocally controlled by central alpha- and beta-adrenergic actions.

Although the model is an elegant one, the data on which the model for thirst are currently based must be considered highly suspect. First, the published reports by Leibowitz indicate that a very high central dose of isoproterenol (40 μg) was used to induce thirst, and an even higher central dose of the beta-adrenergic blocking agent propranolol (84 μg) was required for even a minimal suppression of natural thirst. Since Lehr et al. (1967) reported that delivery of as little as 5 μg of isoproterenol to the periphery of the rat induced drinking, and since we have obtained good drinking in some rats following peripheral injection of 1 μg or less, it is essential to consider the possibility that enough of the centrally injected substance is leaking into the periphery to explain the apparent central action in quite different terms. Also, the beta-adrenergic blocking agent utilized by Leibowitz in her studies is a potent local anesthetic, so that her reports of partial inhibition of natural thirst and blockade of beta-adrenergic *and* of cholinergic drinking following central injection of this agent must also be interpreted with great caution. We have attempted a thorough analysis of the beta-adrenergic relationship to thirst during the past year (Fisher, Antelman, Tarter, & Redgate, 1972), and I will briefly summarize our main findings here.

First, we have found that central isoproterenol drinking is blocked uniformly by nephrectomy (N = 16), while central angiotensin and cholinergic drinking survive nephrectomy in a majority of these same animals (Antelman, Johnson, & Fisher, 1972; Fisher et al., 1972).

Table 6 outlines the results for a series of animals with brain cannulae in the anterolateral hypothalamus or hippocampus. These animals were first tested with a 10-μg brain injection of isoproterenol in 1 μl saline. If they did not respond by drinking 4 cc or more in the next 90 minutes, they were retested on subsequent days with 20 and then 40 μg, or until they met criterion. Subsequently, they were tested with 50 ng of angiotensin and .5 μg of carbachol (on separated days) at the same neural site. Following nephrectomy, animals were retested at the highest isoproterenol level they had received previously and were then given the next higher dose on the same test day when they failed to drink within an hour. Water intake was then recorded for an additional 90 minutes. Following this stage, those animals that had proved positive to angiotensin and/or carbachol were tested first with angiotensin and later on the same day with carbachol if previous data made such a test appropriate. Data

TABLE 6

Mean Amounts of Water Consumed in the 90 Minutes
Following Central Chemical Stimulation
Before and After Nephrectomy

Stimulation	N	Water consumed, cc	
		Prenephrectomy	Postnephrectomy
Isoproterenol	16	7.4	1.2
Carbachol	8	8.7	7.6
Angiotensin	13	11.4	11.0

include the measures from the last or most positive isoproterenol test, as well as the results on single tests with the other drugs.

These data substantiate and supplement the report by Houpt and Epstein (1971) that the drinking response to peripherally administered isoproterenol is abolished by nephrectomy. Such results make it unlikely that the major drinking response seen following central isoproterenol injection reflects the functioning of a central beta-adrenergic thirst system, but the phenomenon must still be explained. Two of the most likely alternatives to the Leibowitz theory are:

1. That leakage of sufficient centrally injected isoproterenol to the periphery occurs to initiate the events (such as angiotensin formation or afferent feedback from kidney or baroreceptor to brain initiating a supraspinal reflex) that could influence thirst systems indirectly and in the same manner as following peripheral injection of the drug.

2. That the injection of isoproterenol in the hypothalamus induces a sympathetic neural outflow which triggers renin release, the formation of angiotensin, and the direct action of that compound on thirst-related neurons in the brain.

We have made a number of attempts to test the viability of these hypotheses, including a series of cord-transection experiments. Our purpose was to cut the cord at a level which would guarantee a lack of communication between the brain and the peripheral sympathetic system, particularly ganglia innervating the kidney, adrenals, and visceral blood vessels. If the central injections of isoproterenol influenced thirst through local (hypothalamic) initiation of sympathetic outflow which then triggered peripheral renin release, then eliminating the sympathetic signal should eliminate central isoproterenol drinking. So long as we concentrated on hypothalamic placements, that is precisely the result we obtained. Just as in the nephrectomy experiments, centrally induced isoproterenol drinking was abolished in all transected animals with hypothalamic brain cannulations, while central angiotensin and cholinergic drinking survived in a majority of the transected animals. At this stage in our work the results were hearteningly unambiguous, and the sympathetically mediated renin-release hypothesis seemed to have gained formidable support. At this point we proceeded to increase our N, and to work with hippocampal as well as hypothalamic placements. Mountford (1969) first implicated hippocampus in isoproterenol-induced thirst, and we had found it an even more reliable positive site than the hypothalamus. In our first "mixed" series we replicated our previous results for all hypothalamic sites tested, but in two out of five hippocampal animals the central isoproterenol drinking response *survived* transection.

Thus, our hopes for early closure, or at least for a relatively unconfounded outcome went aglimmering. If the response to isoproterenol survives transection in some animals, or at *some* brain placements but not at others, then no single hypothesis or mechanism of action is going to handle all the data. Either the leakage variable and the sympathetic outflow variable are interacting to produce such results, or there is, as Leibowitz has maintained, a direct central action of isoproterenol on thirst-related neurons quite independent of peripheral events.

Our next step was to run a larger series of animals, implanted with hippocampal and hypothalamic cannulae, through the cord-transection experiment. Again, the data were as unequivocal as they were bewildering. This time, central isoproterenol drinking survived in five out of eight animals with hippocampal cannulae, yet the response again failed to survive in any of the hypothalamically cannulated animals. Table 7 provides a summary of data from the experimental groups mentioned above.

Animals were again given pretests with increasing amounts of centrally injected isoproterenol (10, 20, and 40 μg) until they drank 4 cc or more in 90 minutes. After transection, animals were maintained in a 78° environmental room for at least 10 days before testing began. Bladders were evacuated manually every few hours. Animals were retested first at the drug level at which they reached criterion, as well as at a dose which was twice that of the criterion

TABLE 7

Mean Amounts of Water Consumed in the 90 Minutes
Following Central Chemical Stimulation with
Isoproterenol (20 to 40 μg) Before and
After T-1 Cord Transection

Stimulation	N	Water consumed, cc	
		Pretransection	Posttransection
Hypothalamic	15	6.8	.9
Hippocampal	13	7.6	5.0

Note.—Seven of 13 hippocampal animals drank 4 cc or more during posttransection testing. Of 15 hypothalamic animals, none drank 4 cc or more during posttransection testing.

TABLE 8

Average DPM/ml Blood $\times 10^4$ Following Peripheral,
Hypothalamic, and Hippocampal Injection of Dosages of
Tritiated Isoproterenol that Induce Drinking

Site of stimulation	N	Dose	DPM/ml blood $\times 10^4$
Peripheral	3	12 μg	27,500
Hypothalamus	9	25 μg	28,000
Hippocampus[a]	6	25 μg	48,000

[a]Hippocampal animal #53 = 5,200. Range for other hippocampals = 27,500–75,000.

dose. As can be seen, only hippocampal animals gave evidence of survival of isoproterenol drinking. Paradoxically, we seemed to be achieving our only evidence in favor of Leibowitz's "central" hypothesis at a site she has never reported testing. Nevertheless, we also had considerable data to indicate that hippocampal isoproterenol drinking was as completely obliterated by nephrectomy as hypothalamic isoproterenol drinking, so a search for a satisfactory explanation continued.

At this point we began working with radioactive isoproterenol, and although our results are preliminary and further control studies and refinements would be helpful, I believe the answer to the puzzle is becoming evident. We have introduced tritiated isoproterenol into the brain cannulae of animals (1 = μl volume) previously tested for both central and peripheral isoproterenol drinking thresholds. We have then taken peripheral blood samples (from the jugular vein) 30 and 60 minutes after central or peripheral injection of isoproterenol, and prepared such samples for scintillation counting.

To our surprise the data indicate a clear difference in radioactive leakage to the peripheral circulation following hippocampal and hypothalamic injections, and for hippocampal placements, the DPM (disintegrations per minute) adjusted count from such peripheral blood samples is well above the count obtained when enough of the radioactive sample to induce drinking is injected directly into the periphery (see Table 8).

Although the apparent difference in traced leakage between hippocampal and hypothalamic placements is highly suggestive, the evidence that has really convinced me that we are on the right track derives from one unusual animal (see Table 8, hippocampal animal #53). This rat had an extremely low threshold for peripheral elicitation of isoproterenol drinking (1 μg or less), but was the only one in a group of 10 animals, each with a hippocampal cannula, that did not respond to up to 40 μg centrally. If a "leakage" theory was indeed correct, including the hypothesis that the key variable between hippocampal and hypothalamic placements was differential leakage to the periphery, then the failure of this animal to respond to central isoproterenol stimulation appeared to be inexplicable. Later, however, the rat in question was included in a large series of animals to be given central injections of radioactive isoproterenol. The results were dramatic indeed, particularly since no one involved in gathering data knew the experimental history of the animals or that a "special" animal was included in the group. The count obtained from peripheral blood samples taken 30 and 60 minutes after central injections of this animal were from 5 to 15 times *lower* than the counts obtained from other hippocampal animals. Thus, the most parsimonious hypothesis to account for a positive central isoproterenol response from the dorsal hippocampus is peripheral leakage.

As a cautionary note, it should be stated that we do not yet know how much of our peripheral radioactive count is due to intact isoproterenol, although the drinking which follows peripheral injection suggests that metabolic breakdown is not a significant factor—at least during the initial hour.

Some of the implications of these preliminary data concerning rapid leakage of brain-injected substances and/or their metabolites into the periphery are of importance. There has been considerable controversy in our field in recent years about spread of injected substances through brain (i.e., see Routtenberg, 1967; Fisher & Levitt, 1967; Routtenberg, Sladek, & Bondareff, 1968; Grossman, 1969; Myers, Tytell, Kawa, & Rudy, 1971), but little consideration of peripheral leakage. On balance, available evidence now suggests to me that there is a relatively minor effective spread of crystalline or small-volume liquid injections across brain tissue (or into ventricles, unless the cannula passes through one, or unless injections over 1 μl are used). However, a substantial proportion of substances we inject may pass into the peripheral circulation, and rather rapidly. The difference in measured leakage between our hypothalamic and dorsal hippocampal animals may relate to the ease of access to subarachnoid spaces and the superior venous sinuses on the surface of the brain. Recently, we have tried central isoproterenol in "control" placements in medial and lateral cortical regions above the dorsal hippocampus and obtained good drinking responses. Indeed, it is still possible that most, rather than some, central isoproterenol data can be explained by a leakage hypothesis. Another piece of evidence favoring such a position relates to the time of maximal intensity of the isoproterenol drinking response following hippocampal or hypothalamic stimulation in normal animals. Table 9 shows the distribtuion of water intake during 28 (90-minute)

TABLE 9

Distribution of Water Intake for Central Isoproterenol Drinkers
During 90-Minute Tests

Site of stimulation	Mean amount consumed, cc			
	1st 30 minutes	2nd 30 minutes	Final 30 minutes	Total intake
Hippocampal	3.8	2.8	.8	7.4
Lateral hypothalamic	1.0	4.2	1.8	7.0

tests carried out on nine hippocampal and five hypothalamic positive isoproterenol drinkers. Seven of these nine hippocampal animals responded with 5 cc
or more of water intake in the first half-hour on one or both tests, while only
one hypothalamic animal drank over 1 cc during this portion of the tests. Again,
the most parsimonious hypothesis would be that differential rate and amount of
leakage from hippocampal and hypothalamic sites could be responsible for such
latency differences. This is particularly true if we include our evidence that
peripheral (plasma) levels of radioactive isoproterenol 30 and 60 minutes after
central injection show a high point for hypothalamic animals at 60 minutes,
while the highest level for most hippocampal animals is seen at 30 minutes.

The question that confronts an all-inclusive leakage hypothesis is *Why* would
positive hypothalamic sites turn negative after transection? One possible
explanation which favors the leakage theory has emerged. We have noted in
many animals a diminished effectiveness of peripheral isoproterenol after
transection. Such a change could reflect a higher threshold of response to
hypotensive agents due to the prolonged hypotensive state that follows
transection (even though we usually wait at least 7 days after transection before
retesting). If this were a factor, then the high rate and amount of leakage from
the hippocampus may still provide an adequate stimulus for renin release, while
the minimal leakage from hypothalamus may no longer be sufficient to set in
motion the events that trigger drinking.

However, since some positive hypothalamic isoproterenol drinkers have
relatively high peripheral isoproterenol drinking thresholds, and others have
thresholds much lower than those of many hippocampal animals (with the
differential often being greater than the difference in radioactive leakage from
the two types of sites), it is difficult to attribute all of the data to leakage. On
balance, therefore, I believe a case can still be made for the interaction of
leakage to the periphery and autonomic outflow from the hypothalamus in
initiating the events following central isoproterenol stimulation that lead to
drinking. In fact, the observed decrease in response to peripheral isoproterenol
after transection may even reflect a partial dependence on sympathetic neural
feedback to brain from kidney (and other) vasculature for the central
enhancement of an autonomic neural outflow which increases renin release.
Such feedback would also fail to survive transection and would provide another
possible explanation for the loss of the hypothalamic isoproterenol response
after transection.

Considering all evidence, I believe it very likely that kidney-related factor(s),
including angiotensin, are largely responsible for the increased intake of fluid(s)
following central or peripheral isoproterenol. Centrally triggered autonomic
outflow, the hypotensive state itself, and direct action of isoproterenol on kidney
probably all contribute to renin release. Likewise, afferent feedback from kidney
and vasculature to brain in all likelihood interacts with the actions of angiotensin
to enhance the drinking response and to direct the animal toward water, isotonic
or hypertonic preferences.

The main reasons for caution relate to some apparent differences between angiotensin and isoproterenol-induced drinking. However, I believe most such differences are more apparent than real, or can be related to other factors operating following isoproterenol injection. For instance, the relatively high peripheral doses of angiotensin required and/or the long latency to drink after peripheral administration (Fitzsimons & Simons, 1969; but also see Epstein, 1972, for a report of much shorter latencies) may be due in part to the fact that the angiotensin data are taken from replete animals, while isoproterenol (in addition to renin release) produces peripheral effects which should themselves be cues for thirst. The failure of isoproterenol to produce drinking after nephrectomy does not totally discount this argument, since there would be a loss of afferent feedback from the kidney and its vasculature, as well as a lack of angiotensin. Likewise, the argument that angiotensin-induced drinking and isoproterenol-induced drinking are separable because the first is accompanied by an increase in urine flow and the second by a decrease, can be countered by the fact that angiotensin infusion into a normal animal increases blood pressure, while isoproterenol would create a hypotensive state leading to oliguria. In most cases, we are finding congruence between isoproterenol and angiotensin drinking wherever we look. Thus, central anticholinergic stimulation blocks neither angiotensin nor isoproterenol drinking that has been centrally induced, but peripheral anticholinergic stimulation partially blocks peripheral isoproterenol drinking and also has a partial blocking effect on both central angiotensin and isoproterenol-induced drinking at dosage levels that leave eating unaffected. Also, a majority of our animals given central isoproterenol injections in either hippocampal or lateral hypothalamic sites drink a higher isotonic saline to water ratio than they do under ad-lib conditions or when water-deprived. As previously mentioned, (see Table 2), we obtain similar results following central angiotensin injections. Conversely, however, I am at a loss to explain the results obtained recently by Fitzsimons and Stricker (1971) in which animals treated with peripheral isoproterenol showed a strong preference for water over isotonic saline. Our own data on effects of peripheral isoproterenol are incomplete, but do not reflect such a preference for water. Since an obvious difference between the studies is in dosage level (Fitzsimons and Stricker used doses of .33 mg/kg, which translates to from 85 to 115 μg/rat, while our dose range has been 1 to 20 μg/rat), we intend to determine whether fluid preference varies as a function of dosage. We have found that doses higher than 40 μg severely debilitate the animal and are often lethal, so there is a real possibility that high doses of isoproterenol produce side effects that impair an adaptive or typical response to the primary action(s) of the drug.

There is one other aspect to the central isoproterenol drinking phenomenon which deserves consideration. Leibowitz now suggests (1971b; 1972) that there are two separable central adrenergic drinking responses, including a very short latency response to isoproterenol, that can also be demonstrated in some animals (prior to eating) when norepinephrine is given centrally. The theory is that the beta-adrenergic properties of norepinephrine are faster acting, and bring about a facilitation of drinking prior to the alpha-adrenergic facilitation of eating. We have seen such responses, as have others (Myers, 1964; Miller, 1965), but in our hands a short latency response to isoproterenol, in particular, is an occasional and quite unreliable phenomenon. Although final judgment must be reserved, I believe the most parsimonious explanation is that beta-adrenergic agents, in affecting a reasonably well documented inhibition of neurons related to hunger (Conte, Lehr, Goldman, & Krukowski, 1968; Leibowitz, 1970), secondarily lower the threshold of drinking-related neurons that are subject to inhibitory influences from collaterals of hunger-related neurons. Since studies are typically done on nondeprived animals, reduction of only one of a number of inhibitory influences on thirst-related neurons could be expected to have a relatively minimal and highly variable effect on drinking behavior, which is the result observed thus far in our laboratory. Leibowitz's latest suggestion (1972) that the dual beta- and alpha-adrenergic properties of norepinephrine may be the basis for food-related drinking is an intriguing one, but not necessarily dependent on a direct facilitatory effect of beta-adrenergic agents on central thirst-related neurons.

Finally, I must question both the validity of Leibowitz's (1971a) report that beta-adrenergic blocking agents effectively attenuate cholinergic as well as beta-adrenergic drinking, and the attendant hypothesis that this proves a cholinergic thirst mechanism is subsidiary to a beta-adrenergic thirst mechanism in the rat.

As Fitzsimons and Setler (1971) have pointed out, the agent used by Leibowitz (propranolol) is a potent local anesthetic. Fitzsimons and Setler found that the d-isomer of propranolol (which has local anesthetic but *no* beta-adrenergic properties) was as effective as the l-isomer in partially blocking cholinergic and angiotensin drinking. They therefore felt it doubtful that either blockade could be attributed to specific antiadrenergic action.

In our laboratory (Clifford & Fisher, unpublished data, 1972) we have tested a more potent beta-adrenergic blocking agent that has minimal local anesthetic actions (pindolol—LB-46, Sandoz; see Giudicelli, Schmitt, & Boissier, 1969). We find no effect on central cholinergic drinking when pindolol is given peripherally (56 μg), although the same dosage of the drug blocked 70% of the drinking induced by 20 μg of peripheral isoproterenol. When pindolol was introduced prior to carbachol or isoproterenol at a central site, results were variable. In one study we saw no effect of pindolol (14 to 56 μg) on drinking induced by 1 μg of carbachol, while in a second study, pindolol in a central site (56 μg) proved equally effective against either carbachol (1 μg) or isoproterenol (20 μg), blocking 40 to 50% of the drinking response shown to either drug alone. However, a number of drugs show partial blockade of cholinergic drinking when both are applied centrally (Levitt, 1969), but none approach the complete blockade produced when an anticholinergic drug is applied at either the same or a distant positive site. The overall data give us no reason to conclude that beta-adrenergic blocking agents have a major effect on cholinergic drinking. Also, the partial blockade by pindolol of central isoproterenol drinking is not strong evidence for a central action of isoproterenol, since the blocking agent is a small molecule which would have as ready access to the periphery as isoproterenol itself.

A SUMMATION AND A POINT OF VIEW

In light of the data reported and reviewed here, the following conclusions seem appropriate.

1. When the rat is used as the animal model, cholinergic neurons appear to play some role in *all* aspects of thirst, but probably do not play a crucial or exclusive role in any single aspect of thirst. On balance, the evidence suggests a heavier cholinergic involvement in central mediation of cell dehydration thirst (with a resultant shift toward preference for water) than in extracellular thirst.

In other mammals, the identity of a transmitter subserving similar functions remains unknown, but is probably not cholinergic.

2. Dopaminergic neurons also appear to be involved in a number of thirst-related phenomena, but apparently play a more crucial role in extracellular thirst.

3. Although exceptions exist (see Stricker, 1971a, on caval ligation), experimental manipulations that selectively implicate extracellular thirst mechanisms typically produce a rapid enhancement of preference for or intake of an isotonic mix of materials which could best repair an extracellular (serum) deficit.

4. Our data indicate that chemical changes that may produce or mimic events relating to extracellular thirst, including injections of low dosages of isoproterenol or of central angiotensin, also produce or further increase a preference for isotonic saline over water.

5. Most data now suggest that angiotensin will join baroreceptor feedback as a primary stimulus or modulator for extracellular thirst.

6. Our data do not indicate that beta-adrenergic agents play a major role in thirst that is independent of angiotensin, although they are almost certainly involved, both directly and indirectly, in the release of angiotensin.

The point of view I choose to take at this time is that the proliferation of data, and of potentially relevant variables that now inundate us is making it increasingly difficult to see the forest for the trees—and that some attempt at a simplification, though hazardous, may already be in order. It is human nature for each of us to become obsessed with our own pet "primary" stimuli, transmitters, or thirst components and to experience an almost irresistible urge to build an elaborate and "separate" conceptual framework in which to house them. Unfortunately, it is possible to separate virtually anything if one sets about it diligently enough, including phenomena that ultimately are as interrelated in their dependence on a single mechanism or unifying principle as night and day. With that as a premise, what is the most parsimonious model that might account for *most* of the data being generated and, hopefully, might provide guidelines for further work or for a search for artifacts in data which fail to fit?

First, I would make the assumption that although there are clearly a number of stimuli for thirst (both primary and secondary, and cellular and extracellular), there is as yet no pressing need to endow our model or our animal with more than one basic neural substrate for mediating water ingestion. Thus, the neural substrate for extracellular thirst may still prove to be integrated with, part of, and thus dependent upon the cellular dehydration thirst system, in the sense that the consumption of water and dilute solutions relative to extracellular thirst may be mediated through parts of the same neuronal network subserving cellular thirst.

I also believe it premature to assume that angiotensin-related thirst is totally different or separate from hypovolemic thirst, though there are assuredly other factors and stimuli that interact with angiotensin to produce a given behavioral outcome to specific extracellular challenges.

Given the above assumptions, the only additional or subsidiary mechanism that would be required to handle both cellular and extracellular thirst would be one subserving sodium appetite. In order for the model I am going to propose to remain viable, however, it will be necessary to demonstrate that the current belief that sodium appetite is slow to develop (6 to 10 hours after a hypovolemic challenge—see Stricker & Wolf, 1966; Stricker & Jalowiec, 1970) is not the whole story. These investigators have certainly documented the fact that an appetite for strongly hypertonic Na^+ solutions has latencies of this order, but it is possible that a preference, or the overcoming of aversion, for increasing concentrations of sodium develops gradually over time following most extra-cellular challenges and the release of renin. This would be reflected by a progressive increase in preference for isotonic solution or mixes and, if called for later by the persistence of a real or simulated sodium deficit, an appetite for increasing concentrations of sodium.

Figure 4a and 4b represent an attempt to provide both a simplified and a more complex schematic model for the substrate I am proposing. The major properties of the model are discussed in the figure legend and below.

1. Water ingestion would be under the control of a system of neurons that had direct input from central osmoreceptors, neural feedback from peripheral baroreceptors and other thirst-related inputs, and a sensitivity (at several levels) to facilitatory actions of angiotensin. Crucial neurons in this system would have the property of responding to the sensitizing influences of angiotensin when dehydrated or in isotonic balance, but not at all when overhydrated.

The fact that overhydration of cells appears sufficient to halt ingestion of water during most extracellular challenges (even though the initiating stimuli are still operating and *no inhibitory mechanism has been found*) suggests to me that

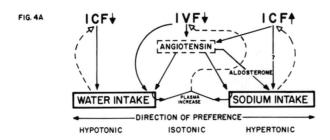

FIG. 4A

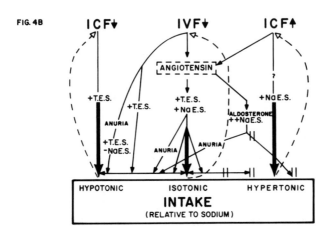

FIG. 4B

ICF↓ = INTRACELLULAR FLUID DECREASE (AND/OR Na⁺INCREASE) IN MONITOR NEURONS
ICF↑ = INTRACELLULAR FLUID INCREASE (AND/OR Na⁺DECREASE) IN MONITOR NEURONS
IVF↓ = INTRAVASCULAR FLUID VOLUME (AND/OR PRESSURE) DECREASE
T.E.S. = THIRST EXCITATORY SYSTEM
NaE.S. = SODIUM APPETITE EXCITATORY SYSTEM
→ = FACILITATORY EFFECT
--▷ = INHIBITORY (NEGATIVE FEEDBACK) EFFECT
▶ = PREFERRED FLUID INTAKE
II II = SHIFTING SODIUM TASTE AVERSION THRESHOLD
? = PATHWAY UNCERTAIN OR INTERMEDIARY UNKNOWN

FIG. 4. Figure 4a is a watered-down version of the model for the central control of thirst, and should be largely self-explanatory. In both Figure 4a and 4b, provision is made for plasma volume deficits to facilitate fluid intake via two routes, one of which is independent of kidney-related angiotensin formation. It remains to be determined whether a brain-based renin-angiotensin system is a necessary contributor to this latter pathway.

Note that negative feedback mechanisms lead directly to the removal of all facilitatory signals in both figures and no separate inhibitory mechanisms have been postulated.

The important additions to the model in Figure 4b include (1) a portrayal of shifts in sodium-aversion threshold (and/or an increased preference for sodium) attributed to rapid (direct) and delayed (indirect, via aldosterone) actions of angiotensin, and (2) a shift away from sodium intake and toward water intake which occurs as a consequence of natural or experimenter-imposed anuria.

the same system of neurons is involved in signaling for water ingestion during both cellular dehydration and hypovolemic thirst and that overhydration of cells in the system simply removes the signal to ingest water.

2. The ingestion of sodium-containing fluids would be under the control of neurons which are also subject to both direct and indirect (aldosterone-related) facilitatory influences by angiotensin, as well as to additional cues which relate to Na^+ balance. Once cells in the water-thirst system become overhydrated, angiotensin would have a dominant and gradually increasing influence on cells mediating sodium intake. Any resultant hypertonicity, however, would reactivate the cellular thirst mechanism, thus permitting the animal to alternate between available sources of fluid and electrolytes until extracellular initiating stimuli were removed. More rapid adjustments and changes in preference might be mediated by central monitoring of and feedback to taste receptors.

Finally, how would the model respond if an isotonic solution is made available to the typical animal in a balanced state, or during an extracellular challenge but in the absence of a concomitant cellular dehydration or of other confounding influences? Then, angiotensin would exert an influence on both mechanisms outlined above so that the integrated outcome would be a heightened preference for or sustained intake of the isotonic solution until eliciting cues were removed or were overruled by competing peripheral cues.

What are the main problems such a model faces? First, some recent studies suggest that substrates for angiotensin, hypovolemic, and hypertonic drinking are anatomically separable, almost certainly on the input side (Blass & Epstein, 1971; Peck, 1971) and perhaps in a more absolute sense as well. However, although I could handily retreat beyond the primary central receptor level and suggest that baroreceptor and angiotensin input can facilitate cells farther into the systems, I will at least pause to make the point that much of the evidence for a neurological separation of cellular and of several types of extracellular thirst deserves careful reconsideration. For example, in the Blass and Epstein (1971) study on the effects of lateral preoptic (LPO) lesions, the extracellular stimulus that was used produced a very minimal drinking response relative to the cellular challenge. Later, the postlesion water intake of those animals that showed a marked depression of cellular thirst and little change in extracellular thirst was actually about the same for both challenges. This could represent the survival of a 2- to 3-cc response-to-water capability, rather than a clear separation of cellular and extracellular thirst. Also, and more important, Johnson's (1972) elegant demonstration that angiotensin appears to mediate its effects *within* the ventricles and to be ineffective in previously implicated sites such as the LPO and hypothalamus should cause us to reassess carefully some of the mapping and lesion/stimulation studies that have led us to favor separatist hypotheses, and an overly discrete anatomical locus of action for primary thirst stimuli.

In the Blass and Epstein paper, for example, the most positive sites for eliciting cellular *or* extracellular thirst tend to be directly under the lateral ventricles. Since up to 2 μl of solution was typically inserted simultaneously into each preoptic area in order to obtain results, it is virtually certain that there was a marked spillover into ventricles, and that receptor cells lining the ventricles may turn out to be the primary target tissue for hypertonic stimuli as well as angiotensin. One compelling clue may have been provided in the Blass and Epstein paper by the statement that the only two animals in an LPO group that failed to respond to angiotensin were also the only two to fail to respond to bilateral intracranial injections of hypertonic saline. This was interpreted as evidence for tissue damage under the cannulae. However, in light of Johnson's finding that the LPO area is negative to angiotensin stimulation unless the cannula guide shaft has pierced and provided access to a ventricle, a more provocative hypothesis would be that the lateral ventricles were missed or maximally disrupted in these two animals, and that the response to hypertonicity, as well as to angiotensin depends on ventricular access. If that should be the case, the sites, mechanisms of action, and degree of independence of the substrates involved remain to be elucidated. I might add that our laboratory has *never* been successful in eliciting thirst from specific brain sites with hypertonic crystals, a stimulus that has its drawbacks and control problems, but involves minimal escape from the site of injection. Paradoxically, cholinergic drinking has probably successfully outlived the ventricular involvement hypothesis, since higher concentrations of cholinergic drugs are required in ventricles than in many tissue sites to produce effects on thirst. It would be whimsical indeed if the chemical which precipitated the ventricular involvement controversy escapes unscathed while other central dipsogenic stimuli (which, unlike cholinergic stimuli, are plasma-borne) do not.

Even if, as would be reasonable to expect, data continue to indicate a clear separation and lack of interaction of the effects of separate stimuli on individual receptor inputs to a thirst system, it is not likely that separate postreceptor substrates are involved. In fact, the pharmacological blocking data presented earlier in this paper would seem to favor, at least slightly, the idea that we are dealing with a single complex system with multiple inputs and chemical messengers. Thus, except at specific central sites where differentiation of function and input would be expected, blocking agents which have *any* effect seem to partially depress *all* aspects or components of thirst, as if the net output from a single system was being modulated by suppression of some, but not all, of the elements feeding toward a final common path. The many reports of additivity of the effects of different thirst stimuli (e.g., see Fitzsimons, 1972) could also be handled reasonably well by a unitary model endowed with multiple inputs.

Some of the apparent strengths of the proposed model relate to: (*a*) the fact that only minimal amounts of pure water are accepted following *most* extracellular challenges, while a magnified response to isotonic saline can be demonstrated to occur rapidly and some time before acceptance of hypertonic solutions; (*b*) the fact that for extracellular stimuli, only the ingestive responses to isotonic saline appear to be additive—there is no increase in the intake of water when several extracellular stimuli are given in combination; (c) the fact that the most persistent efforts have failed to uncover the whereabouts of one or more central inhibitory systems which could effectively inhibit the intake of water following an extracellular challenge, and without involving a cellular dehydration mechanism—the present model would not require central satiety mechanisms, but could operate by the simple removal of adequate stimuli, and changes in responsiveness to angiotensin; (d) the fact that any continued ingestion of water (or preference over an isotonic mix containing sodium) is biologically nonadaptive under hypovolemic or hypotensive conditions, since most of the water will overhydrate cells rather than increase plasma volume.

For a biologically oriented scientist, the "wisdom of the body" principle provides good and sufficient reason to carry out more than the ordinary search for artifacts and relevant side effects when one seems to have devised manipulations which were planned to provide a relatively "pure" extracellular stimulus, but which produce outcomes very different from those of other such challenges or manage to "fool" the homeostatic mechanisms. Thus, if PG is a "pure" hypovolemic stimulus, the model cannot predict clearly the survival of much of PG-induced drinking after nephrectomy, except by assuming the somewhat weak position that PG provides a more powerful and effective stimulus than other such challenges, and either is not as dependent on renal angiotensin or can more readily recruit the still-mysterious brain renin-angiotensin system.

Similarly, the extended preference for water and/or suppression of isotonic saline intake which has been reported to follow caval ligation (Stricker, 1971a) would be difficult for this model to handle, although other data reported here by Stricker (this volume Fig. 3) indicates that a developing "thirst" for isotonic saline and suppression of water intake is demonstrable during the hours immediately following caval ligation, at least in a single-bottle test.

We find very variable effects on drinking following caval ligation, and there may be a number of factors involved in "confusing" the system. For example, cavally ligated rats in the 1971 Stricker studies (1971a, 1971b) were essentially anuric during the first 9 hours after ligation. When PG-treated rats were made anuric by bladder puncture, they also showed a water preference and a suppression of isotonic saline intake that was not evident without anuria. Even more crucial, there has as yet been no actual monitoring of the course of renin output or angiotensin levels following caval ligation, a problem that Stricker now has under investigation (see Stricker, this volume).

We will need to pay closer attention to monitoring as many relevant physiological variables as possible during adaptive or nonadaptive changes in fluid intake which follow our often drastic peripheral or central manipulations. Thus, blood pressure, effective osmolarity of blood and cerebrospinal fluid, and plasma renin activity should be monitored much more extensively in our studies, especially when results appear at odds with homeostatic principles.

In closing, let me say that my main aim, other than to present data for others to criticize, has been to suggest alternatives to present theories and interpretations of data. In some subareas I have found this a difficult enterprise with less than convincing outcomes. It may well be that the mainstream in thirst research is already on the right course, and that swimming against the current or trying to divert it is a foolish exercise. Nevertheless, I perceive us to be at a stage where a devil's advocate approach, though at times beyond my powers, is well worth the effort. There *are* misinterpretations, misdirections, and a needless proliferation of variables in our literature, and we will not find the answers we seek until we can differentiate the real from the apparently real. I remain optimistic that that goal can be approximated during the present decade, with or without the revolution predicted in my opening paragraphs.

REFERENCES

Almli, C. R. Hyperosmolarity accompanies hypovolemia: A simple explanation of additivity of stimuli for drinking. *Physiology and Behavior,* 1970, 5, 1021–1028.

Andersson, B., & Eriksson, L. Conjoint action of sodium and angiotensin on brain mechanisms controlling water and salt balances. *Acta Physiologica Scandinavica,* 1971, 81, 18–29.

Antelman, S. M., Johnson, A. K., & Fisher, A. E. Survival of cholinergic drinking following nephrectomy. *Physiology and Behavior,* 1972, 8, 1169–1170.

Blass, E. M., & Epstein, A. N. A lateral preoptic osmosensitive zone for thirst in the rat. *Journal of Comparative and Physiological Psychology,* 1971, 76, 378–394.

Block, M. L., & Fisher, A. E. Anticholinergic central blockade of salt-aroused and deprivation-induced thirst. *Physiology and Behavior,* 1970, 5, 525–527.

Conte, M., Lehr, D., Goldman, W., & Krukowski, M. Inhibition of food intake by beta-adrenergic stimulation. *Pharmacologist,* 1968, 10, 180.

Epstein, A. N. Drinking induced by low doses of intravenous angiotensin. *Physiologist,* 1972, 15, 127. (Abstract)

Epstein, A. N., Fitzsimons, J. T., & Simons, B. J. Drinking caused by the intracranial injection of angiotensin into the rat. *Journal of Physiology (London),* 1969, 200, 98–100.

Fisher, A. E. Chemical stimulation of the brain. *Scientific American,* 1964, 210, 60–68.

Fisher, A. E. The role of limbic structures in the central regulation of eating and drinking behavior. In P. J. Morgane (Ed.), Neural regulation of food and water intake. *Annals of the New York Academy of Sciences,* 1969, 157(2), 894–901.

Fisher, A. E., Antelman, S. M., Tarter, J. M., & Redgate, E. S. An analysis of the beta-adrenergic facilitation of thirst. *Physiologist,* 1972, 15, 134. (Abstract)

Fisher, A. E., & Coury, J. N. Cholinergic tracing of a central neural circuit underlying the thirst drive. *Science,* 1962, 138, 691–693.

Fisher, A. E., & Coury, J. N. Chemical tracing of neural pathways mediating the thirst drive. In M. J. Wayner (Ed.), *Thirst: Proceedings of the First International Symposium on Thirst in the Regulation of Body Water.* Oxford: Pergamon Press, 1964. Pp. 515–529.

Fisher, A. E., & Levitt, R. A. Drinking induced by carbachol: Thirst circuit or ventricular modification? An answer to Routtenberg. *Science,* 1967, 157, 838–841.

Fitzsimons, J. T. The renin-angiotensin system in the control of drinking. In L. Martini, M. Motta, & F. Fraschini (Eds.), *The hypothalamus.* New York: Academic Press, 1970. Pp. 195–212.

Fitzsimons, J. T. Thirst. *Physiological Reviews,* 1972, **52**,(2), 468–561.

Fitzsimons, J. T., & Setler, P. E. Catechol-aminergic mechanisms in angiotensin-induced drinking. *Journal of Physiology (London),* 1971, **218**, 43–44.

Fitzsimons, J. T., & Simons, B. J. The effect on drinking in the rat of intravenous infusion of angiotensin, given alone or in combination with other stimuli of thirst. *Journal of Physiology (London),* 1969, **203**, 45–57.

Fitzsimons, J. T., & Stricker, E. M. Sodium appetite and the renin-angiotensin system. *Nature,* 1971, **231**, 58–60.

Franklin, K. B. J., & Quartermain, D. Comparison of the motivational properties of deprivation induced drinking elicited by central carbachol stimulation. *Journal of Comparative and Physiological Psychology,* 1970, **71**, 390–395.

Gandelman, R. J., Panksepp, J., & Trowill, J. Preference behavior differences between water deprivation-induced and carbachol-induced drinkers. *Communications in Behavioral Biology,* 1968, Part A, **1**, 341–346.

Ganten, D., Minnich, J. L., Granger, P., Hayduk, K., Brecht, H. M., Barbeau, A., Boucher, R., & Genest, J. Angiotensin-forming enzyme in brain tissue. *Science,* 1971, **173**, 64–65.

Giardina, A. R., & Fisher, A. E. Effect of atropine on drinking induced by carbachol, angiotensin and isoproterenol. *Physiology and Behavior,* 1971, **7**, 653–655.

Giudicelli, J. F., Schmitt, H., & Boissier, J. R. Studies on dl-4-(2-Hydroxy-3-isopropylamino-propoxy)-Indole (LB-46), a new potent beta-adrenergic blocking drug. *Journal of Pharmacology and Experimental Therapeutics,* 1969, **168**, 116–126.

Grace, J. E., & Stevenson, J. A. F. Thermogenic drinking in the rat. *American Journal of Physiology,* 1971, **220**, 1009–1015.

Grossman, S. P. Eating or drinking elicited by direct adrenergic or cholinergic stimulation of hypothalamus. *Science,* 1960, **132**, 301–302.

Grossman, S. P. Intracranial drug implants: An autoradiographic analysis. *Science,* 1969, **166**, 1410–1412.

Hainsworth, F. R., Stricker, E. M., & Epstein, A. N. Water metabolism of rats in the heat: Dehydration and drinking. *American Journal of Physiology,* 1968, **214**, 983–989.

Houpt, K. A., & Epstein, A. N. The complete dependence of beta-adrenergic drinking on the renal dipsogen. *Physiology and Behavior,* 1971, **7**, 897–902.

Johnson, A. K. Localization of angiotensin in sensitive areas for thirst within the rat brain. Paper read at the meeting of the Eastern Psychological Association, Boston, April 27, 1972.

Johnson, A. K., & Fisher, A. E. Taste preferences for sucrose solutions and water under cholinergic and deprivation thirst. *Physiology and Behavior,* 1973, in press. (a)

Johnson, A. K., & Fisher, A. E. Tolerance for quinine under cholinergic versus deprivation induced thirst. *Physiology and Behavior,* 1973, in press. (b)

Lehr, D., Mallow, J., & Krukowski, M. Copious drinking and simultaneous inhibition of urine flow elicited by beta-adrenergic stimulation and contrary effect of alpha-adrenergic stimulation. *Journal of Pharmacology and Experimental Therapeutics,* 1967, **158**, 150–163.

Leibowitz, S. F. Reciprocal hunger-regulating "circuits" involving alpha- and beta-adrenergic receptors located, respectively, in the ventromedial and lateral hypothalamus. *Proceedings of the National Academy of Sciences,* 1970, **67**, 1063–1070.

Leibowitz, S. F. Hypothalamic alpha- and beta-adrenergic systems regulate both thirst and hunger in the rat. *Proceedings of the National Academy of Sciences,* 1971, **68**, 332–334. (a)

Leibowitz, S. F. Hypothalamic beta-adrenergic "thirst" system mediates drinking induced by carbachol and transiently by norepinephrine. *Federation Proceedings,* 1971, **30**, 481. (b)

Leibowitz, S. F. Hypothalamic beta-adrenergic receptors and their interaction with alpha receptors in the regulation of drinking. Paper read at the meeting of the Eastern Psychological Association, Boston, April 29, 1972.

Levitt, R. A. Biochemical blockade of cholinergic thirst. *Psychonomic Science,* 1969, **15**, 274–276.

Levitt, R. A., & Fisher, A. E. Anticholinergic blockade of centrally induced thirst. *Science,* 1966, **154**, 520–522.

Miller, N. E. Chemical coding of behavior in the brain. *Science,* 1965, **148**, 328–338.

Mook, D. G. Some determinants of preference and aversion in the rat. *Annals of the New York Academy of Sciences,* 1969, **152**(2), 1158–1175.

Mountford, D. Alterations in drinking following isoproterenol stimulation of hippocampus. *Physiologist,* 1969, **12**, 309.

Myers, R. D., Tytell, M., Kawa, A., & Rudy T. Micro-injection of ^{3}H-Acetylcholine, Wayner (Ed.), *Thirst: Proceedings of the First International Symposium on Thirst in the Regulation of Body Water.* Oxford: Pergamon Press, 1964. Pp. 533–549.

Myers, R. D., Tytell, M., Kawa, A., & Rudy, T. Micro-injection of ^{3}H-Acetylcholine, ^{14}C-Serotonin and ^{3}H-Norepinephrine into the hypothalamus of the rat: Diffusion into tissue and ventricles. *Physiology and Behavior,* 1971, **7**, 743–751.

Peck, J. W. Separation of kidney-dependent from kidney-independent extracellular thirsts by brain lesions in rats. Paper read at the meeting of the Eastern Psychological Association, New York, April 16, 1971.

Routtenberg, A. Drinking induced by carbachol: Thirst circuit or ventricular modification? *Science,* 1967, **157**, 838–839.

Routtenberg, A., Sladek, J., & Bondareff, W. Histochemical flourescence after application of neurochemicals to caudate nucleus and septal area in vivo. *Science,* 1968, **161**, 272–273.

Smith, D. F., & Stricker, E. M. The influence of need on the rat's preference for dilute NaCl solutions. *Physiology and Behavior,* 1969, **4**, 407–410.

Stein, L., & Seifter, J. Muscarinic synapses in the hypothalamus. *American Journal of Physiology,* 1962, **202**, 751–756.

Stricker, E. M. Effects of hypovolemia and/or caval ligation on water and NaCl solution drinking by rats. *Physiology and Behavior,* 1971, **6**, 299–305. (a)

Stricker, E. M. Inhibition of thirst in rats following hypovolemia and/or caval ligations. *Physiology and Behavior,* 1971, **6**, 293–298. (b)

Stricker, E. M., & Jalowiec, J. E. Restoration of intravascular fluid volume following acute hypovolemia in rats. *American Journal of Physiology,* 1970, **218**, 191–196.

Stricker, E. M., & Wolf, G. Blood volume and tonicity in relation to sodium appetite. *Journal of Comparative and Physiological Psychology,* 1966, **62**, 275–279.

7
THE ROLE OF
CATECHOLAMINES IN THIRST[1]

Paulette E. Setler
University of Cambridge

INTRODUCTION

Since the innovative studies of Grossman (1962a, 1962b), it has become clear that certain drugs which are neurotransmitters or modifiers of synaptic transmission are, when administered directly into the brain, capable of facilitating or inhibiting ingestive behavior. Neuropharmacological manipulation of synaptic function has become an important technique in studies of the central neural mechanisms underlying thirst and drinking.

Grossman discovered the potent dipsogenic effects of cholinergic drugs and the appetite-stimulating effects of the catecholamines epinephrine and norepinephrine. The catecholamines were found to be antidipsogenic when given to thirsting rats. The antagonistic effects of centrally administered adrenergic and cholinergic agents on ingestive behavior led to the theory of chemical coding of ingestive behavior, that drinking, or thirst, is mediated by cholinergic neurons and inhibited by adrenergic neurons, while adrenergic neurons mediate eating, or hunger, which is in turn inhibited by cholinergic neurons. It soon became apparent, however, that under some circumstances adrenergic agonists acted as dipsogens and that the concept of chemical coding is an oversimplified view. The role of the catecholamines in thirst has, however, proved to be elusive since the effects of catecholamines and their antagonists on drinking are often paradoxical.

The experiments to be discussed in this chapter were designed to investigate the effects of catecholamines on drinking and the interaction of catecholaminergic agonists and antagonists with other dipsogenic substances. In

[1] This work was supported by a Medical Research Council grant to Dr. J. T. Fitzsimons.

all experiments, male Wistar rats were used. One stainless steel cannula was stereotaxically implanted in either the preoptic area of the brain or in the right lateral ventricle of each rat. Experiments were begun after a 1-week recovery period. Between experiments the rats had free access to food and water unless stated otherwise; no food was available during drinking tests unless stated otherwise. The animals were used repeatedly, receiving no more than two injections within 24 hours. Drugs were given into the preoptic area in a volume of 1 μl and into the ventricle in a volume of 10 to 20 μl. Whenever possible, each rat served as its own control.

ANTIDIPSOGENIC EFFECTS OF CATECHOLAMINES

Norepinephrine attenuates, but does not abolish, drinking in response to overnight water deprivation. Following overnight water deprivation, during which they had access to food, rats were injected through cannulas implanted in the medial preoptic area of the brain (as shown in Figure 1) with norepinephrine bitartrate dissolved in 1 μl of 0.9% saline. Five minutes later they were given

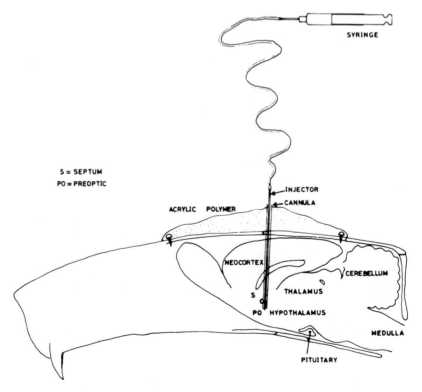

FIG. 1. Schematic drawing of a rat's brain showing the site of injection of substances given into the preoptic area.

TABLE 1

Effects of Injection of Catecholamines in the Preoptic Area on Drinking
Induced by Water Deprivation

Drug	Dose (nmoles)	N	Cumulative water intake (ml ± SEM)		
			60 minutes	120 minutes	180 minutes
Norepinephrine	0	18	13.4 ± 1.0	14.4 ± 1.0	15.2 ± 0.9
	16.3	6	11.8 ± 1.3	12.5 ± 1.4	12.5 ± 1.4
	32.5	6	5.7 ± 0.7*	7.5 ± 1.0*	8.4 ± 0.9*
	65.0	6	7.8 ± 1.1*	8.5 ± 1.1*	9.0 ± 1.1*
Dopamine	0	10	14.3 ± 1.2	15.1 ± 1.0	16.7 ± 1.4
	32.5	5	10.9 ± 1.1	11.3 ± 1.0	12.4 ± 1.0
	65.0	5	14.4 ± 2.0	14.8 ± 2.3	15.4 ± 2.2
Isoproterenol	0	10	15.0 ± 1.6	15.9 ± 1.5	16.3 ± 1.4
	32.5	5	12.5 ± 2.4	13.2 ± 2.3	13.5 ± 2.2
	65.0	5	11.8 ± 1.5	12.0 ± 1.4	12.3 ± 1.4

$*p < .05.$

access to water in graduated drinking tubes. In Table 1 the amounts of water
drunk after norepinephrine treatment are compared with the amounts drunk by
the same animals in control experiments in which no injection was given.

Inhibition of drinking was evident in the first 15 minutes and continued
throughout the 3-hour testing period, although the onset of drinking was
immediate whether the animals were given norepinephrine or were untreated.
The maximum inhibition of drinking occurred in the first hour, and the most
effective dose of norepinephrine was 32.5 nmoles. All doses of norepinephrine
produced some ataxia, excitement, increased motor activity, and biting of cage
and water spout during the first 30 to 45 minutes after injection, but there was
no correlation between degree of excitement and degree of inhibition of
drinking. The maximum inhibition of drinking in this experiment is similar to
that observed after implants of crystalline norepinephrine into the perifornical
region of the lateral hypothalamus (Grossman, 1962a).

Two other catecholamines, dopamine and isoproterenol, were compared with
norepinephrine in an identical experiment to determine whether antidipsogenic
activity is a general property of catecholamines or specific for norepinephrine.
Neither dopamine nor isoproterenol significantly inhibited drinking. The results
are included in Table 1. None of the three catecholamines increased drinking in
this experiment.

If the antidipsogenic effect of norepinephrine is due to a direct specific action
of norepinephrine on adrenergic receptors at or near the site of injection, the
effects of norepinephrine should be blocked by intracranial injection of
adrenergic antagonists. An *alpha*-adrenergic antagonist, phentolamine, and a
beta-adrenergic, antagonist MJ-1999, were given at doses of 5 and 10 µg through

the preoptic cannula 10 to 15 minutes before norepinephrine (32.5 nmoles). The *alpha*-adrenergic receptor blocker was the more effective agent in restoring drinking to control levels; when norepinephrine was preceded by either dose of phentolamine, the amount of water drunk by thirsty rats was not significantly different from that of untreated rats. MJ-1999 only partially attenuated the antidipsogenic effects of norepinephrine.

Water deprivation may be a complex stimulus involving activation of cellular and extracellular thirst systems. To determine whether the antidipsogenic effect of norepinephrine is a general effect or is specific for cellular or extracellular thirst, rats were pretreated with 32.5 nmoles of norepinephrine, the most effective inhibitory dose in water deprivation experiments, before being challenged with hypertonic saline (2 ml of 2 M NaCl, ip), a cellular stimulus of thirst, or polyethylene glycol (2 ml 50% [w/w], ip) or isoproterenol (50 μg/kg isoproterenol HC1, sc), extracellular thirst stimuli. Animals were allowed water immediately. The results are shown in Table 2. Norepinephrine inhibited drinking in response to hypertonic saline but had no effect on drinking in response to polyethylene glycol or isoproterenol, even though these extracellular thirst stimuli were less potent dipsogens.

Because angiotensin is believed to mediate the drinking response to extracellular thirst stimuli (Fitzsimons, 1969) the effects of norepinephrine on angiotensin-induced drinking were also studied. Norepinephrine, 32.5 nmoles, was injected into the preoptic area 5 minutes before angiotensin II. Two doses of angiotensin were used: 100 ng, which has approximately the same dipsogenic potency as overnight water deprivation; and 10 ng, which is equidipsogenic with the doses of isoproterenol and polyethylene glycol used in the experiments

TABLE 2

Effects of Preoptic Injection of Norepinephrine (NE) on
Drinking Induced by Cellular and Extracellular Stimuli

Dipsogen	N	Water intake (ml/hr ± SEM)	
		Control	32.5 nmoles NE
Hypertonic saline[a]	8	10.8 ± 0.6	5.5 ± 0.8*
Polyethylene glycol[b]	5	4.4 ± 0.8	4.1 ± 0.8
Isoproterenol[c]	7	4.5 ± 0.6	5.4 ± 0.4
Carbachol, 300 ng	9	9.6 ± 1.1	5.2 ± 1.4*
Carbachol, 33 ng	9	7.5 ± 0.7	4.5 ± 0.9*
Angiotensin, 100 ng	7	12.8 ± 0.9	10.1 ± 1.4
Angiotensin, 10 ng	10	5.2 ± 0.6	6.0 ± 1.3

[a]2 ml 2 M NaCl, ip.
[b]2 ml 50% (W/w) PG, ip.
[c]50 μg/kg isoproterenol, sc.
*$p < .05$.

discussed above. The results are included in Table 2. Norepinephrine did not significantly alter the drinking induced by either dose of angiotensin II, confirming the lack of inhibition by norepinephrine of drinking related to extracellular thirst.

It has been suggested (Giardina & Fisher, 1971) that cholinergic drinking may be related to cellular thirst. If so, norepinephrine should inhibit carbachol-induced drinking as well as drinking induced by hypertonic saline, and this was found to be so. Two dose levels of carbachol were tested; 300 and 33 ng of carbachol were injected into the preoptic area 5 minutes after 32.5 nmoles of norepinephrine. The drinking responses to both doses of carbachol were depressed by norepinephrine, as shown in Table 2. The average inhibition was about 45%, which is equal to the degree of inhibition of drinking in response to hypertonic saline or to water deprivation.

Neither isoproterenol nor dopamine, given in a dose of 32.5 nmoles, affected the drinking response to either angiotensin or carbachol.

In summary, the results of these experiments confirm reports (Grossmann, 1962a; Leibowitz, 1971) that norepinephrine inhibits drinking by water-deprived rats and show that the inhibition is specific for norepinephrine and may be blocked by adrenergic antagonists. Norepinephrine also attenuates drinking induced by cellular thirst stimuli and carbachol, but has no effect on drinking elicited by extracellular thirst stimuli or angiotensin.

DIPSOGENIC EFFECTS OF CATECHOLAMINES

Several lines of evidence indicated that stimulation as well as inhibition of drinking may involve activation of adrenoceptive neurons. Because isoproterenol, a catecholamine and a *beta*-adrenergic agonist, causes water intake when given systemically (Lehr, Mallow, & Krukowski, 1967) or centrally (Leibowitz, 1971), the suggestion has been made that drinking may be mediated by *beta*-adrenergic neurons in the brain. More recent evidence indicates that drinking induced by isoproterenol requires the participation of a renal factor, presumably the renin-angiotensin system (Houpt & Epstein, 1971). The actual dipsogen appears to be angiotensin formed by renin which is released from the kidney in response to isoproterenol.

Although norepinephrine depresses drinking by water-deprived and salt-loaded rats, it has been reported that intracranial administration of norepinephrine sometimes causes drinking in satiated, water-replete rats (Coury, 1967; Slangen & Miller, 1969). In their experiments both eating and drinking were observed, but drinking often preceded eating and was unlikely to have been secondary to the ingestion of dry food.

To confirm and extend these observations, norepinephrine was given via a cannula in the preoptic area to two groups of satiated, water-replete rats. One group which received doses ranging from 32.5 to 130 nmoles of norepinephrine had access to food and water; the second group received 32.5 nmoles and had access to water alone. As shown in Table 3, all doses of norepinephrine caused drinking as well as eating, and the drinking response to 32.5 nmoles occurred even in the absence of food. The norepinephrine-induced drinking was, therefore, a direct effect of norepinephrine. All animals showed ataxia, muscle weakness, excitement, vocalization, and cage biting; cage biting was especially prevalent in animals without access to food.

Initially, it seemed that norepinephrine, even though its effects were modest in comparison with the dipsogenic effects of much smaller doses of angiotensin II or carbachol, was the only endogenous catecholamine which was an effective dipsogen when given intracranially. Isoproterenol is not an endogenous catecholamine, and its dipsogenic effects seem to depend on the renal dipsogen, as discussed above. Injection of dopamine into the preoptic area of the satiated, water-replete rat produced less drinking than injection of norepinephrine, and very high doses were required to produce any effect. When injected into the lateral ventricle, however, dopamine proved to be a more effective dipsogen than norepinephrine. Dopamine and noradrenaline were given in a volume of 10 μl into the lateral ventricle of water-replete rats; the results are listed in Table 4. Dopamine, at doses of 260 and 520 nmoles, produced a significant increase in water intake. The rats became very weak with marked ataxia and had difficulty in crawling to the water spouts to drink. There was no excitement or increase in motor activity, and cage biting and teeth grinding were observed only rarely. All animals recovered within 60 minutes. No dose of norepinephrine up to 130 nmoles caused a significant increase in water intake. In addition, two rats were given 260 nmoles of norepinephrine and were given access to food and water; although they ate large amounts of food—5.1 and 6.1 g of food,

TABLE 3

Effects of Injection of Catecholamines into the Preoptic Area on Water and Food Intake of Satiated Rats

Drug	Dose (nmoles)	N	No. of rats drinking	Mean intake (ml/hr ± SEM)	No. of rats eating	Mean intake (g/hr ± SEM)
Control	—	8	3	0.3 ± 0	0	0
Norepinephrine	32.5	19	14	1.7 ± 0.3	18	2.6 ± 0.3
	65.0	25	19	1.7 ± 0.4	25	1.6 ± 0.2
Only water available						
Control	—	3	2	0.4 ± 0.2	—	—
Norepinephrine	32.5	11	10	1.8 ± 0.7	—	—
Dopamine	32.5	4	0	0	—	—
	65.0	4	2	0.6 ± 0.4	—	—
	130.0	8	6	1.0 ± 0.3	—	—
	260.0	9	7	1.0 ± 0.4	—	—

TABLE 4

Effect of Intraventricular Injection of Catecholamines on Water
Intake by Water-Replete Rats

Drug	Dose (nmoles)	N	No. of rats drinking	Mean water intake (ml/hr)
Control	—	6	4	1.2 ± 0.6
Norepinephrine	32.5	4	2	0.1 ± 0.1
	65.0	6	5	2.0 ± 1.0
	130.0	5	4	1.0 ± 0.5
Dopamine	130.0	6	5	1.2 ± 0.5
	260.0	6	6	3.5 ± 0.7*
	520.0	6	6	4.0 ± 1.1*

*$p < .05$.

respectively—they drank little, 0 and 1.3 ml, respectively. Because of the severity of the side effects, which included intense peripheral vasoconstriction as well as the usual parameters of excitement and ataxia, use of this dose was discontinued. It is worth noting the dissimilarity of effects produced by the two catecholamines. Dopamine never produced the excitement typical of norepinephrine, although both drugs caused muscle weakness and ataxia. When dopamine-treated animals were given access to food, they ate less than animals given norepinephrine. Dopamine, at 130 nmoles, elicited a mean intake of 0.7 ± 0.3 ($N = 6$) grams of food, and at 260 nmoles, 1.3 ± 0.4 grams ($N = 6$). Intraventricular norepinephrine, at 130 nmoles, elicited a mean intake of 4.3 ± 0.4 grams ($N = 6$), and 5.6 g at 260 nmoles ($N = 2$; see above).

In summary, the predominant effect of intracranially administered norepinephrine, whether given into the preoptic area or into the ventricular system, is eating; but norepinephrine also causes drinking which is not secondary to eating. Dopamine has little effect on eating but does cause water-replete rats to drink. Injections of dopamine into the lateral ventricle are more effective in this respect than preoptic area injections, suggesting that the preoptic area may not be the site of action of dopamine or that simultaneous activation of dopaminoceptive neurons in more than one region of the brain is required to produce drinking.

Catecholamine-containing nerve terminals are found in the diencephalon and telencephalon, especially in structures adjacent to the lateral ventricles (Fuxe, 1965). These terminals possess specific uptake mechanisms for catecholamines (Snyder, Kuhar, Green, Coyle, & Shaskan, 1970). It may be possible for injected norepinephrine to activate dopaminergic receptors by displacement of exogenous dopamine from nerve terminals onto its own receptors (Andén, Engel, & Rubenson, 1972), or similarly, injections of dopamine may indirectly activate noradrenergic receptors. It is possible that both norepinephrine and dopamine cause drinking by activating a single receptor type. Dopamine, when given into the ventricle, seems to produce little activation of adrenergic receptors. Even at very high doses, it causes no excitement and very little eating, which are the predominant effects of norepinephrine. Intraventricular norepinephrine elicits less drinking than dopamine and may do so by indirect activation of dopaminergic receptors. This suggestion requires experimental verification.

In view of the relatively small dipsogenic effect of the catecholamines, the observations discussed above would appear to be of doubtful significance were it not for evidence from other experiments to indicate that one or another of the endogenous catecholamines may mediate the drinking response to various thirst stimuli.

Because angiotensin is known to affect the release and/or reuptake of catecholamines in the brain (Palaic & Khairallah, 1968), it seemed worthwhile to investigate the possibility that catecholaminergic neurons might mediate angiotensin-induced drinking and thus also mediate drinking in response to extracellular thirst stimuli.

TABLE 5

Effects of Depletion of Catecholamines on Drinking Induced by
Angiotensin or Carbachol

Treatment	N	Mean water intake (ml/hr ± SEM)				% Depletion ± SEM	
		Before 6-OHDA[a]		After 6-OHDA		NE[b]	DA[c]
		100 ng angio	300 ng carb	100 ng angio	300 ng carb		
8 μg 6-OHDA (preoptic area)	15	6.2 ± 0.8	7.2 ± 0.9	1.9 ± 0.5*	9.6 ± 0.9	preoptic ($N = 8$)	
						46 ± 4	30 ± 5
2 × 250 μg 6-OHDA (intraventricular)	4	8.2 ± 1.2	6.2 ± 1.1	2.2 ± 1.5*	6.4 ± 1.3	whole brain	
						79 ± 4	75 ± 3
DMI[d] + Pargyline[e] 150 μg 6-OHDA (intraventricular)	4	7.0 ± 1.0	5.7 ± 1.0	4.4 ± 1.4*	6.1 ± 0.6	12 ± 12	83 ± 3
3 × 25 μg 6-OHDA (intraventricular)	4	6.3 ± 0.6	5.6 ± 0.4	6.2 ± 0.6	6.1 ± 0.6	90 ± 9	25 ± 3
Control	4	6.2 ± 1.4	4.8 ± 1.2	6.1 ± 1.3	4.4 ± 0.7	0	0

Note.—Results of intraventricular experiments from Evetts, 1973. Depletion figures refer to whole brain.

[a]6-OHDA = 6-hydroxydopamine.
[b]NE = norepinephrine.
[c]DA = dopamine.
[d]DMI = desmethylimipramine, 15 mg/kg, ip.
[e]Pargyline, 50 mg/kg, ip.
*$p < .05$.

Rats were tested for their responsiveness to preoptic injection of angiotensin II and carbachol before and for several weeks after a single unilateral preoptic injection of 8 μg of 6-hydroxydopamine, which specifically destroys catecholaminergic neurons. The results are shown in Table 5. Partial depletion of norepinephrine and dopamine resulted in abolition or attenuation of drinking in response to angiotensin II, although the response to carbachol was unaffected. Similar results were obtained by giving massive doses of 6-hydroxydopamine into the lateral ventricle. Two injections of 250 μg of 6-hydroxydopamine were given into the lateral ventricle with a 2- to 3-day interval. The effects on angiotensin- and carbachol-induced drinking are included in Table 5. Independent depletions of dopamine were obtained by giving 150 μg of 6-hydroxydopamine after pretreatment with pargyline and desmethylimipramine, and depletion of noradrenaline alone by giving 3 doses of 25 μg of 6-hydroxydopamine. (Evetts, 1973). Animals with dopamine depletions of 50% and nearly normal norepinephrine levels drank significantly less in response to angiotensin than they had prior to treatment with 6-hydroxydopamine, but responded normally to carbachol (see Table 4). Animals with low levels of residual norepinephrine but only very slight depletion of dopamine responded normally to both angiotensin and carbachol. It appears that an intact dopaminergic system is required for angiotensin-induced drinking but not for carbachol-induced drinking.

Attempts to inhibit drinking in response to angiotensin and carbachol with catecholamine receptor blocking agents yielded a similar conclusion (Fitzsimons & Setler, 1971). As shown in Table 6, neither angiotensin-induced drinking nor carbachol-induced drinking was significantly attenuated by *alpha-* or *beta*-adrenergic antagonists, but angiotensin-induced drinking was reduced by centrally administered haloperidol, which is a dopamine antagonist with some norepinephrine receptor blocking activity (Andén, Butcher, Corrodi, Fuxe, & Ungerstedt, 1970). Haloperidol had no significant effect on carbachol-induced drinking. The only receptor blocking agent which blocked the drinking response to carbachol was atropine, a potent anticholinergic drug, which had little or no effect on angiotensin-induced drinking.

Additional experiments were performed to determine whether haloperidol would also attenuate drinking induced by water deprivation, isoproterenol, or hypertonic saline. Haloperidol, injected into the preoptic area at a dose of 5 μg, reduced drinking induced by water deprivation and isoproterenol-induced drinking, as shown in Table 6. There was no attenuation by haloperidol of drinking induced by hypertonic saline (1 ml, 2 M NaCl, ip). This dose of hypertonic saline is a more potent thirst stimulus than isoprenaline and should be tested with higher, bilateral doses of dopamine antagonists before it can be concluded with certainty that dopamine antagonists have no effect on cellular thirst.

Unilateral injections of 5 μg of haloperidol into the preoptic area had no significant effect on deprivation-induced eating or on eating stimulated by

TABLE 6

Effects of Receptor Blocking Drugs on Drinking Induced by Angiotensin or Carbachol

Receptor blocking		Dipsogen			
		Angiotensin 100 ng		Carbachol 300 ng	
		N	ml/hr $\pm$ SEM	N	ml/hr $\pm$ SEM
Atropine	0	47	8.3 $\pm$ 0.6	37	8.4 $\pm$ 0.7
	1 μg	12	6.0 $\pm$ 1.7	14	1.2 $\pm$ 1.2*
	10 μg	14	8.3 $\pm$ 1.4	—	
	100 μg	10	1.8 $\pm$ 1.0*	—	
Phentolamine	0	14	8.4 $\pm$ 0.9	14	9.8 $\pm$ 1.3
	10 μg	5	10.8 $\pm$ 2.8	5	8.5 $\pm$ 0.9
	20 μg	5	8.9 $\pm$ 1.7	6	3.9 $\pm$ 2.3 (toxic)
	40 μg	5	0.3 $\pm$ 0.3 (toxic)	4	0.8 $\pm$ 0.8 (toxic)
MJ-1999	0	7	7.8 $\pm$ 0.9	6	11.4 $\pm$ 2.5
	20 μg	5	8.6 $\pm$ 4.0	6	10.6 $\pm$ 2.4
	40 μg	3	1.1 $\pm$ 1.1 (toxic)	1	toxic
Haloperidol	0	14	8.8 $\pm$ 1.0	7	10.0 $\pm$ 1.8
	2.5 μg	4	3.0 $\pm$ 1.3*	—	
	5 μg	5	2.8 $\pm$ 1.2*	—	
	10 μg	5	0.5 $\pm$ 0.3*	7	8.5 $\pm$ 1.4

Note.—All drugs injected into the preoptic area; blocker injected 10 to 15 minutes before dipsogen.

*$p < .05$.

TABLE 7

Effects of Haloperiodol on Eating and Drinking

Treatment		Control		Haloperidol, 5 μg	
	N	Water (ml/hr $\pm$ SEM)		N	Water (ml/hr $\pm$ SEM)
Water Deprivation	6	11.4 $\pm$ 1.6		6	7.4 $\pm$ 1.3*
2 M NaCl	6	5.4 $\pm$ 1.4		6	5.1 $\pm$ 0.6
Isoproterenol, 50 μg/kg, sc	5	5.8 $\pm$ 0.8		5	2.1 $\pm$ 0.7*
		Food (gm/hr $\pm$ SEM)			Food (gm/hr $\pm$ SEM)
Food Deprivation	5	6.6 $\pm$ 1.1		5	5.5 $\pm$ 1.0
Norepinephrine, 32.5 nmoles in POA	6	3.3 $\pm$ 0.8		6	3.5 $\pm$ 1.0

*$p < .05$.

injection of 32.5 nmoles of norepinephrine (see Table 7), indicating that the effects of this dose of haloperidol were probably due to dopamine receptor blockade rather than an antiadrenergic effect.

Systemic administration of haloperidol in doses from 0.1 to 1.0 mg/kg appeared to depress, at least partially, drinking in response to deprivation, cellular thirst stimuli, and extracellular thirst stimuli, as well as deprivation-induced eating. These doses of haloperidol also caused sedation, and the antidipsogenic effect could not be distinguished from a general depressant effect.

Ungerstedt (1971) has reported that depletion of forebrain catecholamines by electrolytic lesions or by injection of 6-hydroxydopamine along the course of the nigrostriatal bundle produces aphagia and adipsia and a condition similar to the lateral hypothalamic syndrome. The most severely affected animals sustained degeneration of the nigrostriatal system and of ascending noradrenergic pathways, causing depletion of both catecholamines in diencephalon and telecephalon. Depletion of noradrenaline without damage to dopaminergic systems produced no aphagia or adipsia. Selective depletion of dopamine from the *nucleus accumbens septi* and *tuberculum olfactorium* caused only hypophagia and hypodipsia. Smith, Strohmayer, and Reis (1972) have shown that rats made aphagic and adipsic by injections of 6-hydroxydopamine into the lateral hypothalamus failed to drink in response to cellular (hypertonic saline) or extracellular (isoproterenol) thirst stimuli. Rats which recovered from 6-hydroxydopamine–induced aphagia and adipsia drank less than control rats when food was not available, as do rats which have recovered from electrolytic lesions of the lateral hypothalamus (Teitelbaum & Epstein, 1962). These experiments provide compelling evidence that catecholaminergic neurons are involved in the control of drinking.

CONCLUSIONS

The results of the experiments discussed above indicate that catecholamines play an important role in thirst and the control of drinking. The results suggest that the most obvious effect of injected norepinephrine on drinking is inhibitory and that norepinephrine specifically depresses drinking in response to stimuli related to cellular thirst. There is, as yet, no experimental evidence to indicate whether this is a physiological effect of noradrenergic neurons in the forebrain or a pharmacological effect of injection of large amounts of norepinephrine into the brain.

The results show that both catecholamines endogenous to the central nervous system, norepinephrine and dopamine, have dipsogenic activity, possibly through activation of a single type of receptor. Results from experiments using receptor-blocking drugs and chemical lesions of catecholaminergic neurons suggest that dopaminergic and dopaminaceptive neurons may function in mediating the responses to extracellular thirst stimuli. Without doubt, intact catecholaminergic systems in the forebrain are required for normal ingestive behaviour in rats.

Yet the awkward paradox remains that while the anti-dipsogenic effects of diminished catecholaminergic activity are profound, the dipsogenic effects of intracranially injected catecholamines are weak, much weaker than the effects of the extracellular thrist stimuli which seem to depend on adequate catecholaminergic function.

Finally, these experiments emphasize the differences between the neuropharmacology of cellular thirst mechanisms and the neuropharmacology of extracellular thirst. Drinking responses to cellular thirst stimuli are blocked or attenuated by cholinergic antagonists and by norepinephrine, an *alpha*-adrenergic agonist. The same is true of drinking in response to preoptic injections of carbachol. Neither carbachol-induced nor hypertonic saline–induced drinking is significantly attenuated by the dopamine receptor blocker, haloperidol. Carbachol-induced drinking is unaffected by chemical destruction of catecholaminergic pathways.

Drinking in response to extracellular thirst stimuli and to angiotensin, which is thought to participate in extracellular thirst, is not significantly attenuated by intracranial injection of norepinephrine or anticholinergics. Angiotensin-induced and isoproterenol-induced drinking are reduced by dopamine receptor blockade and destruction of catecholaminergic nerve terminals.

In short, drinking in response to cellular thirst seems to be mediated by a cholinergic system, whereas drinking in response to those extracellular thirst stimuli related to angiotensin may depend on catecholaminergic (perhaps dopaminergic) nerve pathways, and to be independent of cholinergic mechanisms.

REFERENCES

Andén, N. E., Butcher, S. G., Corrodi, H., Fuxe, K., & Ungerstedt, U. Receptor activity and turnover of dopamine and noradrenaline after neuroleptics. *European Journal of Pharmacology,* 1970, **11**, 303–314.

Andén, N. E., Engel, J., & Rubenson, A. Mode of action of L-DOPA on central noradrenaline mechanisms. *Nauyn-Schmiedeberg's Archives of Pharmacology,* 1972, **273**, 1–10.

Coury, J. N. Neural correlates of food and water intake in the rat. *Science,* 1967, **156**, 1763–1765.

Evetts, K. D. The effects of 6-hydroxydopamine on brain amines and behavior in the rat. Unpublished doctoral dissertation, University of Cambridge, 1973.

Fitzsimons, J. T. The role of a renal thirst factor in drinking induced by extracellular stimuli. *Journal of Physiology,* 1969, **201**, 349–368.

Fitzsimons, J. T., & Setler, P. E. Catecholaminergic mechanisms in angiotensin-induced drinking. *Journal of Physiology,* 1971, **218**, 43–44P.

Fuxe, K. Evidence for the existence of monamine neurons in the central nervous system. IV. Distribution of monoamine nerve terminals in the central nervous system. *Acta Physiologica Scandinavica,* 1965, **64**, Supplement 247.

Giardina, A. R., & Fisher, A. E. Effect of atropine on drinking induced by carbachol, angiotensin and isoproterenol. *Physiology and Behavior,* 1971, 7, 653–655.

Grossman, S. P. Direct adrenergic and cholinergic stimulation of hypothalamic mechanisms. *American Journal of Physiology,* 1962, **202**, 872–882. (a)

Grossman, S. P. Effects of adrenergic and cholinergic blocking agents on hypothalamic mechanisms. *American Journal of Physiology,* 1962, **202**, 1230–1236. (b)

Houpt, K. A., & Epstein, A. N. The complete dependence of *beta*-adrenergic drinking on the renal dipsogen. *Physiology and Behavior,* 1971, 7, 897–902.

Lehr, D., Mallow, J., & Krukowski, M. Copious drinking and simultaneous inhibition of urine flow elicited by *beta*-adrenergic stimulation and contrary effect of *alpha*-adrenergic stimulation. *Journal of Pharmacology and Experimental Therapeutics,* 1967, **158**, 150–163.

Leibowitz, S. F. Hypothalamic *alpha* and *beta*-adrenergic systems regulate both thirst and hunger in the rat. *Proceedings of the National Academy of Sciences,* 1971, **68**, 332–334.

Palaic, D., & Khairallah, P. A. Inhibition of norepinephrine re-uptake by angiotensin in brain. *Journal of Neurochemistry,* 1968, **15**, 1195–1202.

Slangen, J. L., & Miller, N. E. Pharmacological tests for the function of hypothalamic norepinephrine in eating behavior. *Physiology and Behavior,* 1969, **4**, 543–552.

Smith, G. P., Strohmeyer, A. J., & Reis, D. J. Effect of lateral hypothalamic injections of 6-hydroxydopamine on food and water intake in rats. *Nature,* 1972, **235**, 27–29.

Snyder, S. H., Kuhar, M. J., Green, A. I., Coyle, J. T., & Shaskan, E. G. Uptake and subcellular localization of neurotransmitters in the brain. *International Review of Neurobiology,* 1970, **13**, 127–158.

Teitelbaum, P., & Epstein, A. N. The lateral hypothalamic syndrome: Recovery of feeding and drinking after lateral hypothalamic lesions. *Psychological Reviews,* 1962, **69**, 74–90.

Ungerstedt, U. Adipsia and aphagia after 6-hydroxydopamine induced degeneration of the nigro-striatal dopamine system. *Acta Physiologica Scandinavica,* 1971, Supplement 367, 95–122.

DISCUSSION:
USE OF THE ABLATION METHOD
IN THE PHARMACOLOGICAL
ANALYSIS OF THIRST[1]

John A. Harvey
University of Iowa

The application of pharmacologic techniques to the study of thirst is certainly an important endeavor since it should allow us to specify the chemical nature of the fiber systems and the synaptic transmitters involved in the central regulation of fluid balance. The intraventricular or intracerebral injection of various putative synaptic transmitters or their presumed antagonists has been the most common approach to this problem. Unfortunately, the results obtained with this approach remain difficult to interpret because the assumptions on which the technique is based have not been verified. This chapter will first of all present a critique of methods employing central administration of chemicals, and secondly describe a relatively new approach involving the chemical and pharmacological analysis of the effects of brain lesions.

CENTRAL ADMINISTRATION OF DRUGS

One of the problems involved in the central application of putative synaptic transmitters is the discrepancy between the amounts being applied and the actual endogenous content in the brain. The average value for norepinephrine in the rat is .42 μg/g of brain tissue (Table 1). Thus for a rat whose brain weighs 1.8 grams, the total brain content of norepinephrine would be .76 μg. Norepinephrine is typically injected intracerebrally at a dosage of 10 μg, a quantity that is more than 13 times the entire amount of norepinephrine in the brain of a rat. Since all of the putative synaptic transmitters have an uneven

[1] Supported by Research Scientist Award MH-21849-03 and USPHS Grant MH 16941-03.

TABLE 1

Contents of Putative Synaptic Transmitters in Brain

Compound and molecular weight	Average brain content, $\mu g/g$	Highest regional content	
		ng/mm^3	$pmol/mm^3$
Acetylcholine (146)	2.90	4.4	30
Dopamine (153)	.60	9.0	59
Norepinephrine (169)	.42	2.4	14
Serotonin (176)	.63	2.3	13

Note.— Data taken from Takahashi & Aprison (1964), McIlwain & Bachelard (1971), and Moore, Bhatnagar, & Heller (1971).

distribution in the brain, Table 1 also presents the highest contents that have been obtained expressed either as nanograms or picomoles of the compound per cubic millimeter of tissue. For acetylcholine and dopamine the highest contents are found in the neostriatum, while the diencephalon contains the highest contents of serotonin and norepinephrine. Within these areas one finds that a cubic millimeter of tissue (approximate weight of 1 mg) contains between 2 to 9 ng of the various putative synaptic transmitters, or between 13 and 59 pmol. If one accepts the common assumption that an intracerebrally injected compound will diffuse into approximately 1 to 2 mm^3 of tissue (Grossman & Stumpf, 1969), then an injection of 10 μg of norepinephrine into the hypothalamus would result in a local concentration of between 5 to 10 μg/mm^3 of tissue, an amount that is at least 2,000 times the endogenous content. Looked at another way, the tissue is initially exposed to an approximately 32-mM concentration of norepinephrine. It is difficult to understand why such large amounts would be required to produce an effect on thirst, unless one concludes that the effects are due to nonspecific actions of these compounds on neural tissue. Furthermore, it is clear that such large amounts are not always necessary to produce effects on drinking. Epstein, Fitzsimons, and Rolls (1970) have reported drinking produced by injection of 5 ng of angiotensin, and reliable drinking following 50 ng. If one employs the same assumptions concerning diffusion as before and if one takes into account the molecular weight of angiotensin (ca. 1000), then these dosages would represent between 2.5 and 25 pmol/mm^3 of brain tissue, an amount well within the normal content of putative synaptic transmitters in brain. The need to apply the much larger quantities of various compounds in order to produce an effect on drinking suggests that we should remain quite cautious in our interpretation of the results.

There are powerful uptake mechanisms for all of the compounds listed in Table 1. It is possible therefore that a large proportion of the compounds being applied to the brain are being taken up by neuronal as well as glial elements so that their final concentration in the extracellular space is lower than the previous calculations would suggest. However, at the concentrations of compounds employed in most experiments, these uptake mechanisms would not be very specific. For example, at low concentrations serotonin is primarily taken up by serotonergic neurons; but if application of serotonin leads to a content of approximately .2 ng/mm^3 of tissue, the uptake would be primarily into noradrenergic neurons. Thus the application of even nanogram amounts of serotonin into cerebral tissue would be expected to affect the activity of noradrenergic neurons. Similarly, the application of even nanogram quantities of norepinephrine or dopamine into the brain would be expected to produce a large inhibition (50% or more) of serotonin uptake, thus possibly affecting serotonergic neurons in the brain (Shaskan & Snyder, 1970). It is therefore necessary to know more about the precise distribution of the putative synaptic transmitters after they have been placed into the brain, both in terms of the extent of diffusion and in terms of their distribution in various cellular and subcellular compartments at the time that a behavioral effect is noted. In addition, recent experiments suggest that one must also take into account the possible diffusion of these compounds out of brain and into the general circulation with a consequent pharmacologic effect on peripheral tissues (Houpt & Epstein, 1971).

It is commonly assumed that an intracerebrally applied putative synaptic transmitter produces its effects by an action on some postsynaptic site. Blocking of the effects of a compound such as norepinephrine by an adrenergic blocking agent is put forth as further evidence for a postsynaptic locus of action. There is, however, no evidence to support such an interpretation, since we have no knowledge concerning the possible effects of these compounds on neural activity. When the electrophysiological response of cells is monitored during microelectrophoretic administration of various compounds, one finds that each of the putative synaptic transmitters listed in Table 1 can produce excitation of some cells and inhibition of others. The type of response depends on the area of the brain and the type of cell being examined. It is thus not clear whether the intracerebral injection of the much larger quantities of putative synaptic transmitters produce their effects on drinking by neural excitation, inhibition, or both. Furthermore, the putative synaptic transmitters and their antagonists do not always produce effects on the electrophysiological response of central neurons that would be predicted from their pharmacologic classification (Curtis & Crawford, 1969; Bloom, Hoffer, Nelson, Sheu, & Siggins, 1972). Acetylcholine applied to central neurons can produce a desensitization of receptors (Curtis & Ryall, 1966). The effect of norepinephrine on cell firing in the brainstem or pyriform cortex is often not antagonized by either *alpha*- or *beta*-adrenergic blocking agents (Curtis & Crawford, 1969). Atropine has effects on central neurons that are not due to a specific muscarinic blockade, but rather are similar to the neuronal depression produced by procaine, a local anesthetic (Curtis & Phillis, 1960). In some cases blocking agents can have effects not seen in the peripheral nervous system. Both atropine and scopolamine have been shown to produce an increased release of acetylcholine from brain with a concomitant decrease in its brain content. This effect is noted whether the compounds are applied systemically or directly onto the cortex (Giarman & Pepeu, 1962, 1964; Mitchell, 1963; Szerb, 1964). The classification of agonists and antagonists has been established by experiments conducted on the peripheral autonomic nervous system or on the neuromuscular junction. It is becoming increasingly obvious that this classification system will not be identical for neurons of the central nervous system. Furthermore, as noted above, any given agent has multiple actions, and thus the precise action obtained in any given experiment will depend on dosage.

Even if one could demonstrate that these compounds are indeed producing their effects on some postsynaptic site, one cannot conclude that they are the normal synaptic transmitters. For example, γ-aminobutyric acid (GABA), a presumed synaptic transmitter, has been shown to have a potent electrophysiological effect on the cells of the nodose ganglion, and this effect can be blocked by bicuculline, an antagonist of GABA (De Groat, 1972). Nevertheless, it is clear that GABA cannot be a synaptic transmitter in this ganglion since there is no endogenous GABA present. For this reason one must at least be able to demonstrate that the cells being exposed to an intracerebral injection of norepinephrine are indeed innervated by noradrenergic nerve terminals.

It is clear from what has been said that we do not yet understand the series of events occurring between the application of a compound into the brain and the elicitation or blocking of thirst. The intracerebral application of compounds, then, may provide us with some interesting data, but it cannot serve as the sole basis for inferring neurochemical functions without either the use of alternative methods or an analysis of the precise pharmacological and electrophysiological effects occurring when substances are applied in this manner to the brain.

USE OF LESIONS IN THE PHARMACOLOGICAL ANALYSIS OF THIRST

The first demonstration of a monoamine pathway in brain came from ablation work which demonstrated the existence of a serotonergic fiber system that followed the distribution of the medial forebrain bundle. Lesions placed in the dorsomedial tegmentum (raphe nuclei), ventral tegmentum, medial forebrain bundle, and septal area produced significant decreases in brain content of serotonin. This effect of the lesions followed a time course compatible with the time required for the degeneration of small nonmyelinated fibers (Heller, Harvey, & Moore, 1962; Harvey, Heller, & Moore, 1963). A similar approach demonstrated the existence of a noradrenergic system of fibers (Heller & Harvey, 1963). The application of the histochemical method of Falck and Hillarp (1959) led to the mapping of these monoaminergic fiber systems (Dahlstrom & Fuxe, 1964; Ungerstedt, 1971b). The pathways that have been tentatively described are presented in Figure 1. These neural systems are quite analogous to the peripheral autonomic nervous system, in that they constitute a chemically identifiable series of distinct fiber systems originating from discrete groups of cells in the brainstem and innervating specific diencephalic and telencephalic structures. One can therefore employ lesions to produce a denervation of specific cell bodies in the brain. The effectiveness of the lesion can be assessed qualitatively by examining the loss of fluorescent terminals in the areas denervated, or quantitatively by measuring the loss of the monoamines in various regions by chemical analysis. The chemical changes produced by lesions can be quite large as well as reasonably specific with respect to the compound affected. Lesions in the raphe nuclei will produce decreases of 80% or more in the telencephalic content of serotonin without affecting the other monoamines. Similarly, lesions in the locus coeruleus will produce decreases of 70% or more in telencephalic content of norepinephrine only. It is clear that this use of lesions enhances the application of the ablation technique to the study of thirst and other behaviors, since one can now not only describe the locus of destruction but also the specific chemical changes occurring outside the locus of destruction. It is possible therefore to determine whether the behavioral effect of a lesion is due to the interruption of specific monoaminergic or cholinergic pathways in the brain. Indeed, the measurement of these chemical changes following a lesion provides the most sensitive method for assessing degenerative changes, since current silver stains to not appear to detect terminal degeneration of such small fibers (Ungerstedt, 1971b). This approach has been employed in our laboratory for several years and has allowed us to demonstrate that lesions having a common effect of interrupting the serotonergic system and thus decreasing telencephalic content of serotonin also produce a common behavioral effect, an increased sensitivity to painful stimuli (Harvey & Lints, 1965, 1971). We have recently utilized this approach to examine the neurochemical effects of lesions that alter an animal's ability to respond to levels of hydration.

Our initial interest was focused on the possibility that the permanent loss of water regulation associated with the lateral hypothalamic syndrome of Teitelbaum and Epstein (1962) might be due to the interruption of the nigrostriatal bundle. This fiber bundle originates primarily from cells located in the pars compacta of the substantia nigra (see Figure 1) and travels through the medial portions of the internal capsule and the immediately adjacent portions of the lateral hypothalamus before swinging laterally and passing through the globus pallidus and finally terminating in the caudate nucleus. The distribution of the nigrostriatal bundle corresponds exactly with the "critical forebrain area" described by Gold (1967), destruction of which produces the lateral hypothalamic syndrome of aphagia and adipsia as defined by Teitelbaum and Epstein (1962). This is demonstrated in Figure 2, where the circle represents the critical forebrain area at its most caudal level, and the stippling represents the fibers of the nigrostriatal bundle. Evidence for this hypothesis was provided by Ungerstedt (1971a) who demonstrated that lesions or local injection of

A. NORADRENERGIC PATHWAYS

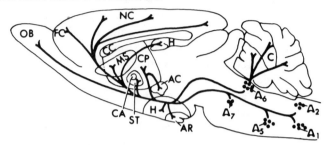

B. DOPAMINERGIC PATHWAYS

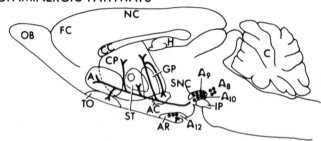

C. SEROTONERGIC PATHWAYS

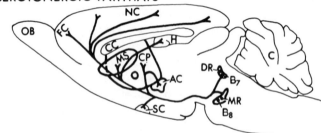

D. CHOLINERGIC PATHWAYS

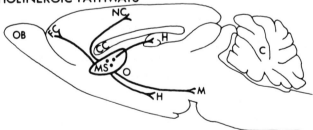

FIG. 1. Schematic representation of the major pathways of putative synaptic transmitters in brain. *Black dots* represent the location of cell bodies and *solid lines* the pathways. Cell bodies are numbered according to Dahlstrom and Fuxe (1964), the letter *A* indicating catecholamine and the letter *B* serotonin cell bodies.   *(Continued)*

FIG. 1A. Noradrenergic pathway (Dahlstrom & Fuxe, 1964; Heller & Moore, 1968; Ungerstedt, 1971b): (1) Dorsal pathway. From cells located primarily in locus coeruleus (A-6) via ventral tegmentum and medial forebrain bundle and innervating; cerebellum, geniculate bodies, thalamic nuclei, hypothalamus (sparse), and entire telencephalon including septum, caudate-putamen, amygdala, hippocampus, cingulate cortex, and entire neocortex. (2) Ventral pathway. From cells located primarily in medulla oblongata and Pons (cell groups A-1, A-2, A-5, A-7) via the ventral tegmentum and medial forebrain bundle and innervating: the brainstem, especially hypothalamic structures such as nucleus dorsalis medialis, nucleus periventricularis, area ventral to the fornix, arcuate nucleus, interstitial layer of median eminence, retro-chiasmatic area, nucleus paraventricularis, nucleus supraopticus, as well as the preoptic area and the interstitial nucleus of the stria terminalis, ventral part.

FIG. 1B. Dopaminergic pathway (Ungersted, 1971b; Moore, Bhatnagar, & Heller, 1971): (1) Nigrostriatal bundle. From cells located in the pars compacta of the substantia nigra (A-9) and in the ventral tegmentum (A-8) via the ventral tegmentum, medial forebrain bundle, internal capsule, and globus pallidus to the caudate-putamen, and amygdala. (2) Meso-limbic pathway. From cells located dorsal to the interpeduncular nucleus (A-10) via the ventral tegmentum and medial forebrain bundle to the accumbens nucleus, interstitial nucleus of the stria terminalis, dorsal part, and olfactory tubercle. (3) Tubero-infundibular pathway. From cells in arcuate nucleus (A12) to the external layer of the median eminence.

FIG. 1C. Serotonergic pathway (Heller, Harvey, & Moore, 1962; Heller & Moore, 1968; Dahlstrom and Fuxe, 1964; Ungerstedt, 1971b): (1) Forebrain pathway. From cells located in the dorsal and median raphe nuclei (B-7 and B-8) via the ventral tegmentum and medial forebrain bundle and innervating: suprachiasmatic nucleus and entire telencephalon including septum, caudate-putamen, amygdala, hippocampus, cingulate cortex, and entire neocortex.

FIG. 1D. Cholinergic pathway (Shute & Lewis, 1967; Lewis & Shute, 1967; Pepeu, Mulas, Ruffi, & Sotgiu, 1971; Sorensen & Harvey, 1971. The dorsal and ventral tegmental pathways have not been verified and so are not shown in the figure.): (1) Dorsal tegmental pathway. From cells located in nucleus cuniformis to tectum and thalamus. (2) Ventral tegmental pathway. From cells located in ventral tegmental area and substantia nigra to subthalamus, hypothalamus, and basal forebrain areas. (3) Septal projections. From cells in medial septal nuclei to the hippocampus, and from cells within the septal area (origin not certain) to cerebral cortex, hypothalamus, and mesencephalon.

Abbreviations used in text figure: *A*, accumbens nucleus; *AC*, central amygdaloid nucleus; *AR*, arcuate nucleus; *C*, cerebellum; *CA*, anterior commissure; *CC*, corpus callosum; *CP*, caudate-putamen; *DR*, dorsal raphe nucleus; *FC*, frontal cortex; *GP*, globus pallidus; *H*, hypothalamus; *HIP*, hippocampus; *IP*, interpeduncular nucleus; *M*, mesencephalon; *MR*, median raphe nucleus; *MS*, medial septal nucleus; *NC*, neocortex; *OB*, olfactory bulb; *SC*, suprachiasmatic nucleus; *SNC*, substantia nigra, pars compacta; *ST*, interstitial nucleus of the stria terminalis; *TO,* olfactory tubercle.

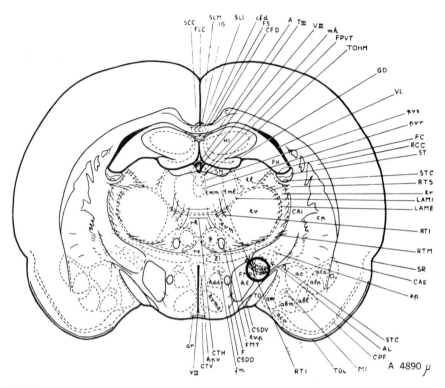

FIG. 2. Area within circle denotes Gold's (1967) forebrain area in the rat, at its most caudal level. The stippling within the just dorsal to the circle represents the degeneration seen following placement of lesions in the substantia nigra (Ungerstedt, 1971b; Moore, Bhatnagar, & Heller, 1971). Abbreviations are: *CAIR*, internal capsule, pars retrolenticularis; *F*, columns of the fornix; *FMP*, medial forebrain bundle; *TO*, olfactory tract; *ZI*, zona incerta; *ep*, entopeduncular nucleus; and *hl*, lateral hypothalamic nucleus. For remaining abbreviations, see Konig and Klippel (1970).

6-hydroxydopamine that led to degeneration of the bundle produced a severe aphagia and adipsia in rats and concluded that this was due to the interruption of the dopaminergic fibers within the nigrostriatal bundle.

Two problems arise from this conclusion. First, while the nigrostriatal bundle consists primarily of dopaminergic fibers innervating the caudate nucleus, where more than 90% of the brain content of dopamine is localized, fibers from other monoaminergic systems do join this bundle at caudal levels of the hypothalamus. Thus serotonergic fibers from the raphe nuclei and noradrenergic fibers from the locus coeruleus travel along with the nigrostriatal bundle to innervate the caudate nucleus. Consequently, lesions aimed at the nigrostriatal bundle would be expected to decrease the caudate content of all 3 monoamines; and to the extent that such lesions invade the medial forebrain bundle, they would also interrupt the ascending monoaminergic systems going to other portions of the telencephalon as well (see Figure 1). Second, the neurochemical effects of such lesions reach their maximum effects by 10 days, after which there is no further change. In contrast, the lateral hypothalamic syndrome passes through several stages (Teitelbaum & Epstein, 1962), with the major permanent effect being the loss of water regulation. Oltmans and Harvey (1972) therefore, placed lesions in the medial forebrain bundle and nigrostriatal bundle and examined the ability of the recovered animal to regulate water intake. After completion of behavioral testing, the animals were decapitated and the telencephalon divided into a striatal and nonstriatal portion, each of which was then analyzed for its content of the monoamines. The brain stem of each rat was placed in formaldehyde for reconstruction of the lesions. The lesions are depicted in Figure 3. The nigrostriatal bundle lesions were well placed and distinctly more lateral than the lesions in the medial forebrain bundle. Both lesions did, however, tend to destroy the portion of the lateral hypothalamus immediately adjacent to the internal capsule through which some of the dopaminergic fibers are known to pass.

In agreement with the results of Ungerstedt (1971a), lesions in the nigrostriatal bundle produced a more severe aphagia and adipsia than did lesions in the medial forebrain bundle. After all animals had passed into Stage IV of Teitelbaum and Epstein (1962), their water consumption was determined during

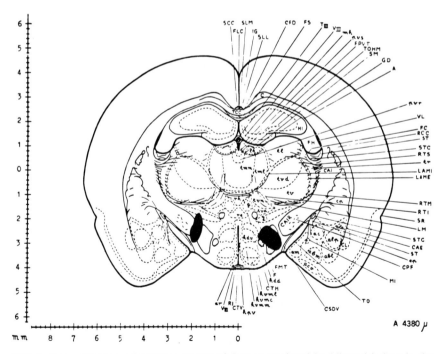

FIG. 3. Reconstruction of common extent of damage produced by bilateral lesions in the medial forebrain bundle, *right side* of figure, and in the nigrostriatal bundle, *left side* of figure. Abbreviations as in Figure 2.

TABLE 2

Effect of Medial Forebrain Bundle (MFB) and Nigrostriatal Bundle (NSB)
Lesions on Water Consumption in the Absence of Food and
Catecholamine Content of Neostriatal and Nonstriatal
Sections of Telencephalon

Experimental group	N	24-hour water con- sumption (no food) ml ± S.D.	Neostriatal Section		Nonstriatal Section
			Dopamine content $\mu g/g \pm$ S.D.	Norepinephrine content $\mu g/g \pm$ S.D.	Norepinephrine content $\mu g/g \pm$ S.D.
Sham-operated	20	31 ± 12	1.98 ± 0.70	0.56 ± 0.10	0.26 ± 0.05
MFB lesion	16	19 ± 9[a]	1.35 ± 0.49[a]	0.36 ± 0.09[a]	0.22 ± 0.07[a]
NSB lesion	16	13 ± 7[b]	0.49 ± 0.26[b]	0.26 ± 0.09[b]	0.14 ± 0.07[b]

[a]Mean significantly different from the mean of sham-operated controls ($p < 0.05$).
[b]Mean significantly different from the mean of sham-operated controls and the mean of MFB lesion group ($p < 0.01$, for each comparison).

a 24-hour period when food was absent from the cage. The data obtained from this test of nonprandial drinking is presented in Table 2, along with the neurochemical effects of the lesions. Lesions in the nigrostriatal bundle produced the largest effect on drinking in the absence of food as well as on the catecholamine contents of the striatal and nonstriatal portions of the telencephalon. In addition, the effects of this lesion on the catecholamines was significantly correlated with the ability of the animal to drink water in the absence of food (Table 3). Results with a second group of animals indicated that interruption of the serotonergic system was not responsible for the loss of ability

TABLE 3

Correlations Between 24-Hour Water Consumption in
the Absence of Food and Catecholamine Levels in
Rats with NSB Lesions[a]

Brain section and monoamine	Correlation with water consumption (no food)[a]	p
Neostriatal-dopamine	.73	< 0.002
Neostriatal-norepinephrine	.72	< 0.002
Nonstriatal-norepinephrine	.66	< 0.01

Note.—24 Hour water consumption in the absence of food was expressed for each rat as a percent of its 24-hour water consumption in the presence of food during the previous 3-day period.
[a]Pearson product-moment correlation coefficients, $N = 16$.

TABLE 4

Effect of MFB and NSB Lesions on Brain Content of Serotonin

Experimental group	N	24-hour water consumption (no food), ml ± S.D.	Serotonin content	
			Neostriatal section, μg/g ± S.D.	Nonstriatal section, μg/g ± S.D.
Sham-operated	8	26 ± 10	0.96 ± 0.10	0.64 ± 0.10
MFB lesion	4	17 ± 3	0.42 ± 0.17[a]	0.24 ± 0.07[a, b]
NSB lesion	4	13 ± 4	0.55 ± 0.12[a]	0.48 ± 0.13

[a]Mean significantly different from mean of sham-operated controls ($p < 0.001$).

[b]Mean significantly different from mean of NSB lesion group ($p < 0.05$).

to drink water in the absence of food (Table 4). There was no relationship between the effect of the lesions on serotonin content and drinking, nor was there a significant correlation between these two measures. These results suggest that the ascending dopaminergic and noradrenergic fibers associated with the nigrostriatal bundle form part of the neural circuit involved in the regulation of thirst. Since the correlation between the decrease in dopamine and norepinephrine was .80 and .67 for the neostriatal and nonstriatal portions of the telencephalon, respectively, it is impossible at this time to determine whether thirst is dependent on one or the other catecholamine.

The results of these studies do, however, demonstrate the manner in which lesions can be employed to determine the chemical nature and distribution of the fiber systems involved in the regulation of thirst. A second example comes from an analysis of the cholinergic systems in brain.

On the basis of histochemical staining for acetylcholinesterase and on the changes in staining following interruption of various fiber systems, a description of possible cholinergic pathways in brain has been published (Shute & Lewis, 1967; Lewis & Shute, 1967). Since the occurrence of cholinesterase in a neuron does not necessarily imply the existence of acetylcholine, these maps must be viewed as pioneering first steps. Corroboration will require the demonstration that interruption of these pathways results in a decrease in acetylcholine content of areas they innervate. Such a corroboration has recently been provided for the cholinergic projections from the septum proposed by Lewis and Shute (1967; see Figure 1). Lesions in the septal area have been found to produce significant decreases of approximately 20% in whole brain content of acetylcholine (Pepeu, Mulas, Ruffi, & Sotgiu, 1971; Sorensen & Harvey, 1971). The decreases occur in telencephalon as well as in diencephalon and the rostral portions of the mesencephalon. These results demonstrate that a significant portion of the acetylcholine content of brain is regulated by a fiber system originating in or passing through the septal area.

Lesions in the septal area are known to produce a hyperdipsia as measured by an increased 24-hour ad libitum water consumption (Harvey & Hunt, 1965). The increased water consumption appears to be due to an essential hyperdipsia resulting from an effect on volemic rather than osmotic mechanisms (Blass & Hanson, 1970). Since several investigators have proposed that thirst is mediated by a cholinergic system in brain, Sorensen and Harvey (1971) examined the effects of septal lesions both on water consumption and on brain content of acetylcholine. Acetylcholine was measured by a modified leech muscle preparation, using morphine to stabilize the muscle and increase sensitivity. These experiments were conducted on 14 rats with septal lesions and 14 sham-operated controls. All animals were housed one per cage. The 24-hour water intake of each animal was recorded from the 5th to the 19th day after surgery. Beginning at 19 days after surgery, animals were decapitated, brains homogenized, and acetylcholine extracted from the whole brain.

Lesions in the septal area produced a significant (51%) increase in daily water intake. These lesions also produced a significant (20%) decrease in acetylcholine content of brain. Using the criterion of Blass and Hanson (1970), the lesioned rats were classified as hyperdipsic if their mean daily water intake exceeded that of sham-operated controls by two standard deviations. Using this criterion, the 14 lesioned rats could be divided into 9 hyperdipsic and 5 nonhyperdipsic rats. The 9 hyperdipsic rats had a 35% decrease in brain acetylcholine, while there

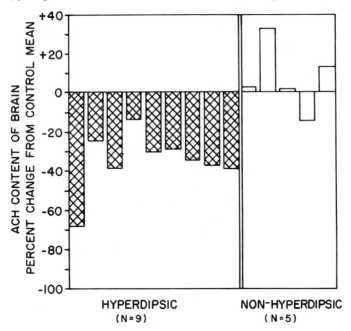

FIG. 4. Percentage decrease in acetylcholine content for nine hyperdipsic (*left panel*) and five nonhyperdipsic (*right panel*) rats with septal lesions.

was no significant decrease in the 5 nonhyperdipsic rats. These data are summarized in Figure 4. To test the degree of association between acetylcholine content of brain and water consumption in lesioned rats, a Pearson product-moment coefficient or correlation was calculated between these two measures. A correlation of -0.73 $(df = 13; p < 0.005)$ was obtained. These data suggest, therefore, that the cholinergic system affected by septal lesions normally exerts an inhibitory influence on thirst.

It can be seen from the two examples given above that the increasing knowledge concerning the monoaminergic and cholinergic pathways in brain can provide important information concerning the distribution of the thirst circuits and their pharmacological nature. Not only can such maps allow us to selectively interrupt various chemical fiber systems and assess changes in thirst regulation, but in addition they provide clues as to the areas in which chemical application of various putative synaptic transmitters might be expected to affect thirst. The combination of the ablation technique with that of the intracerebral application of drugs could therefore provide a more powerful approach to the pharmacological analysis of thirst.

REFERENCES

Blass, E. M., & Hanson, D. G. Primary hyperdipsia in the rat following septal lesions. *Journal of Comparative and Physiological Psychology,* 1970, **70**, 87–93.

Bloom, F. E., Hoffer, B. J., Nelson, C., Sheu, Y-s., & Siggins, G. R. The physiology and pharmacology of serotonin mediated synapses. In J. Barchus & E. Usdin (Eds.), *Serotonin and behavior.* Springfield: Academic Press, 1972, in press.

Curtis, D. R., & Crawford, J. M. Central synaptic transmission: Microelectorphoretic studies. *Annual Review of Pharmacology,* 1969, **9**, 209–240.

Curtis, D. R., & Phillis, J. W. The action of procaine and atropine on spinal neurones. *Journal of Physiology (London),* 1960, **153**, 17–34.

Curtis, D. R., & Ryall, R. W. The synaptic excitation of Renshaw cells. *Experimental Brain Research,* 1966, **2**, 81–96.

Dahlstrom, A., & Fuxe, K. Evidence for the existence of monoamine-containing neurons in the central nervous system. I. Demonstration of monoamines in the cell bodies of brain stem neurons. *Acta Physiologica Scandinavica,* 1964, **62**, Sup. 232, 1–55.

De Groat, W. C. GABA-depolarization of a sensory ganglion: Antagonism by picrotoxin and bicuculline. *Brain Research,* 1972, **38**, 429–432.

Epstein, A. N., Fitzsimons, J. T., & Rolls, B. J. Drinking induced by injection of angiotensin into the brain of the rat. *Journal of Physiology (London),* 1970, **210**, 457–474.

Falck, B., & Hillarp, N.-A. On the cellular localization of catecholamines in the brain. *Acta Anatomica,* 1959, **38**, 277–279.

Giarman, N. J., & Pepeu, C. Drug induced changes in brain acetylcholine. *British Journal of Pharmacology,* 1962, **19**, 226–234.

Giarman, N. J., & Pepeu, G. The influence of centrally acting cholinolitic drugs on brain acetylcholine levels. *British Journal of Pharmacology,* 1964, **23**, 123–130.

Gold, R. M. Aphagia and adipsia following unilateral and bilaterally asymmetrical lesions in rats. *Physiology and Behavior,* 1967, **2**, 211–220.

Grossman, S. P., & Stumpf, W. E. Intracranial drug implants: An autoradiographic analysis of diffusion. *Science,* 1969, **166**, 1410–1412.

Harvey, J. A., Heller, A., & Moore, R. Y. The effect of unilateral and bilateral medial forebrain bundle lesions on brain serotonin. *Journal of Pharmacology and Experimental Therapeutics*, 1963, **140**, 103–110.

Harvey, J. A., & Hunt, H. F. Effect of septal lesions on thirst in the rat as indicated by water consumption and operant responding for water reward. *Journal of Comparative and Physiological Psychology*, 1965, **59**, 49–56.

Harvey, J. A., & Lints, C. E. Lesions in the medial forebrain bundle: Delayed effects on sensitivity to electric shock. *Science*, 1965, **148**, 250–252.

Harvey, J. A., & Lints, C. E. Lesions in the medial forebrain bundle: Relationship between pain sensitivity and telencephalic content of serotonin. *Journal of Comparative and Physiological Psychology*, 1971, **74**, 28–36.

Heller, A., & Harvey, J. A. Effect on CNS lesions on brain norepinephrine. *Pharmacologist*, 1963, **5**, 261.

Heller, A., Harvey, J. A., & Moore, R. Y. A demonstration of a fall in brain serotonin following central nervous system lesions in the rat. *Biochemical Pharmacology*, 1962, **11**, 859–866.

Heller, A., & Moore, R. Y. Control of brain serotonin and norepinephrine by specific neural systems. *Advances in Pharmacology*, 1968, **6**, 191–206. (Part A)

Houpt, K. A., & Epstein, A. N. The complete dependence of beta-adrenergic drinking on the renal dipsogen. *Physiology and Behavior*, 1971, **7**, 897–902.

Konig, J. F. R., & Klippel, R. A. *The rat brain.* New York: Krieger, 1970.

Lewis, P. R., & Shute, C. C. D. The cholinergic limbic system: Projections to hippocampal formation, medial cortex, nuclei of the ascending cholinergic reticular system, and the subfornical organ and supra-optic crest. *Brain*, 1967, **40**, 521–540.

McIlwain, H., & Bachelard, H. S. *Biochemistry and the central nervous system.* (4th ed.) London: Churchill Livingstone, 1971.

Mitchell, J. P. The spontaneous and evoked release of acetylcholine from the cerebral cortex. *Journal of Physiology (London)*, 1963, **165**, 98–116.

Moore, R. Y., Bhatnagar, R. K., & Heller, A. Anatomical and chemical studies of a nigro-neostriatal projection in the cat. *Brain Research*, 1971, **30**, 119–135.

Oltmans, G. A., & Harvey, J. A. LH syndrome and brain catecholamine levels after lesions of the nigrostriatal bundle. *Physiology and Behavior*, 1972, **8**, 69–78.

Pepeu, G., Mulas, A., Ruffi, A., & Sotgiu, P. Brain acetylcholine levels in rats with septal lesions. *Life Sciences*, 1971, **10**, 181–184.

Shaskan, E. G., & Snyder, S. H. Kinetics of serotonin accumulation into slices from rat brain: Relationship to catecholamine uptake. *Journal of Pharmacology and Experimental Therapeutics*, 1970, **175**, 404–418.

Shute, C. C. D., & Lewis, P. R. The ascending cholinergic reticular system: Neocortical, olfactory and subcortical projections. *Brain*, 1967, **40**, 497–520.

Sorensen, J. P., Jr., & Harvey, J. A. Decreased brain acetylcholine after septal lesions in rats: Correlation with thirst. *Physiology and Behavior*, 1971, **6**, 723–725.

Szerb, J. C. The effect of tertiary and quaternary atropine on cortical acetylcholine output and on the electroencephalogram in cats. *Canadian Journal of Physiology and Pharmacology*, 1964, **42**, 303–314.

Takahashi, R., & Aprison, M. H. Acetylcholine content of discrete areas of the brain obtained by a near-freezing method. *Journal of Neurochemistry*, 1964, **11**, 887–898.

Teitelbaum, P., & Epstein, A. N. The lateral hypothalamic syndrome: Recovery of feeding and drinking after lateral hypothalamic lesions. *Psychological Review*, 1962, **69**, 74–90.

Ungerstedt, U. Adipsia and aphagia after 6-hydroxydopamine induced degeneration of the nigro-striatal dopamine systems. *Acta Physiologica Scandinavica*, 1971, Supplement 367, 95–122. (a)

Ungerstedt, U. Stereotaxic mapping of the monoamine pathways in the rat brain. *Acta Physiologica Scandinavica*, 1971, Supplement 367, 1–48. (b)

INVITED COMMENT: COMMENTS TO PAPERS ON "THIRST" BY DRS. FISHER, HARVEY, AND SETLER

David Lehr
New York Medical College

As a pharmacologist and experimental pathologist who has spent the main phase of his scientific life with work on the cardiovascular system and the kidney, and who stumbled into the area of brain research less than 7 years ago, by the serendipitous discovery in the albino rat of copious drinking and simultaneous inhibition of water diuresis by isoproterenol (Lehr, Mallow, Krukowski, & Colon, 1966), I feel doubly humble and appreciative to have been asked to comment on these three very excellent papers on thirst presented from laboratories which are internationally renowned for their many notable contributions to this field. In view of the editorially prescribed space limitations, I shall confine my remarks to a few selected aspects of these presentations which either are most directly related to my own work, or which, from the standpoint of the pharmacologist, touch upon essential concepts and thus might benefit from reemphasis and elaboration.

Drs. Fisher, Harvey, and Setler have all given due credit to Grossman (1960) for his outstanding contribution to the study of consummatory behavior, with his introduction of pharmacological methodology to intracerebral stimulation. Local drug application by brain cannula has undoubtedly advanced our knowledge of brain function and has often made it possible to distinguish anatomically as well as bioelectrically inseparable neural pathways. Yet, this methodology, variously modified and refined, has perhaps been too enthusiastically and sometimes uncritically employed. I quite agree with Harvey that in studies with putative synaptic transmitters in the brain, the dosage selected for intracerebral administration must have some realistic and acceptable relationship to the endogenous concentrations of such putative transmitters in the brain tissue, and that the effects of dosages far in excess of physiological concentrations are not always representative of the specific action sought and may, in fact, constitute toxic manifestations. Yet, caution is in order against misinterpretation of Harvey's very valid argument. To elaborate upon his example, the fact alone that angiotensin is active upon local application to the brain in nanogram amounts, which means in the physiological range of activity, whereas norepinephrine may require many times the endogenous concentration if given by this route, does not necessarily indicate that the response to this larger dose of norepinephrine is less specific than that of angiotensin. This is as true for putative synaptic transmitters in the brain as it is with proven transmitters in the periphery.

Even the most delicate and well-aimed application via brain cannula can at best only represent a crude simulation of transmitter release at junctional clefts of specifically coded neuronal circuits. The ultimate availability of any agent, administered by brain cannula in the biophase of the receptor at which it is aimed, is dependent to a large extent upon its physical and chemical characteristics, its stability, and the mechanisms for its removal and inactivation available in the particular location.

In the special instance under discussion, angiotensin might be expected to remain extracellular and thus to be available in full concentration at a receptor site, its removal depending primarily upon degradation by angiotensinase. Noradrenaline, on the other hand, is subject to effective and rapid removal by uptake into adrenergic neurons, in addition to the well-known mechanisms of enzymic biotransformation. Hence, local application of norepinephrine to a brain site which, for the sake of argument, may contain dense populations of adrenergically coded circuits, most of which may not even be involved in the drinking mechanism or any other behavior under examination, would sharply reduce the availability at the intended receptor site. This may help to explain the need for greater and often "unphysiological" dosage of this particular putative brain transmitter.

These considerations notwithstanding, the argument should not be used to excuse the total disregard for acceptable dosage ranges in claims of the discovery of specific chemical coding of brain "centers," as has been done by some investigators. It is significant that such uncritical employment of intracerebral drug application is not infrequently coupled with unqualified acceptance of its superiority and disdain for any data concerning effects upon the brain, obtained with the *peripheral* route of drug administration, though this is the very route used exclusively in human therapy with all CNS-active drugs.

Moreover, differences encountered by these two routes are not necessarily due to lack of penetration through the blood-brain barrier, but can, on the contrary, often be explained by the ready entry of the systemically administered drug into the brain and thus a far more comprehensive and complicated activation of neuronal circuits than is accomplished by arbitrary cannulation of a single brain site. This applies, for instance, to amphetamine, which readily enters the brain from the periphery. As we have pointed out earlier (Lehr & Goldman,

1971), results obtained by brain cannulation alone have led to the erroneous assumption of beta-adrenergic activation as the mechanism of amphetamine anorexia (Leibowitz, 1970a).

Finally, referring to the observations of Houpt and Epstein (1971), Harvey makes the important point that intracerebrally adminstered compounds may diffuse into the general circulation and induce peripheral pharmacological effects. Fisher rightfully cites isoproterenol-induced drinking as a case in point. The sound experimental evidence which he presents certainly lends considerable weight to the "leakage" hypothesis. Recent data obtained in my laboratory point in the same direction (Lehr, Goldman, & Casner, unpublished data, 1972). Since isoproterenol is an extremely potent vasodilator, causing a highly significant blood-pressure fall after the subcutaneous injection of as little as 1.0 μg per rat, we employed the drop in blood pressure as a sensitive "bioassay" of isoproterenol leakage from the brain in acute experiments with brain-cannulated rats. Injection of 30 μg of isoproterenol (in volumes of 1 μl) into the lateral hypothalamus or hippocampus produced prompt hypotension of nearly equal magnitude, though of shorter duration than when injected subcutaneously. Application of 60 μg caused profound long-lasting hypotension. Local pretreatment with xylocaine (20 to 40 μg) did not block the hypotensive responses, a fact which speaks against the possibility of a *locally* elicited blood pressure drop and supports the concept of "leakage" of pharmacologically active isoproterenol into the periphery.

In an additional study, groups of albino rats with intracerebral cannulas directed towards the lateral hypothalamus were injected with 20, 40, or 60 μg of isoproterenol per rat (Figure 1a). Significant drinking occurred with 60 μg only, an amount which caused considerable ataxia and prostration and which, if injected systemically, induced copious drinking. Thus systemic potency exceeded intracerebral potency.

It is of interest that Fisher, after fully expounding the leakage hypothesis, still arrives at the conclusion that interaction of leakage to the periphery and autonomic outflow from the hypothalamus are the initiating events following central isoproterenol stimulation that lead to drinking. Though I still adhere to our early postulate for the existence of central beta-adrenergically coded thirst circuits, I fully agree with Fisher's view that to date, "no one has reported inducing central isoproterenol drinking reliably at dosage levels at or below the effective peripheral dose." I also share his reluctance to accept the excessive intracerebral dosages used by Leibowitz (1970a, 1970b, 1971) in her model, in which both eating and drinking are reciprocally controlled by central apha- and beta-adrenergic actions. This 1970-71 Leibowitz model, incidentally, bears an uncanny resemblance to our concepts of reciprocal alpha- and beta-adrenergic activity in the brain in regard to both drinking and eating, published in 1967 and 1968 (Lehr, Mallow, & Krukowski, 1967; Conte, Lehr, Goldman, & Krukowski, 1968). Leibowitz differentiates her model from ours by dismissing drinking following *peripheral* isoproterenol administration as not related to that after

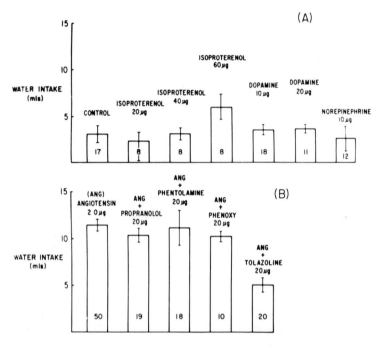

FIG. 1. (*A*) The effects of isoproterenol (ISOP), dopamine (DA), and norepinephrine (NE) on 1-hour water intake following injection into the preoptic area are depicted. ISOP at 20 and 40 μg did not elicit significant drinking; at 60 μg per rat, however, water intake was significantly increased (*p* < .05). Neither DA nor NE produced significant drinking in the dosage employed. Doses, number of animals, and standard error are indicated. Water intake is expressed in milliliters per rat. (*B*) The response to angiotensin after preoptic injection and alterations of its effect by pretreatment with alpha- and beta-adrenergic antagonists (15 min) are shown. Only tolazoline pretreatment significantly modified angiotensin drinking (*p* < .01). The one-hour water intake is expressed in milliliters per rat.

intracerebral application, because the former is abolished in nephrectomized rats. As Fisher's data prove, there is, in fact, no difference between our peripheral and Leibowitz's centrally induced isoproterenol drinking in this respect, since bilateral nephrectomy blocks the responses from both routes.

Though Fisher stresses the "congruence" of angiotensin- and isoproterenol-induced thirst, it is difficult to fully accept the validity of his arguments. We have shown (Goldman & Lehr, 1969) that hypotension itself does not cause drinking in the albino rat and that its sustained presence is also not essential in isoproternol-induced drinking. Thus, denying the water-replete rat access to water for 1 and 2 hours following a single subcutaneous injection of isoproterenol, in no way diminishes the extent of the drinking response at either interval, although the hypotensive phase lasts only 50 to 60 minutes (blood pressure measurements were made with indwelling chronic carotid cannulas in the conscious, unrestrained rat).

The explanation that antidiuresis following isoproterenol and diuresis following angiotensin are due to the contrasting hemodynamic effects of these two agents appears reasonable. However, the type of hypotensive response elicited by isoproterenol does not in itself consistently result in the complete and sustained cessation of the urinary flow. It was this very fact and the observed depletion of antidiuretic hormone from the pituitary (Goldman, 1969) that made us think of a true water-sparing phenomenon. Furthermore, in contrast to Fisher, we did not find any substantial interference with peripherally induced isoproterenol drinking by peripheral atropine blockage (Lehr et al., 1967), whereas this latter measure, in agreement with Fisher's observations, significantly inhibited central angiotensin drinking (Goldman, Lehr, & Frank, 1972).

This vital point of difference in our observations decisively affects the acceptability of the proposed isoproterenol-angiotensin link. We have used atropine exclusively for cholinergic blocking effects. Fisher seems to favor scopolamine, which not only is the far more potent anticholinergic, but also is about *100 times* as potent as atropine in depressing the *reticular activating system.* Hence its selective use in human therapy as "chemical straightjacket" and with morphine in "twilight sleep." Interference with isoproterenol drinking may therefore be based on effects other than the anticholinergic activity of scopolamine. It is of particular interest in this connection that, according to Fisher's Table 5, scopolamine shares with haloperidol the highly effective inhibition also of salt-induced and deprivation-induced as well as hypovolemic drinking. These findings, together with our observations that peripheral chlorpromazine, in mildly sedating dosage, is likewise a potent inhibitor of isoproterenol-, angiotensin-, and carbachol-induced drinking (Lehr & Goldman, 1972), would seem to point towards participation of depression of the reticular activating system which scopolamine has in common with the two major tranquilizers, as the most parsimonious explanation for the suppression of various thirst stimuli.

I was puzzled by Fisher's observation that the *peripheral* injection of more than 0.04 mg of isoproterenol severely debilitated his rats and was often lethal, since we have regularly employed 5.25 mg/kg and 85 mg/kg isoproterenol subcutaneously for the production of disseminated and infarctoid myocardial necrosis in the albino rat for many years with a very low overall mortality (Lehr, 1969, and 1972). The actual MLD for isoproterenol in the albino rat is close to 700 mg/kg sc.

Despite my untrammelled admiration for Fitzsimons' and Epstein's fascinating work with the "renal dipsogen" (Epstein, Fitzsimons, & Simons, 1969; Fitzsimons, 1970; Epstein, 1972), there are additional incongruities which make it difficult to accept the renin-angiotensin system as the intermediary of isoproterenol-drinking.

For one, P. Casner and H. W. Goldman, in my laboratory, have found recently that a dose response curve with reasonable amounts of renin can be obtained only in the nephrectomized rat, and that renin-induced drinking, like that elicited by angiotensin, is strongly inhibited by peripheral atropine and not by alpha- and beta-adrenergic blockade (see Table 1). Interestingly, atropine did not reduce the diuretic action of peripheral renin.

Furthermore, there are important differences in the effect of renin or angiotensin as compared to isoproterenol upon hematocrit and serum osmolarity in the albino rat. Goldman (1969) has shown that isoproterenol (.33 mg/kg sc.) causes a significant *decrease* of the hematocrit within 30 to 60 minutes after injection, the values remaining below control levels for about 3 hours. Serum osmolarity remains unchanged. When animals are denied access to water, the intravascular volume *increases* by about 20%.

These findings are in marked contrast to the *increase* in hematocrit values found by Haefli and Peters (1971) after peripheral injection of renin or angiotensin. In fact, these authors attribute the dipsogenic action of renin and angiotensin to a calculated 22% *diminution* in intravascular volume. In view of these divergent observations, it is difficult to see how isoproterenol could exert its effect via the renin-angiotensin system.

TABLE 1

The Influence of Autonomic Blocking Agents upon
Renin-Induced Drinking in the Intact and Reniprival Rat

# of Rats	Autonomic antagonist (pretreatment 15 min) mg/kg BW sc		Renin units/100 gm BW intraperitoneally	Water intake (3-hour total) ml/100 gm BW
Intact animals				
12			1.0	0.84 ± 0.18
12			3.0	1.02 ± 0.31
18			6.0	2.39 ± 0.43[a]
10	Atropine	5.5	6.0	0.75 ± 0.30[b]
20	Tolazoline	8.5	6.0	2.12 ± 0.37
10	Propranolol	6.2	6.0	1.76 ± 0.43
18			Saline control	0.56 ± 0.17
Nephrectomized animals				
10			1.0	2.07 ± 0.21[a]
10			2.0	3.76 ± 0.25[a]
10			3.0	6.81 ± 0.84[a]
5	Atropine	5.0	3.0	1.00 ± 0.29[b]
30			Saline control	1.23 ± 0.32

[a]Significant difference from control.
[b]Significant difference from highest renin dose.

The interesting observation of Setler on the interaction in the brain of catecholaminergic agonists and antagonists with angiotensin, lead her to conclude that catecholamines play an important role in thirst and the control of drinking, and specifically that the endogenous catecholamines norepinephrine and dopamine have dipsogenic activity, possibly through activation of a single type of receptor.

We are in agreement with Setler on the unimpressive dipsogenic potency of both dopamine and norepinephrine at angiotensin-sensitive sites in the brain (Figure 1*a*). Yet, our observations that intracerebral tolazoline, a rapidly acting, short-duration alpha-adrenergic blocking agent, significantly inhibited intracerebral angiotensin drinking (Figure 1*b*) prompted us to concur with Fitzsimons and Setler's (1971) view that a catecholaminergic mechanism plays an important role in mediating such drinking. However, we have since confirmed the findings of these authors that neither phentolamine nor phenoxybenzamine, both potent peripheral alpha-adrenergic antagonists, have any influence upon the dipsogenic activity of angiotensin. It is conceivable, therefore, that the tolazoline effect in the brain is based on a mechanism unrelated to its specific peripheral action. This problem is presently under investigation.

REFERENCES

Conte, M., Lehr, D., Goldman, H. W., & Krukowski, M. Inhibition of food intake by beta-adrenergic stimulation. *Pharmacologist,* 1968, **10**, 180.

Epstein, A. N. Drinking induced by low doses of intravenous angiotensin. *Physiologist,* 1972, **15**, 127.

Epstein, A. N., Fitzsimons, J. T., & Simons, B. J. Drinking caused by the intracranial injection of angiotensin into the rat. *Journal of Physiology (London),* 1969, **200**, 98–100.

Fitzsimons, J. T. The renin-angiotensin system in the control of drinking. In L. Martini, M. Motta, & F. Fraschini, (Eds.), *The hypothalamus.* New York: Academic Press, 1970. Pp. 195–212.

Fitzsimons, J. T., & Setler, P. E. Catechol-aminergic mechanisms in angiotensin-induced drinking. *Journal of Physiology (London),* 1971, **218**, 43–44.

Goldman, H. W. Correlation of the hemodynamic actions of alpha- and beta-adrenergic amines and other vasoactive substances with their effects on the thirst drive and urine flow in the albino rat. Unpublished doctoral dissertation, New York Medical College, 1969.

Goldman, H. W., & Lehr, D. Possible contribution of blood pressure changes to contrasting effects of alpha- and beta-adrenergic amines upon water balance. *The Pharmacologist,* 1969, **9**, 249.

Goldman, H. W., Lehr, D., & Frank, E. Pharmacologic characterization of the dipsogenic property of angiotensin II. *Federation Proceedings,* 1972, **31**, 573.

Grossman, S. P. Eating and drinking elicited by direct adrenergic and cholinergic stimulation of the hypothalamus. *Science,* 1960, **132**, 301–302.

Haefli, L., & Peters, G. Induction of hypovolemia by thirst-inducing doses of renin or angiotensin II. *British Journal of Pharmacology,* 1971, **42**, 25–30.

Houpt, K. A., & Epstein, A. N. The complete dependence of beta-adrenergic drinking on the renal dipsogen. *Physiology and Behavior,* 1971, **7**, 897–902.

Lehr, D. Tissue electrolyte alterations in disseminated myocardial necrosis. *Annals of the New York Academy of Sciences*, 1969, **156**, 344–378.

Lehr, D. About the healing of myocardial necrosis caused by sympathomimetic amines. *Myocardiology*, 1972, **1**, 526–550.

Lehr, D., & Goldman, H. W. Sympathetic regulation of fluid balance and food intake by reciprocal activity of alpha and beta-adrenergically coded hypothalamic centers. *Proceedings of the International Union of Physiological Sciences*, 1971, **9**.

Lehr, D., & Goldman, H. W. Continued pharmacologic analysis of consummatory behavior in the albino rat. *European Journal of Pharmacology*, in press.

Lehr, D., Mallow, J., & Krukowski, M., Copious drinking and simultaneous inhibition of urine flow elicited by beta-adrenergic stimulation and contrary effect of alpha-adrenergic stimulation. *Journal of Pharmacology and Experimental Therapeutics*, 1967, **158**, 150–163.

Lehr, D., Mallow, J., Krukowski, M., & Colon, R. Drinking elicited by beta-adrenergic stimulation. *Federation Proceedings*, 1966, **25**, 624.

Leibowitz, S. F. Amphetamine's anorexic versus hunger-inducing effects mediated respectively by hypothalamic beta- versus alpha-adrenergic receptors. *Proceedings*, 78th Annual APA Convention, 1970, 813–814. (a)

Leibowitz, S. F. Reciprocal hunger-regulating "circuits" involving alpha- and beta-adrenergic receptors located, respectively, in the ventromedial and lateral hypothalamus. *Proceedings of the National Academy of Sciences*, 1970, **67**, 1063–1070. (b)

Leibowitz, S. F. Hypothalamic beta-adrenergic "thirst" system mediates drinking induced by carbachol and transiently by norepinephrine. *Federation Proceedings*, 1971, **30**, 481.

EPILOGUE:
RETROSPECT AND PROGNOSIS[1]

Alan N. Epstein
University of Pennsylvania

We are in the midst of a new era of thirst research. The dry-mouth idea is far behind us, and we are beyond the view that thirst is little more than the response of brain osmoreceptors to their own water loss, itself an important advance of the early 1950s. The work summarized in this volume, most of it done in the last decade, shows that we have new precedents for research and that we are enjoying more satisfactory answers to our basic question: What is the nature of thirst in animals like ourselves?

Our progress and optimism is due largely to the fact that we have a powerful new concept and the techniques to pursue its full meaning. We are calling the concept the *double depletion hypothesis of thirst.* It is grounded in the basic fact of the division of body water into two separate compartments, and it asserts that thirst is stimulated by depletions of each. In the first part of this essay, I will review the hypothesis by taking a look at its historical roots and by outlining its physiological basis with a set of simplified diagrams. Then I will prognosticate about problems for the future.

THE DOUBLE DEPLETION HYPOTHESIS OF THIRST

The double depletion hypothesis takes as already well established that: (*a*) thirst goes on in the brain, (*b*) the neurological machine for thirst integrates multiple inputs, and (*c*) from these inputs a specific motivational state arises and

[1] The writing of this essay and the original research of the author were supported by a Grant-in-Aid of Research from the Nutrition Foundation and by grants from NINDS (03469 to A. N. Epstein) and NIGMS (5 GM 281 to the Institute of Neurological Sciences).

drives the animal to seek water and to ingest it. The hypothesis adds, as major new concepts, that the principal inputs that control thirst: (*a*) arise from depletions of each of the two major water phases of the body, (*b*) reach the brain mechanism of thirst as neural afferents from peripheral receptors, as direct effects on receptors in the brain itself, and as the hormone angiotensin, and (*c*) also control the mechanisms of water conservation such that input is integrated with control of output to maintain body water constancy.

Historical Antecedents

Historically, the double depletion hypothesis is in the line of research begun at the turn of the century by A. Mayer and H. Wettendorff, (see Fitzsimons, this volume) who showed that thirst was associated with increases in the osmotic pressure of the blood (Mayer, 1900) and that an ultimate cause of thirst was dehydration of the tissues (Wettendorff, 1901). Wettendorff recognized that the rise in osmotic pressure of the blood during water privation was not great enough to account for the avid drinking and large volume intake of the thirsty dog. He concluded that dehydration of the cells, not of the blood, was the cause of thirst. Gilman (1937) made this idea part of our thinking with his marvelously simple and appropriate experiment comparing the powerful effects on drinking of solutes that are excluded from cells with the weak effects of solutes such as urea that enter cells and do not effectively alter the osmotic gradient across their membranes.

But this work was overshadowed by Cannon's dry-mouth theory, which dominated thinking about thirst for more than 30 years in tribute to the immense authority of its author and to the excellence of his work elsewhere in physiology. The undeniable association in common sense and physiological fact between reduced salivary flow and states of dehydration in man and other mammals has kept the idea alive among Cannon's followers (Cizek, 1968), but it has proved to be an intellectual cul-de-sac. Thirst is no more caused by a dry mouth than is hunger caused by contractions of the empty stomach or sleep caused by heaviness of the eyelids, as Schiff (1867) insisted more than 100 years ago.

Andersson's important studies of the mid-1950s (summarized in Andersson, 1967) continued the advance made by Mayer, Wettendorff, and Gilman. With this, the era of the neurological investigation of thirst was begun, and interest in cellular dehydration reached its acme. Andersson and his colleagues showed with lesion studies (Andersson & McCann, 1956; Andersson & Larsson, 1956) that the effects of cell dehydration were exerted directly on the brain and that both thirst and urine concentration (ADH release) were provoked by the same central stimuli. Although his dramatic reports of immediate and vigorous thirst after injection of small amounts of extracellular solute into the hypothalamus (Andersson, 1953) were very likely due to nonspecific stimulation of the thirst system (Peck & Novin, 1971), his work enthroned cell dehydration and hypothalamic osmoreceptors in the center of our thinking about thirst, where they remain for most students of brain function and behavior. Ironically, Andersson is not now among them (see Peck, this volume, and Andersson, this volume).

There were intimations of an influence of extracellular depletion in the background of our thinking from before World War II (McCance, 1936), but it remained for Fitzsimons (1961) to show that volume depletion is as physiologically real and potent a stimulus of thirst as cell dehydration. The studies from Columbia (Holmes & Cizek, 1951; Cizek, Semple, Huang, & Gregersen, 1951; Huang, 1955) published in the early 1950s were prescient. Dogs and rabbits were shown to drink excessively to challenges (chronic sodium depletion and peritoneal dialysis with glucose) that could not have produced cell dehydration. But the case made by these studies for hypovolemia as an independent control of thirst was not convincing: first, because they were used by the Columbia group to criticize the suggestion that thirst is caused by cell dehydration (Cizek et al., 1951) and to support the dry-mouth theory, rather than as evidence for an independent role for reduced plasma volume; secondly, because in the context of the early 1960s, the drinking could have been the result of sodium deficiency (Falk & Herman, 1961) rather than of hypovolemia; and, last, because hemorrhage, the most direct and most easily quantified technique for the reduction of blood volume, did not reliably produce thirst, and negative reports of its use came from the Columbia group (Holmes & Montgomery, 1951). Fitzsimons' extensive work, confirmed by Stricker (this volume), established hypovolemia as an independent and potent stimulus of thirst and elevated it to equal status with cell dehydration. He assembled a set of techniques including hyperoncotic colloid deposition, caval ligation, and hemorrhage that have in common the effect of hypovolemia. All produce thirst without increasing serum osmotic pressure and therefore without cell dehydration.

The Parallel with ADH Release

In parallel with our appreciation of the dual nature of the stimuli of thirst, ADH release was being shown to be under the control of cell dehydration and volume depletion. Again the history begins with a clear demonstration of the effectiveness of cell dehydration operating through brain osmoreceptors (Verney, 1947). Then volume receptors in the walls of the capacitance vessels of the thorax (pulmonary artery and left atrium) were implicated, and volume changes were shown to effect ADH release in the absence of water loss from cells. In this system we have the most direct evidence for peripheral volume receptors (Share, 1969). They are apparently mechanoreceptors in the walls of the left atrium (and pulmonary artery), whose integrated output holds ADH under tonic inhibition (Gupta, Henry, Sinclair, & von Baumgarten, 1966; Henry, Gupta Meehan, Sinclair, & Share, 1968). Reduction of their output during decreased vascular filling releases ADH.

The diagrams that follow summarize our current understanding of the physiologic mechanisms for the cellular and extracellular controls of thirst. A

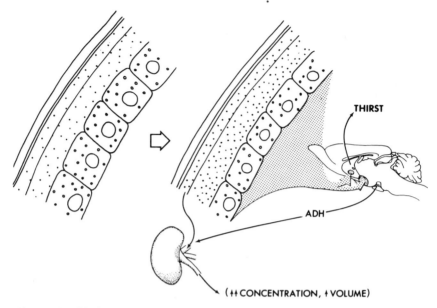

FIG. 1. Simplified schema for the cellular dehydration control of thrist and ADH release.

fuller discussion will be found in Fitzsimons' authoritative and complete review (1972). The diagrams include the parallel ADH system to emphasize the intimacy in brain function between both input and output controls of body water balance.

The Mechanism of Cellular Thirst

Figure 1 depicts the cellular system (see Blass, this volume). A body water diagram is at the left. It emphasizes the two major compartments (while taking great liberties with their relative sizes) and shows that the extracellular compartment (divided into an interstitial space, adjacent to the cells, and a smaller intravascular space) contains solute (the small black dots) that is excluded from the cells. The osmotic pressure of the extracellular compartment can be increased either by solute addition or by water loss. Water loss is probably the more frequent cause. It occurs as the result of transpiration through the skin, respiratory expiration, and evaporation of saliva either in panting or saliva spreading. All these are losses of pure water that increase the osmolality of the remaining extracellular fluid. Solute addition occurs naturally as the result of postprandial absorption from the gut and can be produced experimentally by injection of a solute (sodium chloride, sucrose) that is excluded from the cells. Increasing the extracellular osmotic pressure (shown by the increased density of dots in the altered body water diagram at the right in Figure 1), either by water loss or by addition of solute, draws water from the cells, and they shrink. The dehydration and shrinkage of the cells is, of course, global throughout the body, but as is suggested by the shaded, double-headed arrow, it is sampled by two sets of receptors in the brain (the rat brain is shown in medial view) that stimulate ADH release and mobilize thirst. Although they are partially overlapping (see Peck, this volume), the two sets of osmosensitive cells are shown as anatomically separate to emphasize their different effector outputs, thirst, and ADH release. Water is ingested, and the urine is concentrated (the kidney is represented below, with artery above, ureter below, and vein in the middle). Urine volume will increase in the example shown because of the excess solute load; but when cellular thirst is generated by the more natural circumstance of pure water loss, the urine will be small in volume as well as more concentrated.

The Mechanism of Extracellular Thirst

The extracellular system is more complex (see Stricker, this volume). A receptor has been added to the vascular space in the body water diagram (see Figure 2). It is represented as an innervated mechanoreceptor firing tonically to normovolemia. Volume depletion without loss of cell water simultaneously alters volume receptor output (shown here as an inhibition from the ADH work) and releases renal renin which generates circulating angiotensin (angio II). Together, the renal hormone and the afferents from the vascular receptors stimulate thirst and release ADH. At the lower right, emerging from the brainstem (again, forgive the anatomical liberty), I have suggested an autonomic outflow to the kidney for renin release, since it is known that renin can be

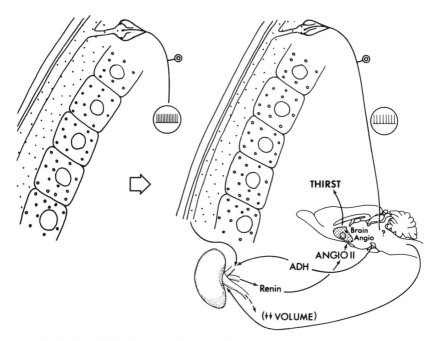

FIG. 2. Simplified schema for the extracellular control of thirst and ADH release.

released reflexly (Vander, 1967); and this phenomenon may be involved in thirst (Fisher, Antelman, Tarter, & Redgate, 1972; and see Fisher, this volume). The neural mechanism by which the vascular afferents effect thirst and ADH release is unknown, hence the question mark in the general vicinity of the brainstem. Angiotensin is shown reaching a broad area in the anterior forebrain from which thirst is aroused. It also participates in the release of ADH (see Peck, this volume). The role of the vascular afferents and the nature of the hormone's interaction with the brain are both problems marked by more ignorance than understanding. We have only the most preliminary information at present, and it is discussed below. Lastly, I have not included a possible mechanism for sodium appetite which is discussed by Stricker (this volume) and Fisher (this volume).

Concurrent Double Depletion during Natural Water Loss

Loss of isotonic extracellular fluid occurs as postprandial secretions, in pathology (vomiting, diarrhea, hemorrhage), or by design in the laboratory. Under natural circumstances in the healthy mammal, body water is lost either as pure water or as hypotonic secretions (sweat, whole saliva), the result being the concurrent loss of both cell water and extracellular volume. We should therefore expect thirst and urine concentration to be mobilized by the brain in response to simultaneous inputs from both water compartments. This is suggested in Figure 3, which combines the mechanisms of both the cellular and the extracellular controls. Notice the overlap in the anterior forebrain of the receptive area for peripheral angiotensin and the osmoreceptive zones for thirst and ADH release. The concurrent activation of these forebrain areas plus the stimulation from the vascular afferents leads to a decrease in urine volume, to an increase in its concentration, and to the drive for water.

This is as far as the facts will allow me to go. But to prepare for the future, I have included an acknowledgement of the presence of the renin-angiotensin system within the brain (Fisher-Ferraro, Nahmod, Goldstein, & Finkielman, 1971), and endogenous to the brain (Ganten, Marquez-Julio, Granger, Hayduk, Karsunky, Boucher, & Genest, 1971). It is, like norepinephrine, represented in parallel in the brain and periphery. Could the brain's own angiotensin be the ultimate dipsogen? Can we expect the most potent dipsogenic substance known (and a most potent releaser of ADH as well) to be present in the brain and have nothing to do with thirst? I will return to these questions later.

Summary of the Double Depletion Hypothesis

For the moment, and subject certainly to revision as more facts emerge, the double depletion hypothesis can be summarized as follows: Recent work has distinguished two quite different kinds of thirst of physiological origin. Both are hydrational in that they are induced by alterations in body water, and both are regulatory in that they contribute to the constancy of body water. But each is linked to only one of the two compartments for water in the mammalian body,

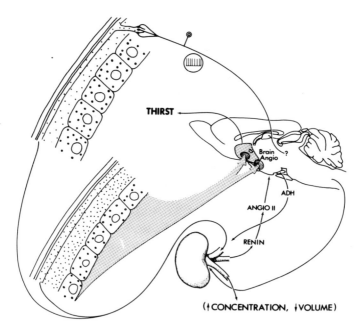

FIG. 3. Combined schema for the defense of body water by thirst and
ADH release, emphasizing the double depletion hypothesis.

and each has a qualitatively different physiological mechanism. One arises from
depletions of extracellular volume (hypovolemia) and is stimulated by a synergy
of neural and hormonal inputs to the brain from the periphery. Hypovolemia
affects thoracic, low-pressure baroreceptors and releases renin-angiotensin from
the kidney. Together these signals generate drinking. The other kind of thirst
arises from depletions of intracellular water (cellular or cell dehydration) and is
stimulated by central receptors in the preoptic area that sample the general cell
dehydration and mobilize drinking. It is, therefore, simpler than hypovolemic
thirst, having no hormonal basis and being entirely cerebral in the detection of
the hydrational stimulus and in the generation of drinking. Both extracellular and
cellular depletions stimulate ADH release by the posterior pituitary, thus giving
the brain command of water conservation by urine concentration. The brain,
using behavior and the kidney, orchestrates the body's defenses against water
loss.

A FORECAST OF URGENT PROBLEMS

So much for review. I now want to prognosticate a bit, to forecast the
problems that I think remain. Some are immediate, and some are long-range; but
all are urgent for the complete understanding of thirst.

The Volume Receptors in the Low-Pressure Circulation

First, we need direct studies of the receptors in the capacitance circulation of the thorax (pulmonary vessels, right heart, and left atrium) that we have burdened, by inference, with a role in extracellular thirst. An additional stimulus for hypovolemic thirst is needed because nephrectomy does not reduce the drinking of hyperoncotic colloid dialysis (Fitzsimons, 1961; Fitzsimons & Stricker, 1971) and only attenuates the thirst of caval ligation (Fitzsimons, 1964). In the absence of angiotensin, something else must be operating. The low-pressure baroreceptors are good candidates. They are innervated by the vagus and lie in the walls of the largest vessels of the low-pressure circulation which contains most of the blood, about 80% in animals like ourselves. The vessel walls are thin and readily distorted by changes in blood volume. Increases in blood volume can lower plasma ADH levels, but resting levels are low, and this point is disputed. But there is general agreement that thoracic hypovolemia inhibits the receptor discharge, and blood loss of 10% or less is a ready stimulus for ADH release. And the effect does not occur after vagotomy (Share, 1969). But we have no published evidence of a role for these receptors in thirst. Kozłowski reported informally at the Fourth International Conference on the Regulation of Food and Water Intake at Cambridge that the influence of blood volume reduction on thirst (a potentiation of cell dehydration thirst) no longer occurs in dogs with only left cervical vagotomy (Kozłowski & Sobocińska, 1971). This is all the direct evidence we have.

The Role of Peripheral Angiotensin

Angiotensin appears to be a hormone of thirst and, as such, it is the first hormone to be directly implicated in ingestive behavior. We need more extensive study of this exciting new idea. Angiotensin is produced by the synthetic process diagrammed in Figure 4. Note that the hormone of the kidney is an enzyme called renin whose substrate is angiotensinogen, a terminal polypeptide of an alpha-2 globulin of the plasma proteins. A synthetic tetradecapeptide angiotensinogen is shown in Figure 4. Renin acts on angiotensinogen to produce the decapeptide angiotensin I which is then enzymatically converted in capillary beds (the lungs, in particular) to the octapeptide angiotensin II. After acting on its target tissues, it is rapidly degraded by peptidases. (See Page & McCubbin, 1968, for a monographic discussion of the renin-angiotensin system). The evidence for angiotensin as a hormone of thirst is: (a) a potent dipsogenic substance can be extracted from the kidney and is indistinguishable from renin (Fitzsimons, 1969); (b) extracellular volume depletions that release renin (Vander, 1967) are potent dipsogenic treatments (Fitzsimons, 1972); (c) several such treatments depend either completely (isoproterenol—see Houpt & Epstein, 1971) or partially (caval ligation—see Fitzsimons, 1964) on the kidney for their dipsogenic effect; (d) both renin and angiotensin are dipsogenic when given

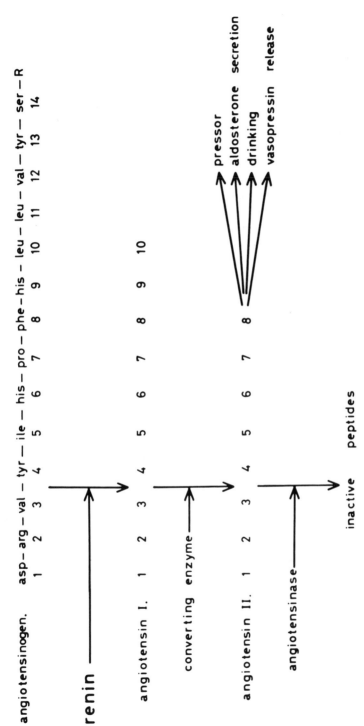

FIG. 4. The synthetic sequence of the renin-angiotensin system, beginning with angiotensinogen (*above*) and proceeding to degradation of the octapeptide. (Courtesy of James T. Fitzsimons.)

intravenously to rats (Fitzsimons & Simons, 1969; Fitzsimons, 1966); (*e*) angiotensin is the most potent dipsogen known when applied directly to the anterior forebrain (Epstein, Fitzsimons, & Rolls, 1970); and (*f*) intracranial angiotensin produces drinking that has the motivational properties of natural thirst (McFarland & Rolls, 1972; Rolls, Jones, & Fallows, 1972).

Until recently the intravenous evidence was the least convincing fact in this chain. The doses necessary for drinking were too high (10 μg/rat in the Fitzsimons and Simons study, 1969) and have been an obstacle to acceptance of peripheral angiotensin as a natural dipsogen. We have some good news on this score. By treating rats less aggressively than Fitzsimons and Simons did, and by more closely imitating the physiological geography of the hormone, we have reduced the effective dipsogenic dose to more satisfactory levels. Instead of infusing our animals immediately after recovery from anesthesia and in a novel chamber, we did so the morning after surgery and in their home cages. In addition, our animals had been stimulated to drink by pharmacological release of the renal dipsogen (100 μg/kg isoproterenol, sc) at least twice during the week before intravenous testing. And lastly, we infused angiotensin I, not angiotensin II. As Figure 5 shows, this simulates the natural course of the hormone in the circulation. Beginning at the left, the decapeptide angiotensin I is shown being formed in the kidney and the venous return to the heart by the interaction of renin an enzyme with its substrate. Enzymatic conversion to the octapeptide occurs in capillary beds, and the first bed to be reached by the angiotensin I is that of the lungs, which convert the decapeptide to angiotensin II. But, unlike all other organs studied, the lungs convert but do not significantly degrade the octapeptide (Hebert, Fouron, Boileau, & Biron, 1972). The lungs therefore return newly formed angiotensin II to the left heart, which then injects it into the systemic circulation where it reaches its target organs, acts, and is rapidly degraded. Any decapeptide that has escaped conversion in the lungs is converted in peripheral capillary beds, and renin can presumably act throughout the circulation. Figure 5 is therefore a simplification, but it does illustrate the fact that it is physiologically more appropriate to infuse angiotensin I, rather than

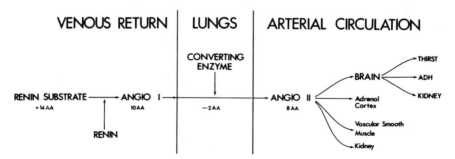

FIG. 5. The physiological geography of the renin-angiotensin system in its course through the circulation.

TABLE 1

Latency to Drinking, Total Cumulative Dose
to the Time of Drinking, and Water Intake
of Rats Infused with 40 ng/min of
Angiotensin I for 20 Minutes

Rat	Latency (min)	Cumulative initiating dose (ng/rat)	Intake in 20 min (ml)
16	7.43	297.2	2.1
18	15.35	614.0	1.8
19	4.12	164.8	1.6
20	16.45	658.0	3.3
25	5.93	237.2	0.2
27	16.45	658.0	3.3
33	8.97	358.8	3.2
35	10.40	416.0	1.4
$\overline{M}$	10.6	425.5	2.1

angiotensin II, into the right side of the heart. Combining these procedures
(and frankly, we do not yet know which are necessary), we have produced
drinking in our animals after 10 minutes of infusion with 40 ng/min, or
with a total cumulative dose of approximately 400 ng/rat of angiotensin I
(1 μg/kg for a 400-gram animal). The data are shown in Table 1. Eight
animals were studied. All had catheters in the superior vena cava at the
entrance to the right auricle. They all drank to the 40 ng/min infusion and
at the moment of drinking had received an average total of 425.5 ng of
angiotensin I (Ile[5], Schwarz/Mann). In our most recent attempts with
Sigmund Hsiao of the University of Arizona, our rats drink to 100 ng if
they have had one prior infusion. We have therefore reduced the dipsogenic
dose 100-fold and are in the range of doses by which angiotensin produces
its hypertensive effects (Gross, Bock, & Turrian, 1961). Experiments that
add mild cell dehydration or brief water deprivation to the hormone
infusion should lower the dose further. The evidence now heavily favors the
suggestion that angiotensin of renal origin is a natural dipsogen.

How does it interact with the brain? This is our most urgent problem. The
hormone acts rapidly as if it were stimulating receptors, so we should be alert for
some specific chemosensory tissue in the brain. But it does not enter the brain in
the conventional manner, and would be exceptional among peptides if it did. It
is excluded by the blood-brain barrier. We were unable to find evidence for its
concentration in the brain by scintillation studies of freshly dissected rat brain
after intravenous injection of radioactive hormone (Osborne, Pooters, Angles
d'Auriac, Epstein, Worcel, & Meyer, 1971) and radioautographic studies confirm
its failure to enter the brain parenchyma (Volicer & Loew, 1971). We must be
imaginative in finding this crucial piece of our puzzle and cannot use the model

of the steroid hormones that penetrate the brain from the blood, accumulate on nerve cell nuclei, and there influence brain function.

Kim Johnson (1972) in my laboratory has recently provided a lead. He showed clearly that the lateral cerebral ventricle is as sensitive as any other area of the brain to angiotensin as dipsogen. Rats drank reliably to the lowest effective dose (1 ng) of hormone when the injection was made unilaterally into the ventricular CSF. Moreover, he found that high or low sensitivity of brain tissue was very much a function of whether or not the cannula in use had traversed the lateral ventricle. Regions such as caudate, previously believed to be negative, (Epstein et al., 1970) were dramatically converted to sensitive regions if the cannula trajectory was angled sharply across the brain in order to traverse the ventricle; and positive sites such as preoptic area lost much of their special quality when the cannula opening into them did *not* enter the ventricle. Our injection work is done with hormone in aqueous solution, and reflux up the outside of the cannula is likely. Could our previous mapping studies have been maps of the readiness by which injected solutions reached the overlying ventricular space? Could the sensitive tissue be in contact with or have easy access to the CSF, and is the CSF therefore the portal of entry into the brain for peripheral hormone? The hormone may pass from blood to CSF to brain tissue, rather than from blood to brain tissue directly. The fluid compartment studies of Volicer and Lowe (1971) suggest this, and their preliminary radioautographs show concentration of isotope in the choroid plexi and periventricular structures that are in the brain but *outside* the barrier. Could these be the sensitive tissues? One of them, the subfornical organ (SFO), has recently been implicated in the drinking induced by intracranial angiotensin. John B. Simpson and Aryeh Routtenberg (personal communication, 1973) find, first, that the SFO is exceptionally sensitive to angiotensin. Drinking is produced reliably by injection of 10^{-13} moles of angiotensin directly into the organ. Secondly, they find that the drinking produced by angiotensin injection into the preoptic area (with subsequent leak into the CSF, as discussed above) is abolished by destruction of the SFO. This important lead requires confirmation and extension. In particular, we need to know what other dipsogenic treatments are less effective in rats without the subfornical organ, and we need to understand the relation between the SFO and the preoptic area. As described by Peck (this volume), preoptic damage blocks the dipsogenic effects of intravenous angiotensin in some animals.

There is one last intrigue here. We did find an extraordinary concentration of radioactivity in the pituitary after intravenous injection of hormone (Osborne et al., 1971). It was as great and as long-lasting as is found in the conventional target organs of the hormone (adrenal cortex and kidney). Centripetal vascular pathways are described from pituitary to median eminence (Török, 1964; Jazdowska & Dobrowski, 1965). Could they be the route of entry for the hormone, particularly for its role as releaser of ADH?

Having entered the brain, what then? How does angiotensin work to mobilize thirst? And what relation does the process initiated by peripheral angiotensin have to the renin-angiotensin system that is endogenous to the brain (Ganten et al., 1971)? What a marvelous fact that is! The most potent dipsogen known (and a most potent releaser of ADH) is packaged in the brain ready for use. Could it be unwrapped by thirst stimuli and angiotensin reaching it from the periphery and therefore be the ultimate extracellular dipsogen? The capacity for specific or competitive inhibition of each of the peptides or proteins in the renin-angiotensin sequence will be a great aid here. Inhibitors exist for the converting enzyme (Miller, Samuels, Haber, & Barger, 1972) and for angiotensin II (Türker, Hall, Yamamoto, Sweet, & Bumpus, 1972), and antibodies can be produced to renin, angiotensin I, and angiotensin II (Page & McCubbin, 1968). They can be used either in the brain or by intravenous infusion, and the barrier will permit selective blockade either of the endogenous system in the brain or of the peripheral hormone. We can examine the effects on thirst of paralyzing the hormonal system either in the brain or in the systemic circulation, at any stage in the conversion sequence from renin to angiotensin II. Epstein, Fitzsimons, and Johnson (1972) have recently taken the first step here using high titer antiangiotensin II rabbit plasma donated by our colleague, Philippe Meyer, of the Broussais Hospital in Paris. We blocked the dipsogenic effect of intracranial angiotensin II with antibody in the brain. Animals that drank to 1 to 5 ng received immune plasma at the dipsogenic locus just before hormone injection and did not drink to intracranial doses as high as 100 ng for an average of 64 minutes. This result shows that the dipsogen is antigenically active angiotensin II and that the technique of antibody blockade is feasible for our questions.

Fitzsimons (1971) has shown that all components of the renin-angiotensin system, including renin itself and synthetic angiotensinogen, as well as angiotensin I and II, are dipsogenic by intracranial injection. In the periphery, angiotensin II is the active material, and the principle may hold for the brain. The precursors of angiotensin II may be active in the brain because of the presence there of renin and the converting enzyme. On the other hand, the brain may be a unique target organ, directly sensitive to angiotensin I. That, at least, is the suggestion of recent work of Fitzsimons using a pentapeptide inhibitor of the converting enzyme. He finds (J. T. Fitzsimons, personal communication, 1972) that prior injection of the pentapeptide at intracranial loci from which thirst is elicited by angiotensin II does *not* block the drinking produced by angiotensin I. In the presence of the inhibitor, conversion to octapeptide is unlikely, and the decapeptide may therefore be a directly active dipsogen in the brain.

The Nonhomeostatic Controls

The double depletion hypothesis is a satisfactory working model for homeostatic thirst; but as Kissileff (this volume) makes very clear in his chapter, signals generated by body water depletion do not account for all of the powerful controls of drinking. He and Oatley (this volume) have given us a splendid review of the nonhomeostatic controls, and I want only to forecast a word or two about the dry mouth and thirst. We have rejected its exaggerated role in our thinking which was the result of Cannon's authority. But having expelled the idea in its prodigal form, we should prepare to welcome it back as a modest member of the family of important controls of drinking. I am struck by the fact that the desalivate rat drinks *less* than normal under several thirst-stimulating circumstances and does not drink excessively except when it must swallow dry food from a dry mouth. It drinks less to water deprivation (Epstein, Spector, Samman, & Goldblum, 1964), hypovolemia (Stricker & Wolf, 1969; Gutman, Benzakein, & Chaimovitz, 1967), constant access to water in the absence of food (Vance, 1965), and in the heat (Hainsworth, Stricker, & Epstein, 1968). The only apparent exception is the desalivate's normal response to cell dehydration (Epstein et al., 1964). In other words, the desalivate appears to be less thirsty than normal. Could the desalivation have deprived him of a facilitation of thirst that operates in the normal mammal? Mouth and throat dryness may serve as an early warning signal of dehydration that contributes to the drive for water. Having a chronically dry oropharynx, or at least one in which decreases in surface hydration are greatly attenuated, the desalivate may no longer experience the increase in dryness that accompanies dehydrations and that drives the intact animal to water and provides the pleasure of drinking. The desalivate may therefore drink only minimally, relying on renal conservation to defend body water constancy, except when saliva is necessary to avoid dysphagia (Epstein, 1971, pp. 275–276). The idea could be tested with techniques for controlling the hydration of the oropharynx, such as those developed by Kissileff (1969).

The Neurological Mechanisms of Thirst

I can do little more here than state the obvious problem of our almost total ignorance of the neurological systems that mediate thirst. We know that damage to the lateral hypothalamus and adjacent structures such as the medial internal capsule and subthalamus produces a complete and permanent adipsia (Epstein, 1971). The animals drink again in order to swallow, but they do not respond to hydrational depletions. And we have evidence for an inhibitory system for extracellular thirst in the septum (Harvey & Hunt, 1965; Blass & Hanson, 1970). The model I have sketched for the double depletion hypothesis points to the anterior forebrain, and to the preoptic area in particular, as a major receptor zone for osmotic dehydration and angiotensin sensitivity. Are there projections posteriorly from these putative receptive zones and from the septal inhibitory system into the lateral hypothalamus, and is the separation between the systems for the cellular and extracellular signals preserved in the motivational and effector apparatus for thirst? And what is the anatomical substrate for the nonhomeostatic controls, for the pleasures of drinking, the anticipation of dehydration?

The Ontogeny and Phylogeny of Thirst

We need better understanding of the development of the adult capacity for thirst. Drinking of free water occurs late in ontogeny (Adolph, 1957). Newborn mammals, without exception, eat before they drink, and the acceptance of free water is delayed in maturation just as is the capacity for urine concentration (Falk, 1955). But what is the time schedule of the development of the separate controls of water intake? Is there a difference in the chronology of development of the cellular and extracellular controls, and in the nonhomeostatic controls? Do they in fact have the same physiological basis in the suckling and weanling mammal as they do in the adult? Is there, perhaps, a difference in the ontogeny of reflexive consummatory responses in the immature mammal versus the more facultative, appetitive behaviors of the adult? And projecting ontogenetic issues into adulthood, what is the influence of early nutritional history on the characteristic temporal patterns of water intake seen in the adult and on the defense of preferred levels of body weight?

Thirst is also later in phylogeny. It occurs indisputably (are marine fish thirsty when they swallow sea water?) only in the fully terrestrial animals—insects, reptiles, birds, and mammals. And even among them it may be absent, such as from some of the desert rodents and the marine mammals (Schmidt-Nielsen, 1962—63). We should be prepared for diversity of the physiological mechanisms for thirst and may find it simpler in reptiles, where it apparently first emerged among animals like ourselves, or among vertebrates that have adapted to life in the absence of fresh water.

The Problem of Motivation

My last forecast of future work is more of a plea than a program of research. We must not lose sight of the necessity to retain the concept of motivation in our thinking. Animals like ourselves do not drink reflexly, like automatons in response to the adequate physiological stimuli. When we have completely defined all the physiological controls of thirst and have complete understanding of where and how they are integrated in the brain, and when we have understood how these inputs are transformed into the coordinated effector output of drinking, we will still have to know how the urge to drink arises in the brain with both its anticipatory and hedonic aspects. What compels the animals to anticipate the ingestion of water and to take risks and solve problems to reach it? After all, animals become thirsty (or hungry or sexy) in the *absence* of the consummatory object. They are not simply aroused by adequate stimulation in the immediate environment as would be the case if the behavior of thirst were merely reflexive. And what creates the hedonic state of thirst from the economics of water movement, nerve impulse, and hormone action? Having reached water, what makes the thirsty animal ingest it avidly? What gives rise to the excitement of need and the pleasures of consumption? We will not fully understand our basic phenomenon if we do not continuously confront the fact of motivation and the elusive neurological problem it poses.

REFERENCES

Adolph, E. F. Ontogeny of physiological regulations in the rat. *Quarterly Review of Biology*, 1957, **32**, 89–137.

Andersson, B. The effect of injections of hypertonic NaCl-solutions in different parts of the hypothalamus of goats. *Acta Physiologica Scandinavica*, 1953, **28**, 188–201.

Andersson, B. The thirst mechanism as a link in the "milieu interieur." In Masson (Ed.), *Les concepts de Claude Bernard sur le milieu interieur*. Paris: Masson & Cie, 1967. Pp. 13–26.

Andersson, B., & Larsson, S. Water and food intake and the inhibitory effect of amphetamine on drinking and eating before and after "prefrontal lobotomy" in dogs. *Acta Physiologica Scandinavica*, 1956, **38**, 22–30.

Andersson, B., & McCann, S. M. The effect of hypothalamic lesions on the water intake of the dog. *Acta Physiologica Scandinavica*, 1956, **35**, 312–320.

Blass, E. M., & Hanson, D. G. Primary hyperdipsia in the rat following septal lesions. *Journal of Comparative and Physiological Psychology*, 1970, **70**, 87–93.

Cizek, L. J. Total water balance: Thirst, fluid deficits, and excesses. In V. B. Mountcastle (Ed.), *Medical physiology*. St. Louis: Mosby, 1968. Pp. 350–369.

Cizek, L. J., Semple, R. E., Huang, K. C., & Gregersen, M. I. Effect of extracellular electrolyte depletion on water intake in dogs. *American Journal of Physiology*, 1951, **164**, 415–422.

Epstein, A. N. The lateral hypothalamic syndrome: Its implications for the physiological psychology of hunger and thirst. In E. Stellar & J. M. Sprague (Eds.), *Progress in physiological psychology*. New York: Academic Press, 1971. Pp. 263–317.

Epstein, A. N., Fitzsimons, J. T., & Johnson, A. K. Prevention by angiotensin II antiserum of drinking induced by intracranial angiotensin. *Journal of Physiology (London)*, Proceedings, 1972, in press.

Epstein, A. N., Fitzsimons, J. T., & Rolls, B. J. Drinking induced by injection of angiotensin into the brain of the rat. *Journal of Physiology (London)*, 1970, **210**, 457–474.

Epstein, A. N., Spector, D., Samman, A., & Goldblum, C. Exaggerated prandial drinking in the rat without salivary glands. *Nature*, 1964, **201**, 1342–1343.

Falk, G. Maturation of renal function in infant rats. *American Journal of Physiology*, 1955, **181**, 157–170.

Falk, J. L., & Herman, T. S. Specific appetite for NaCl without postingestional repletion. *Journal of Comparative and Physiological Psychology*, 1961, **54**, 405–408.

Fischer-Ferraro, C., Nahmod, V. E., Goldstein, D. J., & Finkielman, S. Angiotensin and renin in rat and dog brain. *Journal of Experimental Medicine*, 1971, **133**, 353–361.

Fisher, A. E., Antelman, S. M., Tarter, J. M., & Redgate, E. S. An analysis of the beta-adrenergic facilitation of thirst. *The Physiologist*, 1972, **15**, 134.

Fitzsimons, J. T. Drinking by rats depleted of body fluid without increase in osmotic pressure. *Journal of Physiology (London)*, 1961, **159**, 297–309.

Fitzsimons, J. T. Drinking caused by constriction of the inferior vena cava in the rat. *Nature*, 1964, **204**, 479–480.

Fitzsimons, J. T. Hypovolaemic drinking and renin. *Journal of Physiology (London)*, 1966, **186**, 130–131P.

Fitzsimons, J. T. The role of renal thirst factor in drinking induced by extracellular stimuli. *Journal of Physiology (London)*, 1969, **201**, 349–368.

Fitzsimons, J. T. The effect on drinking of peptide precursors and of shorter chain peptide fragments of angiotensin II injected into the rat's diencephalon. *Journal of Physiology (London)*, 1971, **214**, 295–303.

Fitzsimons, J. T. Thirst. *Physiological Reviews*, 1972, **52**, 468–561.

Fitzsimons, J. T., & Simons, B. J. The effect on drinking in the rat of intravenous infusions of angiotensin, given alone or in combination with other stimuli of thirst. *Journal of Physiology (London)*, 1969, **203**, 45–57.

Fitzsimons, J. T., & Stricker, E. M. Sodium appetite and the renin-angiotensin system. *Nature New Biology,* 1971, **231**, 58–60.

Ganten, D., Marquez-Julio, A., Granger, P., Hayduk, K., Karsunky, K. P., Boucher, R., & Genest, J. Renin in dog brain. *American Journal of Physiology,* 1971, **221**, 1733–1737.

Gilman, A. The relation between blood osmotic pressure, fluid distribution and voluntary water intake. *American Journal of Physiology,* 1937, **120**, 323–328.

Gross, F., Bock, K. D., & Turrian, H. Untersuchen über die Blutdruckwirkung von Angiotensin. *Helvetica Physiologika Acta,* 1961, **19**, 42–57.

Gupta, P. D., Henry, J. P., Sinclair, R., & von Baumgarten, R. Responses of the atrial and aortic baroreceptors to nonhypotensive hemorrhage and to transfusion. *American Journal of Physiology,* 1966, **211**, 1429–1437.

Gutman, Y., Benzakein, F., & Chaimovitz, M. Kidney factors affecting water consumption in the rat. *Israel Journal of Medical Science,* 1967, **3**, 910–911.

Hainsworth, F. R., Stricker, E. M., & Epstein, A. N. Water metabolism of rats in the heat: Dehydration and drinking. *American Journal of Physiology,* 1968, **214**, 983–989.

Harvey, J. A., & Hunt, H. F. Effects of septal lesions on thirst in rats as indicated by water consumption and operant responding for water reward. *Journal of Comparative and Physiological Psychology,* 1965, **59**, 49–56.

Hebert, F., Fouron, J. C., Boileau, J. C., & Biron, P. Pulmonary fate of vasoactive peptides in fetal, newborn, and adult sheep. *American Journal of Physiology,* 1972, **223**, 20–23.

Henry, J. P., Gupta, P. D., Meehan, J. P., Sinclair, R., & Share, L. The role of afferents from the low-pressure system in the release of antidiuretic hormone during non-hypotensive hemorrhage. *Canadian Journal of Physiology and Pharmacology,* 1968, **46**, 287–295.

Holmes, J. H., & Cizek, L. J. Observations on sodium chloride depletion in the dog. *American Journal of Physiology,* 1951, **164**, 407–414.

Holmes, J. H., & Montgomery, A. V. Observations on relations of hemorrhage to thirst. *American Journal of Physiology,* 1951, **167**, 796.

Houpt, K. A., & Epstein, A. N. The complete dependence of beta-adrenergic drinking on the renal dipsogen. *Physiology and Behavior,* 1971, **7**, 897–902.

Huang, K. C. Effect of salt depletion and fasting on water exchange in the rabbit. *American Journal of Physiology,* 1955, **181**, 609–615.

Jazdowska, B., & Dobrowski, W. Vascularization of the hypophysis in sheep. *Endokrynologia Polska,* 1965, **16**, 269–282.

Johnson, A. K. Localization of angiotensin sensitive areas for thirst in the rat brain. Paper read at the meeting of the Eastern Psychological Association, Boston, 1972.

Kissileff, H. R. Oropharyngeal control of prandial drinking. *Journal of Comparative and Physiological Psychology,* 1969, **67**, 309–319.

Kozłowski, S., & Sobocińska, J. Thirst in regulation of blood volume in dogs. In: Fourth International Conference on the Regulation of Food and Water Intake, Cambridge, 1971.

Mayer, A. Variations de la tension osmotique du sang chez les animaux privés de liquides. *Comptes Rendus des Séance de la Société de Biologie,* 1900, **52**, 153–155.

McCance, R. A. Experimental sodium chloride deficiency in man. *Proceedings of the Royal Society (London),* Series B, 1936, **119**, 245–268.

McFarland, D. J., & Rolls, B. J. Suppression of feeding by intracranial injections of angiotensin. *Nature,* 1972, **236**, 172–173.

Miller, E. D., Samuels, A. I., Haber, E. A., & Barger, A. C. Inhibition of angiotensin conversion in experimental renovascular hypertension. *Science,* 1972, **177**, 1108–1109.

Osborne, M. J., Pooters, N., Angles d'Auriac, G., Epstein, A. N., Worcel, M., & Meyer, P. Metabolism of tritiated angiotensin II in anaesthetized rats. *Pflügers Archiv,* 1971, **326**, 101–114.

Page, I. H., & McCubbin, J. W. *Renal hypertension.* Chicago: Yearbook, 1968.

Peck, J. W., & Novin, D. Evidence that osmoreceptors mediating drinking in rabbits are in the lateral preoptic area. *Journal of Comparative and Physiological Psychology,* 1971, **74**, 134–147.

Rolls, B. J., Jones, B. P., & Fallows, D. J. A comparison of the motivational properties of thirst induced by intracranial angiotensin and by water deprivation. *Physiology and Behavior,* 1972, 9, in press.

Schiff, M. Leçons sur la physiologie de la digestion, faites au Muséum d'Histoire Naturelle de Florence. E. Levier (Ed.). Florence: Loescher, 1867. Vol. 1, 41–42.

Schmidt-Nielsen, K. Osmotic regulation in higher vertebrates. *The Harvey Lectures,* 1962–63, Series 58, 53–93.

Share, L. Extracellular fluid volume and vasopressin secretion. In W. F. Ganong, & L. Martini (Eds.), *Frontiers in neuroendocrinology 1969.* New York: Oxford University Press, 1969. Pp. 183–210.

Simpson, J. B., & Routtenberg, A. Subfornical organ: Dipsogenic site of action of angiotensin II. Submitted to *Science,* 1973.

Stricker, E. M., & Wolf, G. Behavioral control of intravascular fluid volume: Thirst and sodium appetite. In P. J. Morgane (Ed.), Neural Regulation of Food and Water Intake. *Annals of the New York Academy of Sciences,* 1969, 157, 553–567.

Török, B. Structure of the vascular connections of the hypothalamo-hypophyseal region. *Acta Anatomica,* 1964, 59, 84–89.

Türker, R. K., Hall, M. M., Yamamoto, M., Sweet, C. S., & Bumpus, F. M. A new, long-lasting competitive inhibitor of angiotensin. *Science,* 1972, 177, 1203–1204.

Vance, W. B. Observations on the role of salivary secretions in the regulation of food and fluid intake in the white rat. *Psychological Monographs* (Princeton), 1965, 5.

Vander, A. J. Control of renin release. *Physiological Reviews,* 1967, 47, 359–382.

Verney, E. B. The antidiuretic hormone and the factors which determine its release. *Proceedings of the Royal Society* (*London*), Series B, 1947, 135, 25–106.

Volicer, L., & Loew, C. G. Penetration of angiotensin II into the brain. *Neuropharmacology,* 1971, 10, 631–636.

Wettendorff, H. Modifications du sang sous l'influence de la privations d'eau: Contribution à l'étude de la soif. *Travaux du Laboratoire de Physiologie, Instituts Solvay,* 1901, 4, 353–484.

AUTHOR INDEX

Numbers in italics refer to the pages on which the complete references are listed.

J

Jacoby, F., 193, *196*
Jalowiec, J. E., 76, 81, 85, 88, *96, 97,* 106, *112,* 271, *278*
James, W., xiv, *xv*
Janssen, S., 25, *32*
Jazdowska, B., 326, *331*
Jewell, P. A., 107, *111,* 220, *222*
Jobin, M., 101, *111*
Johnson, A. K., 92, *96,* 248, 249, 262, 273, *276, 277,* 326, 327, *330, 331*
Johnson, J. A., 92, *96,* 105, *112*
Johnson, M. W., 37, *71*
Jones, B. P., 324, *332*
Jordan, E. F., 114, *116*

K

Kaada, B. R., 130, *140*
Kahler, O., 13, *32*
Kakolewski, J. W., 21, *33,* 62, 63, 65, *70, 71,* 125, 130, *142,* 144, 146, 147, 152–*154,* 158, 159, *161,* 180, *196,* 217, *221, 222*
Kalat, J. W., 106, *112,* 179, *197*
Kanter, G. S., 28, *32,* 41, *71*
Kaplinsky, M., 127, *140*
Karsunky, K. P., 320, 327, *331*
Kavanau, J. L., 219, *222*
Kawa, A., 266, *278*
Kawamura, Y., 128, *142*
Kay, R. N. B., 88, *94*
Keller, A. D., 19, *33*
Khairallah, P. A., 286, *291*
Kissileff, H. R., 50, 61, 69, *71,* 109, *112,* 164–166, 168, 173, 174, 176, 180, 182–192, *196,* 217, *222,* 328, *331*
Kitayama, M., 68, *72*
Kitsikis, A., 236, *240*
Kleeman, C. R., 101, *112*
Klippel, R. A., 300, *306*
Kobayashi, N., 128, *141*
Kolmodin, C.-G., 115, *116*
Konig, J. F. R., 300, *306*
Kozłowski, S., 322, *331*
Kozub, F. J., 178, *197*
Krieckhaus, E. E., 105, *112*
Krukowski, M., 247, 261, 262, 269, *276, 277,* 283, *291,* 307, 309, 311, *313*
Kuhar, M. J., 285, *291*
Kuhn, T. S., 143, *153*

L

Langelier, P., 236, *240*
Larsson, S., 48, 51, *69,* 316, *330*
Lashley, K. S., xiv, *xv,* 193, *196,* 200, *222*
Latta, T., 7, *32*
Leaf, A., 74, *96*
Leeson, C. R., 193, *196*
Lehr, D., 247, 261, 262, 269, *276, 277,* 283, *291,* 307–311, *313, 314*
Leibowitz, S. F., 248, 262, 268, 269, *277,* 283, *291,* 309, *314*
Le Magnen, J., 180, *195, 196,* 209, 213, 215, 217, *222*
Lepkovsky, S., 190, *196*
Leschke, E., 15, *32*
Levak, M., 144, *153,* 156, *160*
Levin, B. E., 237, *240*
Levin, E., 101, *112*
Levitt, R. A., 244, 266, 269, *276, 278*
Lewinska, M. K., 134–136, *140*
Lewis, P. R., 232, *240,* 299, 303, *306*
Lincoln, D. W., 128, *140*
Lints, C. E., 237, *240,* 297, *306*
Lishajko, F., 235, *240*
Livneh, P., 78, *95*
Loew, C. G., 105, *112,* 325, 326, *332*
Long, C. N. H., 19, *31*
Longet, F. A., 7, 10, *32*
Lonsbury, B., 236, *240*
Lorens, S. A., 124, *141*
Lorenz, K. Z., 214, *222*
Lowe, R. D., 75, *96*
Lubar, J. F., 120, 128, *140*
Luschei, E. S., 68, *70*
Lynch, J. R., 19, *33*
Lyon, M., 124, *140*
Lytle, L. D., 236, *240*

M

Mabry, P. D., 120, *140*
McCance, R. A., 26, *33,* 317, *331*
McCann, S. M., 19, 21, *31,* 48, 50, *69,* 91, *94,* 107, *111,* 120, *138,* 316, *330*
McCleary, R. A., 176, *196*
McCubbin, J. W., 322, 327, *331*
McFarland, D. J., 166, *196,* 209, *222,* 324, *331*
McFarland, F. J., 209, *222*
McHenry, L. C., 10, *33*
Machne, X., 128, *139, 140*

SUBJECT INDEX

A

Ablation method, 293
Absorption, 210
Acetylcholine, 237, 244, 294, 295, 303, 304
Acetylcholinesterase, 303
ACTH (*see* Adrenocorticotropic hormone)
Action potentials, 131
Active avoidance response
one-way, 237
Activity
appetitive, 214
locomotor, 215
ADH (*see* Antidiuretic hormone)
Adipsia, 25, 90, 110, 123, 124, 125, 233, 236, 237, 289, 300, 328
Adrenal corticosteroids, 237
Adrenal insufficiency, 74
Adrenalectomy, 75
Adrenals, 263
Adrenergic agents, 25, 231, 279, 309
eating, 25
Adrenergic blocking agent, 295
Adrenocorticotropic hormone, 75, 93
Adulteration
quinine, 239
Afferent feedback, 267

Afferents
oral, 69
Aggression, 227
Air licking, 175
water deprivation, 175
Aldosterone, 30, 75, 76, 86, 90, 93, 252
Alpha-adrenergic antagonists, 281, 313
Alpha-adrenergic blockers, 287, 295
(*See also* Blocking agents, beta-adrenergic)
Alpha-adrenergic stimulation, 262
Ammonium chloride, 101, 114
Amphetamine, 237, 308, 309
Amygdala, 119, 124, 134
ingestive behaviors, 134
inhibitory effects, 134
short-term satiety, 136
Anemia, 77
Anesthetics, 25
Angiotensin, 29, 49, 78, 80, 81, 90, 91, 92, 93, 99, 100, 102, 103, 115, 237, 243, 245, 250, 255, 267, 270, 274, 275, 282, 287, 294, 308, 316, 319, 322, 327
blood-borne, 30
central, 251
circulating, 103, 105
converting enzyme, 105